# Current Debates in International Relations

## Second Edition

### Eric B. Shiraev
*George Mason University*

### Vladislav M. Zubok
*London School of Economics and Political Science*

New York      Oxford
OXFORD UNIVERSITY PRESS

Oxford University Press is a department of the University of Oxford.
It furthers the University's objective of excellence in research, scholarship,
and education by publishing worldwide. Oxford is a registered trade mark of
Oxford University Press in the UK and certain other countries.

Published in the United States of America by Oxford University Press
198 Madison Avenue, New York, NY 10016, United States of America.

**Library of Congress Cataloging-in-Publication Data**

CIP data is on file at the Library of Congress
978-0-19-085540-6

Printing number: 9 8 7 6 5 4 3 2 1
Paperback printed by Marquis, Canada

# Contents

# Preface

This reader can be used as a main or supplementary source for various courses in the fields of international relations, global affairs, foreign policy, and international politics. It introduces fine examples of scholarship and provides pedagogical tools to assist instructors and students in teaching and learning about international relations.

As editors, we pursued several interconnected goals. First, we intended to give the reader a concise yet comprehensive overview of recent studies and contemporary debates in international relations. The research and discussions in this field have become far more complex, dynamic, and less conclusive since the end of the Cold War, especially since 2001. The field of international relations is embracing new interdisciplinary approaches and novel methodological tools, including the methods and models adopted from economics, history, political psychology, anthropology, and comparative cultural studies. At the same time, many fields remain underdeveloped, including new nuclear arms threats or cybersecurity, to name a few. New international developments constantly bring new intellectual challenges and surprises.

Second, we wanted to revisit and reintroduce several classical works in this field. We hoped to examine the ability of these works to address and explain several key issues in international relations of the past century or even a more distant past. We also wanted to look at the contemporary applications of these works. Indeed, some of their assumptions and conclusions appear quite relevant today.

Third, we intended to remind students of the fundamental concepts of international relations such as states, sovereignty, power, and international structure. At the same time, we also brought and discussed several new concepts, those that have been the focus of growing attention since the beginning of the twenty-first century: international terrorism, environmental issues and policies, humanitarian issues and policies, and human rights, as well as culture and identity in a context of international politics. New concepts constantly emerge, and our goal with this reader was to forecast and reflect on them. Overall, the field has certainly became more diverse since the early 2000s. However, it is difficult to say whether studies in international relations have become more effective in terms of reacting to present events and predicting the future.

Finally, while describing problems, challenges, and threats in today's world, we also sought success stories in the field of international relations. We wanted to highlight teachable moments involving good and inspirational examples of conflict resolution, peaceful growth, democratic governance, and international cooperation.

In a general sense, this book can also be used as a basic source of knowledge for the current generation of students, who have unprecedented access to global information yet often lack the background to fully understand and evaluate it. We want to guide students through this information while paying special attention to critical evaluation of studies, facts, and theories. This reader will assist students in navigating major international issues, offer contending approaches, and consider real-world applications of theory.

We hold the view that the complexities of the global world are not likely to fit a single approach or theory. Therefore, this reader includes educational tools to equip students not only with facts and concepts for a solid background, but also with the skills for critical thinking. We encourage students, with the help of case studies and questions, to cross the boundaries of research traditions in search of new answers.

As we stated earlier, we welcome a wide range of explanatory approaches from different fields of knowledge, relevant to the problems of today's world. These approaches are complementary rather than antagonistic: They all add something unique, useful, and critical to the study of international relations. Students are welcome to multitask by studying and discussing data, opinions, and their applications obtained from different fields.

With all this in mind, we present a consistent framework to keep students focused and facilitate their learning.

## THREE PARTS: AN OVERVIEW

The reader has three major parts divided into eleven sections. Based on our teaching experience, each section may be studied in approximately one week during a standard one-semester or one-quarter course. Some sections may require more attention and time, while others may be studied more expeditiously—all depending on the instructors' preferences and the structure of their course.

Part I, "Approaching and Exploring International Relations" (Sections 1–4), introduces the field and emphasizes different, often contrasting ways of thinking and reasoning about international relations. The first section of Part I discusses sovereignty as a concept and a contested political issue in today's world. This section also discusses the contrasting processes of *globalization* and *antiglobalization* in international relations and looks at the ways the events on the ground complement and challenge most established theories. The following three sections present the debates in historical contexts associated with major perspectives on international relations—realism, liberalism—as well as several other approaches, including constructivism, conflict theories, feminism, and political psychology. Recent international developments suggest that realism, one of the traditional perspectives deemed outdated before the 2010s, has become quite topical again.

Part II, "Three Facets of International Relations" (Sections 5–7), discusses the three major, most essential facets of international relations: war and security, international law and international community, and international political economy. The section on war and security discusses both the traditional issues related to armed conflicts and new developments involving asymmetrical threats and cyberwarfare and security. The next section focuses on international law and its development and addresses debates about international community and extraterritoriality. The section about international political economy deals with the application of key economic theories to recent developments, such as globalization and its discontents, emerging new economies, and the blurring of the traditional North–South gap.

Part III, "Twenty-First-Century Challenges" (Sections 8–11), explores the significant and complex challenges of today's world, the challenges that are likely to impact the international relations of tomorrow. One section addresses environmental problems and environmental policies. The next one directs attention to human rights and humanitarian policies. The discussion focuses on liberal concepts such as the *responsibility to protect* and universal jurisdiction, among others. The next section emphasizes the identity issue in international politics and focuses

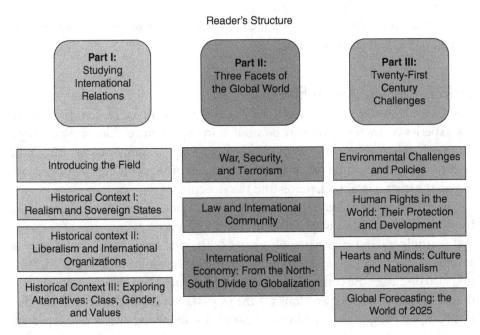

Figure P.1   Reader's Structure

on culture, nationalism, and the meaning of *hearts and minds* in today's world. The concluding section of the book provides critical evaluations of various theoretical predictions about the future of international relations.

## ARTICLES: AN OVERVIEW

Each section contains original research articles, essays, commentaries, or sizable excerpts from such articles, published by outstanding scholars. At least three types of articles have been selected for this book.

The **first type** includes key theoretical and other fundamental works that describe the structure and dynamics of international relations, key actors and institutions, major international events, and key approaches to their understanding. We can call these works *classical* because of their known impact on past and current debates in the discipline. These classical articles or book chapters are presented in full or shortened.

The **second type** includes contemporary research articles, social commentaries, and essays that focus on specific theoretical and applied issues of contemporary studies of international relations and their applications.

The **third type** is mostly illustrative. The articles are selected from academic and nonacademic sources. These entries provide factual materials and opinions as practical applications of theory to contemporary international relations.

In addition, a selection of critical commentaries—relevant to each section of the book—appears on the companion website. Some of these materials refer to key historic documents, such as treaties and international agreements. Other materials serve as illustrations to most contemporary international events. We hope that the accompanying site will be an important supplementary and illustrative source for this reader.

An overview and critical-thinking questions for class use or homework assignments accompany each section. These overviews comment on the debates in specific fields in the discipline of international relations and refer to contemporary developments relevant to the section's articles.

The majority of works selected for this volume were published in the United States or the United Kingdom. Do these choices reveal a deliberate bias in our selection of the articles? We do not think so. For several decades, the United States has been the world leader in studies of international relations. The openness and innovativeness of the American research and educational system rooted in universities, both public and private, have strengthened the academic community involved in the study of international relations. American and British professional, peer-reviewed journals invite contributions from all authors, with different perspectives, from all countries and regions. Many talented scholars writing and publishing in English are from Latin America, Africa, China, India, Pakistan, Hong Kong, and Russia, as well as several other countries and regions. These scholars—their names and works appear in this reader—contribute to the scientific discussion by bringing fresh perspectives, multidisciplinary methods, and, of course, critical thinking.

## THINKING CRITICALLY WITH THE READER

Critical thinking is not simply passing skeptical judgments. It is a set of skills that we all can master. It is a process of inquiry based on the important virtues of *curiosity*, *doubt*, and *intellectual honesty*. Curiosity helps us dig below the surface to distinguish facts from opinions. Doubt keeps us from being satisfied with overly simple explanations. And intellectual honesty helps in recognizing and addressing discrepancy or even bias in our own opinions.

### Distinguishing Facts from Opinions

The study of international relations is not basic science, like physics or biology. The behavior of states, nongovernment organizations, and international organizations is often difficult to describe in mathematical formulas and to test in controlled experiments. A single event can be judged from many different angles. However, we still should learn to separate facts from opinions. Facts are verifiable events and developments. Opinions are speculations or intuitions about how and why such developments have taken place.

Distinguishing facts and opinions is not so easy. Some facts are deliberately hidden or distorted by government authorities or interest groups. Other facts remain in dispute. In 1945, the British novelist and journalist George Orwell wrote about the uncertainty of information with regard to the events of the Second World War:

> There can often be a genuine doubt about the most enormous events. [. . .] The calamities that are constantly being reported—battles, massacres, famines, revolutions—tend to inspire in the average person a feeling of unreality. [. . .] One has no way of verifying the facts, one is not even fully certain that they have happened, and one is always presented with totally different interpretations from different sources. ("Notes on Nationalism," *Polemic*, May 1945)

Orwell's warnings are even more valid today. The Internet has lowered information barriers and we are now flooded with news, reports, and opinions. Yet anyone seeking information on the Internet must be especially cautious: Often, seemingly reliable reports can be full of speculation presented as "fact," but in reality, it is just opinion. Even more often, facts are presented in a selective, one-sided way. However, this does not mean that the reports constitute "fake news." Take, for example, an ongoing conflict such as that in Syria or Ukraine and see how different the accounts of the conflict are in the eyes of the opposing sides. As viewers and listeners, we tend to embrace the facts we like but ignore or criticize information that contradicts our views. As an example, a passionate supporter of democracy may gladly read and suggest to others an article describing how democracy is associated with stability and peace. However, the same person could easily overlook facts showing that a transition to democracy, especially in countries with a history of ethnic and religious hostility, could contribute to even greater violence. Could you suggest a few specific examples showing a selective bias in people's choices of facts?

Our desire to be objective is often constrained by the limits of language. Because people use language to communicate, they frequently *frame* facts, or put them into a convenient arrangement. Reports about international politics are often framed so that contradictory and confusing information becomes simple: "bad" countries are supposed to act badly; "good" countries are supposed to conduct virtuous policies. Uncertainties and gray areas are often omitted. Framing by the mass media works with remarkable effectiveness, camouflaging incomplete or even biased selection of facts and opinions.

Separating facts from opinions should help you navigate the sea of information related to world events. It can start with you looking for new and more reliable sources of facts. Whenever possible, try to establish as many facts as possible related to the issue you are studying. Do not limit yourself only to the facts that are easily available. Check your sources: How reliable are they? If there is a disagreement about the facts in two reports, discuss why these differences occur. Pay attention to the web address of the source: If it is unknown, its reliability should be verified. Check how the articles frame the facts and opinions in a certain direction. What are the motivations that have contributed to a certain point of view? The more often you ask yourself these questions, the more accurate your analysis of the received information will be.

### Looking for Multiple Causes

Why do countries go to war? You often hear simple and categorical explanations and statements such as, "This war took place because of this country's oil-driven interests," "That war happened because of that country's imperial ambitions," and so on. In fact, every war is a result not only of someone's interests and ambitions, but also of many interconnected developments. Moreover, virtually any international event—not only war—has many underlying reasons or causes. As critical thinkers studying international relations, we must consider a wide range of possible influences and factors, all of which could be involved to varying degrees in the shaping of international events and global developments. For example, some tend to explain the collapse of Communism in eastern Europe and the Soviet Union in the late 1980s using President Ronald Reagan's unrelenting military and economic pressure on those countries. Although this pressure was real, the Soviet Union's demise was caused not by one policy, but rather by several intertwining factors, including people's disillusionment with Communist ideology, a growing economic and financial crisis, and the disastrous domestic policies of Soviet leadership.

### Being Aware of Bias

We must keep in mind that our opinions, as well as the opinions of people around us, may be inaccurate. Every interpretation of the facts is made from someone's point of view. And people tend to avoid information that challenges their assumptions while gravitating to information that supports their views. When it comes to international relations, it is easy to support leaders we like and to oppose the policies of those we dislike. Our personal attachments, interests, preferences, and values have a tremendous impact on the facts we gather and judgments we make about international events. Ask your professor which online or printed periodical she or he read first with that morning's tea or coffee. Opinion polls show that people's party affiliation is correlated with their choice of news sources.

Bias is often caused by different experiences and life circumstances. Personal emotions can deepen misunderstandings and disagreements by causing us to refuse to learn new facts and accept new information. Parochialism, a worldview limited to the small piece of land on which we live, necessarily narrows the experiences we can have. It is a powerful roadblock in the study and practice of international relations.

An emphasis on critical thinking will help all of us as students of international relations. You will learn to retrieve verifiable knowledge from apparently endless fountains of information, from media reports to statistical databanks. You will also learn to be an informed skeptic and a decision-maker.

## KEY PEDAGOGICAL TOOLS: AN OVERVIEW

- In addition to this introduction, each of the three parts of the book starts with critical introductory remarks, which contain a preview of the topics and selected articles.
- These introductory remarks also provide critical-thinking questions for class discussions or reading assignments.
- Critical-thinking questions relating to the articles appear at the end of each part of the book.
- Practice test questions accompany every section of the book and appear on the companion website.
- The companion website contains additional sources relevant to the articles in the book and current media reports to better illustrate or critically discuss the contents of the articles. PowerPoint slides posted on the site summarize the articles in the book.
- There are other web-based interactive tools relevant to successful teaching and learning.

## CONTENTS

Again, the reader contains three parts, each further divided into eleven sections. The first part introduces the major approaches to the field of international relations. The second part examines three major facets of international relations. The third part refers to the three most important domestic, regional, and global challenges and emphasizes the importance of knowledge and global understanding in the practice of international relations.

In sum, we hope that the current reader addresses at least two main challenges to teaching introductory international relations or similar courses.

We believe that our students should learn to appreciate the classical as well as the latest professional achievements in the field and, in their understanding of international relations, take a variety of factors into account. On the one hand, we believe it is crucial to show the relevance of these approaches to real-world problems. On the other hand, we do not want to overwhelm undergraduates with a deluge of theoretical nuances.

Second, students must become informed skeptics and develop a critical view toward discussions of world events. Statistics, video clips, tweets, maps, eyewitness reports, theoretical articles, and biographies—all are just a click away. We try to bank on this opportunity while paying special attention to critical evaluation of facts and theories. We seek to focus on the development of basic skills of critical fact analysis and theoretical thinking—a major task in understanding and teaching international relations today.

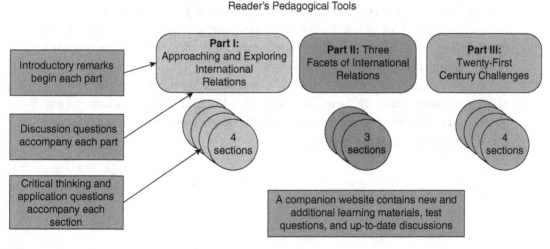

Figure P.2   Reader's Pedagogical Tools

## TO THE STUDENT

We always ask students who take our classes to imagine that they have obtained the power to travel back in time and space. Could you do the same right now? How far back and where would you go? Would you pick a seat in an inaugural session of the United Nations? Or would you choose to be a fly on the wall in the White House, listening to a president's top-secret discussion of a new global strategy? Or would you prefer to climb atop the Berlin Wall on November 9, 1989, to chip off a chunk of the monstrous barrier, the symbol of the Cold War? Or would you rather listen to the discussion in the White House about the decision to kill bin Laden? Would you want to be among the few physicians contemplating Doctors without Borders in 1971? Or maybe you would like to attend the NATO meeting when the decisions to bomb Libya in 2011 were reached? Or you would like to be in the White House in 2019, when tariffs on China were discussed?

Too many choices, too many people . . . But even if you saw everything you wanted and met everyone you planned, what exactly could you learn from that experience? And what lessons could you draw when everything in the world is so rapidly changing? Do you feel that there are too many opinions, judgments, and suggestions made every minute on television and on the web about the evolving world?

We believe that this book will not only help you in your study of international relations, but also provide you with at least three crucial advantages over many commentators in the media and cyberspace. First, we believe that you will adopt the right language to speak about and explain international relations, beginning with crucial terms such as *anarchy*, *states*, *balance of power*, *interests*, *cooperation*, *security*, and several others. Second, you will be able to gain and strengthen your knowledge about how governments and international organizations respond to crises and wars. Third, you will better understand why the world of today remains unstable, unpredictable, and even dangerous.

Finally, we hope that in your studies of international relations, in our analyses of great decisions and significant mistakes, we will build your confidence in our ability to contribute to a more secure, peaceful, and prosperous world of the future. It is up to you to accept the challenge.

# Acknowledgments

We received assistance and guidance from many great individuals, colleagues, and friends whose discussions, suggestions, and backing were very important when we were working on this book. We are grateful for the insightful comments and critical advice of our many reviewers and research assistants. And, of course, not much could have been done without the patience and understanding of our family members. We also acknowledge the great and consistent support we have been receiving for many years at virtually every stage of this project's improvement and refinement from the team at Oxford University Press. Executive editor Jennifer Carpenter initiated this project and directed it at every stage. Editorial assistant Patrick Keefe provided week-by-week management and saw to the numerous details; and production editor Brad Rau guided the book through production. We appreciate the work of our copyeditor, Susan Brown and our indexer, Mary Harper. Thank you for your care and efficiency.

Particular thanks go to our colleagues: William Wohlforth from Dartmouth University; Mark Pollack, Richard Immerman, and Petra Goedde from Temple University; Mark Kramer from Harvard, Mary Sarotte from Henry A. Kissinger Center for Global Affairs ; Norman Naimark, David Holloway, Mikhail Bernstam, and Cheryl Koopman from Stanford University; Thomas Blanton from the National Security Archive; William Taubman from Amherst College; Odd Arne Westad from Yale University, Mike Cox from the LSE-IDEAS; Matthew Jones, Piers Ludlow, Svetozar Rajak and Peter Trubowitz from the London School of Economics, John Ikenberry from Princeton University; Ted Hopf from the National University of Singapore; David Sears from the University of California–Los Angeles; James Sidanius from Harvard University; David Levy from Pepperdine University; Bob Dudley, Colin Dueck, Eric McGlinchey, and Ming Wan from George Mason University; Philip Tetlock from the University of Pennsylvania; Christian Ostermann, Robert Litwak, and Blair Ruble from the Woodrow Wilson Center; Andrew Kuchins from the Center for Strategic and International Studies; Alan Whittaker from the National Defense University; and Scott Keeter from the Pew Research Center, as well as John Haber for inspiring us early and throughout our careers.

We received constant help, critical advice, and validation from our colleagues and friends in the United States and around the world. We express our gratitude to Mark Katz, Dimitri Simes, Paul Saunders, Henry Hale, Stephen E. Hanson, James

Goldgeier, Eric John, Peter Mandaville, Jason Smart, Richard Sobel, Henry Nau, Martijn Icks, Stanislav Eremeev, Konstantin Khudoley, Jennifer Keohanne, Sergei Samoilenko, and Vitaly Kozyrev. A word of appreciation goes to Olga Chernyshev, Elena Vitenberg, Michael Zubok, John and Judy Ehle, Dmitry Shiraev, Dennis Shiraev, and Nicole Shiraev. Our work will continue!

# PART I

# APPROACHING AND EXPLORING INTERNATIONAL RELATIONS

## Main Perspectives: Their Evolution and Relevance Today (Editorial Introduction)

Everywhere we have taught international relations over the past twenty years—in Washington, DC, and Philadelphia, Rome and Warsaw, Tartu and Amsterdam, London and Moscow—we often heard similar questions from our students early in the course: Why do we have to study these theories and perspectives of the past? Could we just skip them and turn to the urgent issues of the day? The obvious impatience of a young person who is dreaming about a career in diplomacy, international politics, economic development and business, or international law is understandable. All their thoughts are about the present and the future, not the past. Besides, today's global world is evolving faster than ever. Following and understanding its rapid developments become increasingly challenging and at times even frustrating. And on top of history comes the theory. *Who needs it?*

Eventually, most of our skeptical students change their minds. After a semester of lectures and class discussions, they realize that studying these approaches and theories makes sense. Not only do these approaches and theories help them understand the dramatic events of 1914, 1941, 1989, and 2001, but also this conceptual thinking helps them critically evaluate the international challenges, tragedies, and triumphs that unfold before our eyes, right at this moment. The students see that their knowledge of international relations theory serves as a much-needed "navigator" in understanding today's world.

As an academic discipline, international relations is relatively young. It took its early, steady steps only in the twentieth century. Several dramatic developments and collective experiences impacted the growth of this discipline. The world's periods of peace and prosperity took turns with economic breakdowns and two world wars. The Cold War—a major confrontation between the Soviet bloc and Western states— threatened humankind with a nuclear Armageddon. Yet suddenly the Soviet Union had fallen and the United States remained the only superpower standing. About the same time, China began its rapid economic and political ascendance. For two decades, the international liberal order, protected by NATO, the European Union, and multiple trade agreements, expanded without major conflicts and problems. However, after economic slump of 2008-2009, the signs of a crisis of international order have appeared. What are the causes of this disorder? How can it be addressed?

The world is evolving, and so is the discipline of international relations. This means that the theories and approaches that we study today are not immutable, time-less "laws," but rather conceptual lodestars guiding us in the fast-evolving world. Every new generation, every new cohort of scholars, tests these principal approaches, compares them to the current developments, and updates them accordingly. Without them, we would become like ancient seafarers who sailed the seas without a compass or even a lodestar.

The two approaches that dominated the study of international relations in the universities of the United States and Great Britain since the 1960s are realism and lib-eralism (sometimes called international liberalism). Realism focuses on the power of states (sovereign countries), their interests, and their search for security. According to this theoretical approach, the very nature of international relations is anarchic. This means that main actors, such as powerful sovereign states, can act on the world stage more or less as they want, without any authority above them. These sovereign states react to anarchy by defending their core interests. They protect their resources, create alliances with other states, respond to outside threats, and, if necessary, impose their will on others. States, according to the followers of realism, are constantly preoccupied with *balance of power* and look for the best position within the international order. They also balance one another by trying to prevent other states from gaining a signifi-cant advantage over others. Among common instruments of this balancing are strate-gic alliances, armament increases, threats of using military force, and, ultimately, war.

Liberalism is a different approach. It claims that international anarchy does not necessarily lead to conflicts and wars. It may result in cooperation among states. It should take education, expanding political freedom, and goodwill—which are interconnected—to build a prosperous and conflict-free world. Liberalism emphasizes international collaboration, economic ties, international law, and shared values. International institutions should play a big role too. Liberalism also sees nonstate actors, such as nongovernment organizations and public opinion, as influencing state choices and policies.

Modern realism and liberalism may differ substantially from their original for-mulations. Back in 1948, Hans Morgenthau, a refugee from Germany who had found a new life in the United States, formulated his famous *six principles of realism.*

To propose these principles, Morgenthau first synthesized his broad knowledge of European and ancient Greco-Roman history as well as the tragic experiences of the two world wars of the twentieth century. He taught that leaders of sovereign states should conduct foreign policy in terms of their state's interests defined through power. Ethical principles that guide the behavior of individuals should not necessarily be tied to states' actions. Moral values still may play an important role in foreign policy, but in most cases, states should pursue these two interconnected goals: maximize their benefits and reduce their losses in relations with other states. Morgenthau's ideas gained significant support. Many American and British textbooks on international relations discussed and endorsed his ideas, which seemed timely and very much appropriate.

Yet just thirty years after Morgenthau introduced his principles, the world was very different. A new international system had emerged that was shaped by the Cold War. The world's affairs were dominated by the United States and the Soviet Union, which were commonly called *superpowers*. Reflecting on and critically rethinking that global change, the American political scientist Kenneth Waltz redesigned the concept of realism. Analyzing the Cold War, Waltz concluded that the most important single factor that shaped international relations was the distribution of power, which resulted in a certain *structure* of international relations. He then argued that sovereign states respond to the condition of international anarchy by seeking more security for themselves, rather than more power, in an existing international system. Because the system was bipolar during the Cold War, shaped by the global rivalry between the two key global powers—the United States and the Soviet Union—all other states had to adapt to this structure. The followers of Waltz were labeled *structural realists* or *neorealists* (see Figure 1).

Liberalism, like realism, was rooted in European history and the twentieth-century experience. It stemmed from the principles of liberal idealism (related to humanism and Enlightenment) and political liberalism. Liberal thinkers believed that human reason and transparency in international relations could bring about an international system of peaceful and prosperous sovereign states. Political liberals formed a powerful social and political movement that originated in the nineteenth century; it challenged inherited privileges of the nobility and called for universal political rights.

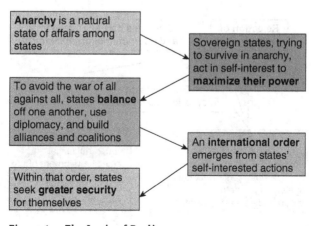

Figure 1.   The Logic of Realism

Although the problems of security and the challenges of the arms race dominated the foreign policy agenda of many countries during the Cold War, liberal views became increasingly influential. A certain belief was gaining strength in Western Europe and the United States: If mutual interests and common values were to drive countries' foreign policy, this could reduce international tensions and bring substantial benefits to all countries. In the 1950s and 1960s, Western democracies enjoyed tremendous economic growth, in part because of increasing international trade and technological exchanges. War, power balancing, and arms races were frequently seen as outdated phenomena from the past. The growing economic prosperity, the increasing prominence of international organizations, and the ongoing European economic integration began to influence and even challenge the old realist agenda of power balance, deterrence, and containment. Military competition—especially the nuclear buildup—seemed to many an outdated and counterproductive strategy.

Supporters of liberalism, while continuing their criticism of realism, focused on states' cooperation. Liberal scholars followed several conceptual paths. Some scholars, such as Robert Keohane, showed that the growth of economic dependence among sovereign countries was becoming increasingly complex and multilayered. Others, like Hedley Bull, focused on the rising influence of intergovernmental and nongovernmental organizations, as well as the emergence of a so-called international society where sovereign states voluntarily followed common norms of behavior to enhance their security and prosperity (see Figure 2).

Other liberal scholars turned to human rights, environmental challenges, and international law. Individual actions of sovereign states, in the view of these scholars, should become history. These were the areas, they argued, that should alter the nature of international relations and lead to some new international settings called *global governance*. Another important debate emerged among supporters of liberalism who argued whether the global spread of democracy would diminish the danger of major wars. Scholars like Michael Doyle argued that developed, prosperous democracies do not go to war against each other. To put it simply, the more democratic countries emerge, the more stable the world's peace becomes. Does democracy give an answer to

Figure 2.   The Logic of Liberalism

mitigating the anarchic nature of international relations? Critics argued that countries that can be characterized as young or unstable democracies in fact tend to go to war more frequently than nondemocracies. The debates on this subject continue.

The concepts of realism and liberalism have always been based on several broad assumptions and key concepts such as states (or sovereign countries), state interests, international anarchy, and balance of power. Most scholars of these two approaches rarely probed such assumptions. In contrast, several alternative approaches and theories did so: They looked at international relations quite differently than liberalism and realism.

From the nineteenth century, Marxism has remained the strongest conceptual framework or inspiration for some alternative approaches. Marxist ideas, developed by thinkers such as Vladimir Lenin in Russia, Antonio Gramsci in Italy, and others, rejected the assumptions that states were independent actors in world politics. Instead, they argued, states reflected the interests of dominant social groups (or *ruling classes* in Marxist's terminology), including industrial and financial elites, international corporations, banks, and even big, influential, international organizations. Several neo-Marxist scholars, particularly from Latin America, argued that the structure of international relations—and trade in particular—makes it impossible for poor countries to move out of poverty by following Western models of development and modernization. The free market keeps poor states excessively dependent on rich states, while supplying the latter with cheap labor and raw materials. Such dependency can be reduced only if states build their own industries and substitute their products for foreign goods. These views became the foundation of *dependency theory,* by the Argentine economist Raul Prebisch. Advancing similar arguments, several sociologists created *world-systems theory,* according to which the world is divided into a core, consisting of the wealthy developed states and the periphery, including former colonies and underdeveloped and chronically poor states. Using the neo-Marxist concept of hegemony in international relations, Immanuel Wallerstein claimed that a small group of wealthy Western states have for many decades maintained their supremacy over the rest of the world. Supporters of these views also maintained that the "real" conflict in international relations has not been between the West and the East (the Soviet bloc), but rather between the wealthy "North" and the poor "South." Sovereign states, as the British political scientist Susan Strange contended, could not be viewed as main actors in international relations: Instead, they sacrificed their sovereignty in the economic and financial sphere to international financial organizations.

Since the 1970s, many international relations scholars have turned to the identity factor in politics. Feminism emerged as a powerful school of thought. Feminist scholars have produced a wealth of innovative work linking gender and gender inequality to international relations. Feminist authors like Ann Tickner, Carol Cohn, and others asserted that defense and security policies reflect a masculine culture that translates into confrontation, war, and violence, rather than consensus and peace. For centuries, ruling elites did not take into consideration women's values and priorities. Feminist authors also argued that domestic gender inequality and violence against women are highly correlated with states' choices between violence and cooperation and peace and war in international affairs.

Most of the concepts described earlier emerged in the shadow of the Cold War between the Soviet bloc and the alliance of Western states. The end of the Cold War and the collapse of the Soviet Union produced new challenges and uncertainties in international relations. Structural realists were poorly prepared to explain a surprising end to the twentieth century's global rivalry. To add to the list of challenges for realists, the terrorist attacks on September 11, 2001, demonstrated that the new threats to the international system could come not only from sovereign countries but also from nonstate networks such as al-Qaeda that remain clandestine while empowered by radical ideologies.

The end of the Cold War brought numerous challenges to thinkers of liberalism, too. Some of them were probably overwhelmed by their optimism when the Soviet bloc and the Soviet Union collapsed: It seemed that most significant sources for international tensions had been eliminated. Some, like Francis Fukuyama, who were inspired by the fall of Communism, claimed the coming of "the end of history." The democratic West, as he had anticipated, governed by principles of liberal freedoms, would no longer face a serious ideological challenge from other countries. These scholars assumed that the traditional priorities of Cold War international relations, such as political and military security, nuclear deterrence, proxy wars, the arms race, and arms control, should be replaced by a new agenda emphasizing economic and social development, trade, education, human rights, and environmental security. The rapid and seemingly successful integration of a large group of countries into the European Union produced a new flow of optimistic arguments about the end of the international system based on sovereign states and balance of power.

When a chain of ethnic wars erupted in the Balkans, Africa, and other regions in the 1990s, liberal scholars argued that it was now the responsibility of the *international community* (meaning the United Nations, but also NATO and the European Union) to stop ethnic violence and tribal genocide. They further maintained that sovereignty as a key concept of international relations might be disregarded if there are legitimate grounds for an international intervention to stop massive violence and save lives threatened by governments or nongovernmental groups. Scores of experts and journalists began to use a new language, where *promotion of democracy, humanitarian intervention*, and the *responsibility to protect* replaced the traditional *containment, nuclear deterrence*, and *balance of power* from the Cold War days. Liberal authors preferred using concepts such as *common rules, values*, and *networks* instead of *power*. They spoke about *intergovernmental organizations* and deemphasized the importance of sovereign states and central governments in international affairs.

However, the realities on the ground revealed serious limitations of liberal concepts and approaches to international relations. The intergovernmental organizations and nongovernmental organizations, as it turned out, could not effectively replace states and alliances of states. The United States and its NATO allies, such as the United Kingdom and France, carried out almost all significant interventions of the past two decades involving the use of force or requiring massive and urgent assistance. The general expectation about the inevitable erosion of national sovereignty, as Stephen Krasner underlined, proved to be premature. International anarchy seems hard to avoid. Because of continuing disagreements among Russia, China, and the United States, it is difficult to set common rules of global governance. The much-hoped-for democratization of the Middle East in 2011–13 did not happen. Instead, radical nonstate groups such as ISIS—a jihadist network operating in Iraq and Syria—threatened to replace the old dictatorships in several Arab countries. And in 2014, the liberal order in Europe was openly challenged by Russia's actions against Ukraine. The president of Russia, Vladimir Putin, showed that he put his country's security interests, domination, and territorial control above international law and liberal values. In Syria, the Russian military helped the dictator Bashar al-Assad to restore power and re-establish control over much of the country.

Most important, the rise of China, India, and Brazil and the ambitious behavior of Russia seemed to put an end to the idea of a US-led liberal global order and produced a tough intellectual challenge to some American, British, and other liberal scholars. They argued that an eagerly proclaimed new international system based on liberal principles of peace and cooperation was declining along with the decline of Western countries' power. Responding to this argument, the American scholar G. John Ikenberry contended that the emerging international society requires its own "liberal Leviathan," or more specifically, the United States as a global leader. This strong country would guarantee that the rest of the world, and above all other economically powerful states, would continue to abide by rules of international cooperation developed predominantly in the West.

The continuing conflicts in Afghanistan and Iraq, however, weakened the authority of the United States as leader of the global liberal order. And the most surprising challenge to the liberal hopes came from within: The presidential victory of Donald Trump in 2016 put an open critic of liberalism in the White House. Trump turned to nationalism and unilateralism in foreign policy. He also turned against international alliances, organizations, and trade agreements that for decades had been the pillars of the international liberal order. Trump supporters argued that it was the right move: The existing international order needed a massive overhaul because it no longer served the United States' interests. However, critics of Trump warned that his policies not only would harm the established liberal alliances but also would undermine the American authority, which allowed the United States to set global rules. At about the same time, the European Union experienced a similar challenge from the inside: The referendum in the United Kingdom in 2016 produced a surprising victory for those who wanted to restore the British *full sovereignty* and leave European common market and other historic arrangements among European countries. In 2017, the British government initiated the *Brexit* from Europe, the outcome of which is likely to remain uncertain and highly contentious for years. The analysts wonder why two established democracies such as the United States and the United Kingdom, the long-term promoters of liberal values, transformed so rapidly into hotbeds of polarization and discontent.

At the point of this writing, neither the blithe predictions of spread of liberalism nor the dire warnings of realism had come true. The liberal international order appeared to be in trouble, yet the opposition to Trump's policies in the United States was strong, and his ability to radically transform the country's foreign policy was constrained. The European Union was hurt by rising nationalism and financial problems, but it appears that it would survive with or without Brexit. For years, some structural realists forecast the emergence of another center of power, an alternative to the United States. They argued that America's unipolarity of the 1990s should have been only a brief moment in history. Yet there was no clear indication by the third decade of the twenty-first century that any of the rising economic powers, including China, was prepared to replace American global leadership and form a new multipolar system. Russia, despite its assertive international actions and statements that often generate media headlines, remains a regional oil-rich power that is wrestling with its own economic decline and conflicting with its neighbors. Apparently, neither realism nor liberalism provides a one-size-fits-all explanation of the world's dynamics of today's international world.

The collapse of Communist states in the late 1980s also meant the rapid decline in popularity of neo-Marxist concepts and their derivatives, such as dependency theory and world-systems theory. The number of studies and journal articles based on alternative approaches has plummeted. At the same time, a new and increasingly popular approach called constructivism emerged in the 1990s. One of its founders, Alexander Wendt, postulated that states' actions and policies are based on how leaders, bureaucracies, and societies interpret or construct the information available to them. This does not mean that politicians could easily manipulate realities and images of realities to affect their countries' foreign policy (although some political psychologists claim that this is often the case). Constructivism posits that power, anarchy, and security are socially created, within a cultural process where people's interests and identities are formed. For that reason, these key notions of international relations should have different meanings for different states. One state (country) may see a serious foreign threat where others see only a positive development. Like individuals, states can exaggerate external threats, undervalue them, or completely overlook them—all based on how they interpret these threats. During the past twenty years, constructivism became a third major theoretical approach to international relations, and some scholars believe it has even become a serious rival to both realism and liberalism (see Figure 3).

New theories have also appeared that emphasized cultural factors, such as identity, and differences between ethnic and cultural groups. Samuel Huntington and his followers argued that the major conflicts in world politics are not between states, but rather between *civilizations* unified by cultural or spiritual values. Iran and Saudi Arabia, in this view, struggle not over oil or influence in the region, but rather because of a deep-seated animosity between Persian and Arab civilizations. Similarly, some

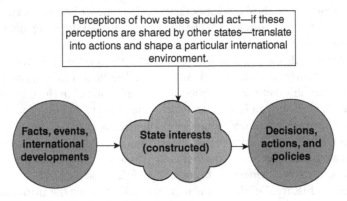

Figure 3.   The Logic of Constructivism

countries of Europe have for centuries treated Russia with great suspicion not just because of its policies, but also because they viewed the culture as alien and dangerous.

Almost every recent international development reveals other problems and issues that affect international relations as a discipline and its applications. Other developments reflect the discipline itself, such as the choice of research methods or the gap between university-based theoretical studies, on the one hand, and foreign policy agenda on the other. A significant proportion of contemporary studies rely mostly on sophisticated quantitative approaches incorporating advanced statistics. The process of quantification of knowledge is a positive development because it helps in establishing trends and verifying research hypotheses. At the same time, we should not forget that formulas and regressions are just a tool in advancing scientific knowledge. Statistical correlations cannot replace an expert's historical erudition and his or her ability for critical thinking, analysis, generalizations, creativity, and moral judgment. The trend toward mathematization of international relations should not lead to the advancement of science for science's sake if it remains detached from specific policies and, most essentially, the interests and rights of human beings. There are strong voices among scholars warning that the gap between international relations as a field and international realities has grown since the end of the Cold War in 1989-91.

So what must we do to bring research closer to the needs of the young generation that is exploring and entering the field of international relations? A good start will be to learn the skills of our predecessors in this discipline: their capacity for bold, innovative thinking and generalizations, their reliance on the knowledge in modern and contemporary history, and their ability to conduct interdisciplinary research and apply it to the challenging realities of the evolving world.

## GENERAL DISCUSSION QUESTIONS RELATED TO THE READINGS ON MAIN PERSPECTIVES, THEIR EVOLUTION, AND RELEVANCE

These general questions are for class discussions as well as individual assignments. The discussion of these questions should help students think more critically and better understand the materials in this section. Other, more specific critical-thinking and practice questions related to the reading materials appear at the end of Part I.

- Why is it important that the international relations discipline is drawing from a variety of fields such as sociology, behavioral economics, history, and political psychology?
- Consider several international events or developments of the past five or ten years. Which approach—realist or liberal—is more suitable, from your perspective, for interpreting these developments?

    - Iran's nuclear program and the debates around it
    - An international military operation in Libya in 2011
    - Territorial claims of several counties in the Arctic region
    - Events in and around Ukraine in 2014–19 and later
    - Events in Egypt, Syria, and Iraq in 2013–19 and later

- The disagreement between realists and liberal internationalists is about when and how force should be used in international relations. Discuss two or three (a) realist and (b) liberal arguments that should justify, in your view, the use of military force of one country against other countries. In other words, when can war be justified?
- Liberalism argues that cooperation, not confrontation such as military threats or annexation of territory, should foster international stability. Find and discuss facts from recent history or today's developments to (a) support and (b) challenge this assertion.
- What are the shortcomings of realism and liberalism in understanding international relations?
- Propose your own theory that will creatively blend the key principles of realism and liberalism. Use your theory to explain any international development of this year.
- Compose a list of major international military conflicts from 1990 (the end of the Cold War) until today. Which countries have been directly involved? List these countries and divide them into three categories: *established democracies*, *developing democracies*, and *nondemocracies*. Use the Democracy Index (available online) to judge the selected countries. Based on this list, discuss the liberal thesis that democracies do not go to war against one another.
- Kenneth Waltz argued that sovereign states respond to the condition of international anarchy according to an existing structure for an international system. During the Cold War, the system was bipolar. Consider the following:

  - What system do you envision in ten years and why?
  - Will it be bipolar, unipolar, tripolar, or multipolar?
  - Which countries will be in these poles?

- Dependency and Marxist theories seem to have regained their popularity in recent years. Why is this happening, from your standpoint? Which international and domestic developments in various countries could you explain using these theories?
- How many male and female secretaries of state have been there since 1992? Find this information on the web, including http://www.state.gov. Do your findings suggest that feminist criticisms of contemporary politics are no longer valid when applied to US foreign policy? Explain your opinion.
- Americans often criticize their presidents for their foreign policy actions or inaction. Would you criticize the current president? If so, for which specific foreign policies?

Introducing the Field

# The Clash of Civilizations?

SAMUEL P. HUNTINGTON

## THE NEXT PATTERN OF CONFLICT

World politics is entering a new phase, and intellectuals have not hesitated to proliferate visions of what it will be—the end of history, the return of traditional rivalries between nation states, and the decline of the nation state from the conflicting pulls of tribalism and globalism, among others. Each of these visions catches aspects of the emerging reality. Yet they all miss a crucial, indeed a central, aspect of what global politics is likely to be in the coming years.

It is my hypothesis that the fundamental source of conflict in this new world will not be primarily ideological or primarily economic. The great divisions among humankind and the dominating source of conflict will be cultural. Nation states will remain the most powerful actors in world affairs, but the principal conflicts of global politics will occur between nations and groups of different civilizations. The clash of civilizations will dominate global politics. The fault lines between civilizations will be the battle lines of the future.

Conflict between civilizations will be the latest phase in the evolution of conflict in the modern world. For a century and a half after the emergence of the modern international system with the Peace of Westphalia, the conflicts of the Western world were largely among princes—emperors, absolute monarchs and constitutional monarchs attempting to expand their bureaucracies, their armies, their mercantilist economic strength and, most important, the territory they ruled. In the process they created nation states, and beginning with the French Revolution the principal lines of conflict were between nations rather than princes. In 1793, as R. R. Palmer put it, "The wars of kings were over; the wars of peoples had begun." This nineteenth-century pattern lasted until the end of World War I. Then, as a result of the Russian Revolution and the reaction against it, the conflict of nations yielded to the conflict of ideologies, first among communism, fascism-Nazism and liberal democracy, and then between communism and liberal democracy. During the Cold War, this latter conflict became embodied in the struggle between the two superpowers, neither of which was a nation state in the classical European sense and each of which defined its identity in terms of its ideology.

These conflicts between princes, nation states and ideologies were primarily conflicts within Western civilization, "Western civil wars," as William Lind has labeled them. This was as true of the Cold War as it was of the world wars and the earlier wars of the seventeenth, eighteenth and nineteenth centuries. With the end of the Cold War, international politics moves out of its Western phase, and its centerpiece becomes the interaction between the West and non-Western civilizations and among non-Western civilizations. In the politics of civilizations, the peoples and governments of non-Western civilizations no longer remain the objects of history as targets of Western colonialism but join the West as movers and shapers of history.

## THE NATURE OF CIVILIZATIONS

During the Cold War the world was divided into the First, Second and Third Worlds. Those divisions are no longer relevant. It is far more meaningful now to group countries not in terms of their political or economic systems or in terms of their level of economic development but rather in terms of their culture and civilization.

What do we mean when we talk of a civilization? A civilization is a cultural entity. Villages, regions, ethnic groups, nationalities, religious groups, all have distinct cultures at different levels of cultural heterogeneity. The culture of a village in southern Italy may be different from that of a village in northern Italy, but both will share in a common Italian culture that distinguishes them from German villages. European communities, in turn, will share cultural features that distinguish them from Arab or Chinese communities. Arabs, Chinese and Westerners, however, are not part of any broader cultural entity. They constitute civilizations. A civilization is thus the highest cultural grouping of people and the broadest level of cultural identity people have short of that which distinguishes humans from other species. It is defined both by common objective elements, such as language, history, religion, customs, institutions, and by the subjective self-identification of people. People have levels of identity: a resident of Rome may define himself with varying degrees of intensity as a Roman, an Italian, a Catholic, a Christian, a European, a Westerner. The civilization to which he belongs is the broadest level of identification with which he intensely identifies. People can and do redefine their identities and, as a result, the composition and boundaries of civilizations change.

Civilizations may involve a large number of people, as with China ("a civilization pretending to be a state," as Lucian Pye put it), or a very small number of people, such as the Anglophone Caribbean. A civilization may include several nation states, as is the case with Western, Latin American and Arab civilizations, or only one, as is the case with Japanese civilization. Civilizations obviously blend and overlap, and may include sub-civilizations. Western civilization has two major variants, European and North American, and Islam has its Arab, Turkic and Malay subdivisions. Civilizations are nonetheless meaningful entities, and while the lines between them are seldom sharp, they are real. Civilizations are dynamic; they rise and fall; they divide and merge. And, as any student of history knows, civilizations disappear and are buried in the sands of time.

Westerners tend to think of nation states as the principal actors in global affairs. They have been that, however, for only a few centuries. The broader reaches of human history have been the history of civilizations. In *A Study of History*, Arnold Toynbee identified 21 major civilizations; only six of them exist in the contemporary world.

## WHY CIVILIZATIONS WILL CLASH

Civilization identity will be increasingly important in the future, and the world will be shaped in large measure by the interactions among seven or eight major civilizations. These include Western, Confucian, Japanese, Islamic, Hindu, Slavic-Orthodox, Latin American and possibly African civilization. The most important conflicts of the future will occur along the cultural fault lines separating these civilizations from one another.

Why will this be the case?

First, differences among civilizations are not only real; they are basic. Civilizations are differentiated from each other by history, language, culture, tradition and, most important, religion. The people of different civilizations have different views on the relations between God and man, the individual and the group, the citizen and the state, parents and children, husband and wife, as well as differing views of the relative importance of rights and responsibilities, liberty and authority, equality and hierarchy. These differences are the product of centuries. They will not soon disappear. They are far more fundamental than differences among political ideologies and political regimes. Differences do not necessarily mean conflict, and conflict does not necessarily mean violence. Over the centuries, however, differences among civilizations have generated the most prolonged and the most violent conflicts.

*The conflicts of the future will occur along the cultural fault lines separating civilizations.*

Second, the world is becoming a smaller place. The interactions between peoples of different civilizations are increasing; these increasing interactions intensify civilization consciousness and awareness of differences between civilizations and commonalities within civilizations. North African immigration to France generates hostility among Frenchmen and at the same time increased receptivity to immigration by "good" European

Catholic Poles. Americans react far more negatively to Japanese investment than to larger investments from Canada and European countries. Similarly, as Donald Horowitz has pointed out, "An Ibo may be . . . an Owerri Ibo or an Onitsha Ibo in what was the Eastern region of Nigeria. In Lagos, he is simply an Ibo. In London, he is a Nigerian. In New York, he is an African." The interactions among peoples of different civilizations enhance the civilization-consciousness of people that, in turn, invigorates differences and animosities stretching or thought to stretch back deep into history.

Third, the processes of economic modernization and social change throughout the world are separating people from longstanding local identities. They also weaken the nation state as a source of identity. In much of the world religion has moved in to fill this gap, often in the form of movements that are labeled "fundamentalist." Such movements are found in Western Christianity, Judaism, Buddhism and Hinduism, as well as in Islam. In most countries and most religions the people active in fundamentalist movements are young, college-educated, middle-class technicians, professionals and business persons. The "unsecularization of the world," George Weigel has remarked, "is one of the dominant social facts of life in the late twentieth century." The revival of religion, "la revanche de Dieu," as Gilles Kepel labeled it, provides a basis for identity and commitment that transcends national boundaries and unites civilizations.

Fourth, the growth of civilization-consciousness is enhanced by the dual role of the West. On the one hand, the West is at a peak of power. At the same time, however, and perhaps as a result, a return to the roots phenomenon is occurring among non-Western civilizations. Increasingly one hears references to trends toward a turning inward and "Asianization" in Japan, the end of the Nehru legacy and the "Hinduization" of India, the failure of Western ideas of socialism and nationalism and hence "re-Islamization" of the Middle East, and now a debate over Westernization versus Russianization in Boris Yeltsin's country. A West at the peak of its power confronts non-Wests that increasingly

have the desire, the will and the resources to shape the world in non-Western ways.

In the past, the elites of non-Western societies were usually the people who were most involved with the West, had been educated at Oxford, the Sorbonne or Sandhurst, and had absorbed Western attitudes and values. At the same time, the populace in non-Western countries often remained deeply imbued with the indigenous culture. Now, however, these relationships are being reversed. A de-Westernization and indigenization of elites is occurring in many non-Western countries at the same time that Western, usually American, cultures, styles and habits become more popular among the mass of the people.

Fifth, cultural characteristics and differences are less mutable and hence less easily compromised and resolved than political and economic ones. In the former Soviet Union, communists can become democrats, the rich can become poor and the poor rich, but Russians cannot become Estonians and Azeris cannot become Armenians. In class and ideological conflicts, the key question was "Which side are you on?" and people could and did choose sides and change sides. In conflicts between civilizations, the question is "What are you?" That is a given that cannot be changed. And as we know, from Bosnia to the Caucasus to the Sudan, the wrong answer to that question can mean a bullet in the head. Even more than ethnicity, religion discriminates sharply and exclusively among people. A person can be half-French and half-Arab and simultaneously even a citizen of two countries. It is more difficult to be half-Catholic and half-Muslim.

Finally, economic regionalism is increasing. The proportions of total trade that were intraregional rose between 1980 and 1989 from 51 percent to 59 percent in Europe, 33 percent to 37 percent in East Asia, and 32 percent to 36 percent in North America. The importance of regional economic blocs is likely to continue to increase in the future. On the one hand, successful economic regionalism will reinforce civilization-consciousness. On the other hand, economic regionalism may succeed only when it is rooted in a common civilization. The European Community rests on the shared foundation of European culture and Western

Christianity. The success of the North American Free Trade Area depends on the convergence now underway of Mexican, Canadian and American cultures. Japan, in contrast, faces difficulties in creating a comparable economic entity in East Asia because Japan is a society and civilization unique to itself. However strong the trade and investment links Japan may develop with other East Asian countries, its cultural differences with those countries inhibit and perhaps preclude its promoting regional economic integration like that in Europe and North America.

Common culture, in contrast, is clearly facilitating the rapid expansion of the economic relations between the People's Republic of China and Hong Kong, Taiwan, Singapore and the overseas Chinese communities in other Asian countries. With the Cold War over, cultural commonalities increasingly overcome ideological differences, and mainland China and Taiwan move closer together. If cultural commonality is a prerequisite for economic integration, the principal East Asian economic bloc of the future is likely to be centered on China. This bloc is, in fact, already coming into existence. As Murray Weidenbaum has observed,

> Despite the current Japanese dominance of the region, the Chinese-based economy of Asia is rapidly emerging as a new epicenter for industry, commerce and finance. This strategic area contains substantial amounts of technology and manufacturing capability (Taiwan), outstanding entrepreneurial, marketing and services acumen (Hong Kong), a fine communications network (Singapore), a tremendous pool of financial capital (all three), and very large endowments of land, resources and labor (mainland China).... From Guangzhou to Singapore, from Kuala Lumpur to Manila, this influential network—often based on extensions of the traditional clans—has been described as the backbone of the East Asian economy.[1]

Culture and religion also form the basis of the Economic Cooperation Organization, which brings together ten non-Arab Muslim countries: Iran, Pakistan, Turkey, Azerbaijan, Kazakhstan, Kyrgyzstan, Turkmenistan, Tadjikistan, Uzbekistan and Afghanistan. One impetus to the revival and expansion of this organization, founded originally in the 1960s by Turkey, Pakistan and Iran, is the realization by the leaders of several of these countries that they had no chance of admission to the European Community. Similarly, Caricom, the Central American Common Market and Mercosur rest on common cultural foundations. Efforts to build a broader Caribbean-Central American economic entity bridging the Anglo-Latin divide, however, have to date failed.

As people define their identity in ethnic and religious terms, they are likely to see an "us" versus "them" relation existing between themselves and people of different ethnicity or religion. The end of ideologically defined states in Eastern Europe and the former Soviet Union permits traditional ethnic identities and animosities to come to the fore. Differences in culture and religion create differences over policy issues, ranging from human rights to immigration to trade and commerce to the environment. Geographical propinquity gives rise to conflicting territorial claims from Bosnia to Mindanao. Most important, the efforts of the West to promote its values of democracy and liberalism as universal values, to maintain its military predominance and to advance its economic interests engender countering responses from other civilizations. Decreasingly able to mobilize support and form coalitions on the basis of ideology, governments and groups will increasingly attempt to mobilize support by appealing to common religion and civilization identity.

The clash of civilizations thus occurs at two levels. At the micro-level, adjacent groups along the fault lines between civilizations struggle, often violently, over the control of territory and each other. At the macro-level, states from different civilizations compete for relative military and economic power, struggle over the control of international institutions and third parties, and competitively promote their particular political and religious values.

## THE FAULT LINES BETWEEN CIVILIZATIONS

The fault lines between civilizations are replacing the political and ideological boundaries of the Cold War as the flash points for crisis and bloodshed. The Cold War began when the Iron Curtain divided Europe politically and ideologically. The Cold War ended with the end of the Iron Curtain. As the ideological division of Europe has disappeared, the cultural division of Europe between Western Christianity, on the one hand, and Orthodox Christianity and Islam, on the other, has reemerged. The most significant dividing line in Europe, as William Wallace has suggested, may well be the eastern boundary of Western Christianity in the year 1500. This line runs along what are now the boundaries between Finland and Russia and between the Baltic states and Russia, cuts through Belarus and Ukraine separating the more Catholic western Ukraine from Orthodox eastern Ukraine, swings westward separating Transylvania from the rest of Romania, and then goes through Yugoslavia almost exactly along the line now separating Croatia and Slovenia from the rest of Yugoslavia. In the Balkans this line, of course, coincides with the historic boundary between the Hapsburg and Ottoman empires. The peoples to the north and west of this line are Protestant or Catholic; they shared the common experiences of European history—feudalism, the Renaissance, the Reformation, the Enlightenment, the French Revolution, the Industrial Revolution; they are generally economically better off than the peoples to the east; and they may now look forward to increasing involvement in a common European economy and to the consolidation of democratic political systems. The peoples to the east and south of this line are Orthodox or Muslim; they historically belonged to the Ottoman or Tsarist empires and were only lightly touched by the shaping events in the rest of Europe; they are generally less advanced economically; they seem much less likely to develop stable democratic political systems. The Velvet Curtain of culture has replaced the Iron Curtain of ideology as the most significant dividing line in Europe. As the events in Yugoslavia show, it is not only a line of difference; it is also at times a line of bloody conflict.

Conflict along the fault line between Western and Islamic civilizations has been going on for 1,300 years. After the founding of Islam, the Arab and Moorish surge west and north only ended at Tours in 732. From the eleventh to the thirteenth century the Crusaders attempted with temporary success to bring Christianity and Christian rule to the Holy Land. From the fourteenth to the seventeenth century, the Ottoman Turks reversed the balance, extended their sway over the Middle East and the Balkans, captured Constantinople, and twice laid siege to Vienna. In the nineteenth and early twentieth centuries as Ottoman power declined Britain, France, and Italy established Western control over most of North Africa and the Middle East.

After World War II, the West, in turn, began to retreat; the colonial empires disappeared; first Arab nationalism and then Islamic fundamentalism manifested themselves; the West became heavily dependent on the Persian Gulf countries for its energy; the oil-rich Muslim countries became money-rich and, when they wished to, weapons-rich. Several wars occurred between Arabs and Israel (created by the West). France fought a bloody and ruthless war in Algeria for most of the 1950s; British and French forces invaded Egypt in 1956; American forces went into Lebanon in 1958; subsequently American forces returned to Lebanon, attacked Libya, and engaged in various military encounters with Iran; Arab and Islamic terrorists, supported by at least three Middle Eastern governments, employed the weapon of the weak and bombed Western planes and installations and seized Western hostages. This warfare between Arabs and the West culminated in 1990, when the United States sent a massive army to the Persian Gulf to defend some Arab countries against aggression by another. In its aftermath NATO planning is increasingly directed to potential threats and instability along its "southern tier."

This centuries-old military interaction between the West and Islam is unlikely to decline. It could become more virulent. The Gulf War left some Arabs feeling proud that Saddam Hussein had attacked Israel and stood up to the West. It also left many feeling humiliated and resentful of the West's military presence in the Persian Gulf, the West's overwhelming military dominance, and their apparent inability to shape their own destiny. Many

Arab countries, in addition to the oil exporters, are reaching levels of economic and social development where autocratic forms of government become inappropriate and efforts to introduce democracy become stronger. Some openings in Arab political systems have already occurred. The principal beneficiaries of these openings have been Islamist movements. In the Arab world, in short, Western democracy strengthens anti-Western political forces. This may be a passing phenomenon, but it surely complicates relations between Islamic countries and the West.

Those relations are also complicated by demography. The spectacular population growth in Arab countries, particularly in North Africa, has led to increased migration to Western Europe. The movement within Western Europe toward minimizing internal boundaries has sharpened political sensitivities with respect to this development. In Italy, France and Germany, racism is increasingly open, and political reactions and violence against Arab and Turkish migrants have become more intense and more widespread since 1990.

On both sides the interaction between Islam and the West is seen as a clash of civilizations. The West's "next confrontation," observes M. J. Akbar, an Indian Muslim author, "is definitely going to come from the Muslim world. It is in the sweep of the Islamic nations from the Maghreb to Pakistan that the struggle for a new world order will begin." Bernard Lewis comes to a similar conclusion:

We are facing a mood and a movement far transcending the level of issues and policies and the governments that pursue them. This is no less than a clash of civilizations—the perhaps irrational but surely historic reaction of an ancient rival against our Judeo-Christian heritage, our secular present, and the worldwide expansion of both.[2]

Historically, the other great antagonistic interaction of Arab Islamic civilization has been with the pagan, animist, and now increasingly Christian black peoples to the south. In the past, this antagonism was epitomized in the image of Arab slave dealers and black slaves. It has been reflected in the on-going civil war in the Sudan between Arabs and blacks, the fighting in Chad

between Libyan-supported insurgents and the government, the tensions between Orthodox Christians and Muslims in the Horn of Africa, and the political conflicts, recurring riots and communal violence between Muslims and Christians in Nigeria. The modernization of Africa and the spread of Christianity are likely to enhance the probability of violence along this fault line. Symptomatic of the intensification of this conflict was the Pope John Paul II's speech in Khartoum in February 1993 attacking the actions of the Sudan's Islamist government against the Christian minority there.

On the northern border of Islam, conflict has increasingly erupted between Orthodox and Muslim peoples, including the carnage of Bosnia and Sarajevo, the simmering violence between Serb and Albanian, the tenuous relations between Bulgarians and their Turkish minority, the violence between Ossetians and Ingush, the unremitting slaughter of each other by Armenians and Azeris, the tense relations between Russians and Muslims in Central Asia, and the deployment of Russian troops to protect Russian interests in the Caucasus and Central Asia. Religion reinforces the revival of ethnic identities and restimulates Russian fears about the security of their southern borders. This concern is well captured by Archie Roosevelt:

Much of Russian history concerns the struggle between the Slavs and the Turkic peoples on their borders, which dates back to the foundation of the Russian state more than a thousand years ago. In the Slavs' millennium-long confrontation with their eastern neighbors lies the key to an understanding not only of Russian history, but Russian character. To understand Russian realities today one has to have a concept of the great Turkic ethnic group that has preoccupied Russians through the centuries.[3]

The conflict of civilizations is deeply rooted elsewhere in Asia. The historic clash between Muslim and Hindu in the subcontinent manifests itself now not only in the rivalry between Pakistan and India but also in intensifying religious strife within India between increasingly militant Hindu groups and India's substantial Muslim minority. The destruction of the Ayodhya mosque in December 1992 brought to the fore the issue of whether India will remain a secular democratic state or become a Hindu one. In East Asia, China has outstanding territorial disputes with most of its neighbors. It has pursued a ruthless policy toward the Buddhist people of Tibet, and it is pursuing an increasingly ruthless policy toward its Turkic-Muslim minority. With the Cold War over, the underlying differences between China and the United States have reasserted themselves in areas such as human rights, trade and weapons proliferation. These differences are unlikely to moderate. A "new cold war," Deng Xaioping reportedly asserted in 1991, is under way between China and America.

*The crescent-shaped Islamic bloc, from the bulge of Africa to central Asia, has bloody borders.*

The same phrase has been applied to the increasingly difficult relations between Japan and the United States. Here cultural difference exacerbates economic conflict. People on each side allege racism on the other, but at least on the American side the antipathies are not racial but cultural. The basic values, attitudes, behavioral patterns of the two societies could hardly be more different. The economic issues between the United States and Europe are no less serious than those between the United States and Japan, but they do not have the same political salience and emotional intensity because the differences between American culture and European culture are so much less than those between American civilization and Japanese civilization.

The interactions between civilizations vary greatly in the extent to which they are likely to be characterized by violence. Economic competition clearly predominates between the American and European subcivilizations of the West and between both of them and Japan. On the Eurasian continent, however, the proliferation of ethnic conflict, epitomized at the extreme in "ethnic cleansing," has not been totally random. It has been most frequent and most violent between

groups belonging to different civilizations. In Eurasia the great historic fault lines between civilizations are once more aflame. This is particularly true along the boundaries of the crescent-shaped Islamic bloc of nations from the bulge of Africa to central Asia. Violence also occurs between Muslims, on the one hand, and Orthodox Serbs in the Balkans, Jews in Israel, Hindus in India, Buddhists in Burma and Catholics in the Philippines. Islam has bloody borders.

## CIVILIZATION RALLYING: THE KIN-COUNTRY SYNDROME

Groups or states belonging to one civilization that become involved in war with people from a different civilization naturally try to rally support from other members of their own civilization. As the post-Cold War world evolves, civilization commonality, what H. D. S. Greenway has termed the "kin-country" syndrome, is replacing political ideology and traditional balance of power considerations as the principal basis for cooperation and coalitions. It can be seen gradually emerging in the post-Cold War conflicts in the Persian Gulf, the Caucasus and Bosnia. None of these was a full-scale war between civilizations, but each involved some elements of civilizational rallying, which seemed to become more important as the conflict continued and which may provide a foretaste of the future.

First, in the Gulf War one Arab state invaded another and then fought a coalition of Arab, Western and other states. While only a few Muslim governments overtly supported Saddam Hussein, many Arab elites privately cheered him on, and he was highly popular among large sections of the Arab publics. Islamic fundamentalist movements universally supported Iraq rather than the Western-backed governments of Kuwait and Saudi Arabia. Forswearing Arab nationalism, Saddam Hussein explicitly invoked an Islamic appeal. He and his supporters attempted to define the war as a war between civilizations. "It is not the world against Iraq," as Safar Al-Hawali, dean of Islamic Studies at the Umm Al-Qura University in Mecca, put it in a widely circulated tape. "It is the West against Islam."

Ignoring the rivalry between Iran and Iraq, the chief Iranian religious leader, Ayatollah Ali Khamenei, called for a holy war against the West: "The struggle against American aggression, greed, plans and policies will be counted as a jihad, and anybody who is killed on that path is a martyr." "This is a war," King Hussein of Jordan argued, "against all Arabs and all Muslims and not against Iraq alone."

The rallying of substantial sections of Arab elites and publics behind Saddam Hussein caused those Arab governments in the anti-Iraq coalition to moderate their activities and temper their public statements. Arab governments opposed or distanced themselves from subsequent Western efforts to apply pressure on Iraq, including enforcement of a no-fly zone in the summer of 1992 and the bombing of Iraq in January 1993. The Western-Soviet-Turkish-Arab anti-Iraq coalition of 1990 had by 1993 become a coalition of almost only the West and Kuwait against Iraq.

Muslims contrasted Western actions against Iraq with the West's failure to protect Bosnians against Serbs and to impose sanctions on Israel for violating U.N. resolutions. The West, they alleged, was using a double standard. A world of clashing civilizations, however, is inevitably a world of double standards: people apply one standard to their kin-countries and a different standard to others.

Second, the kin-country syndrome also appeared in conflicts in the former Soviet Union. Armenian military successes in 1992 and 1993 stimulated Turkey to become increasingly supportive of its religious, ethnic and linguistic brethren in Azerbaijan. "We have a Turkish nation feeling the same sentiments as the Azerbaijanis," said one Turkish official in 1992. "We are under pressure. Our newspapers are full of the photos of atrocities and are asking us if we are still serious about pursuing our neutral policy. Maybe we should show Armenia that there's a big Turkey in the region." President Turgut Özal agreed, remarking that Turkey should at least "scare the Armenians a little bit." Turkey, Özal threatened again in 1993, would "show its fangs." Turkish Air Force jets flew reconnaissance flights along the Armenian border; Turkey suspended food shipments and air

flights to Armenia; and Turkey and Iran announced they would not accept dismemberment of Azerbaijan. In the last years of its existence, the Soviet government supported Azerbaijan because its government was dominated by former communists. With the end of the Soviet Union, however, political considerations gave way to religious ones. Russian troops fought on the side of the Armenians, and Azerbaijan accused the "Russian government of turning 180 degrees" toward support for Christian Armenia.

Third, with respect to the fighting in the former Yugoslavia, Western publics manifested sympathy and support for the Bosnian Muslims and the horrors they suffered at the hands of the Serbs. Relatively little concern was expressed, however, over Croatian attacks on Muslims and participation in the dismemberment of Bosnia-Herzegovina. In the early stages of the Yugoslav breakup, Germany, in an unusual display of diplomatic initiative and muscle, induced the other 11 members of the European Community to follow its lead in recognizing Slovenia and Croatia. As a result of the pope's determination to provide strong backing to the two Catholic countries, the Vatican extended recognition even before the Community did. The United States followed the European lead. Thus the leading actors in Western civilization rallied behind their coreligionists. Subsequently Croatia was reported to be receiving substantial quantities of arms from Central European and other Western countries. Boris Yeltsin's government, on the other hand, attempted to pursue a middle course that would be sympathetic to the Orthodox Serbs but not alienate Russia from the West. Russian conservative and nationalist groups, however, including many legislators, attacked the government for not being more forthcoming in its support for the Serbs. By early 1993 several hundred Russians apparently were serving with the Serbian forces, and reports circulated of Russian arms being supplied to Serbia.

Islamic governments and groups, on the other hand, castigated the West for not coming to the defense of the Bosnians. Iranian leaders urged Muslims from all countries to provide help to Bosnia; in violation of the U.N. arms embargo, Iran supplied weapons and men for the Bosnians; Iranian-supported Lebanese groups sent guerrillas to train and organize the Bosnian forces. In 1993 up to 4,000 Muslims from over two dozen Islamic countries were reported to be fighting in Bosnia. The governments of Saudi Arabia and other countries felt under increasing pressure from fundamentalist groups in their own societies to provide more vigorous support for the Bosnians. By the end of 1992, Saudi Arabia had reportedly supplied substantial funding for weapons and supplies for the Bosnians, which significantly increased their military capabilities vis-à-vis the Serbs.

In the 1930s the Spanish Civil War provoked intervention from countries that politically were fascist, communist and democratic. In the 1990s the Yugoslav conflict is provoking intervention from countries that are Muslim, Orthodox and Western Christian. The parallel has not gone unnoticed. "The war in Bosnia-Herzegovina has become the emotional equivalent of the fight against fascism in the Spanish Civil War," one Saudi editor observed. "Those who died there are regarded as martyrs who tried to save their fellow Muslims."

Conflicts and violence will also occur between states and groups within the same civilization. Such conflicts, however, are likely to be less intense and less likely to expand than conflicts between civilizations. Common membership in a civilization reduces the probability of violence in situations where it might otherwise occur. In 1991 and 1992 many people were alarmed by the possibility of violent conflict between Russia and Ukraine over territory, particularly Crimea, the Black Sea fleet, nuclear weapons and economic issues. If civilization is what counts, however, the likelihood of violence between Ukrainians and Russians should be low. They are two Slavic, primarily Orthodox peoples who have had close relationships with each other for centuries. As of early 1993, despite all the reasons for conflict, the leaders of the two countries were effectively negotiating and defusing the issues between the two countries. While there has been serious fighting between Muslims and Christians elsewhere in the former Soviet Union and much tension and some fighting between Western and Orthodox Christians in the Baltic states, there has been virtually no violence between Russians and Ukrainians.

Civilization rallying to date has been limited, but it has been growing, and it clearly has the potential to spread much further. As the conflicts in the Persian Gulf, the Caucasus and Bosnia continued, the positions of nations and the cleavages between them increasingly were along civilizational lines. Populist politicians, religious leaders and the media have found it a potent means of arousing mass support and of pressuring hesitant governments. In the coming years, the local conflicts most likely to escalate into major wars will be those, as in Bosnia and the Caucasus, along the fault lines between civilizations. The next world war, if there is one, will be a war between civilizations.

## THE WEST VERSUS THE REST

The West is now at an extraordinary peak of power in relation to other civilizations. Its superpower opponent has disappeared from the map. Military conflict among Western states is unthinkable, and Western military power is unrivaled. Apart from Japan, the West faces no economic challenge. It dominates international political and security institutions and with Japan international economic institutions. Global political and security issues are effectively settled by a directorate of the United States, Britain and France, world economic issues by a directorate of the United States, Germany and Japan, all of which maintain extraordinarily close relations with each other to the exclusion of lesser and largely non-Western countries. Decisions made at the U.N. Security Council or in the International Monetary Fund that reflect the interests of the West are presented to the world as reflecting the desires of the world community. The very phrase "the world community" has become the euphemistic collective noun (replacing "the Free World") to give global legitimacy to actions reflecting the interests of the United States and other Western powers.[4] Through the IMF and other international economic institutions, the West promotes its economic interests and imposes on other nations the economic policies it thinks appropriate.

In any poll of non-Western peoples, the IMF undoubtedly would win the support of finance ministers and a few others, but get an overwhelmingly unfavorable rating from just about everyone else, who would agree with Georgy Arbatov's characterization of IMF officials as "neo-Bolsheviks who love expropriating other people's money, imposing undemocratic and alien rules of economic and political conduct and stifling economic freedom."

Western domination of the U.N. Security Council and its decisions, tempered only by occasional abstention by China, produced U.N. legitimation of the West's use of force to drive Iraq out of Kuwait and its elimination of Iraq's sophisticated weapons and capacity to produce such weapons. It also produced the quite unprecedented action by the United States, Britain and France in getting the Security Council to demand that Libya hand over the Pan Am 103 bombing suspects and then to impose sanctions when Libya refused. After defeating the largest Arab army, the West did not hesitate to throw its weight around in the Arab world. The West in effect is using international institutions, military power and economic resources to run the world in ways that will maintain Western predominance, protect Western interests and promote Western political and economic values.

*The very phrase "world community" has become a euphemism to give legitimacy to the actions of the West.*

That at least is the way in which non-Westerners see the new world, and there is a significant element of truth in their view. Differences in power and struggles for military, economic and institutional power are thus one source of conflict between the West and other civilizations. Differences in culture, that is basic values and beliefs, are a second source of conflict. V. S. Naipaul has argued that Western civilization is the "universal civilization" that "fits all men." At a superficial level much of Western culture has indeed permeated the rest of the world. At a more basic level, however, Western concepts differ fundamentally from those prevalent in other civilizations. Western ideas of individualism, liberalism, constitutionalism, human rights, equality, liberty, the rule of law, democracy, free markets, the separation of church and state, often have little resonance in Islamic, Confucian, Japanese, Hindu, Buddhist or Orthodox cultures. Western efforts to propagate such ideas produce instead a reaction against "human rights imperialism" and a reaffirmation of indigenous values, as can be seen in the support for religious fundamentalism by the younger generation in non-Western cultures. The very notion that there could be a "universal civilization" is a Western idea, directly at odds with the particularism of most Asian societies and their emphasis on what distinguishes one people from another. Indeed, the author of a review of 100 comparative studies of values in different societies concluded that "the values that are most important in the West are least important worldwide."[5] In the political realm, of course, these differences are most manifest in the efforts of the United States and other Western powers to induce other peoples to adopt Western ideas concerning democracy and human rights. Modern democratic government originated in the West. When it has developed in non-Western societies it has usually been the product of Western colonialism or imposition.

The central axis of world politics in the future is likely to be, in Kishore Mahbubani's phrase, the conflict between "the West and the Rest" and the responses of non-Western civilizations to Western power and values.[6] Those responses generally take one or a combination of three forms. At one extreme, non-Western states can, like Burma and North Korea, attempt to pursue a course of isolation, to insulate their societies from penetration or "corruption" by the West, and, in effect, to opt out of participation in the Western-dominated global community. The costs of this course, however, are high, and few states have pursued it exclusively. A second alternative, the equivalent of "band-wagoning" in international relations theory, is to attempt to join the West and accept its values and institutions. The third alternative is to attempt to "balance" the West by developing economic and military power and cooperating with other non-Western societies against the West, while preserving indigenous values and institutions; in short, to modernize but not to Westernize.

## THE TORN COUNTRIES

In the future, as people differentiate themselves by civilization, countries with large numbers of peoples of different civilizations, such as the Soviet Union and Yugoslavia, are candidates for dismemberment. Some other countries have a fair degree of cultural homogeneity but are divided over whether their society belongs to one civilization or another. These are torn countries. Their leaders typically wish to pursue a bandwagoning strategy and to make their countries members of the West, but the history, culture and traditions of their countries are non-Western. The most obvious and prototypical torn country is Turkey. The late twentieth-century leaders of Turkey have followed in the Attatürk tradition and defined Turkey as a modern, secular, Western nation state. They allied Turkey with the West in NATO and in the Gulf War; they applied for membership in the European Community. At the same time, however, elements in Turkish society have supported an Islamic revival and have argued that Turkey is basically a Middle Eastern Muslim society. In addition, while the elite of Turkey has defined Turkey as a Western society, the elite of the West refuses to accept Turkey as such. Turkey will not become a member of the European Community, and the real reason, as President Özal said, "is that we are Muslim and they are Christian and they don't say that." Having rejected Mecca, and then being rejected by Brussels, where does Turkey look? Tashkent may be the answer. The end of the Soviet Union gives Turkey the opportunity to become the leader of a revived Turkic civilization involving seven countries from the borders of Greece to those of China. Encouraged by the West, Turkey is making strenuous efforts to carve out this new identity for itself.

During the past decade Mexico has assumed a position somewhat similar to that of Turkey. Just as Turkey abandoned its historic opposition to Europe and attempted to join Europe, Mexico has stopped defining itself by its opposition to the United States and is instead attempting to imitate the United States and to join it in the North American Free Trade Area. Mexican leaders are engaged in the great task of redefining Mexican identity and have introduced fundamental economic reforms that eventually will lead to fundamental political change. In 1991 a top adviser to President Carlos Salinas de Gortari described at length to me all the changes the Salinas government was making. When he finished, I remarked: "That's most impressive. It seems to me that basically you want to change Mexico from a Latin American country into a North American country." He looked at me with surprise and exclaimed: "Exactly! That's precisely what we are trying to do, but of course we could never say so publicly." As his remark indicates, in Mexico as in Turkey, significant elements in society resist the redefinition of their country's identity. In Turkey, European-oriented leaders have to make gestures to Islam (Özal's pilgrimage to Mecca); so also Mexico's North American-oriented leaders have to make gestures to those who hold Mexico to be a Latin American country (Salinas' Ibero-American Guadalajara summit).

Historically Turkey has been the most profoundly torn country. For the United States, Mexico is the most immediate torn country. Globally the most important torn country is Russia. The question of whether Russia is part of the West or the leader of a distinct Slavic-Orthodox civilization has been a recurring one in Russian history. That issue was obscured by the communist victory in Russia, which imported a Western ideology, adapted it to Russian conditions and then challenged the West in the name of that ideology. The dominance of communism shut off the historic debate over Westernization versus Russification. With communism discredited Russians once again face that question.

President Yeltsin is adopting Western principles and goals and seeking to make Russia a "normal" country and a part of the West. Yet both the Russian elite and the Russian public are divided on this issue. Among the more moderate dissenters, Sergei Stankevich argues that Russia should reject the "Atlanticist" course, which would lead it "to become European, to become a part of the world economy in rapid and organized fashion, to become the eighth member of the Seven, and to put particular emphasis on Germany and the United States as the two dominant members of the Atlantic alliance." While also rejecting an exclusively Eurasian policy, Stankevich nonetheless argues that Russia should give priority to the protection of Russians in other countries, emphasize its Turkic and Muslim connections, and promote "an appreciable redistribution of our resources, our options, our ties, and our interests in favor of Asia, of the eastern direction." People of this persuasion criticize Yeltsin for subordinating Russia's interests to those of the West, for reducing Russian military strength, for failing to support traditional friends such as Serbia, and for pushing economic and political reform in ways injurious to the Russian people. Indicative of this trend is the new popularity of the ideas of Petr Savitsky, who in the 1920s argued that Russia was a unique Eurasian civilization.[7] More extreme dissidents voice much more blatantly nationalist, anti-Western and anti-Semitic views, and urge Russia to redevelop its military strength and to establish closer ties with China and Muslim countries. The people of Russia are as divided as the elite. An opinion survey in European Russia in the spring of 1992 revealed that 40 percent of the public had positive attitudes toward the West and 36 percent had negative attitudes. As it has been for much of its history, Russia in the early 1990s is truly a torn country.

To redefine its civilization identity, a torn country must meet three requirements. First, its political and economic elite has to be generally supportive of and enthusiastic about this move. Second, its public has to be willing to acquiesce in the redefinition. Third, the dominant groups in the recipient civilization have to be willing to embrace the convert. All three requirements in large part exist with respect to Mexico. The first two in large part exist with respect to Turkey. It is not clear that any of them exist with respect to Russia's joining the West. The conflict between liberal democracy and Marxism-Leninism was between ideologies which, despite their major differences, ostensibly shared ultimate goals of freedom, equality and prosperity. A traditional, authoritarian, nationalist Russia could have quite different goals. A Western democrat could carry on an intellectual debate with a Soviet Marxist. It would be virtually impossible for him to do that with a Russian traditionalist. If, as the Russians stop behaving like Marxists, they reject liberal democracy and begin behaving like Russians but not like Westerners, the relations between Russia and the West could again become distant and conflictual.[8]

## THE CONFUCIAN-ISLAMIC CONNECTION

The obstacles to non-Western countries joining the West vary considerably. They are least for Latin American and East European countries. They are greater for the Orthodox countries of the former Soviet Union. They are still greater for Muslim, Confucian, Hindu and Buddhist societies. Japan has established a unique position for itself as an associate member of the West: it is in the West in some respects but clearly not of the West in important dimensions. Those countries that for reason of culture and power do not wish to, or cannot, join the West compete with the West by developing their own economic, military and political power. They do this by promoting their internal development and by cooperating with other non-Western countries. The most prominent form of this cooperation is the Confucian-Islamic connection that has emerged to challenge Western interests, values and power.

Almost without exception, Western countries are reducing their military power; under Yeltsin's leadership so also is Russia. China, North Korea and several Middle Eastern states, however, are significantly expanding their military capabilities. They are doing this by the import of arms from Western and non-Western sources and by the development of indigenous arms industries. One result is the emergence of what Charles Krauthammer has called "Weapon States," and the Weapon States are not Western states. Another result is the redefinition of arms control, which is a Western concept and a Western goal. During the Cold War the primary purpose of arms control was to establish a stable military balance between the United States and its allies and the Soviet Union and its allies. In the post-Cold War world the primary objective of arms control is to prevent the development by non-Western societies of military capabilities that could threaten Western interests. The West attempts to do this through international agreements, economic pressure and controls on the transfer of arms and weapons technologies.

The conflict between the West and the Confucian-Islamic states focuses largely, although not exclusively, on nuclear, chemical and biological weapons, ballistic missiles and other sophisticated means for delivering them, and the guidance, intelligence and other electronic capabilities for achieving that goal. The West promotes non-proliferation as a universal norm and nonproliferation treaties and inspections as means of realizing that norm. It also threatens a variety of sanctions against those who promote the spread of sophisticated weapons and proposes some benefits for those who do not. The attention of the West focuses, naturally, on nations that are actually or potentially hostile to the West.

*A Confucian-Islamic connection has emerged to challenge Western interests, values and power.*

The non-Western nations, on the other hand, assert their right to acquire and to deploy whatever weapons they think necessary for their security. They also have absorbed, to the full, the truth of the response of the Indian defense minister when asked what lesson he learned from the Gulf War: "Don't fight the United States unless you have nuclear weapons." Nuclear weapons, chemical weapons and missiles are viewed, probably erroneously, as the potential equalizer of superior Western conventional power. China, of course, already has nuclear weapons; Pakistan and India have the capability to deploy them. North Korea, Iran, Iraq, Libya and Algeria appear to be attempting to acquire them. A top Iranian official has declared that all Muslim states should acquire nuclear weapons, and in 1988 the president of Iran reportedly issued a directive calling for development of "offensive and defensive chemical, biological and radiological weapons."

Centrally important to the development of counter-West military capabilities is the sustained expansion of China's military power and its means to create military power. Buoyed by spectacular economic development, China is rapidly increasing its military spending and vigorously moving forward with the modernization of its armed forces. It is purchasing weapons from the former Soviet states; it is developing long-range missiles; in 1992 it tested a one-megaton nuclear device. It is developing power-projection capabilities, acquiring aerial refueling technology, and trying to purchase an aircraft carrier. Its military buildup and assertion of sovereignty over the South China Sea are provoking a multilateral regional arms race in East Asia. China is also a major exporter of arms and weapons technology. It has exported materials to Libya and Iraq that could be used to manufacture nuclear weapons and nerve gas. It has helped Algeria build a reactor suitable for nuclear weapons research and production. China has sold to Iran nuclear technology that American officials believe could only be used to create weapons and apparently has shipped components of 300-mile-range missiles to Pakistan. North Korea has had a nuclear weapons program under way for some while and has sold advanced missiles and missile technology to Syria and Iran. The flow of weapons and weapons technology is generally from East Asia to the Middle East. There is, however, some movement in the reverse direction; China has received Stinger missiles from Pakistan.

A Confucian-Islamic military connection has thus come into being, designed to promote acquisition by its members of the weapons and weapons technologies needed to counter the military power of the West. It may or may not last. At present, however, it is, as Dave McCurdy has said, "a renegades' mutual support pact, run by the proliferators and their backers." A new form of arms competition is thus occurring between Islamic-Confucian states and the West. In an old-fashioned arms race, each side developed its own arms to balance or to achieve superiority against the other side. In this new form of arms competition, one side is developing its arms and the other side is attempting not to balance but to limit and prevent that arms build-up while at the same time reducing its own military capabilities.

## IMPLICATIONS FOR THE WEST

This article does not argue that civilization identities will replace all other identities, that nation states will disappear, that each civilization will become a single coherent political entity, that groups within a civilization will not conflict with and even fight each other. This paper does set forth the hypotheses that differences between civilizations are real and important; civilization-consciousness is increasing; conflict between civilizations will supplant ideological and other forms of conflict as the dominant global form of conflict; international relations, historically a game played out within Western civilization, will increasingly be de-Westernized and become a game in which non-Western civilizations are actors and not simply objects; successful political, security and economic international institutions are more likely to develop within civilizations than across civilizations; conflicts between groups in different civilizations will be more frequent, more sustained and more violent than conflicts between groups in the same civilization; violent conflicts between groups in different civilizations are the most likely and most dangerous source of escalation that could lead to global wars; the paramount axis of world politics will be the relations between "the West and the Rest"; the elites in some torn non-Western countries will try to make their countries part of the West, but in most cases face major obstacles to accomplishing this; a central focus of conflict for the immediate future will be between the West and several Islamic-Confucian states.

This is not to advocate the desirability of conflicts between civilizations. It is to set forth descriptive hypotheses as to what the future may be like. If these are plausible hypotheses, however, it is necessary to consider their implications for Western policy. These implications should be divided between short-term advantage and long-term accommodation. In the short term it is clearly in the interest of the West to promote greater cooperation and unity within its own civilization, particularly between its European and North American components; to incorporate into the West societies in Eastern Europe and Latin America whose cultures are close to those of the West; to promote and maintain cooperative relations with Russia and Japan; to prevent escalation of local inter-civilization conflicts into major inter-civilization wars; to limit the expansion of the military strength of Confucian and Islamic states; to moderate the reduction of Western military capabilities and maintain military superiority in East and Southwest Asia; to exploit differences and conflicts among Confucian and Islamic states; to support in other civilizations groups sympathetic to Western values and interests; to strengthen international institutions that reflect and legitimate Western interests and values and to promote the involvement of non-Western states in those institutions.

In the longer term other measures would be called for. Western civilization is both Western and modern. Non-Western civilizations have attempted to become modern without becoming Western. To date only Japan has fully succeeded in this quest. Non-Western civilizations will continue to attempt to acquire the wealth, technology, skills, machines and weapons that are part of being modern. They will also attempt to reconcile this modernity with their traditional culture and values. Their economic and military strength relative to the West will increase. Hence the West will increasingly have to accommodate these non-Western modern civilizations whose power approaches that of the West but whose values and interests differ significantly from those of the West. This will require the West to maintain the economic and military power necessary to protect its interests in relation to these civilizations. It will also, however, require the West to develop a more profound understanding of the basic religious and philosophical assumptions underlying other civilizations and the ways in which people in those civilizations see their interests. It will require an effort to identify elements of commonality between Western and other civilizations. For the relevant future, there will be no universal civilization, but instead a world of different civilizations, each of which will have to learn to coexist with the others.

## Notes

[1] Murray Weidenbaum, *Greater China: The Next Economic Superpower?*, St. Louis: Washington University Center for the Study of American Business, Contemporary Issues, Series 57, February 1993, pp. 2–3.

[2] Bernard Lewis, "The Roots of Muslim Rage," *The Atlantic Monthly*, vol. 266, September 1990, p. 60; *Time*, June 15, 1992, pp. 24–28.

[3] Archie Roosevelt, *For Lust of Knowing*, Boston: Little, Brown, 1988, pp. 332–333.

[4] Almost invariably Western leaders claim they are acting on behalf of "the world community." One minor lapse occurred during the run-up to the Gulf War. In an interview on "Good Morning America," Dec. 21, 1990, British Prime Minister John Major referred to the actions "the West" was taking against Saddam Hussein. He quickly corrected himself and subsequently referred to "the world community." He was, however, right when he erred.

[5] Harry C. Triandis, *The New York Times*, Dec. 25, 1990, p. 41, and "Cross-Cultural Studies of Individualism and Collectivism," Nebraska Symposium on Motivation, vol. 37, 1989, pp. 41–133.

[6] Kishore Mahbubani, "The West and the Rest," *The National Interest*, Summer 1992, pp. 3–13.

[7] Sergei Stankevich, "Russia in Search of Itself," *The National Interest*, Summer 1992, pp. 47–51; Daniel Schneider, "A Russian Movement Rejects Western Tilt," *Christian Science Monitor*, Feb. 5, 1993, pp. 5–7.

[8] Owen Harries has pointed out that Australia is trying (unwisely in his view) to become a torn country in reverse. Although it has been a full member not only of the West but also of the ABCA military and intelligence core of the West, its current leaders are in effect proposing that it defect from the West, redefine itself as an Asian country and cultivate close ties with its neighbors. Australia's future, they argue, is with the dynamic economies of East Asia. But, as I have suggested, close economic cooperation normally requires a common cultural base. In addition, none of the three conditions necessary for a torn country to join another civilization is likely to exist in Australia's case.

# The Sovereign State Is Just About Dead

FROM, "SOVEREIGNTY" BY STEPHEN D. KRASNER

**Very wrong.** Sovereignty was never quite as vibrant as many contemporary observers suggest. The conventional norms of sovereignty have always been challenged. A few states, most notably the United States, have had autonomy, control, and recognition for most of their existence, but most others have not. The polities of many weaker states have been persistently penetrated, and stronger nations have not been immune to external influence. China was occupied. The constitutional arrangements of Japan and Germany were directed by the United States after World War II. The United Kingdom, despite its rejection of the euro, is part of the European Union.

Even for weaker states—whose domestic structures have been influenced by outside actors, and whose leaders have very little control over transborder movements or even activities within their own country—sovereignty remains attractive. Although sovereignty might provide little more than international recognition, that recognition guarantees access to international organizations and sometimes to international finance. It offers status to individual leaders. While the great powers of Europe have eschewed many elements of sovereignty, the United States, China, and Japan have neither the interest nor the inclination to abandon their usually effective claims to domestic autonomy.

In various parts of the world, national borders still represent the fault lines of conflict, whether it is Israelis and Palestinians fighting over the status of Jerusalem, Indians and Pakistanis threatening to go nuclear over Kashmir, or Ethiopia and Eritrea clashing over disputed territories. Yet commentators nowadays are mostly concerned about the erosion of national borders as a consequence of globalization. Governments and activists alike complain that multilateral institutions such as the United Nations, the World Trade Organization, and the International Monetary Fund overstep their authority by promoting universal standards for everything from human rights and the environment to monetary policy and immigration. However, the most important impact of economic globalization and transnational norms will be to alter the scope of state authority rather than to generate some fundamentally new way to organize political life.

## SOVEREIGNTY MEANS FINAL AUTHORITY

**Not anymore, if ever.** When philosophers Jean Bodin and Thomas Hobbes first elaborated the notion of sovereignty in the 16th and 17th centuries, they were concerned with establishing the legitimacy of a single hierarchy of domestic authority. Although Bodin and Hobbes accepted the existence of divine and natural law, they both (especially Hobbes) believed the word of the sovereign was law. Subjects had no right to revolt. Bodin and Hobbes realized that imbuing the sovereign with such overweening power invited tyranny, but they were predominately concerned with maintaining domestic order, without which they believed there could be no justice. Both were writing in a world riven by sectarian strife. Bodin was almost killed in religious riots in France in 1572. Hobbes published his seminal work, *Leviathan,* only a few years after parliament (composed of Britain's emerging wealthy middle class) had executed Charles I in a civil war that had sought to wrest state control from the monarchy.

This idea of supreme power was compelling, but irrelevant in practice. By the end of the 17th century, political authority in Britain was divided between king and parliament. In the United States, the Founding Fathers established a constitutional structure of checks and balances and multiple sovereignties distributed among local and national interests that were inconsistent with hierarchy and supremacy. The principles of justice, and especially order, so valued by Bodin and Hobbes, have best been provided by modern democratic states whose organizing principles are antithetical to the idea that sovereignty means uncontrolled domestic power.

If sovereignty does not mean a domestic order with a single hierarchy of authority, what does it mean? In the contemporary world, sovereignty primarily has been linked with the idea that states are autonomous and independent from each other. Within their own boundaries, the members of a polity are free to choose their own form of government. A necessary corollary of this claim is the principle of nonintervention: One state does not have a right to intervene in the internal affairs of another.

More recently, sovereignty has come to be associated with the idea of control over transborder movements. When contemporary observers assert that the sovereign state is just about dead, they do not mean that constitutional structures are about to disappear. Instead, they mean that technological change has made it very difficult, or perhaps impossible, for states to control movements across their borders of all kinds of material things (from coffee to cocaine) and not-so-material things (from Hollywood movies to capital flows).

Finally, sovereignty has meant that political authorities can enter into international agreements. They are free to endorse any contract they find attractive. Any treaty among states is legitimate provided that it has not been coerced.

## THE PEACE OF WESTPHALIA PRODUCED THE MODERN SOVEREIGN STATE

**No, it came later.** Contemporary pundits often cite the 1648 Peace of Westphalia (actually two separate treaties, Münster and Osnabrück) as the political big bang that created the modern system of autonomous states. Westphalia—which ended the Thirty Years' War against the hegemonic power of the Holy Roman Empire—delegitimized the already waning transnational role of the Catholic Church and validated the idea that international relations should be driven by balance-of-power considerations rather than the ideals of Christendom. But Westphalia was first and foremost a new constitution for the Holy Roman Empire. The preexisting right of the principalities in the empire to make treaties was affirmed, but the Treaty of Münster stated that "such Alliances be not against the Emperor, and the Empire, nor against the Publick Peace, and this Treaty, and without prejudice to the Oath by which every one is bound to the Emperor and the Empire." The domestic political structures of the principalities remained embedded in the Holy Roman Empire. The Duke of Saxony, the Margrave of Brandenburg, the Count of Palatine, and the Duke of Bavaria were affirmed as electors who (along with the archbishops of Mainz, Trier, and Cologne) chose the emperor. They did not become or claim to be kings in their own right.

Perhaps most important, Westphalia established rules for religious tolerance in Germany. The treaties gave lip service to the principle (*cuius regio, eius religio*) that the prince could set the religion of his territory—and then went on to violate this very principle through many specific provisions. The signatories agreed that the religious rules already in effect would stay in place. Catholics and Protestants in German cities with mixed populations would share offices. Religious issues had to be settled by a majority of both Catholics and Protestants in the diet and courts of the empire. None of the major political leaders in Europe endorsed religious toleration in principle, but they recognized that religious conflicts were so volatile that it was essential to contain rather than repress sectarian differences. All in all, Westphalia is a pretty medieval document, and its biggest explicit innovation—provisions that undermined the power of princes to control religious affairs within their territories—was antithetical to the ideas of national sovereignty that later became associated with the so-called Westphalian system.

## UNIVERSAL HUMAN RIGHTS ARE AN UNPRECEDENTED CHALLENGE TO SOVEREIGNTY

**Wrong.** The struggle to establish international rules that compel leaders to treat their subjects in a certain way has been going on for a long time. Over the centuries the emphasis has shifted from religious toleration, to minority rights (often focusing on specific ethnic groups in specific countries), to human rights (emphasizing rights enjoyed by all or broad classes of individuals). In a few instances states have voluntarily embraced international supervision, but generally the weak have acceded to the preferences of the strong: The Vienna settlement following the Napoleonic wars guaranteed religious toleration for Catholics in the Netherlands. All of the successor states of the Ottoman Empire, beginning with Greece in 1832 and ending with Albania in 1913, had to accept provisions for civic and political equality for religious minorities as a condition for international recognition. The peace settlements following World War I included extensive provisions for the protection of minorities. Poland, for instance, agreed to refrain from holding elections on Saturday because such balloting would have violated the Jewish Sabbath. Individuals could bring complaints against governments through a minority rights bureau established within the League of Nations.

But as the Holocaust tragically demonstrated, interwar efforts at international constraints on domestic practices failed dismally. After World War II, human, rather than minority, rights became the focus of attention. The United Nations Charter endorsed both human rights and the classic sovereignty principle of nonintervention. The 20-plus human rights accords that have been signed during the last half century cover a wide range of issues including genocide, torture, slavery, refugees, stateless persons, women's rights, racial discrimination, children's rights, and forced labor. These U.N. agreements, however, have few enforcement mechanisms, and even their provisions for reporting violations are often ineffective.

The tragic and bloody disintegration of Yugoslavia in the 1990s revived earlier concerns with ethnic rights. International recognition of the Yugoslav successor states was conditional upon their acceptance of constitutional provisions guaranteeing minority rights. The Dayton accords established externally controlled authority structures in Bosnia, including a Human Rights Commission (a majority of whose members were appointed by the Western European states). NATO created a de facto protectorate in Kosovo.

The motivations for such interventions—humanitarianism and security—have hardly changed. Indeed, the considerations that brought the great powers into the Balkans following the wars of the 1870s were hardly different from those that engaged NATO and Russia in the 1990s.

## GLOBALIZATION UNDERMINES STATE CONTROL

**No.** State control could never be taken for granted. Technological changes over the last 200 years have increased the flow of people, goods, capital, and ideas—but the problems posed by such movements are not new. In many ways, states are better able to respond now than they were in the past.

The impact of the global media on political authority (the so-called CNN effect) pales in comparison to the havoc that followed the invention of the printing press. Within a decade after Martin Luther purportedly nailed his 95 theses to the Wittenberg church door, his ideas had circulated throughout Europe. Some political leaders seized upon the principles of the Protestant Reformation as a way to legitimize secular political authority. No sovereign monarch could contain the spread of these concepts, and some lost not only their lands but also their heads. The sectarian controversies of the 16th and 17th centuries were perhaps more politically consequential than any subsequent transnational flow of ideas.

In some ways, international capital movements were more significant in earlier periods than they are now. During the 19th century, Latin American states (and to a lesser extent Canada, the United States, and Europe) were beset by boom-and-bust cycles associated with global financial crises. The Great Depression, which had a powerful effect on the domestic politics of all major states, was precipitated by an international collapse of credit. The Asian financial crisis of the late 1990s was not nearly as devastating. Indeed, the speed with which countries recovered from the Asian flu reflects how a better working knowledge of economic theories and more effective central banks have made it easier for states to secure the advantages (while at

the same time minimizing the risks) of being enmeshed in global financial markets.

In addition to attempting to control the flows of capital and ideas, states have long struggled to manage the impact of international trade. The opening of long-distance trade for bulk commodities in the 19th century created fundamental cleavages in all of the major states. Depression and plummeting grain prices made it possible for German Chancellor Otto von Bismarck to prod the landholding aristocracy into a protectionist alliance with urban heavy industry (this coalition of "iron and rye" dominated German politics for decades). The tariff question was a basic divide in U.S. politics for much of the last half of the 19th and first half of the 20th centuries. But, despite growing levels of imports and exports since 1950, the political salience of trade has receded because national governments have developed social welfare strategies that cushion the impact of international competition, and workers with higher skill levels are better able to adjust to changing international conditions. It has become easier, not harder, for states to manage the flow of goods and services.

## GLOBALIZATION IS CHANGING THE SCOPE OF STATE CONTROL

**Yes.** The reach of the state has increased in some areas but contracted in others. Rulers have recognized that their effective control can be enhanced by walking away from issues they cannot resolve. For instance, beginning with the Peace of Westphalia, leaders chose to surrender their control over religion because it proved too volatile. Keeping religion within the scope of state authority undermined, rather than strengthened, political stability.

Monetary policy is an area where state control expanded and then ultimately contracted. Before the 20th century, states had neither the administrative competence nor the inclination to conduct independent monetary policies. The mid-20th century effort to control monetary affairs, which was associated with Keynesian economics, has now been reversed due to the magnitude of short-term capital flows and the inability of some states to control inflation. With the exception of Great Britain, the major European states have established a single monetary authority. Confronting recurrent hyperinflation, Ecuador adopted the U.S. dollar as its currency in 2000.

Along with the erosion of national currencies, we now see the erosion of national citizenship—the notion that an individual should be a citizen of one and only one country, and that the state has exclusive claims to that person's loyalty. For many states, there is no longer a sharp distinction between citizens and noncitizens. Permanent residents, guest workers, refugees, and undocumented immigrants are entitled to some bundle of rights even if they cannot vote. The ease of travel and the desire of many countries to attract either capital or skilled workers have increased incentives to make citizenship a more flexible category.

Although government involvement in religion, monetary affairs, and claims to loyalty has declined, overall government activity, as reflected in taxation and government expenditures, has increased as a percentage of national income since the 1950s among the most economically advanced states. The extent of a country's social welfare programs tends to go hand in hand with its level of integration within the global economy. Crises of authority and control have been most pronounced in the states that have been the most isolated, with sub-Saharan Africa offering the largest number of unhappy examples.

## NGOs ARE NIBBLING AT NATIONAL SOVEREIGNTY

**To some extent.** Transnational nongovernmental organizations (NGOs) have been around for quite awhile, especially if you include corporations. In the 18th century, the East India Company possessed political power (and even an expeditionary military force) that rivaled many national governments. Throughout the 19th century, there were transnational movements to abolish slavery, promote the rights of women, and improve conditions for workers.

The number of transnational NGOs, however, has grown tremendously, from around 200 in 1909 to over 17,000 today. The availability of inexpensive and very fast communications technology has made it easier for such groups to organize and make

an impact on public policy and international law—the international agreement banning land mines being a recent case in point. Such groups prompt questions about sovereignty because they appear to threaten the integrity of domestic decision making. Activists who lose on their home territory can pressure foreign governments, which may in turn influence decision makers in the activists' own nation.

But for all of the talk of growing NGO influence, their power to affect a country's domestic affairs has been limited when compared to governments, international organizations, and multinational corporations. The United Fruit Company had more influence in Central America in the early part of the 20th century than any NGO could hope to have anywhere in the contemporary world. The International Monetary Fund and other multilateral financial institutions now routinely negotiate conditionality agreements that involve not only specific economic targets but also domestic institutional changes, such as pledges to crack down on corruption and break up cartels.

Smaller, weaker states are the most frequent targets of external efforts to alter domestic institutions, but more powerful states are not immune. The openness of the U.S. political system means that not only NGOs, but also foreign governments, can play some role in political decisions. (The Mexican government, for instance, lobbied heavily for the passage of the North American Free Trade Agreement.) In fact, the permeability of the American polity makes the United States a less threatening partner; nations are more willing to sign on to U.S.-sponsored international arrangements because they have some confidence that they can play a role in U.S. decision making.

## SOVEREIGNTY BLOCKS CONFLICT RESOLUTION

**Yes, sometimes.** Rulers as well as their constituents have some reasonably clear notion of what sovereignty means—exclusive control within a given territory—even if this norm has been challenged frequently by inconsistent principles (such as universal human rights) and violated in practice (the U.S.- and British-enforced no-fly zones over Iraq). In fact, the political importance of conventional sovereignty rules has made it harder to solve some problems. There is, for instance, no conventional sovereignty solution for Jerusalem, but it doesn't require much imagination to think of alternatives: Divide the city into small pieces; divide the Temple Mount vertically with the Palestinians controlling the top and the Israelis the bottom; establish some kind of international authority; divide control over different issues (religious practices versus taxation, for instance) among different authorities. Any one of these solutions would be better for most Israelis and Palestinians than an ongoing stalemate, but political leaders on both sides have had trouble delivering a settlement because they are subject to attacks by counterelites who can wave the sovereignty flag.

Conventional rules have also been problematic for Tibet. Both the Chinese and the Tibetans might be better off if Tibet could regain some of the autonomy it had as a tributary state within the traditional Chinese empire. Tibet had extensive local control, but symbolically (and sometimes through tribute payments) recognized the supremacy of the emperor. Today, few on either side would even know what a tributary state is, and even if the leaders of Tibet worked out some kind of settlement that would give their country more self-government, there would be no guarantee that they could gain the support of their own constituents.

If, however, leaders can reach mutual agreements, bring along their constituents, or are willing to use coercion, sovereignty rules can be violated in inventive ways. The Chinese, for instance, made Hong Kong a special administrative region after the transfer from British rule, allowed a foreign judge to sit on the Court of Final Appeal, and secured acceptance by other states not only for Hong Kong's participation in a number of international organizations but also for separate visa agreements and recognition of a distinct Hong Kong passport. All of these measures violate conventional sovereignty rules since Hong Kong does not have juridical independence. Only by inventing a unique status for Hong Kong, which involved the acquiescence of other states, could China claim sovereignty while simultaneously preserving the confidence of the business community.

## THE EUROPEAN UNION IS A NEW MODEL FOR SUPRANATIONAL GOVERNANCE

**Yes, but only for the Europeans.** The European Union (EU) really is a new thing, far more interesting in terms of sovereignty than Hong Kong. It is not a conventional international organization because its member states are now so intimately linked with one another that withdrawal is not a viable option. It is not likely to become a "United States of Europe"—a large federal state that might look something like the United States of America—because the interests, cultures, economies, and domestic institutional arrangements of its members are too diverse. Widening the EU to include the former communist states of Central Europe would further complicate any efforts to move toward a political organization that looks like a conventional sovereign state.

The EU is inconsistent with conventional sovereignty rules. Its member states have created supranational institutions (the European Court of Justice, the European Commission, and the Council of Ministers) that can make decisions opposed by some member states. The rulings of the court have direct effect and supremacy within national judicial systems, even though these doctrines were never explicitly endorsed in any treaty. The European Monetary Union created a central bank that now controls monetary affairs for three of the union's four largest states. The Single European Act and the Maastricht Treaty provide for majority or qualified majority, but not unanimous, voting in some issue areas. In one sense, the European Union is a product of state sovereignty because it has been created through voluntary agreements among its member states. But, in another sense, it fundamentally contradicts conventional understandings of sovereignty because these same agreements have undermined the juridical autonomy of its individual members.

The European Union, however, is not a model that other parts of the world can imitate. The initial moves toward integration could not have taken place without the political and economic support of the United States, which was, in the early years of the Cold War, much more interested in creating a strong alliance that could effectively oppose the

Soviet Union than it was in any potential European challenge to U.S. leadership. Germany, one of the largest states in the European Union, has been the most consistent supporter of an institutional structure that would limit Berlin's own freedom of action, a reflection of the lessons of two devastating wars and the attractiveness of a European identity for a country still grappling with the sins of the Nazi era. It is hard to imagine that other regional powers such as China, Japan, or Brazil, much less the United States, would have any interest in tying their own hands in similar ways. (Regional trading agreements such as Mercosur and NAFTA have very limited supranational provisions and show few signs of evolving into broader monetary or political unions.) The EU is a new and unique institutional structure, but it will coexist with, not displace, the sovereign-state model.

# The Future of American Power

JOSEPH S. NYE JR.

The twenty-first century began with a very unequal distribution of power resources. With five percent of the world's population, the United States accounted for about a quarter of the world's economic output, was responsible for nearly half of global military expenditures, and had the most extensive cultural and educational soft-power resources. All this is still true, but the future of U.S. power is hotly debated. Many observers have interpreted the 2008 global financial crisis as the beginning of American decline. The National Intelligence Council, for example, has projected that in 2025, "the U.S. will remain the preeminent power, but that American dominance will be much diminished."

Power is the ability to attain the outcomes one wants, and the resources that produce it vary in different contexts. Spain in the sixteenth century took advantage of its control of colonies and gold bullion, the Netherlands in the seventeenth century profited from trade and finance, France in the eighteenth century benefited from its large population and armies, and the United Kingdom in the nineteenth century derived power from its primacy in the Industrial Revolution and its navy. This century is marked by a burgeoning revolution in information technology and globalization, and

to understand this revolution, certain pitfalls need to be avoided.

First, one must beware of misleading metaphors of organic decline. Nations are not like humans, with predictable life spans. Rome remained dominant for more than three centuries after the peak of its power, and even then it did not succumb to the rise of another state. For all the fashionable predictions of China, India, or Brazil surpassing the United States in the next decades, the greater threat may come from modern barbarians and nonstate actors. In an information-based world, power diffusion may pose a bigger danger than power transition. Conventional wisdom holds that the state with the largest army prevails, but in the information age, the state (or the nonstate actor) with the best story may sometimes win.

Power today is distributed in a pattern that resembles a complex three-dimensional chess game. On the top chessboard, military power is largely unipolar, and the United States is likely to retain primacy for quite some time. On the middle chessboard, economic power has been multipolar for more than a decade, with the United States, Europe, Japan, and China as the major players and others gaining in importance. The bottom chessboard is the realm of transnational relations. It includes nonstate actors as diverse as bankers who electronically transfer funds, terrorists who traffic weapons, hackers who threaten cybersecurity, and challenges such as pandemics and climate change. On this bottom board, power is widely diffused, and it makes no sense to speak of unipolarity, multipolarity, or hegemony.

In interstate politics, the most important factor will be the continuing return of Asia to the world stage. In 1750, Asia had more than half the world's population and economic output. By 1900, after the Industrial Revolution in Europe and the United States, Asia's share shrank to one-fifth of global economic output. By 2050, Asia will be well on its way back to its historical share. The rise of China and India may create instability, but this is a problem with precedents, and history suggests how policies can affect the outcome.

## HEGEMONIC DECLINE?

It is currently fashionable to compare the United States' power to that of the United Kingdom a century ago and to predict a similar hegemonic decline. Some Americans react emotionally to the idea of decline, but it would be counterintuitive and ahistorical to believe that the United States will have a preponderant share of power resources forever. The word "decline" mixes up two different dimensions: absolute decline, in the sense of decay, and relative decline, in which the power resources of other states grow or are used more effectively.

The analogy with British decline is misleading. The United Kingdom had naval supremacy and an empire on which the sun never set, but by World War I, the country ranked only fourth among the great powers in its share of military personnel, fourth in GDP, and third in military spending. With the rise of nationalism, protecting the empire became more of a burden than an asset. For all the talk of an American empire, the United States has more freedom of action than the United Kingdom did. And whereas the United Kingdom faced rising neighbors, Germany and Russia, the United States benefits from being surrounded by two oceans and weaker neighbors.

Despite such differences, Americans are prone to cycles of belief in their own decline. The Founding Fathers worried about comparisons to the Roman republic. Charles Dickens observed a century and a half ago, "If its individual citizens, to a man, are to be believed, [the United States] always is depressed, and always is stagnated, and always is at an alarming crisis, and never was otherwise." In the last half century, belief in American decline rose after the Soviet Union launched Sputnik in 1957, after President Richard Nixon's economic adjustments and the oil shocks in the 1970s, and after the closing of rust-belt industries and the budget deficits in the Reagan era. Ten years later, Americans believed that the United States was the sole superpower, and now polls show that many believe in decline again.

Pundits lament the inability of Washington to control states such as Afghanistan or Iran, but they allow the golden glow of the past to color their appraisals. The United States' power is not what it used to be, but it also never really was as great as assumed. After World War II, the United States had nuclear weapons and an overwhelming preponderance of economic power but nonetheless was unable to prevent the "loss" of China, to roll back communism in Eastern Europe, to overcome stalemate in the Korean War, to stop the "loss" of North Vietnam, or to dislodge the Castro regime in Cuba. Power measured in resources rarely equals power measured in preferred outcomes, and cycles of belief in decline reveal more about psychology than they do about real shifts in power resources. Unfortunately, mistaken beliefs in decline—at home and abroad—can lead to dangerous mistakes in policy.

## DEBATING DECLINE

Any net assessment of American power in the coming decades will remain uncertain, but analysis is not helped by misleading metaphors of decline. Declinists should be chastened by remembering how wildly exaggerated U.S. estimates of Soviet power in the 1970s and of Japanese power in the 1980s were. Equally misguided were those prophets of unipolarity who argued a decade ago that the United States was so powerful that it could do as it wished and others had no choice but to follow. Today, some confidently predict that the twenty-first century will see China replace the United States as the world's leading state, whereas others argue with equal confidence that the twenty-first century will be the American century. But unforeseen events often confound such projections. There is always a range of possible futures, not one.

As for the United States' power relative to China's, much will depend on the uncertainties of future political change in China. Barring any political upheaval, China's size and high rate of economic growth will almost certainly increase its relative strength vis-à-vis the United States. This will bring China closer to the United States in power resources, but it does not necessarily mean that China will surpass the United States as the most powerful country—even if China suffers no major domestic political setbacks. Projections based on GDP growth alone are one-dimensional. They ignore U.S. advantages in military and soft power, as well as China's geopolitical disadvantages in the Asian balance of power.

Among the range of possible futures, the more likely are those in which China gives the United States a run for its money but does not surpass it in overall power in the first half of this century. Looking back at history, the British strategist Lawrence Freedman has noted that the United States has "two features which distinguish it from the dominant great powers of the past: American power is based on alliances rather than colonies and is associated with an ideology that is flexible.... Together they provide a core of relationships and values to which America can return even after it has overextended itself." And looking to the future, the scholar Anne-Marie Slaughter has argued that the United States' culture of openness and innovation will keep it central in a world where networks supplement, if not fully replace, hierarchical power.

The United States is well placed to benefit from such networks and alliances, if it follows smart strategies. Given Japanese concerns about the rise of Chinese power, Japan is more likely to seek U.S. support to preserve its independence than ally with China. This enhances the United States' position. Unless Americans act foolishly with regard to Japan, an allied East Asia is not a plausible candidate to displace the United States. It matters that the two entities in the world with per capita incomes and sophisticated economies similar to those of the United States—the European Union and Japan—both are U.S. allies. In traditional realist terms of balances of power resources, that makes a large difference for the net position of U.S. power. And in a more positive-sum view of power—that of holding power with, rather than over, other countries—Europe and Japan provide the largest pools of resources for dealing with common transnational problems. Although their interests are not identical to those of the United States, they share overlapping social and governmental networks with it that provide opportunities for cooperation.

On the question of absolute, rather than relative, American decline, the United States faces serious problems in areas such as debt, secondary education, and political gridlock. But they are only part of the picture. Of the multiple possible futures, stronger cases can be made for the positive ones than the negative ones. But among the negative futures, the most plausible is one in which the United States overreacts to terrorist attacks by turning inward and thus cuts itself off from the strength it obtains from openness. Barring such mistaken strategies, however, there are solutions to the major American problems of today. (Long-term debt, for example, could be solved by putting in place, after the economy recovers, spending cuts and consumption taxes that could pay for entitlements.) Of course, such solutions may forever remain out of reach. But it is important to distinguish hopeless situations for which there are no solutions from those that could in principle be solved. After all, the bipartisan reforms of the Progressive era a century ago rejuvenated a badly troubled country.

## A NEW NARRATIVE

It is time for a new narrative about the future of U.S. power. Describing power transition in the twenty-first century as a traditional case of hegemonic decline is inaccurate, and it can lead to dangerous policy implications if it encourages China to engage in adventurous policies or the United States to overreact out of fear. The United States is not in absolute decline, and in relative terms, there is a reasonable probability that it will remain more powerful than any single state in the coming decades.

At the same time, the country will certainly face a rise in the power resources of many others—both states and nonstate actors. Because globalization will spread technological capabilities and information technology will allow more people to communicate, U.S. culture and the U.S. economy will become less globally dominant than they were at the start of this century. Yet it is unlikely that the United States will decay like ancient Rome, or even that it will be surpassed by another state, including China.

The problem of American power in the twenty-first century, then, is not one of decline but what to do in light of the realization that even the largest country cannot achieve the outcomes it wants without the help of others. An increasing number of challenges will require the United States to exercise power with others as much as power over others. This, in turn, will require a deeper understanding of power, how it is changing, and how to construct "smart power" strategies that combine hard- and soft-power resources in an information age. The country's capacity to maintain alliances and create networks will be an important dimension of its hard and soft power.

Power is not good or bad per se. It is like calories in a diet: more is not always better. If a country has too few power resources, it is less likely to obtain its preferred outcomes. But too much power (in terms of resources) has often proved to be a curse when it leads to overconfidence and inappropriate strategies. David slew Goliath because Goliath's superior power resources led him to pursue an inferior strategy, which in turn led to his defeat and death. A smart-power narrative for the twenty-first century is not about maximizing power or preserving hegemony. It is about finding ways to combine resources in successful strategies in the new context of power diffusion and "the rise of the rest."

As the largest power, the United States will remain important in global affairs, but the twentieth century narrative about an American century and American primacy—as well as narratives of American decline—is misleading when it is used as a guide to the type of strategy that will be necessary in the twenty-first century. The coming decades are not likely to see a post-American world, but the United States will need a smart strategy that combines hard- and soft-power resources—and that emphasizes alliances and networks that are responsive to the new context of a global information age.

# Historical Context I: Realism and Sovereign States

# Thomas Hobbes: Man in a State of Nature Is in a State of War

FROM, *LEVIATHAN* BY HOBBES THOMAS (1588–1679)

Nature hath made men so equal in the faculties of body and mind as that, though there be found one man sometimes manifestly stronger in body or of quicker mind than another, yet when all is reckoned together the difference between man and man is not so considerable as that one man can thereupon claim to himself any benefit to which another may not pretend as well as he. For as to the strength of body, the weakest has strength enough to kill the strongest, either by secret machination or by confederacy with others that are in the same danger with himself.

For such is the nature of men that howsoever they may acknowledge many others to be more witty, or more eloquent or more learned, yet they will hardly believe there be many so wise as themselves; for they see their own wit at hand, and other men's at a distance. But this proveth rather that men are in that point equal, than unequal. For there is not ordinarily a greater sign of the equal distribution of anything than that every man is contented with his share.

From this equality of ability ariseth equality of hope in the attaining of our ends. And therefore if any two men desire the same thing, which nevertheless they cannot both enjoy, they become enemies; and in the way to their end (which is principally their own conservation, and sometimes their delectation only) endeavour to destroy or subdue one another. And from hence it comes to pass that where an invader hath no more to fear than another man's single power, if one plant, sow, build, or possess a convenient seat, others may probably be expected to come prepared with forces united to dispossess and deprive him, not only of the fruit of his labour, but also of his life or liberty. And the invader again is in the like danger of another.

So that in the nature of man, we find three principal causes of quarrel. First, competition; secondly, diffidence; thirdly, glory.

The first maketh men invade for gain; the second, for safety; and the third, for reputation. The first use violence, to make themselves masters of other men's persons, wives, children, and cattle; the second, to defend them; the third, for trifles, as a word, a smile, a different opinion, and any other sign of undervalue, either direct in their persons or by reflection in their kindred, their friends, their nation, their profession, or their name.

Hereby it is manifest that during the time men live without a common power to keep them all in awe, they are in that condition which is called war; and such a war as is of every man against every man. For war consisteth not in battle only, or the act of fighting, but in a tract of time, wherein the will to contend by battle is sufficiently known: and therefore the notion of time is to be considered in the nature of war, as it is in the nature of weather. For as the nature of foul weather lieth not in a shower or two of rain, but in an inclination thereto of many days together: so the nature of war consisteth not in actual fighting, but in the known disposition thereto during all the time there is no assurance to the contrary. All other time is peace.

In such condition there is no place for industry, because the fruit thereof is uncertain: and consequently no culture of the earth; no navigation, nor use of the commodities that may be imported by sea; no commodious building; no instruments of moving and removing such things as require much force; no knowledge of the face of the earth; no account of time; no arts; no letters; no society; and which is worst of all, continual fear, and danger of violent death; and the life of man, solitary, poor, nasty, brutish, and short.

It may peradventure be thought there was never such a time nor condition of war as this; and I believe it was never generally so, over all the world: but there are many places where they live so now. For the savage people in many places of America, except the government of small families, the concord whereof dependeth on natural lust, have no government at all, and live at this day in that brutish manner, as I said before. Howsoever, it may be perceived what manner of life there would be, where there were no common power to fear, by the manner of life which men that have formerly lived under a peaceful government use to degenerate into a civil war.

To this war of every man against every man, this also is consequent; that nothing can be unjust. The notions of right and wrong, justice and injustice, have there no place. Where there is no common power, there is no law; where no law, no injustice. Force and fraud are in war the two cardinal virtues. Justice and injustice are none of the faculties neither of the body nor mind. If they were, they might be in a man that were alone in the world, as well as his senses and passions. They are qualities that relate to men in society, not in solitude. It is consequent also to the same condition that there be no propriety, no dominion, no mine and thine distinct; but only that to be every man's that he can get, and for so long as he can keep it. And thus much for the ill condition which man by mere nature is actually placed in; though with a possibility to come out of it, consisting partly in the passions, partly in his reason.

# Politics Among Nations: The Struggle for Power and Peace

HANS J. MORGENTHAU

## SIX PRINCIPLES OF POLITICAL REALISM

**1.** Political realism believes that politics, like society in general, is governed by objective laws that have their roots in human nature. In order to improve society it is first necessary to understand the laws by which society lives. The operation of these laws being impervious to our preferences, men will challenge them only at the risk of failure.

Realism, believing as it does in the objectivity of the laws of politics, must also believe in the possibility of developing a rational theory that reflects, however imperfectly and one-sidedly, these objective laws. It believes also, then, in the possibility of distinguishing in politics between truth and opinion-between what is true objectively and rationally, supported by evidence and illuminated by reason, and what is only a subjective judgment, divorced from the facts as they are and informed by prejudice and wishful thinking.

. . . To give meaning to the factual raw material of foreign policy, we must approach political reality with a kind of rational outline, a map that suggests to us the possible meanings of foreign policy. In other words, we put ourselves in the position of a statesman who must meet a certain problem of foreign policy under certain circumstances, and we ask ourselves what the rational alternatives are from which a statesman may choose who must meet this problem under these circumstances (presuming always that he acts in a rational manner), and which of these rational alternatives this particular statesman, acting under these circumstances, is likely to choose. It is the testing of this rational hypothesis against the actual facts and their consequences that gives theoretical meaning to the facts of international politics.

**2.** The main signpost that helps political realism to find its way through the landscape of international politics is the concept of interest defined in terms of power. This concept provides the link between reason trying to understand international politics and the facts to be understood. It sets politics as an autonomous sphere of action and understanding apart from other spheres, such as economics

New York: Alfred A. Knopf, 1978 pp. 4–15

(understood in terms of interest defined as wealth), ethics, aesthetics, or religion. Without such a concept a theory of politics, international or domestic, would be altogether impossible, for without it we could not distinguish between political and nonpolitical facts, nor could we bring at least a measure of systematic order to the political sphere.

... A realist theory of international politics, then, will guard against two popular fallacies: the concern with motives and the concern with ideological preferences.

To search for the clue to foreign policy exclusively in the motives of statesmen is both futile and deceptive. It is futile because motives are the most illusive of psychological data, distorted as they are, frequently beyond recognition, by the interests and emotions of actor and observer alike. Do we really know what our own motives are? And what do we know of the motives of others?

We cannot conclude from the good intentions of a statesman that his foreign policies will be either morally praiseworthy or politically successful. Judging his motives, we can say that he will not intentionally pursue policies that are morally wrong, but we can say nothing about the probability of their success. If we want to know the moral and political qualities of his actions, we must know them, not his motives. How often have statesmen been motivated by the desire to improve the world, and ended by making it worse? And how often have they sought one goal, and ended by achieving something they neither expected nor desired?

Neville Chamberlain's politics of appeasement were, as far as we can judge, inspired by good motives; he was probably less motivated by considerations of personal power than were many other British prime ministers, and he sought to preserve peace and to assure the happiness of all concerned. Yet his policies helped to make the Second World War inevitable, and to bring untold miseries to millions of men. Sir Winston Churchill's motives, on the other hand, were much less universal in scope and much more narrowly directed toward personal and national power, yet the foreign policies that sprang from these inferior motives were certainly superior in moral and political quality to those pursued by his predecessor. ...

A realist theory of international politics will also avoid the other popular fallacy of equating the foreign policies of a statesman with his philosophic or political sympathies, and of deducing the former from the latter. Statesmen, especially under contemporary conditions, may well make a habit of presenting their foreign policies in terms of their philosophic and political sympathies in order to gain popular support for them. ...

Especially where foreign policy is conducted under the conditions of democratic control, the need to marshal popular emotions to the support of foreign policy cannot fail to impair the rationality of foreign policy itself. Yet a theory of foreign policy which aims at rationality must for the time being, as it were, abstract from these irrational elements and seek to paint a picture of foreign policy which presents the rational essence to be found in experience, without the contingent deviations from rationality which are also found in experience.

The difference between international politics as it actually is and a rational theory derived from it is like the difference between a photograph and a painted portrait. The photograph shows everything that can be seen by the naked eye; the painted portrait does not show everything that can be seen by the naked eye, but it shows, or at least seeks to show, one thing that the naked eye cannot see: the human essence of the person portrayed.

Political realism contains not only a theoretical but also a normative element. It knows that political reality is replete with contingencies and systemic irrationalities and points to the typical influences they exert upon foreign policy. Yet it shares with all social theory the need, for the sake of theoretical understanding, to stress the rational elements of political reality; for it is these rational elements that make reality intelligible for theory. Political realism presents the theoretical construct of a rational foreign policy which experience can never completely achieve.

At the same time political realism considers a rational foreign policy to be good foreign policy; for only a rational foreign policy minimizes risks and maximizes benefits and, hence, complies both with the moral precept of prudence and the political requirement of success. Political realism wants the photographic picture of the political world to resemble as much as possible its painted portrait. . . .

3. Realism assumes that its key concept of interest defined as power is an objective category which is universally valid, but it does not endow that concept with a meaning that is fixed once and for all. The idea of interest is indeed of the essence of politics and is unaffected by the circumstances of time and place . . .

A small knowledge of human nature will convince us, that, with far the greatest part of mankind, interest is the governing principle; and that almost every man is more or less, under its influence. Motives of public virtue may for a time, or in particular instances, actuate men to the observance of a conduct purely disinterested; but they are not of themselves sufficient to produce persevering conformity to the refined dictates and obligations of social duty. Few men are capable of making a continual sacrifice of all views of private interest, or advantage, to the common good.

. . . The same observations apply to the concept of power. Its content and the manner of its use are determined by the political and cultural environment. Power may comprise anything that establishes and maintains the control of man over man. Thus power covers all social relationships which serve that end, from physical violence to the most subtle psychological ties by which one mind controls another. Power covers the domination of man by man, both when it is disciplined by moral ends and controlled by constitutional safeguards, as in Western democracies, and when it is that untamed and barbaric force which finds its laws in nothing but its own strength and its sole justification in its aggrandizement.

Political realism does not assume that the contemporary conditions under which foreign policy operates, with their extreme instability and the ever present threat of large-scale violence, cannot be changed. The balance of power, for instance, is indeed a perennial element of all pluralistic societies, as the authors of *The Federalist* papers well knew; yet it is capable of operating, as it does in the United States, under the conditions of relative stability and peaceful conflict. If the factors that have given rise to these conditions can be duplicated on the international scene, similar conditions of stability and peace will then prevail there, as they have over long stretches of history among certain nations.

What is true of the general character of international relations is also true of the nation state as the ultimate point of reference of contemporary foreign policy. While the realist indeed believes that interest is the perennial standard by which political action must be judged and directed, the contemporary connection between interest and the nation state is a product of history, and is therefore bound to disappear in the course of history. Nothing in the realist position militates against the assumption that the present division of the political world into nation states will be replaced by larger units of a quite different character, more in keeping with the technical potentialities and the moral requirements of the contemporary world. . . .

4. Political realism is aware of the moral significance of political action. It is also aware of the ineluctable tension between the moral command and the requirements of successful political action.

The individual may say for himself: "*Fiat justitia, pereat mundus* (Let justice be done, even if the world perish)," but the state has no right to say so in the name of those who are in its care. Both individual and state must judge political action by universal moral principles, such as that of liberty. Yet while the individual has a moral right to sacrifice himself in defense of such a moral principle, the state has no right to let its moral disapprobation of the infringement of liberty get in the way of successful political action, itself inspired by the moral principle of national survival.

Ethics in the abstract judges action by its conformity with the moral law; political ethics judges action by its political consequences. Classical and medieval philosophy knew this, and so did Lincoln when he said:

I do the very best I know how, the very best I can, and I mean to keep doing so until the end. If the end brings me out all right, what is said against me won't amount to anything. If the end brings me out wrong, ten angels swearing I was right would make no difference.

**5.** Political realism refuses to identify the moral aspirations of a particular nation with the moral laws that govern the universe.

The lighthearted equation between a particular nationalism and the counsels of Providence is morally indefensible, for it is that very sin of pride against which the Greek tragedians and the Biblical prophets have warned rulers and ruled. That equation is also politically pernicious, for it is liable to engender the distortion in judgment which, in the blindness of crusading frenzy, destroys nations and civilizations-in the name of moral principle, ideal, or God himself.

On the other hand, it is exactly the concept of interest defined in terms of power that saves us from both that moral excess and that political folly. For if we look at all nations, our own included, as political entities pursuing their respective interests defined in terms of power, we are able to do justice to all of them. . . .

**6.** The difference, then, between political realism and other schools of thought is real, and it is profound. . . .

Intellectually, the political realist maintains the autonomy of the political sphere, as the economist, the lawyer, the moralist maintain theirs. He thinks in terms of interest defined as power, as the economist thinks in terms of interest defined as wealth; the lawyer, of the conformity of action with legal rules; the moralist, of the conformity of action with moral principles. The economist asks: "How does this policy affect the wealth of society, or a segment of it?" The lawyer asks: "Is this policy in accord with the rules of law?" The moralist asks: "Is this policy in accord with moral principles?" And the political realist asks: "How does this policy affect the power of the nation?" (Or of the federal government, of Congress, of the party, of agriculture, as the case may be.)

In 1939 the Soviet Union attacked Finland. This action confronted France and Great Britain with two issues, one legal, the other political. Did that action violate the Covenant of the League of Nations and, if it did, what countermeasures should France and Great Britain take? The legal question could easily be answered in the affirmative, for obviously the Soviet Union had done what was prohibited by the Covenant. The answer to the political question depends, first, upon the manner in which the Russian action affected the interests of France and Great Britain; second, upon the existing distribution of power between France and Great Britain, on the one hand, and the Soviet Union and other potentially hostile nations, especially Germany, on the other; and, third, upon the influence that the countermeasures were likely to have upon the interests of France and Great Britain and the future distribution of power. France and Great Britain, as the leading members of the League of Nations, saw to it that the Soviet Union was expelled from the League, and they were prevented from joining Finland in the war against the Soviet Union only by Sweden's refusal to allow their troops to pass through Swedish territory on their way to Finland. If this refusal by Sweden had not saved them, France and Great Britain would shortly have found themselves at war with the Soviet Union and Germany at the same time.

The policy of France and Great Britain was a classic example of legalism in that they allowed the answer to the legal question, legitimate within its sphere, to determine their political actions. Instead of asking both questions, that of law and that of power, they asked only the question of law; and the answer they received could have no bearing on the issue that their very existence might have depended upon.

This realist defense of the autonomy of the political sphere against its subversion by other modes of thought does not imply disregard for the existence and importance of these other modes of thought. It rather implies that each should be assigned its proper sphere and function. Political realism is based upon a pluralistic conception of human nature. Real man is a composite of "economic man," "political man," "moral man," "religious man," etc. A man who was nothing but "political man" would be a beast, for he would be completely lacking in moral restraints. A man who was nothing but "moral man" would be a fool, for he would be completely lacking in prudence. A man who was nothing but "religious man" would be a saint, for he would be completely lacking in worldly desires.

Recognizing that these different facets of human nature exist, political realism also recognizes that in order to understand one of them one has to deal with it on its own terms. . . .

It is in the nature of things that a theory of politics which is based upon such principles will not meet with unanimous approval—nor does, for that matter, such a foreign policy. For theory and policy alike run counter to two trends in our culture which are not able to reconcile themselves to the assumptions and results of a rational, objective theory of politics. One of these trends disparages the role of power in society on grounds that stem from the experience and philosophy of the nineteenth century; we shall address ourselves

to this tendency later in greater detail. The other trend, opposed to the realist theory and practice of politics, stems from the very relationship that exists, and must exist, between the human mind and the political sphere . . . the human mind in its day-by-day operations cannot bear to look the truth of politics straight in the face. It must disguise, distort, belittle, and embellish the truth-the more so, the more the individual is actively involved in the processes of politics, and particularly in those of international politics. For only by deceiving himself about the nature of politics and the role he plays on the political scene is man able to live contentedly as a political animal with himself and his fellow men.

# An Interview on a Theory of International Relations and the Role of Structure

KENNETH WALTZ

## THE IMPORTANCE OF STRUCTURE IN IR

Always, until World War II in modern history, there were five or so great powers contending. World War II eventuated in a world in which there were only two: the United States and the Soviet Union. States acting in those two different worlds face different kinds of problems. . . . That is, the difficulty, for example, that previous great powers—countries like Great Britain and France—had coming to terms with the fact that they were no longer great powers, that they were reduced to the level of major powers. . . . It explains how Europe could develop as a somewhat distinct political realm. France no longer had to worry about a possible war with Germany, or, as it had in previous times, a possible war against Britain. We worried about that, and the Soviet Union worried about that . . .

Whole new kinds of behavior become possible for the previous great powers, because they're no longer great powers, just for that simple reason. And the United States assumed new responsibilities that

it never dreamed of assuming. In the 1930s, to tell an American that America would begin to take the responsibility for the security of major parts of the world would have been laughable. Nobody could even imagine such a condition. But when the structure of international politics dramatically changed, we accommodated ourselves to that new condition.

It takes an act of the mind to conceive of how the conditions under which these actions and interactions occur influence the actions and interactions themselves. That's not something that you open your eyes and look at and see, or read about in *The New York Times* every morning. It takes an act of thought to do that.

. . . Looking back, the article on stability of a bipolar world was published in 1964. It was strangely controversial. It made people mad. I first gave the paper as a talk to the Harvard/MIT Arms Control Seminar. There was a lively and heated discussion following the presentation of the simple idea that this has become a world of two powers, in other words, a bipolar world. People were saying, "No, wait a minute. Europe still counts." Well, of course, Europe still counted, but not nearly as much, obviously, as it once did, and not merely as much as the United States and the Soviet Union. Ultimately, the world's fate depended on the United States, the Soviet Union, and the interaction between them.

In economic terms, it was not a world of interdependence at all: the United States and the Soviet Union scarcely traded with one another. Militarily, the interdependence was close, because each could do grievous damage to the other. And in international politics, again, a realm of self-help; ultimately, that's what counts.

Within, I'd say, certainly within ten years, probably less than ten years, it became accepted: "Yes, of course, the world is bipolar." And that makes the really deep controversy by which this article was greeted all the more striking.

. . . One of the striking things about nuclear deterrence is that it has worked, no matter what country we're talking about, no matter what kind of government the country has, no matter what kind of ruler the country has had. The most striking case, of course, is Mao Zedong and the Cultural Revolution. It lasted from 1966 to 1976 in China, where China was in seemingly unheard-of chaos. And yet China, a country with a fair number of nuclear weapons at the time, managed to take care of those weapons very well indeed! The government separated foreign policy to a certain extent, and nuclear policy completely, from the Cultural Revolution.

## AFTER THE SOVIET UNION DISAPPEARED

. . . If you recall, the 1980s was when Reagan and those who agreed with him were saying that the Soviet Union was catching up with us, they were going to pass us. "The Soviet Union has become the most powerful military country in the world"—Reagan, you know. "They passed us on all fronts—strategic and conventional alike."

Well, the opposite was the truth, and one could see it. I mean, you can look at data. You could look at the demographic composition of the Soviet Union, with the Russian component sinking and the non-Russian component of the population rising. You could look at the extent to which the Soviet Union was falling behind in military technology—indeed, in technology across the board, and therefore in military technology as well. It looked to me as though the Soviet Union was on a losing course.

. . . I remember, especially, being in China for the first time in 1982, and presenting this analysis to one of the institutes, which I've now talked at over the years about four or five times. The last time was in 1996, and I reminded them of 1982. What they were saying was, "Hey, the Soviet Union is getting ahead." In fact, that's why China was moving toward the United States, because it felt that the United States was getting weaker, and in order to form a block of sufficient strength against the Soviet Union, they had to edge over toward our side. Again, perceptions of what the structure of international politics is at a given time strongly influence the policy that one follows. So I was saying, "No, the Soviet Union is getting weaker. The United State is getting relatively stronger." And the people at this institute who were charged with thinking about this—this was the purpose of their institute, to think about things like this—had reached the opposite conclusion. They . . . well, they were wrong.

## UNIPOLAR WORLD: THE US AS THE ONLY SUPERPOWER

Checks and balances are supposed to work in the United States; it's ingrained in our thinking. But, in fact, they don't work very well, or at least in my view they are not working very well. They do not place effective constraints on what the government can do abroad. They do not place effective constraints on how much we spend on our military forces. In 1998, for example, we outspent the next eight big spenders. We're now spending about as much as the next fourteen or fifteen. And, according to *The New York Times,* projecting the spending until next year, we will be spending as much as all the other countries in the world combined on our military forces. Now, what do we want all that military force for? Other countries are bound to ask that question. They do ask that question. And they worry about it, because power can be so easily abused.

. . . No combination of other countries and no other country singly in the foreseeable future is going to be able to balance the power of the United States. Now, in the end, power will balance power, and there isn't any doubt that the Chinese are smarting, very uncomfortable with the extent to which the United States dominates the world militarily. I'm not implying that it doesn't bother other countries as well. But China, if it maintains its political coherence, its political capabilities, will have in due course the economic and the technological means of competing. But how far away is that? Certainly, twenty years. Probably more than twenty years.

# China's Unpeaceful Rise

JOHN J. MEARSHEIMER

Can China rise peacefully? My answer is no. If China continues its impressive economic growth over the next few decades, the United States and China are likely to engage in an intense security competition with considerable potential for war. Most of China's neighbors—including India, Japan, Singapore, South Korea, Russia, and Vietnam—will join with the United States to contain China's power.

To predict the future in Asia, one needs a theory of international politics that explains how rising great powers are likely to act and how other states in the system will react to them. That theory must be logically sound and it must account for the past behavior of rising great powers.

My theory of international politics says that the mightiest states attempt to establish hegemony in their region of the world while making sure that no rival great power dominates another region. This theory, which helps explain US foreign policy since the country's founding, also has implications for future relations between China and the United States.

## THE CONTEST FOR POWER

According to my understanding of international politics, survival is a state's most important goal, because a state cannot pursue any other goals if it does not survive. The basic structure of the international system forces states concerned about their security to compete with each other for power. The ultimate goal of every great power is to maximize its share of world power and eventually dominate the system.

The international system has three defining characteristics. First, the main actors are states that operate in anarchy, which simply means that there is no higher authority above them. Second, all great powers have some offensive military capability, which means that they have the wherewithal to hurt each other. Third, no state can know the intentions of other states with certainty, especially their future intentions. It is simply impossible, for example, to know what Germany or Japan's intentions will be toward their neighbors in 2025.

In a world where other states might have malign intentions as well as significant offensive capabilities, states tend to fear each other. That fear is compounded by the fact that in an anarchic system there is no night watchman for states to call if trouble comes knocking at their door. Therefore, states recognize that the best way to survive in such a system is to be as powerful as possible relative to potential rivals. The mightier a state is, the less likely it is that another state will attack it. No Americans, for example, worry that Canada or Mexico will attack the United States, because neither of those countries is powerful enough to contemplate a fight with Washington. But great powers do not merely strive to be the strongest great power, although that is a welcome outcome. Their ultimate aim is to be the hegemon—that is, the only great power in the system.

What exactly does it mean to be a hegemon in the modern world? It is almost impossible for any state to achieve global hegemony, because it is too hard to project and sustain power around the globe and onto the territory of distant great powers. The best outcome that a state can hope for is to be a regional hegemon, and thus dominate one's own geographical area. The United States has been a regional hegemon in the Western Hemisphere since the late 1800s. Although the United States is clearly the most powerful state on the planet today, it is not a global hegemon.

States that gain regional hegemony have a further aim: they seek to prevent great powers in other regions from duplicating their feat. Regional hegemons do not want peers. Instead, they want to keep other regions divided among several great powers, so that these states will compete with each other and be unable to focus on them. In sum, my theory says that the ideal situation for any great power is to be the only regional hegemon in the world.

## THE AMERICAN HEGEMON

A brief look at the history of American foreign policy illustrates the explanatory power of this theory. When the United States won its independence from Britain in 1783, it was a small and weak country comprised of 13 states strung along the Atlantic seaboard. The new country was surrounded by the British and Spanish empires and much of the territory between the Appalachian Mountains and the Mississippi River was controlled by hostile Native American tribes. It was a dangerous, threat-filled environment.

Over the course of the next 115 years, American policy makers of all stripes worked assiduously to turn the United States into a regional hegemon. They expanded America's boundaries from the Atlantic to the Pacific oceans as part of a policy commonly referred to as "Manifest Destiny." The United States fought wars against Mexico and various Native American tribes and took huge chunks of land from them. The nation became an expansionist power of the first order. As Senator Henry Cabot

Lodge put it, the United States had a "record of conquest, colonization, and territorial expansion unequalled by any people in the nineteenth century."

American policy makers in that century were not just concerned with turning the United States into a powerful territorial state. They were also determined to push the European great powers out of the Western Hemisphere and make it clear to them that they were not welcome back. This policy, known as the Monroe Doctrine, was laid out for the first time in 1823 by President James Monroe in his annual message to Congress. By 1898, the last European empire in the Americas had collapsed and the United States had become the first regional hegemon in modern history.

However, a great power's work is not done once it achieves regional hegemony. It then must make sure that no other great power follows suit and dominates its area of the world. During the twentieth century, there were four great powers that had the capability to make a run at regional hegemony: Imperial Germany (1900–1918), Imperial Japan (1931–1945), Nazi Germany (1933–1945), and the Soviet Union during the cold war (1945–1989). Not surprisingly, each tried to match what the United States had achieved in the Western Hemisphere in the nineteenth century.

*America is likely to behave toward China much the way it behaved toward the Soviet Union during the cold war.*

How did the United States react? In each case, it played a key role in defeating and dismantling those aspiring hegemons. The United States entered World War I in April 1917 when Imperial Germany looked like it would win the war and rule Europe. American troops played a critical role in tipping the balance against the Kaiserreich, which collapsed in November 1918. In the early 1940s, President Franklin Delano Roosevelt went to great lengths to maneuver the United States into World War II to thwart Japan's ambitions in Asia and especially Germany's ambitions in Europe. During the war, the United States helped destroy both Axis powers. And after 1945, American policy makers made certain that Germany and Japan remained militarily weak. Finally, during the cold war, the United States steadfastly worked to prevent the Soviet Union from dominating Eurasia, and in the late 1980s helped relegate its empire to the scrap heap of history.

Shortly after the cold war ended, the first Bush administration's "Defense Guidance" of 1992, which was leaked to the press, boldly stated that the United States was now the most powerful state in the world by far and it planned to remain in that exalted position. In other words, the United States would not tolerate a peer competitor.

That same message was repeated in the famous "National Security Strategy" issued by the second Bush administration in October 2002. There was much criticism of this document, especially its claims about "preemptive war." But hardly a word of protest was raised about the assertion that the United States should check rising powers and maintain its commanding position in the global balance of power.

The bottom line is that the United States—for sound strategic reasons—worked hard for more than a century to gain hegemony in the Western Hemisphere. After achieving regional dominance, it has gone to great lengths to prevent other great powers from controlling either Asia or Europe.

What are the implications of America's past behavior for the rise of China? In short, how is China likely to behave as it grows more powerful? And how are the United States and the other states in Asia likely to react to a mighty China?

## PREDICTING CHINA'S FUTURE

China is likely to try to dominate Asia the way the United States dominates the Western Hemisphere. Specifically, China will seek to maximize the power gap between itself and its neighbors, especially Japan and Russia. China will want to make sure that it is so powerful that no state in Asia has the wherewithal to threaten it. It is unlikely that China will pursue military superiority so that it can go on a rampage and conquer other Asian countries, although that is always possible. Instead, it is more likely that China will want to dictate the boundaries of acceptable behavior to neighboring countries, much the way the United

States makes it clear to other states in the Americas that it is the boss. Gaining regional hegemony, I might add, is probably the only way that China will get Taiwan back.

An increasingly powerful China is also likely to try to push the United States out of Asia, much the way the United States pushed the European great powers out of the Western Hemisphere. We should expect China to come up with its own version of the Monroe Doctrine, as Japan did in the 1930s.

These policy goals make good strategic sense for China. Beijing should want a militarily weak Japan and Russia as its neighbors, just as the United States prefers a militarily weak Canada and Mexico on its borders. What state in its right mind would want other powerful states located in its region? Most Chinese surely remember what happened in the past century when Japan was powerful and China was weak. In the anarchic world of international politics, it is better to be Godzilla than Bambi.

Furthermore, why would a powerful China accept US military forces operating in its backyard? American policy makers, after all, become apoplectic when other great powers send military forces into the Western Hemisphere. Those foreign forces are invariably seen as a potential threat to American security. The same logic should apply to China. Why would China feel safe with US forces deployed on its doorstep? Following the logic of the Monroe Doctrine, would not China's security be better served by pushing the American military out of Asia?

Why should we expect China to act any differently from how the United States did? Is Beijing more principled than Washington? More ethical? Less nationalistic? Less concerned about survival? China is none of these things, of course, which is why it is likely to imitate the United States and attempt to become a regional hegemon.

## TROUBLE AHEAD

It is clear from the historical record how American policy makers will react if China attempts to dominate Asia. The United States does not tolerate peer competitors. As it demonstrated in the twentieth century, it is determined to remain the world's only regional hegemon. Therefore, the United States can be expected to go to great lengths to contain China and ultimately weaken it to the point where it is no longer capable of ruling the roost in Asia. In essence, America is likely to behave toward China much the way it behaved toward the Soviet Union during the cold war.

China's neighbors are certain to fear its rise as well, and they too will do whatever they can to prevent the Chinese from achieving regional hegemony. Indeed, there is already substantial evidence that countries like India, Japan, and Russia, as well as smaller powers like Singapore, South Korea, and Vietnam, are worried about China's ascendancy and are looking for ways to contain it. In the end, they will join an American-led balancing coalition to check China's rise, much the way Britain, France, Germany, Italy, Japan, and even China joined forces with the United States to contain the Soviet Union during the cold war.

Finally, given Taiwan's strategic importance for controlling the sea lanes in East Asia, it is hard to imagine the United States, as well as Japan, allowing China to control that large island. In fact, Taiwan is likely to be an important player in the anti-China balancing coalition, which is certain to infuriate China and fuel the security competition between Beijing and Washington.

The picture I have painted of what is likely to happen if China continues its rise is not a pretty one. I actually find it categorically depressing and wish that I could tell a more optimistic story about the future. But the fact is that international politics is a nasty and dangerous business, and no amount of goodwill can ameliorate the intense security competition that sets in when an aspiring hegemon appears in Eurasia. That is the tragedy of great power politics.

# Historical Context II: Liberalism and International Organizations

# Perpetual Peace: A Philosophical Sketch

IMMANUEL KANT

## Perpetual Peace

Whether this satirical inscription on a Dutch inn-keeper's sign upon which a burial ground was painted had for its object mankind in general, or the rulers of states in particular, who are insatiable of war, or merely the philosophers who dream this sweet dream, it is not for us to decide. But one condition the author of this essay wishes to lay down. The practical politician assumes the attitude of looking down with great self-satisfaction on the political theorist as a pedant whose empty ideas in no way threaten the security of the state, inasmuch as the state must proceed on empirical principles; so the theorist is allowed to play his game without interference from the worldly-wise statesman. Such being his attitude, the practical politician—and this is the condition I make—should at least act consistently in the case of a conflict and not suspect some danger to the state in the political theorist's opinions which are ventured and publicly expressed without any ulterior purpose. By this *clausula salvatoria* the author desires formally and emphatically to deprecate herewith any malevolent interpretation which might be placed on his words.

## SECTION I

### Containing the Preliminary Articles for Perpetual Peace Among States

1. "No Treaty of Peace Shall Be Held Valid in Which There Is Tacitly Reserved Matter for a Future War" . . .
2. "No Independent States, Large or Small, Shall Come under the Dominion of Another State by Inheritance, Exchange, Purchase, or Donation" . . .
3. "Standing Armies (*miles perpetuus*) Shall in Time Be Totally Abolished" . . .
4. "National Debts Shall Not Be Contracted with a View to the External Friction of States" . . .

5. "No State Shall by Force Interfere with the Constitution or Government of Another State" . . .
6. "No State Shall, during War, Permit Such Acts of Hostility Which Would Make Mutual Confidence in the Subsequent Peace Impossible: Such Are the Employment of Assassins (*percussores*), Poisoners (*venefici*), Breach of Capitulation, and Incitement to Treason (*perduellio*) in the Opposing State" . . .

## SECTION II

### Containing the Definitive Articles for Perpetual Peace Among States First Definitive Article for Perpetual Peace
*The Civil Constitution of Every State Should Be Republican*

The only constitution which derives from the idea of the original compact, and on which all juridical legislation of a people must be based, is the republican. This constitution is established, firstly, by principles of the freedom of the members of a society (as men); secondly, by principles of dependence of all upon a single common legislation (as subjects); and, thirdly, by the law of their equality (as citizens). The republican constitution, therefore, is, with respect to law, the one which is the original basis of every form of civil constitution. The only question now is: Is it also the one which can lead to perpetual peace?

The republican constitution, besides the purity of its origin (having sprung from the pure source of the concept of law), also gives a favorable prospect for the desired consequence, i.e., perpetual peace. The reason is this: if the consent of the citizens is required in order to decide that war should be declared (and in this constitution it cannot but be the case), nothing is more natural than that they would be very cautious in commencing such a poor game, decreeing for themselves all the calamities of war. Among the latter would be: having to fight, having to pay the costs of war from their own resources, having painfully to repair the devastation war leaves behind, and, to fill up the measure of evils, load themselves with a heavy national debt that would embitter peace itself and that can never be liquidated on account of constant wars in the future. But, on the other hand, in a constitution which is not republican, and under which the subjects are not citizens, a declaration of war is the easiest thing in the world to decide upon, because war does not require of the ruler, who is the proprietor and not a member of the state, the least sacrifice of the pleasures of his table, the chase, his country houses, his court functions, and the like. He may, therefore, resolve on war as on a pleasure party for the most trivial reasons, and with perfect indifference leave the justification which decency requires to the diplomatic corps who are ever ready to provide it.

In order not to confuse the republican constitution with the democratic (as is commonly done), the following should be noted. The forms of a state (*civitas*) can be divided either according to the persons who possess the sovereign power or according to the mode of administration exercised over the people by the chief, whoever he may be. The first is properly called the form of sovereignty (*forma imperii*), and there are only three possible forms of it: autocracy, in which one, aristocracy, in which some associated together, or democracy, in which all those who constitute society, possess sovereign power. They may be characterized, respectively, as the power of a monarch, of the nobility, or of the people. The second division is that by the form of government (*forma regiminis*) and is based on the way in which the state makes use of its power; this way is based on the constitution, which is the act of the general will through which the many persons become one nation. In this respect government is either republican or despotic. Republicanism is the political principle of the separation of the executive power (the administration) from the legislative; despotism is that of the autonomous execution by the state of laws which it has itself decreed. Thus in a despotism the public will is administered by the ruler as his own will.

Of the three forms of the state, that of democracy is, properly speaking, necessarily a despotism, because it establishes an executive power in which "all" decide for or even against one who does not agree; that is, "all," who are not quite all, decide, and this is a contradiction of the general will with itself and with freedom.

Every form of government which is not representative is, properly speaking, without form. The legislator can unite in one and the same person his function as legislative and as executor of his will just as little as the universal of the major premise in a syllogism can also be the subsumption of the particular under the universal in the minor. And even though the other two constitutions are always defective to the extent that they do leave room for this mode of administration, it is at least possible for them to assume a mode of government conforming to the spirit of a representative system (as when Frederick II at least *said* he was merely the first servant of the state). On the other hand, the democratic mode of government makes this impossible, since everyone wishes to be master. Therefore, we can say: the smaller the personnel of the government (the smaller the number of rulers), the greater is their representation and the more nearly the constitution approaches to the possibility of republicanism; thus the constitution may be expected by gradual reform finally to raise itself to republicanism. For these reasons it is more difficult for an aristocracy than for a monarchy to achieve the one completely juridical constitution, and it is impossible for a democracy to do so except by violent revolution.

The mode of governments, however, is incomparably more important to the people than the form of sovereignty, although much depends on the greater or lesser suitability of the latter to the end of [good] government. To conform to the concept of law, however, government must have a representative form, and in this system only a republican mode of government is possible; without it, government is despotic and arbitrary, whatever the constitution may be. None of the ancient so-called "republics" knew this system, and they all finally and inevitably degenerated into despotism under the sovereignty of one, which is the most bearable of all forms of despotism.

## Second Definitive Article for a Perpetual Peace

### *The Law of Nations Shall be Founded on a Federation of Free States*

Peoples, as states, like individuals, may be judged to injure one another merely by their coexistence in the state of nature (i.e., while independent of external laws). Each of them may and should for the sake of its own security demand that the others enter with it into a constitution similar to the civil constitution, for under such a constitution each can be secure in his right. This would be a league of nations, but it would not have to be a state consisting of nations. That would be contradictory, since a state implies the relation of a superior (legislating) to an inferior (obeying), i.e., the people, and many nations in one state would then constitute only one nation. This contradicts the presupposition, for here we have to weigh the rights of nations against each other so far as they are distinct states and not amalgamated into one.

When we see the attachment of savages to their lawless freedom, preferring ceaseless combat to subjection to a lawful constraint which they might establish, and thus preferring senseless freedom to rational freedom, we regard it with deep contempt as barbarity, rudeness, and a brutish degradation of humanity. Accordingly, one would think that civilized people (each united in a state) would hasten all the more to escape, the sooner the better, from such a depraved condition. But, instead, each state places its majesty (for it is absurd to speak of the majesty of the people) in being subject to no external juridical restraint, and the splendor of its sovereign consists in the fact that many thousands stand at his command to sacrifice themselves for something that does not concern them and without his needing to place himself in the least danger. The chief difference between European and American savages lies in the fact that many tribes of the latter have been eaten by their enemies, while the former know how to make better use of their conquered enemies than to dine off them; they know better how to use them to increase the number of their subjects and thus the quantity of instruments for even more extensive wars.

When we consider the perverseness of human nature which is nakedly revealed in the uncontrolled relations between nations (this perverseness being veiled in the state of civil law by the constraint exercised by government), we may well be astonished that the word "law" has not yet been banished from war politics as pedantic, and that no state has yet been bold enough to advocate this point of view. Up to the present, Hugo Grotius, Pufendorf, Vattel, and many other irritating comforters have been cited in justification of war, though their code, philosophically or diplomatically formulated, has not and cannot have the least legal force, because states as such do not stand under a common external power. There is no instance on record that a state has ever been moved to desist from its purpose because of arguments backed up by the testimony of such great men. But the homage which each state pays (at least in words) to the concept of law proves that there is slumbering in man an even greater moral disposition to become master of the evil principle in himself (which he cannot disclaim) and to hope for the same from others. Otherwise the word "law" would never be pronounced by states which wish to war upon one another; it would be used only ironically, as a Gallic prince interpreted it when he said, "It is the prerogative which nature has given the stronger that the weaker should obey him."

States do not plead their cause before a tribunal; war alone is their way of bringing suit. But by war and its favorable issue, in victory, right is not decided, and though by a treaty of peace this particular war is brought to an end, the state of war, of always finding a new pretext to hostilities, is not terminated. Nor can this be declared wrong, considering the fact that in this state each is the judge of his own case. Notwithstanding, the obligation which men in a lawless condition have under the natural law, and which requires them to abandon the state of nature, does not quite apply to states under the law of nations, for as states they already have an internal juridical constitution and have thus outgrown compulsion from others to submit to a more extended lawful constitution according to their ideas of right. This is true in spite of the fact that reason, from its throne of supreme moral legislating authority, absolutely condemns war as a legal recourse and makes a state of peace a direct duty, even though peace cannot be established or secured except by a compact among nations.

For these reasons there must be a league of a particular kind, which can be called a league of peace (*foedus pacificum*), and which would be distinguished from a treaty of peace (*pactum pacis*) by the fact that the latter terminates only one war, while the former seeks to make an end of all wars forever. This league does not tend to any dominion over the power of the state but only to the maintenance and security of the freedom of the state itself and of other states in league with it, without there being any need for them to submit to civil laws and their compulsion, as men in a state of nature must submit.

## The Great Illusion

NORMAN ANGELL

What are the fundamental motives that explain the present rivalry of armaments in Europe, notably the Anglo-German? Each nation pleads the need for defense; but this implies that someone is likely to attack, and has therefore a presumed interest in so doing. What are the motives, which each State thus fears its neighbors may obey?

They are based on the universal assumption that a nation, in order to find outlets for expanding population and increasing industry, or simply to ensure the best conditions possible for its people, is necessarily pushed to territorial expansion and the exercise of political force against others (German naval competition is assumed to be the expression of the growing need of an expanding population for a larger place in the world, a need which will find a realization in the conquest of English Colonies or trade, unless these are defended); it is assumed, therefore, that a nation's relative prosperity is broadly determined by its political power; that nations being competing units, advantage, in the last resort, goes to the possessor of preponderant military force, the weaker going to the wall, as in the other forms of the struggle for life.

The author challenges this whole doctrine. He attempts to show that it belongs to a stage of development out of which we have passed; that the commerce and industry of a people no longer depend upon the expansion of its political frontiers; that a nation's political and economic frontiers do not now necessarily coincide; that military power is socially and economically futile, and can have no relation to the prosperity of the people exercising it; that it is impossible for one nation to seize by force the wealth or trade of another—to enrich itself by subjugating, or imposing its will by force on another; that, in short, war, even when victorious, can no longer achieve those aims for which peoples strive. He establishes this apparent paradox, in so far as the economic problem is concerned, by showing that wealth in the economically civilized world is founded upon credit and commercial contract (these being the outgrowth of an economic interdependence due to the increasing division of labor and greatly developed communication). If credit and commercial contract are tampered with in an attempt at confiscation, the credit-dependent wealth is undermined, and its collapse involves that of the conqueror; so that if conquest is not to be self-injurious it must respect the enemy's property, in which case it becomes economically futile. Thus the wealth of conquered territory remains in the hands of the population of such territory. When Germany annexed Alsatia, no individual German secured a single mark's worth of Alsatian property as the spoils of war. Conquest in the modem world is a process of multiplying by Synopsis xi X, and then obtaining the original figure by dividing by X. For a modern nation to add to its territory no more adds to the wealth of the people of such nation than it would add to the wealth of Londoners if the City of London were to annex the county of Hertford. The author also shows that international finance has become so interdependent and so interwoven with trade and industry that the intangibility of an enemy's property extends to his trade. It results that political and military power can in reality do nothing for trade; the individual merchants and manufacturers of small nations, exercising no such power, compete successfully with those of the great. Swiss and Belgian merchants drive English from the British Colonial market; Norway has, relatively to population, a greater mercantile, marine than Great Britain; the public credit (as a rough-and-ready indication, among others, of security and wealth) of small States possessing no political power often stands higher than that of the Great Powers of Europe, Belgian Three per Cents, standing at 96, and German at 82; Norwegian Three and a Half per Cents, at 102, and Russian Three and a Half per Cents, at 81. The forces which have brought about the economic futility of military power have also rendered it futile as a means of enforcing a nation's moral ideals or imposing social institutions upon a conquered people. Germany could not turn Canada or Australia into German colonies—i.e., stamp out their language, law, literature, traditions, etc.—by "capturing" them. The necessary security in their material possessions enjoyed by the inhabitants of such conquered provinces, quick inter-communication by a cheap press, widely-read literature, enable even small communities to become articulate and effectively to defend their special social or moral possessions, even when military conquest has been complete. The fight for ideals can no longer take the form of fight between nations, because the lines of division on moral questions are within the nations themselves and intersect the political frontiers. There is no modem State which is completely Catholic or Protestant, or liberal or autocratic, or aristocratic or democratic, or socialist or individualist; the moral and spiritual struggles of the modem world go on between citizens of the same State in unconscious intellectual co-operation with corresponding groups in other States, not between the public powers of rival States. This classification by strata involves necessarily a redirection of human pugnacity, based rather on the rivalry of classes and interests than on State divisions. War has no longer the justification that it makes for the survival of the fittest; it involves the survival of the less fit. The idea that the struggle between nations is a part of the evolutionary law of man's advance involves a profound misreading of the biological analogy. The warlike nations do not inherit the earth; they represent the decaying human element. The diminishing of physical force in all spheres of human activity carries with it profound psychological modifications. These tendencies, mainly the outcome of purely modem conditions (e.g. rapidity of communication), have rendered the problems of modern international politics profoundly and essentially different from the ancient; yet our ideas are still dominated by the principles and axioms, images and terminology of the bygone days.

The author urges that these little-recognized facts may be utilized for the solution of the armament difficulty on at present untried lines—by such modification of opinion in Europe that much of the present motive to aggression will cease to be operative, and by thus diminishing the risk of attack, diminishing to the same extent the need for defense. He shows how such a political reformation is within the scope of practical politics, and the methods which should be employed to bring it about.

# Twenty Years of Institutional Liberalism

ROBERT O. KEOHANE

The social purpose of Institutional Liberalism is to promote beneficial effects on human security, human welfare and human liberty as a result of a more peaceful, prosperous and free world. Institutional Liberalism justifies the use of power in constructing institutions on the basis of this conception of social purpose.

Institutional Liberalism is very different from what E. H. Carr, in *The Twenty Years' Crisis*, described as "liberalism." Carr had in mind nineteenth century liberalism, which was based on abstract rational principles taken out of context and therefore believed, in Carr's words, that "public opinion can be relied on to judge rightly on any question rationally presented to it." This form of liberalism, according to Carr, believed in a harmony of interests based on a "synthesis of morality and reason." And it separated power from economics. Carr's critique of this harmony-of-interest form of liberalism was convincing. Contemporary Institutional Liberals, such as myself, have learned from Carr and appropriated his insights. . . .

The roots of Institutional Liberalism lay less in specific views of capitalism and the state than in pluralist conceptions of power and interests that are well expressed in the works of James Madison. Madison was a republican: the people should govern. He did not believe that people are good and easily ruled, but rather that power needs to be checked for fear of the consequences of unchecked power. So domestically, the people should govern, but they need to establish institutions to control themselves, guarding against bad leaders and moments of passion. My views on democracy represent an ethnically, racially and gender-egalitarian adaptation of Madison's arguments. The people, broadly conceived, should rule, but they have to rule through institutions. At some moments, when publics are attuned to political events and leadership is responsive, government "by the people" is very progressive and effective. An American naturally thinks in this respect of the first years of the Civil War in the North, when attitudes toward both slavery and racism changed dramatically along with policy; and the New Deal. But when the people are not engaged, or when they are misled by demagoguery, democracy may merely be, as Churchill is said to have commented, the worst form of government except for all the others.

One of the most important contemporary liberal theorists of international relations, Michael W. Doyle, sees liberalism as resembling "a family portrait of principles and institutions," focused on the essential principle of freedom of the individual and associated with negative freedom (freedom from arbitrary authority), positive freedom (social rights essential for promoting the capacity for freedom), and democratic participation or representation. Institutions are essential for exercising these rights.

Internationally, Institutional Liberals believe that power should be used in the interests of liberal values but with caution and restraint. Institutions serve a crucial social purpose because they are essential for sustained cooperation that enhances the interests of most, if not all, people. In world politics, a sophisticated liberalism is, as I have written, "an antidote to fatalism and a source of hope." Unlike Realism, it strives for, and believes in, improvement of the human condition and provides a rationale for building cooperative institutions that can facilitate better lives for human beings.

## QUESTIONING INSTITUTIONAL LIBERALISM

But I write not to celebrate Institutional Liberalism but to question it. Invoking the ideas and spirit of E. H. Carr, but focusing on a different form of liberalism, I seek to evaluate the last 20 years of liberal dominance in world politics. Only since the collapse of the Soviet Union has it been possible to

Robert Keohane, International Relations (26, 2), pp.56–58, © 2012 by SAGE, Reprinted by Permission of SAGE.

evaluate the impact of liberal institutionalism on world politics.

Before 1991, institution-building by the United States and its allies had a significant security justification: to create economic prosperity and patterns of cooperation that would reinforce the position of the West in the struggle with the Soviet Union. Furthermore, American hegemony was crucial: the international institutions created after World War II "were constructed on the basis of principles espoused by the United States, and American power was essential for their construction and maintenance." Cooperation persisted longer than most Realists would have expected, but as long as the Soviet Union remained a rival and a threat, a Realist emphasis on relative gains was consistent with continued cooperation between the United States and other advanced industrialized countries. The relative gains that mattered were between the West and the Soviet bloc. In other words, an interpretation that explains institutions on the basis of the functions that they serve and a Realist one could both explain the patterns of cooperation that emerged and persisted.

The international institutions that operated during this period facilitated mutually beneficial cooperation on issues ranging from security to monetary cooperation to trade. Most of these institutions were not highly legalized. Sovereignty was not taken away from states, but became a *bargaining resource* that states could negotiate away, to some extent, in order to obtain other benefits, such as influence over other states' regulatory policies. Cooperation occurred on the basis of mutual self-interest and reciprocity, without much legalization.

Yet these patterns of cooperation led to remarkably robust international regimes: sets of principles, norms and rules governing the relations among well-defined sets of actors. Under the international monetary regime that prevailed between 1958 and 1971, for instance, membership in fixed exchange rate regimes was well defined and the rules were followed, with some relatively minor exceptions. Until the early 1970s the international oil regime was also quite clear, although the rules were largely set by major international oil companies,

not by states. Finally, the trade regime built around the General Agreements on Tariffs and Trade (GATT) became progressively stronger as well, at least until the mid-1980s. In the early 1980s both Ruggie and I, despite our different perspectives, anticipated a continuation and gradual strengthening of international institutions grounded in domestic politics and achieving substantial cooperation on the basis largely of specific reciprocity, as in the GATT trade system.

Since the early 1990s we can observe three developments of note: an increase in legalization; increasing legalism and moralism expressed by people leading civil society efforts to create and modify international institutions; and a decline in the coherence of some international regimes along with a failure to increase the coherence of others. Increasing legalism and moralism might have been expected 20 years ago by those of us who studied liberalism; but in different ways the increases in legalization and the recent apparent decline in the coherence of international regimes seem anomalous.

In what follows I reassess Institutional Liberalism in the light of the experience of the last 20 years. Does Institutional Liberalism contain a formerly hidden logic linking legalization, the upsurge of legalism and moralism, and decreased regime coherence? That is, do these apparently contradictory developments all represent manifestations of liberalism, which only became fully evident when it became dominant in world politics? Or do some or all of these tendencies not reflect liberalism as such, but the impact of changes in power structures in tension with liberalism, or of domestic politics? In this latter view, the changes that we see are not direct effects of liberalism but only of the inability of liberal values to be realized in a world of fragmented power and pluralist domestic politics.

Before developing my argument, it is essential that I define what I mean by "legalization," "international regimes," "legalism," and "moralism."

Legalization is a property of *institutions*. The rules of legalized institutions are precise and obligatory, and they provide arrangements for third-party adjudication.[9] . . . legalization has facilitated the progressive extension of rights, and legal protection, to oppressed persons and peoples.

Even in situations when formal legalization is not feasible, an orientation toward legalization can promote the rise of "soft law," which helps reduce uncertainty and facilitate rule-implementation.

*Coherence* is also a property of institutions, but refers more to the relationship among institutions than to the properties of any single institution. Coherent institutions or clusters of institutions have clear lines of authority linking them, so that for any given situation it is clear which rules apply, or at least which adjudicatory institutions are authorized to determine which rules apply. . . .

Finally, there seems to have been a rise in legalism and moralism in the discourse of international relations. Legalism and moralism are not properties of institutions but rather of the *human mind*. Legalism is the belief that moral and political progress can be made through the extension of law. Moralism is the belief that moral principles provide valuable, if not necessarily sufficient, guides to how political actors should behave, and that actions by those in power can properly be judged on the basis of their conformity to general moral principles developed chiefly to govern the actions of individuals.

Although many authors, particularly international legal scholars, have celebrated both legalism and legalization without distinguishing them, I wish to distinguish them from one another in this essay, since I am particularly ambivalent about legalism. I believe with E. H. Carr that law, and its efficacy, always rests on structures of power. So legalism, when taken as the description of a causal process, seems misleading to me in an ideological sense: that is, it can serve as a veil, hiding the exercise of power. In practice, the application of law can become quite uneven under situations of unequal power, leading to a form of what Stephen Krasner calls "organized hypocrisy."

E. H. Carr was critical of utopian thinking, which is often moralistic; and he was also critical of legalism. As he said, "Law is a function of political society, is dependent for its development on the development of that society, and is conditioned by the political presuppositions which that society shares in common." So an appropriate entry-point into our inquiry is to start with Carr's own thinking about morality in world politics and the role of law. What would Carr, observing the revival of legalism and moralism in world politics, make of their revival? We cannot really answer this question, but in this essay I take up some of E. H. Carr's themes to see what insights, and cautions, they may raise about contemporary international liberalism, and the moralistic and legalistic tone that it seems increasingly to be taking.

I begin with the revival of moralism, since it is fundamental—often providing a justification for legalization and legalism—and it seems to me relatively easy to explain. I will then turn to legalization and legalism, seeking to account for their growth as well. Finally, I reflect on what appears to be a counter-trend: the growing incoherence of major international regimes and the failure of coherent regimes to emerge in other areas, where functional arguments might expect them to develop.

## IDEALISM AND INTERESTS: THE REVIVAL OF MORALISM IN WORLD POLITICS

The collapse of the Soviet Union in 1991 made the US and liberal democratic states elsewhere believe that they could construct "a new world order" more consistent with the values and practices of liberal domestic politics. The language of moralism, which had previously been used in conjunction with efforts to stop the spread of Communism during the Cold War, was now detached from great power struggles. Four examples of morally justified activities are as follows:

- The conclusion of a number of major human rights treaties in the decades of the 1960s, 1970s and 1980s, and the continual push for their implementation by nongovernmental organizations committed to human rights and by some governments. These efforts included efforts to protect the rights of women and children in societies with well-entrenched practices adverse to the protection of these rights.
- Efforts by democratic governments and civil society to promote democracy in Eastern

Europe after the Cold War and around the world. These efforts were institutionalized in what Sarah Bush has called "The Democracy Establishment"—a network of individuals in governments and NGOs working to institute democratic practices in countries that were not stable democracies. The institution of extensive international election monitoring provides one notable aspect of the work of the Democracy Establishment.

- The Responsibility to Protect Doctrine, agreed by the Millennium Summit of the United Nations in 2005, which calls on states to protect their populations and provides for UN Security Council action to protect populations if the state with formal jurisdiction fails to do so. R2P, as it is called, has become a strong norm affecting UN action, although it is not a legal rule. R2P is a good example of moralism as I have defined it: the belief that moral principles provide a valuable guide to political action.

- NATO's use of military force to prevent the domination of neighboring peoples by Serbia, and last year to overthrow the Qaddafi regime in Libya. UN Security Council Resolution 1973 of 17 March 2011, authorizing the use of force against the government of Libya, referred to the Libyan government's responsibility to protect its citizens, and expressed the Council's determination to protect civilians, without explicitly invoking the R2P doctrine. In defending his support for military intervention, Barack Obama, on 28 March 2011, declared: "Some nations may be able to turn a blind eye to atrocities in other countries. The United States of America is different. And as President, I refused to wait for the images of slaughter and mass graves before taking action." . . .

So we should give *two cheers for moralism* in an era lacking vital threats to the security of our societies and our democratic institutions. First, moralism provides an impetus to social movements that provide incentives for democratic politicians to promote liberal democratic values abroad. Second, as Carr pointed out, moralism, if enunciated in moderation and practiced more or less consistently, can enhance the legitimacy of hegemonic states and the orders they seek to maintain. But we withhold the third cheer: the Realists are right to point out that power corrupts, so we need to beware that moralism can also generate arrogance, facilitate the distortion of reality, and even conceal nefarious purposes.

## THE REVIVAL OF LEGALISM AND ITS PENUMBRA

Since 1991, as I have noted, Institutional Liberalism has increasingly been legalized. The social movements of democratic liberalism have tried to institute what Ruti Teitel calls "humanity law": the "law of persons and peoples" rather than the law of states.

Liberals naturally turn to law as a constraint on power. For Institutional Liberals, this emphasis on law reflects neither a naïve belief in human goodness nor the automatic power of rules, but the view that human beings require institutional constraints to ensure that they behave well. Since 1991 there has been a remarkable increase in the number and significance of international legal institutions. Four prominent examples include the following:

- The International Criminal Tribunal for the Former Yugoslavia (ICTFY) was founded in May 1993 and is expected to operate for two or three more years.
- World trade law was legalized in the World Trade Organization, which came into force on 1 January 1995.
- The European Court of Human Rights (ECHR) was established on a permanent basis in 1998, with jurisdiction over 800 million people in the 47 member countries of the Council.
- The International Criminal Court (ICC) came into being on 1 July 2002, and now has over 115 member states. . . .

## CHANGES IN STRUCTURE AND THE DECREASING COHERENCE OF INTERNATIONAL ECONOMIC AND ENVIRONMENTAL REGIMES

Realists look for cycles and therefore have a tendency to expect observed changes to reverse themselves, because, as Robert G. Gilpin said 30 years ago, "the fundamental nature of international relations has not changed over the millennia. International relations continue to be a recurring struggle for wealth and power among independent actors in a state of anarchy."

Pursuing this line of thought, John J. Mearsheimer famously, and wrongly, predicted in 1990 that the collapse of the Soviet Union would take the world "back to the future"—to a world of power politics in Europe. The liberal "prediction of peace in a multipolar Europe is flawed." Waltz's theory of balancing would have led us to believe that the dominance of the United States would generate a blocking coalition against it. Neither of these scenarios occurred. But the broader claim of Realism is embedded in balance of power theory: that power generates attempts to counter it. And in this light 9/11 can be seen as supportive of the Realist worldview, which is profoundly cyclical and anti-progressive. Concentrated power does motivate efforts to oppose it. American dominance has been challenged by al-Qaeda, by North Korea and from Iran, and in a less radical but more enduring and fundamental sense there will be a continuing challenge over the next few decades from China. The point is that there is a counter-narrative to the progressive and pacific narrative of Institutional Liberalism. . . .

Countries such as Brazil, China, and India have different interests from those of the established industrialized democracies—with respect to trade, foreign investment, monetary arrangements and governing arrangements for limiting climate change. It is therefore not surprising that the Doha Round trade talks seem permanently stalled, that China and other exporting countries keep their exchange rate undervalued and build up enormous foreign currency reserves, that rivalry rather than cooperation characterizes oil politics, or that

the non-Annex I countries under the Kyoto Protocol, exempted from rules for emissions controls when they were weak and small, refused until the Durban meetings in December 2011 to agree to be governed by common emissions rules despite being the major sources of increases in emissions.

As a generalization, it seems to me that what could have been seen in the mid-1990s as a progressive extension of international regimes, with stronger rules and larger jurisdictions, has been halted if not reversed. The hopes of observers such as John Ikenberry for a revival of liberal regimes under a more capacious form of American hegemony are not, so far, being realized. And here again Realism remains relevant: to understand institutions and international law, we need to peer through the veil of rhetoric and law, to discern the power and interest structures that lie below. Those power and interest structures moved strongly toward greater coherence and uniformity with the collapse of the Soviet Union: when the WTO was formed, the West was at a historic high point of dominance. With the rise of China, India and other emerging economies, structures of power and interest have become more diverse; and as Structural Realism would have anticipated, the institutions that link major powers have been weakened, with more contention over their proper arrangements. Liberal regimes with United States leadership may be easy to join, as Ikenberry asserts; but they can also be rejected by states with sufficient independent power. As institutional theorists anticipated, many of these institutions persist despite changes in patterns of power and interests; but as Realists claimed, it has become increasingly difficult to construct strong new institutions. . . .

## CONCLUSION

At the beginning of this essay I asked whether moralism and legalism, legalization, and declines in the coherence of international regimes reflected intrinsic qualities of liberalism or the impact of changes in structures of power. My answer is mixed. I attribute increased legalization, moralism and legalism to intrinsic features of liberalism and to the dominance since 1991 of liberal states. But I attribute declines in the coherence of international regimes to the anticipated as well as actual diversification of power and interests in world politics as well as the inhibitions on learning built into domestic politics in most countries in an era of slow economic growth and increasing economic inequality. Collapse is avoided because, as Joseph Nye and I wrote in *Power and Interdependence*, "a set of networks, norms and institutions, once established, will be difficult either to eradicate or drastically rearrange." But progress toward more coherent and comprehensive regimes has also come to a halt.

So we see the persistence and in some areas the expansion of legalization, coupled with legalism and moralism, at the same time as urgent problems no longer generate the creation of multilateral regimes. Contradictory patterns continue to appear.

My own liberalism has little in common with either laissez-faire economics or with the notion that liberals are optimists about human nature. It has much more in common with Judith N. Sklar's concept of the "liberalism of fear." As I implied at the beginning of this article, I share much of James Madison's political philosophy. I am a liberal not because I think people are good and easily ruled, but because I think that unchecked power is dangerous and that power-holders therefore need to be held in check. Institutional Liberalism offers not the promise of continuous progress but a source of hope for improvement coupled with institutional checks against retrogression.

Power continues to be important but institutions can help to tame it, and states whose leaders seek both to maintain and use power must be attentive, as E. H. Carr recognized, to issues of legitimacy. At the moment, legalism and moralism thrive, but the comprehensiveness and coherence of multilateral institutions are suffering. We need at this time less to profess and preach legalism and moralism than to figure out how to form coalitions that will build and maintain coherent multilateral institutions to address the major challenges of our time. The fact that these institutions are not foolproof is less a counsel of despair than a motivation to build them on as firm foundations as we can.

# Section 4

Historical Context III: Exploring Alternatives:
Class, Gender, and Values

# Constructing International Politics

ALEXANDER WENDT

Indeed, one of our main objections to neorealism is that it is not structural enough: that adopting the individualistic metaphors of micro-economics restricts the effects of structures to state behavior, ignoring how they might also constitute state identities and interests. Constructivists think that state interests are in important part constructed by systemic structures, not exogenous to them; this leads to a sociological rather than micro-economic structuralism.

Where neorealist and constructivist structuralisms really differ, however, is in their assumptions about what structure is made of. Neorealists think it is made only of a distribution of material capabilities, whereas constructivists think it is also made of social relationships. Social structures have three elements: shared knowledge, material resources, and practices.

First, social structures are defined, in part, by shared understandings, expectations, or knowledge. These constitute the actors in a situation and the nature of their relationships, whether cooperative or conflictual. . . .

Second, social structures include material resources like gold and tanks. In contrast to neorealists' desocialized view of such capabilities, constructivists argue that material resources only acquire meaning for human action through the structure of shared knowledge in which they are embedded. For example, 500 British nuclear weapons are less threatening to the United States than 5 North Korean nuclear weapons, because the British are friends of the United States and the North Koreans are not, and amity or enmity is a function of shared understandings. As students of world politics, neorealists would probably not disagree, but as theorists the example poses a big problem, since it completely eludes their materialist definition of structure. Material capabilities as such explain nothing; their effects presuppose structures of shared knowledge, which vary and which are not reducible to capabilities. Constructivism is therefore compatible with changes in material power affecting social relations, as long as those effects can be shown to presuppose still deeper social relations.

Third, social structures exist, not in actors' heads nor in material capabilities, but in practices. Social structure exists only in process. The Cold War was a structure of shared knowledge that governed great power relations for forty years, but once they stopped acting on this basis, it was "over."

In sum, social structures are real and objective, not "just talk." But this objectivity depends on shared knowledge, and in that sense social life is "ideas all the way down" (until you get to biology and natural resources). Thus, to ask "when do ideas, as opposed to power and interest, matter?" is to ask the wrong question. Ideas always matter, since power and interest do not have effects apart from the shared knowledge that constitutes them as such. . . .

## EXPLAINING WAR AND PEACE

In "Anarchy is What States Make of It" I argued that such behavior is a self-fulfilling prophecy, and that this is due to both agency and social structure. Thus, on the agency side, what states do to each other affects the social structure in which they are embedded, by a logic of reciprocity. If they militarize, others will be threatened and arm themselves, creating security dilemmas in terms of which they will define egoistic identities and interests. But if they engage in policies of reassurance, as the Soviets did in the late 1980s, this will have a different effect on the structure of shared knowledge, moving it toward a security community. The depth of interdependence is a factor here, as is the role of revisionist states, whose actions are likely to be especially threatening. However, on the structural

Alexander Wendt, 'Constructing International Politics', International Security, 20:1 (Summer, 1995), pp.71–81. © 1995 by the President and Fellows of Harvard College and the Massachusetts Institute of Technology side, the ability of revisionist states to create a war of all against all depends on the structure of shared knowledge into which they enter. If past interactions have created a structure in which status quo states are divided or naive, revisionists will prosper and the system will tend toward a Hobbesian world in which power and self-interest rule. In contrast, if past interactions have created a structure in which status quo states trust and identify with each other, predators are more likely to face collective security responses like the Gulf War. *History matters.* Security dilemmas are not acts of God: they are effects of practice. This does not mean that once created they can necessarily be escaped (they are, after all, "dilemmas"), but it puts the causal locus in the right place. . . .

Anarchy as such is not a structural cause of anything. What matters is its social structure, which varies across anarchies. An anarchy of friends differs from one of enemies, one of self-help from one of collective security, and these are all constituted by structures of shared knowledge.

In order to get from anarchy and material forces to power politics and war, therefore, neorealists have been forced to make additional, ad hoc assumptions about the social structure of the international system.

The problem becomes even more acute when neorealists try to explain the relative absence of inter-state war in today's world. If anarchy is so determining, why are there not more Bosnias? Why are weak states not getting killed off left and right? It stretches credulity to think that the peace between Norway and Sweden, or the United States and Canada, or Nigeria and Benin are all due to material balancing.

## RESPONSIBILITY

To say that structures are socially constructed is no guarantee that they can be changed. Sometimes social structures so constrain action that transformative strategies are impossible. This goes back to the collective nature of social structures; structural change depends on changing a system of expectations that may be mutually reinforcing. A key issue in determining policymakers' responsibilities, therefore, is how much "slack" a social structure contains. Neorealists think there is little slack in the system, and thus states that deviate from power politics will get punished or killed by the "logic" of anarchy. Institutionalists think such dangers have been greatly reduced by institutions such as sovereignty and the democratic peace, and that there is therefore more possibility for peaceful change.

The example of Gorbachev is instructive in this respect, since the Cold War was a highly conflictual social structure . . . . What is so important about the Gorbachev regime is that it had the courage to see how the Soviets' own practices sustained the Cold War, and to undertake a reassessment of Western intentions. This is exactly what a constructivist would do, but not a neorealist, who would eschew attention to such social factors as naive and as mere superstructure. Indeed, what is so striking about neorealism is its total neglect of the explanatory role of state practice. It does not seem to matter what states do: Brezhnev, Gorbachev, Zhirinovsky, what difference does it make? The logic of anarchy will always bring us back to square one. This is a disturbing attitude if *realpolitik* causes the very conditions to which it is a response; to the extent that realism counsels *realpolitik*, therefore, it is part of the problem. . . .

To analyze the social construction of international politics is to analyze how processes of interaction produce and reproduce the social structures—cooperative or conflictual—that shape actors' identities and interests and the significance of their material contexts. It is opposed to two rivals: the materialist view, of which neorealism is one expression, that material forces per se determine international life, and the rational choice–theoretic view that interaction does not change identities and interests.

# The Growth and Future of Feminist Theories in International Relations

J. ANN TICKNER

BROWN JOURNAL OF WORLD AFFAIRS: What has been your overall personal experience as a woman feminist theorist in the field of International Relations?

J. ANN TICKNER: I have certainly found the experience very rewarding. It has been wonderful to be part of a community of scholars who are building a new approach in the discipline of International Relations (IR). Feminist approaches got started at the end of the 1980s so we've had about 12 or 13 years and it's been a very exciting and intellectually stimulating time. In 1989, I spent some months at the London School of Economics and it was very interesting that there were scholars and graduate students there who were beginning to think along the same lines, but independently of those of us in the United States. About the same time Jindy Pettman wrote a feminist critique of IR in the *Australian Journal of International Affairs*. It was intriguing that, in three different parts of the world, similar themes were emerging at about the same time.

Since that time there's been some great work in feminist international relations that critiques the discipline from a gendered perspective and articulates some new feminist approaches. There is now a growing body of empirical work that looks at global issues from a feminist perspective and highlights research about women. There are a lot of wonderful scholars in this field and it's been a privilege to be a part of it.

JOURNAL: How has your work evolved throughout your career? How has this process been affected by the way in which your theories are viewed in the greater international community?

TICKNER: My interest in feminism began in the mid-1980s when I was teaching at Holy Cross College, a hospitable environment in which to do non-mainstream work. Each year I taught the introductory undergraduate IR course for our majors. This was during the Cold War so there was a heavy emphasis on security issues and nuclear strategy. I noticed that a number of my female students would come to my office and say, "I'm just not cut out for this kind of stuff." When I asked them to explain why, it would often come down to the fact that they thought the male students were somehow more qualified to talk about weapons and military strategy. Often they felt disempowered around these issues. In trying to understand why they felt this way when many of them did very well in the course, I began to look at some feminist work in other fields to find the answer to this puzzle.

The first book I read that helped me with this puzzle and really influenced my thinking about how IR is a masculine gendered discipline was Evelyn Fox Keller's *Reflections on Gender and Science*. It is a wonderfully perceptive feminist critique of the natural sciences as gendered masculine. When I read the book it made me think that a lot

Courtesy of Brown Journal of World Affairs. Winter/Spring, 10, 2, pg. 47–56 of what Keller had to say about the natural sciences would actually apply to IR. By this I mean the way we construct theories in IR and how we evaluate them. I then started reading more feminist theory, but feminist theory from other disciplines, because feminist IR theory did not really exist at that time. My book, *Gender in International Relations,* was the first singly authored feminist text that critiqued the discipline from a gendered perspective. While, of necessity, I constructed my critique out of feminist theory from other disciplines, I also tried to seriously engage with IR. I have always tried to acknowledge, and engage with, the things that IR can tell us, but there are many things we need to know that it doesn't tell us.

JOURNAL: What are the themes of your current project?

TICKNER: I am undertaking a writing project about feminist research practices for IR. I would like to direct it towards graduate students who, when they want to take up topics having to do with gender, race, and other similar issues, find that there are not many methodological guidelines upon which they can draw—at least not in IR. We need more texts that focus specifically on feminist methodologies for IR.

JOURNAL: Where do you see feminist theory heading in the future?

TICKNER: I am hopeful that feminist theory will continue to flourish, but I am also aware that it is hard for it to gain acceptance, particularly in what I am calling the mainstream of the discipline. As I said before, there is a lot of excellent "second generation" feminist empirical work, but there's also a lot of gate keeping in the discipline. At the moment there is an extremely tight job market in academia and I think that graduate students often feel pressured to adopt more mainstream approaches because they think it will help them find academic jobs. This is too bad because there's so much interest and demand on the part of students, not only for feminist IR, but also for other critical perspectives. The dominance of rational choice and game theory is very strong and the tolerance for critical perspectives, other than a certain form of constructivism, is not very high. It's worrisome.

JOURNAL: As feminist discourse and theories appear to be developing a greater legitimacy within the discipline of IR, how do you see feminist theory best implemented beyond academics in the current world system? Do you think feminist theory runs the risk of being able to speak only to other academics?

TICKNER: I was actually rather heartened that you thought that feminist theory had already achieved this legitimacy! It has amongst some people, but it is still rather precarious as I just mentioned. However, I do notice that a lot of introductory IR textbooks now have a section on feminist approaches. I think we are making progress. I agree with you about the problems of writing for academics. However, I would like to emphasize that I think that more conventional IR theory is also written for academics. I don't think you can talk only about feminists being guilty of this, but maybe that's not what you meant. I think much of IR theory is quite esoteric, removed from the "real world" and hard for lay people to understand. In my view, it is quite astonishing how much of our discipline has so little to tell us about what's actually going on in the real world today.

Feminist theory is a tool for those who want to write about gendered perspectives in IR. It seems unfamiliar and esoteric to some because we are not used to gender analysis and, in IR at least, we don't have the requisite training for it. Gender is a sociological category; it doesn't fit well with the methodologies, more typical of mainstream IR, that draw on microeconomics and rational choice. With its focus on social relations, feminist theory is more akin to sociological perspectives.

A lot of the empirical IR feminist work that's now coming out, is grounded in the "real world." Or maybe we should talk about multiple "real worlds" since the worlds that feminists are writing about have frequently been hidden from the agendas of international politics. Take Kathy Moon's book which talks about military prostitution in Korea, or Elizabeth Prügl's work on home-based labor. Jacqui True has just finished a book on the effects on women of the post-Communist transition in the Czech Republic. And all of Cynthia Enloe's work is grounded in the "real world" although not the same "real world"—the world of states and states*men*—that IR has studied. While some feminist theory may be esoteric, much of it has evolved out of social movements and political practice. Frequently, feminists emphasize constructing theory out of practice, particularly the practice of everyday lives of ordinary people. I think that this is a strength of feminist theory. However, many IR theorists don't think that it's a legitimate way to build knowledge.

JOURNAL: How do you think the greater IR community perceives feminist theory?

TICKNER: I don't think the greater IR community understands feminist theory very well. If you limit the question to mainstream IR, they honestly believe that feminist approaches to IR are not "scientific." I think this is one of the greatest barriers to mutual understanding, and it's why I have begun to work on methodology. IR scholars will often say that it is really interesting to bring women into the picture but that you have to do it in a "scientific" way. The methodological problems are much harder to resolve than the legitimacy of the subject matter. I think that mainstream IR theorists are quite willing to think that they

might learn something from the kind of work we do, but they find the way we go about doing it problematic.

Another problem is that gender is always equated with women. We must understand that gender is also about men and masculinity—something that is central to international politics since so much of the discipline is about men and masculinity. A big problem is that many people who don't understand feminist theory very well assume that it can tell us something about women, but they don't assume that it can tell us anything about global politics more generally. This is important but it is very hard for scholars who don't work in this perspective to understand.

Another obstacle is that gender is something that is very threatening to people's identities. When you talk about feminism or gender, many people feel personally threatened. It's often very difficult to get beyond this personal worry and move on to acknowledge that gender can help us understand the world better. Questions such as, "Oh, so you don't like men?" or "Are you trying to tell me that women are more peaceful than men?" continue to crop-up. But I am hopeful that this problem is diminishing in your generation now that feminist literature is included in more IR courses.

JOURNAL: What is the relationship between marginalization and women in feminist theory?

TICKNER: Feminism *is* a perspective from the margins because so many women throughout the world have been marginalized. Not all women of course. Feminist theory emerges from what we might call a standpoint of those who are disempowered and subordinated but there are certainly other theories that come from similar standpoints—Marxist class analysis, for example. Indeed, certain strands of feminist theory draw on class analysis. Feminisms have emerged out of multiple standpoints. I do think it is useful to analyze the world from marginal perspectives because you see things that you do not see from the center. In fact, 1990s' feminism was very focused on difference—that is women's differing positionality, based on their race, class, ethnic origins, nationalities, etc.

The bigger worry for feminist theory is the danger of seeing women as victims who lack agency. Another related worry is that more empowered women speak for those who have less power and voice. For example, there has been much criticism by Third World feminists of Western feminists' inclination to speak for them. One of the positive aspects of this is the emergence of African-American and post-colonial feminist theories. This has also been a big issue around the Middle East and U.S. foreign policy—the view that women "over there" are helpless victims to whom we need to reach out and offer our enlightened ideas. That is a difficult issue for feminists and women in the Middle East more generally who do need our support but who also ask us to respect their right to liberate themselves in ways that make sense for them.

JOURNAL: How would you compare the Islamic and secular nations based on their structure and views on women?

TICKNER: In general I think that secularism is better for women although one must respect the views of those women who struggle for their rights using a sense of religious identity. There have been some very depressing reports from Iraq recently about how women feel much more insecure post-Saddam Hussein than before. I have read several stories in the *New York Times* which say that things are actually getting worse for women because, as religious fundamentalism is on the rise, women are being pushed back into the private sphere and are suffering from increased sexual violence. Based on interviews with Iraqi women, the

*Times* also stated that the occupation forces have not paid much attention to these problems. Even were there to be a more democratic Iraq we cannot assume that things will be better for women. Very often when you look at what are applauded as progressive transformational moments in history you find that things did not actually improve for women.

JOURNAL: Do you perceive the U.S. occupation of Iraq as a masculine approach to managing conflict?

TICKNER: I would like to talk first about what "a masculine approach to managing conflict" might mean. Certainly no policy maker would use this term. That in itself is something we should find interesting.

Let me begin by discussing the definition of gender, which is very much encoded in our everyday lives and practices. We all know what masculine means but we are not called upon to define it very often. Gender is about a set of relational characteristics that we associate with masculinity and femininity—characteristics such as power, autonomy, rationality, and agency are seen as typically masculine. Other characteristics, such as weakness, dependency, emotion and passivity, are associated with femininity. However, these are not necessarily attributes of individual women and men. In fact, one of the exercises that I do with my undergraduates, who often have never consciously thought about gender in these terms, is to ask them to come up with lists of characteristics they would associate with masculinity and femininity. I write them on the board in two columns. When I ask them which characteristics they identify with, most of the students will identify with the masculine ones, even though the majority of them are women. But they know that these are the characteristics they should display to be successful in the public sphere. So we all know what masculinity means—the norms to which we aspire in our public lives and which come to be seen as universal.

However, I would like to point out that when you say a "masculine approach," it's not *the only* masculine approach. It's what I and others have called "hegemonic masculinity." It's this sort of masculinity that we don't have to explain. We know that it is something that we should try to live up to. But most people don't act this way, including many men who often feel quite uncomfortable with trying to "act like a man." Nevertheless, it legitimates certain ways of behaving and delegitimates others including other forms of masculinity. It is interesting to map these hegemonic masculine characteristics onto the international behavior of states. To me, this is a big problem. It's not that these ways of acting—seeking power, being autonomous—are always bad, but it does tend to delegitimate other valid ways of behaving that use more cooperative, less power-centered strategies. And often these alternative ways for states to behave are judged inferior by being associated with women and femininity.

I think that the way that we're going to get beyond this problem is by questioning these gender stereotypes. We must be able to acknowledge that, while autonomy is important, there may be times when more interdependent, less autonomous, more multilateral strategies might be more appropriate. If you pay attention to academic and media accounts of foreign policy, it's amazing how much of it is described and evaluated in these gendered terms. I ask my students to analyze newspaper articles in terms of this gender coding. They find it all over the place although often they say that they had never noticed it before. Feminism is all about questioning what we normally take for granted.

So to get back to your question, yes, I do think that the war in Iraq is a masculine approach. The emphasis on a strong military response closes off other more conciliatory options. This is not the same thing as saying that men always favor the use of force while women always favor more peaceful responses. Women supported this war, too, although there was a significant gender gap on the issue, at least until the war started. What I am

saying that we are *all* socialized into regarding masculine norms as the correct way to operate—particularly in matters of foreign policy. This has the negative effect of shutting off other options. And the framing of the war on terrorism as good versus evil reflects the kind of dichotomous thinking that feminists find deeply problematic, as I have illustrated with my definition of gender. Feminists have written a great deal about the dangers of either/or categorizations and the tolerance for ambiguity, both of which could be useful here.

> JOURNAL: One of your arguments in your article "Feminist Perspectives on 9/11" was that 9/11 happened in part because al-Qaeda thought the United States was becoming "feminine" and thus vulnerable. How can you incorporate a feminist perspective into current discourse about the war on terror?
>
> TICKNER: I don't think that this was the whole reason why it happened although I don't think that al-Qaeda expected such a massive response from what it perceived as a country unwilling to fight, a view that was often articulated through reference to the "feminization" of the United States. And Bin Laden used gender coding to rally his supporters behind fighting against "weak, wimpy, feminized" Westerners. But he also talked about Westerners as crusaders, which isn't a feminized image. The gender messages were very strong but they were very complicated.

And we feminize Islamic nations. Our foreign policy plays on the notion of feminizing the "Other," but only certain others. We did not feminize the Soviet Union to the same extent. They were our adversaries, but they were rational people to whom we could talk sensibly about not blowing each other up. This selective feminization of other nations is quite racial—we tend to feminize nonwhite nations. There is a fascinating literature about the gendering of colonialism: for example, the British discourse of nineteenth century imperialism was highly gendered with those who were colonized frequently depicted in gendered feminine terms.

An interesting complication today is that, as I said, "they" are also feminizing "us." To quote Osama bin Laden, "Our brothers who fought in Somalia saw wonders about the weakness, feebleness, and cowardliness of the U.S. soldier." In this speech, Bin Laden goes on to berate the U.S. military for having women in it. There's a lot in the rhetoric of al-Qaeda about the West being weak and feminized. And there's a lot of talk in the Middle East about the dangers posed by liberated western women that serves to police Middle Eastern women and keep them out of public life.

But we must remember that religious fundamentalist discourses of all faiths, Christian as well as Muslim, inside as well as outside the United States, talk about the dangers of the United States becoming feminized if women get too much power. And, as I said in the article you mentioned, it gets much more pronounced in times of upheaval and insecurity as it did after 9/11.

> JOURNAL: What influence can women in power have? How can women in positions of power achieve a feminist agenda?
>
> TICKNER: Women *are* in power, though not in large numbers. They are playing all sorts of roles. There have been women presidents, prime ministers, and even ministers of defense. But how much better it will be when we no longer refer to them as "women presidents" but just as "presidents!" Women

have had powerful roles just like men. I am aware that in some countries this is not possible, but in many it is. The big question is why there are *so few* women in positions of power even in countries where legal equality has been in place for a long time. The power that gender role expectations exert can tell us a lot about this.

The question of feminists in power is a different one. It is a much more difficult issue. There has been a lot of speculation about whether women would more likely pursue feminist agendas if they were in a majority of leadership positions. We have so little empirical evidence on this score that it is very hard to say whether it would make a difference. I am intrigued by the Scandinavian states which have a fairly large proportion of women in political power. Could there be a connection with these states' friendliness to social welfare policy—better day care, etc.? It is very hard to say whether these relatively women-friendly policies happened because there were so many women in power, or vice versa. But I do have the sense that it might make a difference if you had a critical mass of women in power.

And if we didn't have such hierarchical gendered societies it would certainly be easier to get things on the agenda that feminists believe in. But it's a big leap to think that people who identify themselves as feminists would be in power anywhere. In the United States, Hillary Clinton has been vilified for being a feminist but she's pretty cautious about this identification. It is very important to think *why* the term "feminist' carries so many negative connotations. This is a very political issue that has a lot to do with preserving power for those who already have it.

# The Kennedy Experiment Revisited

AMITAI ETZIONI

Many of the critical issues and conflicts in international relations today bear a significant resemblance to the geopolitical circumstances that led to the development of the theorem I published in these pages forty years ago. States, grappling over nuclear proliferation and other security issues, still face off against one another, brimming with mutual hostility and mistrust that render it difficult for them to move forward with bilateral or multilateral negotiations. . . . The emergence of nonstate actors as significant players in international relations has even further exacerbated the effects of such suspicion in hampering prospects for negotiations (e.g., Russia and Chechen separatists and Israel and Hamas). In light of these developments, my theorem, which outlines measures that can be taken in the face of such mutual hostility and suspicion in order to reduce the tensions and pave the way to productive negotiations, remains at least as relevant today as when I initially formulated it at the height of the Cold War.

## THE THEOREM OUTLINED

My theorem maps out a certain pattern of action for agents to pursue where they face a situation in which mutual suspicion and hostility effectively prevent progress toward negotiations. Specifically, it points toward a course of (1) *unilateral*, (2) *reciprocal*, and (3) *symbolic* actions between mutually mistrustful agents. This pattern of actions, my theorem suggests, is the best road to travel toward the possibility of "normal" negotiations.

1. Steps down this road are unilateral—states should pursue acts that do not rely on any of the usual give and take of international relations. My theorem stands in contrast to those realists who frown upon such unilateral concessions, believing that they damage one's interest and stature. . . .

2. Steps down the road that my theorem maps out must be reciprocal—if one side does not reciprocate after one or several gestures, the pattern is broken.

3. Finally, and most centrally, steps down the road that my theorem maps out are symbolic—states should pursue actions with predominantly "psychological" weight rather than with significant military, economic, or any other "real" value. In this regard, my theorem stands in contrast to those "grand unilateralists" who posit that, for example, if one nation were to give up its nuclear military capabilities, its adversary would be compelled to do the same. Instead, the idea here is merely to open a window to see if fresh air can be introduced, not to blow off the roof and knock down the walls.

In contrast to major theories of international relations that focus on "real" factors, such as the number of nuclear bombs a nation commands, the size of its military, the rate of its economic growth, and so on, my theorem holds that "psychology" matters a great deal. I do not, however, take the extreme version of this position as held by some social constructivists who argue, for example, that since "war begins in the minds of men," it is exactly there where efforts to end and prevent war must be waged. On my theorem, psychological factors are not taken to be all powerful in this way; I do not argue that if nations ceased to fear or threaten one another, peace would simply break out all over. Instead, psychological factors are best viewed as playing an important but limited role; they can and do have "real" consequences, including helping pave the way toward multilateral negotiations, but are not in and of themselves taken as a cure-all remedy.

In the forty years since my original article was published, the need for foreign policy makers to

Amitai Etzioni, Political Research Quarterly (Vol. 61, No. 1), pp. 20–24, copyright © YEAR by SAGE, Reprinted by Permission of SAGE Publications.

recognize the importance of psychological factors has become increasingly necessary. Specifically, "legitimacy"—the successful drawing of psychological connections between new international facts to people's perceptions and values—has come to matter a great deal. This is in part a result of the spread of education and means of communication ("the CNN factor") that has allowed more people to become more informed and involved in public and international affairs. Yet many policy makers continue to ignore the significance of legitimacy and other psychological factors—usually at their own peril.

For example, a clear and striking pattern has emerged in which important agreements (e.g., the Camp David Accords, the Oslo Agreements, and the proposed European Constitution) that are made without sufficient consideration or accommodation of these factors—the perceptions, sentiments, and values of the public involved—have failed or have subsequently collapsed.

As another example, look at the most common reaction to Yasser Arafat, who is frequently criticized for his rejection of what many consider a very accommodating offer made by then Israeli Prime Minister Ehud Barak but was in fact paying close attention to the psychological factors at play. He recognized (unlike most of his critics) that to sign such an agreement would be tantamount to asking that Palestinians change their perception of Israel overnight, from the evil, dreaded enemy that deserves to be demolished to a partner for peace in a two-state solution. In short, Arafat recognized that acquiring legitimacy for such an agreement would have been impossible. Similarly, Arafat recognized that there was an Israeli minority that was strongly opposed to such a deal and that was not prepared to accept it. In rejecting this deal, Arafat was keenly attuned to the psychological factors at play both among his own people and in his opponents.

These examples show that legitimacy and other psychological factors have become critical factors in evaluating policy making not only in looking to the behavior and actions of opponents but also in looking domestically at one's own people. The *unilateral-reciprocal* model that my theorem lays out can be and is profitably applicable not only to

other actors but also toward the population of one's own state in order to build legitimacy.

## A "NATURAL" EXPERIMENT

President Kennedy was probably unaware of the academic work being done on the unilateral-reciprocal approach to tension reduction and conflict resolution. (However, I did send memos to this effect to his staff, as I believe did Charles Osgood, a colleague who developed a similar theorem.) Hence, the events of 1963 are best viewed as a "natural experiment"—as providing an inadvertent but nevertheless valid test of my theorem. Here follows a brief overview of the pattern of unilateral steps and reciprocations undertaken that cumulatively led to a thawing of the Cold War as well as to bilateral and multilateral negotiated agreements.

On June 10, 1963, in his "Strategy for Peace" speech, Kennedy struck a reconciliatory tone toward the Union of Soviet Socialist Republics (USSR) and announced that the United States would stop all nuclear tests in the atmosphere. The USSR permitted Kennedy's speech to be published in its media outlets and broadcast without interruption—such public exposure was highly unusual for a speech by an American president. The day after this speech, the USSR withdrew its objection to Western-backed proposals to send United Nations (UN) observers to Yemen. Next, the United States withdrew its objection to granting full membership status to the Hungarian delegation to the UN. Four days later, Khrushchev delivered a speech with a reconciliatory tone similar to Kennedy's, welcoming the president's initiative and announcing that the USSR's production of strategic bombers had been halted. Soon thereafter Khrushchev agreed to a U.S.–USSR communications link first proposed by the United States in late 1962 and also announced that the USSR would not test nuclear weapons in the atmosphere (several months prior to the August 1963 treaty on this issue).

Further gestures were made in late September. Kennedy suggested each of the following: a possible exchange of observer posts at key points to reduce the danger of a surprise attack, the expansion of the test treaty to include underground testing, direct flights between Moscow and New York, and the opening of consulates in Leningrad and Chicago. Meanwhile, Soviet foreign minister Andrei Gromyko called for a NATO–Warsaw Pact nonaggression pact and pursued an agreement to foreswear the orbiting of nuclear weapons.

In October, Kennedy called for reducing the trade barriers between East and West and approved the sale of $250 million in wheat to the USSR. The president also declared an agreement in principle not to put nuclear weapons in orbit. By late October, a resolution was passed by the UN General Assembly to this effect.

November marked a slowdown in U.S. unilateral initiatives. The administration was concerned that hope for more USSR–U.S. measures was running too high and wanted to reduce some of the mounting pressure. Allies in Western Europe had begun to voice anxiety about the apparent growing willingness to compromise they observed in U.S. behavior. And perhaps most significantly, Kennedy was about to face elections against a Republican party that viewed conciliatory measures as weakening the nation's resolve and power. Prior to President Kennedy's premature death, it was widely expected that this pattern of reciprocal moves would resume after the 1964 presidential election.

Three points are particularly worth highlighting from this narration:

1. For each unilateral move the United States made, the USSR not only reciprocated but did so proportionally so that over the course of the exchange, neither side made a disproportionate gain in advantage or status.

2. None of the moves was costly in military, economic, or any other "real" terms but were, rather, symbolic or "psychological." For example, the U.S. halting of atmospheric nuclear testing came after the United States had already conducted twice as much testing as the USSR and had amassed enough data to take at least a year of analysis to digest. At the time of Khrushchev's announcement about halting production of the strategic bomber, the USSR was likely planning on phasing out those bombers anyway. In addition, his announcement contained no proposed method of verification for the United States to ensure that production was actually stopped. In terms of the initiatives made regarding East–West trade, overall trade policy was never really in question and did not change, and the total value of the wheat ultimately sold to the USSR was not $250 million but only $65 million. In short, the concessions made by both sides were for the most part highly symbolic.

3. Both sides initiated actions. The USSR offered some initiatives of its own, including the withdrawal of objections to Yemen observers, the proposal for a NATO–Warsaw Pact nonaggression agreement, and the proposal of an air treaty.

Overall, as I found in my paper forty years ago, the unilateral-reciprocal approach led to reduced tensions between the United States and the USSR and paved the way toward multilateral-simultaneous measures. When the pattern of symbolic gestures was interrupted in November 1963, the tension reduction ceased. . . .

## A RANGE OF CONCEPTUAL RESPONSES

My analysis of the "Kennedy Experiment" published on these pages more than a generation ago sparked a debate among my colleagues on the power of psychological or symbolic concessions in international relations. Not all of my colleagues were convinced of the validity of the analysis.

Some realists charged that the effects credited to the applications of the theorem were actually products of deterrence—they argued that the threat of nuclear annihilation itself produced détente. . . .

Still others pointed out that the theorem was not fully specified. For instance, Johan Niezing (1978) wrote,

What happens if the opposite party does not react? The various authors writing on the idea of unilateral steps do not agree. Some, like Etzioni, advocate stopping after several steps. Others propose initiating the process all the same, by taking one big step which the opposing party cannot but interpret as a cognitively dissonant element. . . .

In toto, my theorem has received the kind of varied and relevant observations those who formulate theorems aspire to. My only regret it that there have been very few attempts to apply this theorem to subsequent international conflicts as a tension-reducing tactic; there have, in other words, been too few subsequent "natural experiments" of my theory. Little wonder that various parties find it so difficult to move from hostile confrontations to multilateral negotiations.

# Critical Thinking and Discussion Questions for Part I (Sections 1–4)

## SECTION 1

1. **Huntington wrote in 1993, "The fault lines between civilizations will be the battle lines of the future." Locate on a world map at least four such fault lines.**
   - Which countries do they include?
   - Check the most recent news from these fault lines related to tensions or conflicts.
   - How stable today are the regions on the fault lines compared to other regions?

2. **Huntington offered six reasons why civilizations would clash.**
   - Argue against any one of these reasons.
   - Offer a few counterarguments about why civilizations will not clash.

3. **Explain the kin-country syndrome. From the list of countries below, select three pairs, which, if you apply Huntington's ideas, should be viewed as kin countries:**

   Japan  Vietnam  Libya  Cuba  France  Russia  Mexico  Egypt
   Argentina  Belgium  Serbia  Germany  Venezuela  Ukraine

**Explain your choices.**

4. **Give an example involving two contemporary relations and conflicts: one that proves and the other that disproves the kin-country syndrome.**
   - Suggested cases for starters: Russia's actions in Crimea in 2014 and after; China–Taiwan relations; relations between North Korea and South Korea; relations between the United States and the United Kingdom; or relations between the governments of Syria and Iran.

5. **Provide several examples of today's "torn" countries. Explain your selections. Can you suggest that some countries that struggle with order and security are more torn than others?**

6. **How was the race factor incorporated in US foreign policy before the 1960s? How did it play out recently, in the past three years, in your opinion?**

7. **Explain why globalization, according to Krasner, does not undermine state control. Remember that the article was written some time ago. Do you think globalization is undermining state control today? Use China, the**

74    MAIN PERSPECTIVES: THEIR EVOLUTION AND RELEVANCE TODAY (EDITORIAL INTRODUCTION)

European Union, or the United States as an example. Suggest and discuss other examples.

8. The European Union for many years was viewed as an example for supranational governance. Which cluster of countries outside Europe would you like to see as another model for supranational governance? Explain your choice.

9. Looking at the United States' policies today, why is the analogy with British decline in the 1940s–50s misleading, according to Nye? Do you agree with Nye and why?

10. What are the specific factors in US domestic politics, not mentioned by Nye, that are negatively affecting Washington's foreign policy, based on your opinion?
   - Could you suggest—using your personal opinion—specific factors in US domestic politics (or that of any other country) that are positively affecting its foreign policy?

11. What is absolute and relative decline of a country's power? Give examples.

12. Nye suggests that the United States' "capacity to maintain alliances and create networks will be an important dimension of its hard and soft power." Which alliances and networks would you have in mind if you agree with Nye?

13. Apply (1) Krasner's views of state sovereignty and (2) Huntington's clash of civilizations to suggest how the world should deal with today's (a) global economic inequality among countries, (b) international terrorism, and (b) nuclear disarmament.

## SECTION 2

1. Explain *three principal causes of quarrel* among people according to Hobbes.
   - Suggest three cases from history that support Hobbes's thesis.
   - Suggest three cases from contemporary international relations that support Hobbes's thesis.

2. Hobbes wrote, "Where there is no common power, there is no law; where no law, no injustice."
   - How would you understand and interpret *common power* today?
   - Can you identify places in the world without common power?

3. Suggest current examples to illustrate each of Morgenthau's six points.

4. Discuss the statement: "An individual has a moral right to sacrifice in defense of a moral principle; the state has no right to do so."

5. When in the past, according to Waltz, did multipolar and bipolar worlds exist?

6. In Waltz's view, why did deterrence work during the Cold War?

7. Explain the two reasons suggested by Mearsheimer for why world powers could not commit themselves to the pursuit of a peaceful world order.

8. Using current examples, discuss the two factors (Mearsheimer) that inhibit cooperation among states.

9. Unipolarity, according to realist theories, implies that a single superpower, such as the United States, faces no ideological rival of equal status or influence.
   - In your view, has any other country today offered an ideological alternative that may soon become a model for other states to imitate?
   - Which country do you think could offer such an alternative in the near future?

10. A unipolar power can pursue at least one of three grand strategies: defensive dominance (through diplomacy and negotiations), offensive dominance (through military power and economic sanctions), or disengagement (through noninvolvement in international affairs).
    - Which policy (or a combination of which) does the United States pursue now?
    - Which policy should the United States pursue?

11. Explain why unipolarity possesses much potential for conflict.
    - Provide two contemporary examples to support this argument.
    - Provide an example to disprove this argument.

12. Mearsheimer argues that by claiming regional hegemony, some countries seek to prevent great powers in other regions from duplicating their feat.
    - Discuss this assumption by analyzing US–China relations.
    - Discuss this assumption by analyzing US–Russia relations.
    - Discuss this assumption by analyzing China–Russia relations.

13. What could be China's own version of the Monroe Doctrine in Asia? Suggest a possible scenario.

14. Is Russia using its own version of the Monroe Doctrine to conduct its foreign policy today? What is your view on China's nuclear modernization? Will this modernization contribute to regional or global stability? Will it provoke instability?

## SECTION 3

1. **Immanuel Kant put together six preliminary articles or conditions for perpetual peace among countries. Describe them.**
   - Which of these conditions appear to you more important than others, and why?
   - Which one of these conditions, in your view, appears most advanced (developed) in today's world?

2. **Do you think it would be possible today to implement most of the Kantian peace principles without the use of force, or do you think that from time to time the use of limited force would be necessary?**

3. **Would global free trade—with almost no limitations and tariffs—lead to a global economic prosperity, in your view?**

4. **Norman Angell offered several arguments against war. Discuss them.**
   - Which argument do you find most applicable to today's international relations and why?
   - Which argument by Angell do you consider least compelling?

5. **How did Norman Angell explain his thesis that the fight for ideals can no longer take the form of fight between countries?**
   - Search for examples in recent history and today suggestive of an opposite point that countries continue to fight for ideals. How compelling are these examples?

6. **Provide examples from recent history or contemporary international politics showing countries (other than the United States) governed by liberal democracies that used violence in international affairs.**

7. **Discuss the classical liberal argument that people in democratic countries—mainly because these people bear the costs of war (such as taxes or restrictions)—have a fundamental interest in peace. Provide contemporary examples to support or reject this view.**

8. **Discuss the classical liberal argument that mass publics in democracies, because their voices are heard through opinion polls, grass-roots organizations, social networks, and elections, are a powerful force against war. Do you agree with this view? Why?**

9. **Compile a list of military conflicts in which Canada, Japan, Germany, the United Kingdom, the United States, and Argentina were involved in the past twenty-five years. Discuss your findings in the context of the democratic peace theory.**
   - Did these conflicts involve democratic or nondemocratic countries?
   - What were the causes of these conflicts?
   - What were the outcomes of these conflicts?

10. The liberal international order is not just a collection of liberal democratic states. What does this order have to involve, in your view?

# SECTION 4

1. **Social structures have three elements, according to Wendt. Name them.**
   - Explain them using the Cold War as an example.
   - Explain them using examples from the twenty-first century.

2. **Explain Wendt's suggestion that the meaning of power depends on the underlying structure of shared knowledge.**
   - If you agree with this assertion, provide an example.
   - If you disagree with this assertion, provide an example.

3. **It is assumed that individual decisions of political leaders change social structures and therefore international relations.**
   - Suggest examples from history.
   - Provide examples from contemporary international politics.

4. **In your view, how did the personality of US president Donald Trump affect the United States' foreign policy from 2016 until today?**
   - Compare the individual styles of Barack Obama and Donald Trump. Discuss differences and similarities.

5. **Describe the essence of the *unilateral reciprocal approach* to tension reduction.**
   - Choose a country with which the United States has contentious or tense relations and suggest a contemporary diplomatic strategy based on the unilateral reciprocal approach.
   - Suggest several weaknesses of the unilateral reciprocal approach.
   - What can and should be done when the opposite party (country) does not behave in a reciprocal way?

6. **In the context of the US–China relationship, what do (1) optimistic and (2) pessimistic constructivists generally emphasize?**
   - What is your assessment of the optimistic and pessimistic claims today?

7. **What is gender socialization? Explain using your own case as an example.**
   - When and how did you learn about politics and international relations?
   - Did your views evolve? If so, when and in which direction?

8. **How could gender socialization affect people's views of foreign countries and international politics?**

9. What is the "masculine" approach to international conflicts? Provide a few examples of the masculine approach from contemporary international relations.

10. Suggest alternatives to the masculine approach using several cases from recent history.

# PART II

# THREE FACETS OF THE INTERNATIONAL RELATIONS

## International Security, International Law, and International Political Economy (Editorial Introduction)

In this part we will examine how sovereign countries and international organizations engage in conflicts, resolve them, and pursue security. Then, we will discuss international law as a basic source of formal rules governing international community. Finally, we will review how countries and organizations engage in economic activities in the context of international relations.

*National security* has traditionally been understood as the protection of a state's sovereignty, territorial integrity, and strategic interests. *International security* refers to mutual security issues involving more than one state. Governments historically act to protect their countries' sovereignty and territorial integrity from domestic and foreign threats. Some act alone, relying on their economic might and armed forces. Others seek protection and cooperation from neighbors, more distant countries, like the United States, and international organizations like the United Nations or NATO. To protect their strategic interests and to reduce or eliminate domestic and international threats, individual countries and international organizations develop security policies. Such policies are constantly evolving and typically born out of continuous debates among political elites, security officials, military experts, researchers, and the media. Sometimes security policies can be rooted in arbitrary decisions of powerful political leaders and their close circles.

At least two major and competing perspectives on national and international security have been dominant since the 1970s. According to *realism*, the main postulates of which we discussed in Part I, security is the vital and exclusive responsibility of sovereign countries. They try to maximize their power, tend to act according to their interests, and use these interests in assessing external threats and their own defensive capabilities. Countries create security regimes in which powerful states provide protection to others in exchange for their cooperation. One example of a security regime is NATO. The core element of every state's security, according to realism, is power and the ability to use it in the context of the evolving international situation.

On the contrary, supporters of *liberalism* (also discussed in Part I) recognize the primary role of states in security policies, but also point to the increasing role of international organizations and nonstate actors. Liberals believe that the power of states and security regimes is no longer the only key to lasting peace in today's world. In the liberal view, neither economic nor military power alone can bring long-term security, and military threats are seldom the best choice of action in security policies. Instead, the desire for mutually acceptable outcomes and the complexity of international problems give countries the incentive to cooperate.

Wars, conflicts, and terrorism are the main challenges to international security. A conflict is any antagonism between countries (sovereign states), international organizations, or nongovernmental organizations. Some conflicts remain nonviolent. Other conflicts become war, which is an organized, violent confrontation between states or other social and political entities, such as ethnic or religious groups. Traditionally, debates about conflict and war continue to focus on the nature of war and its types, the causes and consequences of war, offensive and defensive strategies, the possibility of preventing war, and conflict resolution. Today's debates tend to focus on new security threats, especially those related to cybersecurity.

The argument that a country's military strength and its reliance on technologies alone could guarantee victory in a military conflict has a long history. For centuries, countries' leaders associated security policies with military power and its effective use to prevent war or in the time of war. Maintaining the armed forces, obtaining and modernizing weapons, keeping and building new aircraft and battleships, training specialists, and developing mass-mobilization plans were always essential for national security. In most recent times, security experts added to this debate by turning to so-called *revolution in military affairs*, which is the most up-to-date and rapid advance of communications, information, and precision munitions technologies. Military victories during the Gulf War of 1991 and the Kosovo campaign in 1999 have persuaded many specialists that modern technologies have fundamentally changed the nature of war and, therefore, require new types of security policies. These experts assumed that the most advanced modern weapons and technologies alone—if they are used correctly—should win any modern war.

However, almost two hundred years ago, academics and practitioners were already aware of broader aspects of war. Carl von Clausewitz (1780–1831), a Prussian officer and military expert—who is widely regarded as one of the most prominent military theorists—wrote in *On the Nature of War* that wars should not be viewed exclusively in military terms. War is also a complex sociopolitical and even psychological phenomenon. Von Clausewitz furthered the idea that war is an ultimate confrontation, which states constantly use to achieve their political goals. Yet every war, in his view, involves individual decision-making, calculations and guesses, right decisions and mistakes, emotions, and a degree of risk. This idea received additional support in recent studies of important historic cases showing that state leaders often make fateful military decisions—such as declaring war or attacking an opponent—because they misjudge their adversaries' intentions and also exaggerate their own strengths and neglect weaknesses. You can discuss in class which international conflicts demonstrate the misjudgments and misinterpretations of the leaders involved in such conflicts (consider, for example, the Soviet invasion of Afghanistan in 1979 or the United States' escalation in Vietnam in 1964–65 and occupation of Iraq in 2003). Today, the supporters of the *constructivist* view of international relations (which maintains, as you should remember, that countries act according to their collective identities, perceptions, and social norms) argue that separating modern war from its political, cultural, and psychological context and turning military campaigns to "targeting exercises" would likely lead to failure. Factors such as cultural, tribal, and political identities increase complexity and influence the course of events. The validity of all these arguments is being tested in modern conflicts in new contexts. One of these contexts is international terrorism.

Twenty years ago, international terrorism was not a major topic in textbooks and mainstream academic publications. Since the attacks of September 11, 2001, however, this subject has become a distinct field of study, next to the discussion of war and security. Definitions of *terrorism* vary, yet most refer to it as violence by nonstate actors, such as individuals or groups, to achieve radical political goals. It is essentially a form of political radicalism—ideas and methods to produce rapid, dramatic change in the social or political order or address immediate political grievances. Domestic and international terrorism overlap but remain different. Domestic terrorism does not necessarily present a direct and significant danger to other sovereign countries or international organizations. International terrorists, on the contrary, challenge international stability by threatening a country or a group of states.

Effective security strategies to counter terrorism cannot be designed without first understanding the strategic logic that motivates terrorist violence. Terrorist groups are likely to pursue different tactical goals, but most of their strategies remain consistent. There are at least four such strategies identified by political scientists Andrew Kydd and Barbara Walter: (a) intimidation, (b) provocation, (c) attrition, and (d) spoiling. Intimidation is about generating constant fear and uncertainty by demonstrating that the terrorists have the ability—real or imaginary—to harm at any time they want and that the government (such as law enforcement) is powerless to stop them. Provocation strategies aim to draw the government and the public into ineffective, costly, and even dangerous actions (domestic and foreign, such as waging military operations) against the terrorists. Attrition is about persuading and convincing the public that the terrorists are strong, relentless, and determined to consistently inflict serious damage to a country's infrastructure and its people. The goal of a spoiling strategy is to create uncertainty and conflict within the society about how to deal with terrorism: Some will insist on negotiations and bargaining while others will demand violent actions against terrorism. Overall, terrorist strategies can be effective not simply because acts of terrorism spark fear in people, but also because they cause governments, international organizations, and individuals to respond in ways that aid the terrorists' cause.

Terrorism is an evolving phenomenon, which should be studied in a historical perspective. Thus, Michel Wieviorka in "From Classical Terrorism to Global Terrorism" distinguishes between *classical* and contemporary forms of terrorism. The classical form, in his opinion, was perpetrated by radicals of the political Left and the political Right and often took the form of anticapitalist or nationalist movements. This form of terrorism usually operated within separate states and threatened their domestic order, and sometimes their territorial integrity. Modern terrorism emerged in the 2000s. It spreads beyond sovereign borders, and its motives are rooted in religious fundamentalism as well as in a cultural, mostly anti-Western sentiment. Whether this global wave will remain associated exclusively with radical jihadism remains to be seen. Other dangerous forms may also occur.

International terrorism as a term sometimes is misidentified by journalists as well as by politicians. Notice a tendency by some of them to call any violent action or military operation terrorism, which is incorrect. We encourage our students to follow the definition of terrorism provided earlier in these pages.

For example, terrorism differs from guerrilla warfare, which is political violence by identifiable, irregular combat units, usually to seize state power, win autonomy, or found new sovereign states. The discussion of contemporary terrorism and guerilla warfare has revived an old debate about the nature of threats in international relations. Realism teaches that there usually is a balance of forces and threats. This means that an attack by one country causes a symmetrical response from the other. Symmetry helps to maintain international stability, as sovereign states seek a balance between peace and war. Terrorism and guerilla warfare, however, pose an asymmetrical threat to sovereign countries. Because terrorists do not officially represent a government and guerilla fighters often hide among civilians, governments are likely to find it difficult to identify the perpetrators and retaliate effectively. Nonstate actors—either individuals or groups—can disrupt the balance of power in an international context, much like sovereign countries. In an asymmetrical conflict, governments can run two types of risks. First, they may overreact or launch ineffective responses to fight terrorism. Second, inaction in response to terrorism may impact public opinion or encourage terrorists to strike again. Therefore, asymmetrical warfare is often a powerful tool of international destabilization. And it is not necessarily clear to modern theorists what to do to effectively address terrorism and other types of asymmetrical threats (see Figure 4).

Most experts writing about terrorism underline the need to understand strategies that perpetrators of asymmetrical conflicts use. Guerrilla warfare, for example, is not

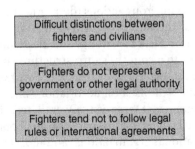

Difficult distinctions between
fighters and civilians

Fighters do not represent a
government or other legal authority

Fighters tend not to follow legal
rules or international agreements

Figure 4.  Key Elements of Asymmetrical Conflicts

a new form of military struggle. In twentieth-century conflicts, several political leaders gained power in their countries by launching protracted guerilla wars. History shows that most guerilla movements hoped to push the superior, better organized, and better equipped enemy close to physical and psychological attrition. New international contexts may favor insurgents and complicate the attempts of states to deal with guerillas. As Max Boot suggests in his article, because mass media in democratic countries report heavily on casualties and destruction caused by insurgency's actions, public opinion in such countries may fast develop a negative view of an ongoing conflict. This may exhaust the will of democratic countries to engage in protracted counterinsurgencies, especially outside their own territory, and heighten the ability of insurgents to survive even after suffering grave military setbacks.

In the past, technology was relatively unimportant in guerrilla war. Today's guerrillas can use sophisticated technological devices, cyberweapons, and mobile phones to detonate bombs; they can also use drones to target governments and civilians. Can governments strike back using similar methods? For several years, debates have persisted about the use of drones in antiterrorist operations. There is evidence that drones are effective and civilian deaths from armed drone strikes are far fewer than deaths from traditional combat aircraft. Yet debates about legal and moral justifications of such policy intensify. The simplest question for you to discuss is, What if other countries adopt the same rationale as the United States for carrying out lethal strikes against individuals outside declared war zones and in violation of territorial sovereignty? What if another country, for example, starts using drones to target and kill certain individuals in Australia or the United Kingdom?

Effective security policies require assessments of emerging security threats. For centuries, it meant the assessment and protection of natural resources and their delivery. Will future threats involve natural resources? Many specialists believe this is the case: The increasing contest for oil and other mineral resources may generate armed conflicts. The new round of struggle for markets, and especially for raw materials, can be intensified by the growth of the economy of China and other countries in Asia, Africa, and South America. What are possible consequences of these developments for global security?

Neorealists suggest that in the unfolding competition for energy resources, new political alliances may emerge. Former ideological and political allies may turn away from their former partners and gravitate toward energy-rich countries, thus weakening some traditional strategic security regimes. New emerging energy alliances could easily be perceived as threats to other states' security. Also, as Charles Glaser in *How Oil Influences U.S. National Security* indicates, energy demands may increase the value of resource-rich territories. Such conflicts may draw the United States into a military confrontation. Further, the United States' energy independence does not necessarily guarantee security. Other countries are likely to make substantial investments in their militaries to protect energy resources. Of particular importance, as Glaser writes, is the potential danger that Chinese oil imports create for US security—China's efforts to protect its sea lines of communication are fueling military competition that could strain US–China relations and increase the probability of conflict between them. Recently we have seen a rivalry between the United States, on the one hand, where the *fracking* type of oil production has grown, and the oil-producing countries of the Middle East (OPEC) that are joining ranks with Russia on the other hand.

Identifying several emerging security threats is just the first step of security policy. The next step is to find a strategy to deal with them. Traditionally, countries used geopolitics—the concept and practice of using geographical position and territorial gains to achieve political power or seek security. Geographical position gave some countries clear advantages in security matters, while others remained vulnerable. Today, however, the meaning of territory is changing. A few individuals located miles away may disrupt the activities of sovereign states, private businesses, and nongovernmental organizations.

Cyberwarfare is a very powerful type of asymmetrical threat. It is about launching paralyzing Internet attacks on political, financial, and economic centers. Cyberwarfare also involves deliberate disinformation and provocation to achieve certain security objectives. Cyberwarfare thus can target public opinion, sway people's beliefs in a particular direction, and can have an impact on voting behavior. Organized online attacks targeting public opinion can help a government achieve political or diplomatic goals. Cyberwarfare has several types. There could be a state-against-state conflict in which one country targets the other's strategic computer assets. It could be a private individuals-against-state or state-to-private war, in which a government attacks the private computer systems of another state. It also can be a private-to-private conflict, involving an exchange of cyberblows between nonstate entities, including nongovernmental organizations and private businesses. Cyberwarfare involves intelligence, offensive, and defensive operations, as well as their combinations. It is different from cybercrime, which typically involves bank accounts and credit card fraud, other financial crimes, and transmission of illegal materials.

Cyberthreats are real and may range from significant theft of data and disruption of computer operations to more serious and even deadly attacks that destroy or paralyze entire energy grids. Cyberattacks undermine a country's military capabilities and may disturb a regional or global order. All in all, the cyberrevolution brings new and significant challenges to international security. In most recent times, cyberattacks, deliberate disinformation via media or social networks, and meddling with other countries' elections, often on a limited scale, can be used by a government to pursue its political goals in international affairs. The ultimate goal of cyberattacks is evolving to not only affect computer systems, but also disrupt or destroy certain social, economic, or government functions.

Feminism offers a fundamentally different, alternative outlook on security. Since the mid-twentieth century, feminists have criticized the government monopoly on security issues. They were particularly wary of realism because it defined national and international security in terms of state sovereignty and domination—two key values associated with masculinity. During the 1980s and later, feminists argued that the male-dominated narrative of force and war should be replaced with other narratives, including individual safety, interdependence, agreement, and shared power. Feminists, for instance, ask to reconsider and reject the whole concept of war as a "natural" way by which sovereign states protect themselves from threats. Security specialists, as it is argued, must consider the value of the golden rule: Do not do to others what you do not want others do to you. Security policies also must be *gender mainstreamed*: More women must be involved in institutional policies, and masculine "values" on conflict and war must be questioned and rejected (see Figure 5).

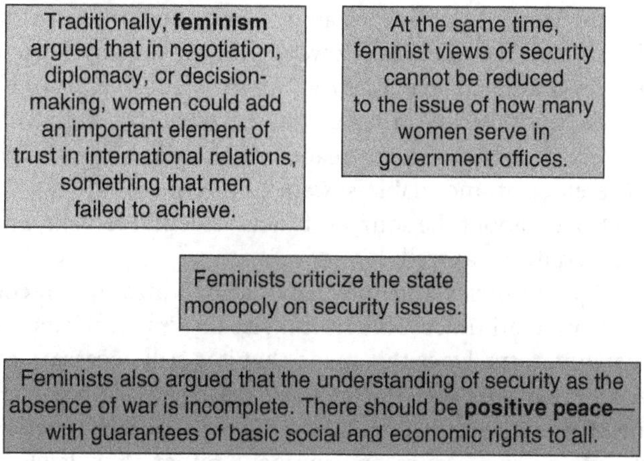

Traditionally, **feminism** argued that in negotiation, diplomacy, or decision-making, women could add an important element of trust in international relations, something that men failed to achieve.

At the same time, feminist views of security cannot be reduced to the issue of how many women serve in government offices.

Feminists criticize the state monopoly on security issues.

Feminists also argued that the understanding of security as the absence of war is incomplete. There should be **positive peace**—with guarantees of basic social and economic rights to all.

Figure 5. Feminist View of International Security

Overall, it is clear that organizing an international effort to deal with a variety of security threats must remain a constant effort, involving governments, nongovernmental organizations, media, and broad segments of the population. Also, there may not be just one winning strategy. Instead, each different case dictates a different mix of policies. They may range from military action and surveillance to public diplomacy, economic sanctions, economic aid, law enforcement, education, training, and application of legal rulings.

The next section of the book is called "Law and International Community" It is about a set of principles, rules, and agreements that regulate the behavior of states and other international actors.

Stephen Neff, in "A Short History of International Law," shows that the meaning of international law has been evolving over centuries. Indeed, an early model that is reflected in international laws today can be found in the law of nations (*jus gentium*)—a codification of Roman law compiled during the rule of the Byzantine emperor Justinian I (482–565). The law of nations was based on natural law—rules that are not only common to the laws of all lands but also reflect universal interests, such as the safety of sea commerce from piracy or honoring treaties. Eleven centuries later, the Dutch diplomat and jurist Hugo Grotius (1583–1645) formulated the principle of freedom of the seas: A state's sovereignty ends at the edge of its territorial waters. This principle survived for centuries. In his later classical work, *On the Law of War and Peace*, Grotius further connected international law to natural law. He argued that wars between sovereign countries could be justifiable, but only under particular circumstances. Like individuals, sovereign countries have the right to self-defense. But even in a state of war, countries should abide by certain rules. Grotius has laid an intellectual foundation for contemporary *just war theory*.

By the twentieth century, as Neff underlines, international law was increasingly understood as a corpus of rules determined by sovereign countries. At that time, formal accords between more than two countries began to play a major role in international affairs. The Hague Peace Conferences of 1899 and 1907 were inspired by the desire of many of the world leaders to establish a set of common rules to reduce the risk of war and diminish its cruelties. However, for all the good intentions of these diplomatic initiatives, wars and atrocities did not stop. The League of Nations created after World War I did not protect against aggressive wars. The founding of the United Nations in 1945, to replace the defunct League of Nations, was a critical step in the building of a more efficient and viable system of international law, the process that continues today. Debates about the sources, functions, enforcement, and effectiveness of international law continue as well.

Not all sovereign countries and international organizations recognize and observe international law at all times. Some countries interpret international laws based on their immediate interests. Does this mean that it is still necessary and practical to have such a law? The answer is yes. At least three reasons explain why. First, countries need a secure international environment. Sovereign states, organizations, businesses, and ordinary people need a secure environment rather than lawlessness. As Jean d'Aspremont argues in "The International Court of Justice and the Irony of System-Design," governments as well as international lawyers turn to rules-based modes of legal reasoning to support their much-cherished idea of an international legal system. States and international organizations set these formal rules and establish sanctions against violations of such rules. Take piracy, for example. It disrupts maritime communication, inhibits trade, and endangers lives. The United States has appealed to international legal norms to fight piracy since the end of the eighteenth century. A significant increase of piracy near Somalia and the Horn of Africa in the beginning of the twenty-first century, as recent history has shown, created a collective and mostly successful international response to uphold and enforce international antipiracy laws.

Second, countries need a way to resolve conflict by peaceful means. Although international actors constantly engage in disputes, they realize that force alone is not the most efficient way to resolve them. Wars are simply too destructive and lead to further conflicts. When international political organizations are incapable or unwilling to move forward, international courts should. Despite difficulties, international law has played and continues to play a significant role in the peaceful settlement of many international disputes. As the records of diplomacy suggest, strong legal arguments play a particularly important role in settling territorial disputes between two countries. For instance, in the 1990s, Yemen and Eritrea fought over control of the Hanish Islands in the Red Sea. Violence was about to erupt. In 1998, the Permanent Court of Arbitration, one of the oldest institutions for dispute resolution, determined that the archipelago belonged to Yemen. Eritrea accepted this legal decision and violence was avoided. Under the right conditions, international law becomes a more powerful force to bring stability, order, and peaceful change than political sanctions or military action.

Third, countries must coordinate domestic laws in a globally interdependent world. Because countries have different constitutional, administrative, criminal, contract, family, and property laws, numerous practical problems and disagreements naturally emerge, especially in an era of global communication, trade, and travel. International law is therefore essential in regulating the relationships (a) among private citizens living in different countries, (b) between private citizens and foreign governments or organizations, and (c) among international organizations. Think of divorce and custody disputes, trademark violations, traffic accidents, financial obligations,

*A need for a secure international environment.*
Countries, organizations, businesses, and ordinary people need a secure environment rather than lawlessness.

*A need for conflict resolution.*
Countries realize that force alone is not the most efficient way to resolve disagreements and disputes.

*A need to coordinate domestic laws in a global world.*
Because countries have different laws, numerous practical problems and disagreements naturally emerge, especially in an era of global trade and travel.

Figure 6.   Why the World Needs International Law

and compensation for faulty products or services. However, there is a need for a strong enforcement mechanism built into international law. If such a mechanism is created, international law should also be more efficiently applied to fight transnational organized crime, including extortion, drug and human trafficking, kidnapping, and money laundering (see Figure 6).

*International Political Economy* studies how politics and economics interact in an international context. One of the key debates in this field focuses on the question, Should there be economic policies developed by experts and state bureaucracies, or should economic development be left to market forces and international trade? Can it be a third way?

Robert Keohane in "The Old IPE and the New" writes that in the 1970s most economists were ignoring international politics, and international relations specialists were dismissing political economy. Yet later it was becoming clear that international economy affects international politics and vice versa. Today, for example, five big changes are taking place within the process of such interaction. In the past, the world was divided into *developing* and *developed* countries. Today, genuine economic development is taking place for much of the world's population. China has emerged early in this century as a big player in international manufacturing, trade, and finance. Volatility in financial and energy markets has been extreme. New global actors emerged: They are global corporations and nongovernmental organizations. And finally, new communication technologies now significantly affect commerce, finance, investment, and, as it appears, politics.

Major concepts and debates in international political economy have been developing for many years. Mercantilism, as one of the oldest economic approaches, calls for the accumulation and protection of available resources in the name of the sovereign country. This economic theory was widely accepted several centuries ago, when absolute monarchies, such as France, followed mercantilist recipes to aggrandize power at the expense of their neighbors. At the heart of mercantilism is the view that maximizing net exports is the best route to national prosperity. Mercantilism is very much alive today: Many countries, including China, use its core principles (such as maximizing domestic employment and subsidizing exports) to adapt to the global market.

Another somewhat old-fashioned concept is so-called Keynesian economics. These are the principles proposed by John M. Keynes (1883–1946), a British economist who was a founder of macroeconomics, that is, a theory of how economy worked within a single sovereign country. Keynes and his followers argued that, contrary to the assumption of the efficiency of free markets, governments should actively regulate business and especially finances. According to Keynesian economics, national governments can ease the undesirable effects of economic recessions by spending more money than their revenues allow. By putting money into the economy, government can fuel business transactions and purchases, stimulate production and consumption, lower unemployment, and create a prosperous middle class. Keynes's principles have played a key role in the understanding of the structure and performance of economics for half of the twentieth century. Today, some influential economists argue in favor of returning to Keynesian economic policies, in view of unstable international markets and because of the decline of middle classes—especially in manufacturing spheres—in most developed countries under the pressure of globalization and cross-border migration. Their argument is that the governments should do more to protect domestic markets and domestic employment.

Economic liberalism is an influential concept that criticizes both mercantilism and Keynesian economics. Liberal economists maintain that the free market would remain the key strategic answer to most economic challenges. The American economist Milton Friedman (1912–2006), in his classic work *Capitalism and Freedom*, asserted that state regulations of economy are inflationary and counterproductive. He contended that people are rational actors and that individual choices of millions of economic actors (businesses, consumers, etc.) work better for economic development than the regulations and policies developed by a few economic experts and state bureaucrats. Friedman, who taught at the University of Chicago, argued that the state does have a limited role to play: It should gradually increase the amount of money in circulation—an idea called monetarism. He was against the gold standard, the guaranteed exchange of paper money for gold in state reserves. He advocated policies under which governments abandoned the gold standard and started to manipulate the supply of money through banking interest rates—a process known as monetary policy. He supported a system of freely floating exchange rates determined by market transactions without governmental intervention.

A serious discussion continues about the direction of economic politics and the revision of the economic and political guidelines offered to developing countries in the past. One such "recipe" has been the maximum deregulation of production and finances to jumpstart stagnant and inefficient economies of a wide range of countries. This approach has been called the *Washington Consensus* (because the International Monetary Fund and other financial institutions that advocated this "consensus" are located in Washington, DC). How successful were such policies? Although liberal economists continue emphasizing the benefits of the "free market," many criticisms of the Washington Consensus deserve attention and careful analysis. Critics, for example, argue that rigid application of the Washington Consensus may unintentionally destroy the middle class, bring instability, jeopardize democracy, and give excessive power to transnational corporations and export-oriented lobbies. In the end, a few enrich themselves at the expense of many others. Economic inequality between countries and regions has always been an important topic of discussion in international relations. Indeed, the pressure on governments today grows to become less focused on the free flow of capital and more concerned with social disruptions caused by global competition for well-paid jobs and by fiscal crises of social safety nets. Although the Washington Consensus did not necessarily disregard social policies, its focus on efficiency and fiscal discipline often led to cuts in social spending, which contributed to excessive pressures on middle classes and social instability. Therefore, governments of developing countries today increasingly turn to *reindustrialization*: They are supporting domestic industries through state subsidies and other incentives.

Marxist economic ideas continue to be influential today, feeding on the discontent about global and domestic economic inequality. Marxism's key economic and political argument is that there is a ruling class that owns the major means of production, natural resources, and services and thus dominates the world. Throughout the twentieth century and after, this ruling class became increasingly global, as capital moved across borders and continents. Vladimir Lenin argued a century ago about the growing threat of strengthening the domination of the "parasitical" financial "oligarchy" and international monopolies trying to establish global economic and political domination. Today Marxist views inspire some activists of the antiglobalist movement who demand high taxes on the rich and rigorous social control over banks and corporations. Marxists claim that international corporations and banks, not the governments of sovereign countries, are the true holders of global power because of their financial resources. States serve the interests of the ruling class of billionaires using diplomacy, international agreements, and international law to manage international relations, which in effect should lead to higher profits.

Supporters of dependency theory maintain that developed nations with modern technologies and capital, called the *core*, have been receiving more benefits from international trade than countries without technology and capital, called the *periphery*. The core countries invest in new technologies and make significant profits. The periphery countries, in contrast, suffer from technological backwardness and their inability to overcome it. As a result, the countries of the global periphery must sell natural resources and provide cheap labor for the core countries. The core countries make the rules of international trade, often by direct political control of the periphery. Local elites in the periphery also are interested in this economic order because they pocket most profits from selling natural resources of their countries to the core countries.

Supporters of these views maintain that the discriminatory structure of the world's global economy and trade is the main cause of global inequality and chronic poverty. The poor agricultural nations of the South (because most of the poorer countries are in the Southern Hemisphere) are completely dependent on the developed industrial North, both economically and politically. Unlike Marxists, supporters of dependency theory accept private property and acknowledge the importance of some elements of a free-market economy. Nevertheless, they believe that the rules governing markets should change and the world's economic order should be restructured.

The demise of Western-style capitalism is probably what supporters of Marxism and world-systems theories hope will take place. Some economists argue that the Washington Consensus did not really intend to help the emerging economies. They also argue that South Korea, Taiwan, Singapore, and then China did not follow the Washington Consensus and achieved spectacular success in their economic development. In their view, liberalization of foreign trade and capital movements benefitted the American economy and the interests of the West most of all. They also believe that the core of the global capitalist system would inevitably shift from the United States to China. When Chinese manufacturing and economy surpass that of the United States, Chinese *yuan* would challenge the US dollar as a world chief currency. The Washington Consensus, based on a neoliberal model of free trade, would be replaced, as the authors think, by a *Beijing consensus* based on state-run capitalism.

These assumptions echo postcolonial studies, in which former colonies were expected to demand an end to Western global domination. They would also be hoping for greater restraints on international capital markets. Susan Strange, a neo-Marxist, while acknowledging that the world is dependent on the market economy, urges us to turn attention to disadvantaged social groups. In today's world, she wrote, some state and nonstate authorities have the power to manage, restrict, exploit, or profit from branches of the world market. Others do not. In her view, the world is still driven by material interests of social classes behind the façade of government (see Figure 7).

International political economists are careful observers of the emerging trends and commonly welcome several viewpoints to critically understand global economic developments. Economist Karl Polanyi wrote decades ago about the great changes in economic relations among the states and the transformations of human institutions and human nature. He also wrote that economic protectionism that grew in the second decade of this century was a natural political response to an unrestrained free market governed by the liberal principles.

The past decade has also brought the realization that the countries of the emerging markets have begun to play a more serious role in global economic affairs on their own. Yet there is no guarantee that their economic growth and stability are sustainable

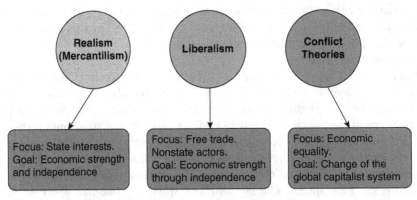

Figure 7.    Major Approaches in International Political Economy

for a long period. The economies of China, India, and Brazil, driven by cheap labor and imported technology in the first fifteen years of the century, have shown signs of slowing down. In many ways, the success or failure of these countries' policies will determine whether a western-style liberal trade system of international economic relations would fall from its pedestal or become stronger.

In the past, a few wealthy states could define economic and financial policies for others as well. For decades, liberal trade and market principles worked well in western Europe, Japan, and North America. More recently, many Asian countries found a way to benefit from an international liberal trade market, while domestically pursuing a combination of mercantilist and Keynesian policies. More than 1.3 billion people have been removed from extreme poverty since the 1990s. Multiple factors have contributed to this progress. However, one-size-fits-all free-market policies can damage rather than help countries. Also, world experience demonstrates that countries must be stable financial, governmental, and social institutions to prosper in the conditions of today's global economy. For example, China kept its authoritarian state intact and gradually liberalized some sections of its economy and trade without liberalizing its politics. China achieved remarkable economic success. In contrast, Russia's attempt to shift rapidly and simultaneously to a liberal market economy and liberal democracy cost it dearly; its productive capacities declined dramatically and the population suffered. Today's studies suggest that each country's political, social, and cultural conditions significantly determine which economic policies are likely to succeed or fail.

Economic theories rise and fall with the tides of history. The global interdependence that has emerged in the first decade of the century seemingly has challenged past theories of political economy. Yet a new tendency has appeared that, yet again, challenged the assumptions of globalization theorists. Some economists ask a very provocative yet timely question: Has globalization faltered? Adjiedj Bakas, the Dutch trend watcher, has coined the term *slowbalization* to describe the global and sustained decline in cross-border exchanges of goods, services, and even ideas. Experts show that since 2010, cross-border investment, trade, loans, and supply chains have been shrinking or idling. The cost of moving products across borders has stopped declining. The global value of cross-border investment by multinational companies decreased—at least for some time. Most activities in the second decade of the century have been shifting toward services, and services are difficult to sell across borders: surgical instruments can be easily transported, but nurses and doctors in one country must become licensed in foreign countries, which is extremely difficult. Chinese manufacturing has increasingly become self-sufficient in the second decade of this century; it must import fewer products. Countries begin to fight again: over rules on privacy, data possession, and espionage. Americans criticize Europe's regulations; Europeans are targeting the tremendous success of Silicon Valley's most successful tech companies, which seek global domination. Washington and Brussels increasingly carefully watch foreign investments to avoid dependency, especially on energy sources and information technologies, for instance, on Chinese-made fifth-generation mobile Internet. China, on its part, had no intentions for many years of allowing foreign firms fair conditions to do business in China. If the process of slowbalization continues, it can affect international relations in many unpredictable ways.

# GENERAL DISCUSSION QUESTIONS RELATED TO THE MATERIALS ABOUT INTERNATIONAL SECURITY, INTERNATIONAL LAW, AND INTERNATIONAL POLITICAL ECONOMY

These general questions are for class discussions as well as individual assignments. The discussion of these questions should help students think critically and better understand the materials in this part of the book. Other, more specific critical-thinking and practice questions related to the reading materials appear at the end of Part II.

- Give an example of a security policy or security-related decision you consider (a) mostly effective and one you consider (b) mostly ineffective. Explain your choices. Suggested examples:

  - US border control policies and the building of the "wall"
  - US occupation of Afghanistan in 2001 and the lingering conflict in the country today
  - Israel–Palestinian conflict today
  - The conflict in Syria

- Select two or three international conflicts to demonstrate the misjudgments and misinterpretations of the leaders involved in such conflicts. World War I comes to mind, as do the 2003 war in Iraq and Russia's annexation of Crimea and the conflict in Eastern Ukraine in 2014. Also ask your professor which conflict she or he could recommend for this analysis.

- Suggest contemporary examples to illustrate *revolution in military affairs*. Discuss the impact that new technological innovations (especially social networks) could have on security policies and diplomacy.

- Suggest several regions or countries in which or around which new conflicts related to energy and resources may occur ten years from now. Will it be the Middle East or the Arctic region? Explain your choices.

- Geographical position gave some countries clear advantages in security matters, while others remained vulnerable. Which countries will remain more vulnerable than others from their security standpoint—including cybersecurity—in the first half of the twenty-first century? Explain your opinion.

- Why are definitions of *terrorism* important today? Discuss this from the position of international law and diplomacy. Suggest and discuss several examples of the actual or potential misuse of the term *terrorism*. Why do people and governments misuse this term?

- Explain why terrorism is an asymmetrical threat. Find and discuss a few examples to illustrate this point.

- Consider the statement "Almost every fundamentalist or radical group supports terrorism." Could you prove or disprove this statement? Do your own research and provide examples of political radicalism and fundamentalism that reject violence.

- Why are the statements of Osama bin Laden (made years ago) important in the study of international relations? How do they relate to the current crisis in Iraq? Explain your view.

- Is it possible to eradicate international terrorism for the most part by 2025? Why or why not? Discuss your view.
- Hugo Grotius formulated the principle of *freedom of the seas*: A state's sovereignty ends at the edge of its territorial waters. Imagine for a moment that territorial waters are no longer recognized.

  - How would this development affect the United States? The United Kingdom? China? Russia?
  - How do you think countries would react to this new legal reality?

- What are the main limitations of international law? Is it necessary or practical to have international law? Explain your answer. Suggest one or two arguments not listed earlier in this book in support of international law.
- The Treaty on the Non-Proliferation of Nuclear Weapons attempts to stop the spread of nuclear weapons. Will it be possible, in your view, to reach a global agreement to eliminate all nuclear weapons in fifteen years?
- Imagine the United Nations passes an international law to ban wars altogether.

  - Will this law be effective? Will most wars stop?
  - Based on what you have read in this part of the book, suggest several conditions under which this new international law could be effective.
  - Which country or organization could be capable of creating and maintaining such conditions, and how?

- What is your view on international economic, financial, and political sanctions and under what circumstances? Discuss the cases of Russia, Iran, and North Korea as examples.
- Discuss the likelihood of replacing the Washington Consensus (based on deregulation of finance and the liberal model of trade) with a Beijing Consensus (based on state controls over trade and finances). Which countries do you think will turn to state-run capitalism and which will not? Consider the period from today until 2025.
- China has become the main beneficiary of economic globalization early in the twenty-first century. Discuss whether a country can be economically successful and relatively isolated at the same time.
- How deep and significant will the process of slowbalization be, in your view?

# Section 5

## War, Security, and Terrorism

# The Changing Face of War: Into the Fourth Generation

WILLIAM S. LIND, COLONEL KEITH NIGHTINGALE (USA), CAPTAIN JOHN F. SCHMITT (USMC),

COLONEL JOSEPH W. SUTTON (USA), AND LIEUTENANT COLONEL GARY I. WILSON (USMCR)

The peacetime soldier's principal task is to prepare effectively for the next war. In order to do so, he must anticipate what the next war will be like. This is a difficult task that gets continuously more difficult. German Gen Franz Uhle-Wettler writes:

> At an earlier time, a commander could be certain that a future war would resemble past and present ones. This enabled him to analyze appropriate tactics from past and present. The troop commander of today no longer has this possibility. He knows only that whoever fails to adapt the experiences of the last war will surely lose the next one.

## THE CENTRAL QUESTION

If we look at the development of warfare in the modern era, we see three distinct generations. In the United States, the Army and the Marine Corps are now coming to grips with the change to the third generation. This transition is entirely for the good. However, third generation warfare was conceptually developed by the German offensive in the spring of 1918. It is now more than 70 years old. This suggests some interesting questions: Is it not about time for a fourth generation to appear? If so, what might it look like? These questions are of central importance. Whoever is first to recognize, understand, and implement a generational change can gain a decisive advantage. Conversely, a nation that is slow to adapt to generational change opens itself to catastrophic defeat.

Our purpose here is less to answer these questions than to pose them. Nonetheless, we will offer some tentative answers. To begin to see what these might be, we need to put the questions into historical context.

## THREE GENERATIONS OF WARFARE

While military development is generally a continuous evolutionary process, the modern era has witnessed three watersheds in which change has been dialectically qualitative. Consequently, modern military development comprises three distinct generations.

First generation warfare reflects tactics of the era of the smoothbore musket, the tactics of line and column. These tactics were developed partially in response to technological factors—the line maximized firepower, rigid drill was necessary to generate a high rate of fire, etc.—and partially in response to social conditions and ideas, e.g., the columns of the French revolutionary armies reflected both the élan of the revolution and the low training levels of conscripted troops. Although rendered obsolete with the replacement of the smoothbore by the rifled musket, vestiges of first generation tactics survive today, especially in a frequently encountered desire for linearity on the battlefield. Operational art in the first generation did not exist as a concept although it was practiced by individual commanders, most prominently Napoleon.

Second generation warfare was a response to the rifled musket, breechloaders, barbed wire, the machinegun, and indirect fire. Tactics were based on fire and movement, and they remained essentially linear. The defense still attempted to prevent all penetrations, and in the attack a laterally dispersed line advanced by rushes in small groups. Perhaps the principal change from first generation tactics was heavy reliance on indirect fire; second generation tactics were summed up in the French maxim, "the artillery conquers, the infantry occupies." Massed firepower replaced massed manpower. Second generation tactics remained the basis of

U.S. doctrine until the 1980s, and they are still practiced by most American units in the field.

While ideas played a role in the development of second generation tactics (particularly the idea of lateral dispersion), technology was the principal driver of change. Technology manifested itself both qualitatively, in such things as heavier artillery and bombing aircraft, and quantitatively, in the ability of an industrialized economy to fight a battle of materiel (*Materialschlacht*).

The second generation saw the formal recognition and adoption of the operational art, initially by the Prussian army. Again, both ideas and technology drove the change. The ideas sprang largely from Prussian studies of Napoleon's campaigns. Technological factors included von Moltke's realization that modern tactical firepower mandated battles of encirclement and the desire to exploit the capabilities of the railway and the telegraph.

Third generation warfare was also a response to the increase in battlefield firepower. However, the driving force was primarily ideas. Aware they could not prevail in a contest of materiel because of their weaker industrial base in World War I, the Germans developed radically new tactics. Based on maneuver rather than attrition, third generation tactics were the first truly nonlinear tactics. The attack relied on infiltration to bypass and collapse the enemy's combat forces rather than seeking to close with and destroy them. The defense was in depth and often invited penetration, which set the enemy up for a counterattack.

While the basic concepts of third generation tactics were in place by the end of 1918, the addition of a new technological element—tanks—brought about a major shift at the operational level in World War II. That shift was blitzkrieg. In the blitzkrieg, the basis of the operational art shifted from place (as in Liddell-Hart's indirect approach) to time. This shift was explicitly recognized only recently in the work of retired Air Force Col John Boyd and his "OODA (observation–orientation–decision–action) theory."

Thus we see two major catalysts for change in previous generational shifts: technology and ideas. What perspective do we gain from these earlier shifts as we look toward a potential fourth generation of warfare?

## ELEMENTS THAT CARRY OVER

Earlier generational shifts, especially the shift from the second to the third generation, were marked by growing emphasis on several central ideas. Four of these seem likely to carry over into the fourth generation, and indeed to expand their influence.

The first is mission orders. Each generational change has been marked by greater dispersion on the battlefield. The fourth generation battlefield is likely to include the whole of the enemy's society. Such dispersion, coupled with what seems likely to be increased importance for actions by very small groups of combatants, will require even the lowest level to operate flexibly on the basis of the commander's intent.

Second is decreasing dependence on centralized logistics. Dispersion, coupled with increased value placed on tempo, will require a high degree of ability to live off the land and the enemy.

Third is more emphasis on maneuver. Mass, of men or fire power, will no longer be an overwhelming factor. In fact, mass may become a disadvantage as it will be easy to target. Small, highly maneuverable, agile forces will tend to dominate.

Fourth is a goal of collapsing the enemy internally rather than physically destroying him. Targets will include such things as the population's support for the war and the enemy's culture. Correct identification of enemy strategic centers of gravity will be highly important.

In broad terms, fourth generation warfare seems likely to be widely dispersed and largely undefined; the distinction between war and peace will be blurred to the vanishing point. It will be nonlinear, possibly to the point of having no definable battlefields or fronts. The distinction between "civilian" and "military" may disappear. Actions will occur concurrently throughout all participants' depth, including their society as a cultural, not just a physical, entity. Major military facilities, such as airfields, fixed communications sites, and large headquarters will become rarities because of their vulnerability; the same may be true of civilian equivalents, such as seats of government, power plants, and industrial sites (including knowledge as well as manufacturing industries). Success will depend heavily on effectiveness in joint operations as lines between responsibility and mission become very blurred. Again, all these elements are present in third generation warfare; fourth generation will merely accentuate them.

## POTENTIAL TECHNOLOGY-DRIVEN FOURTH GENERATION

If we combine the above general characteristics of fourth generation warfare with new technology, we see one possible outline of the new generation. For example, directed energy may permit small elements to destroy targets they could not attack with conventional energy weapons. Directed energy may permit the achievement of EMP (electromagnetic pulse) effects without a nuclear blast. Research in superconductivity suggests the possibility of storing and using large quantities of energy in very small packages. Technologically, it is possible that a very few soldiers could have the same battlefield effect as a current brigade.

The growth of robotics, remotely piloted vehicles, low probability of intercept communications, and artificial intelligence may offer a potential for radically altered tactics. In turn, growing dependence on such technology may open the door to new vulnerabilities, such as the vulnerability to computer viruses.

Small, highly mobile elements composed of very intelligent soldiers armed with high technology weapons may range over wide areas seeking critical targets. Targets may be more in the civilian than the military sector. Front–rear terms will be replaced with targeted–untargeted. This may in turn radically alter the way in which military services are organized and structured.

Units will combine reconnaissance and strike functions. Remote, "smart" assets with preprogrammed artificial intelligence may play a key role. Concurrently, the greatest defensive strengths may be the ability to hide from and spoof these assets.

The tactical and strategic levels will blend as the opponent's political infrastructure and civilian society become battlefield targets. It will be critically important to isolate the enemy from one's own homeland because a small number of people will be able to render great damage in a very short time.

Leaders will have to be masters of both the art of war and technology, a difficult combination as two different mindsets are involved. Primary challenges facing commanders at all levels will include target selection (which will be a political and cultural, not just a military, decision), the ability to concentrate suddenly from very wide dispersion, and selection of subordinates who can manage the challenge of minimal or no supervision in a rapidly changing environment. A major challenge will be handling the tremendous potential information overload without losing sight of the operational and strategic objectives.

Psychological operations may become the dominant operational and strategic weapon in the form of media/information intervention. Logic bombs and computer viruses, including latent viruses, may be used to disrupt civilian as well as military operations. Fourth generation adversaries will be adept at manipulating the media to alter domestic and world opinion to the point where skillful use of psychological operations will sometimes preclude the commitment of combat forces. A major target will be the enemy population's support of its government and the war. Television news may become a more powerful operational weapon than armored divisions.

This kind of high-technology fourth generation warfare may carry in it the seeds of nuclear destruction. Its effectiveness could rapidly eliminate the ability of a nuclear-armed opponent to wage war conventionally. Destruction or disruption of vital industrial capacities, political infrastructure, and social fabric, coupled with sudden shifts in the balance of power and concomitant emotions, could easily lead to escalation to nuclear weapons. This risk may deter fourth generation warfare among nuclear armed powers just as it deters major conventional warfare among them today.

A major caveat must be placed on the possibility of a technologically driven fourth generation, at least in the American context. Even if the technological state of the art permits a high-technology fourth generation—and this is not clearly the case—the technology itself must be translated into weapons that are effective in actual combat. At present, our research, development, and procurement process has great difficulty making this transition. It often produces weapons that incorporate high technology irrelevant in combat or too complex to work in the chaos of combat. Too many so-called "smart" weapons provide examples; in combat they are easy to counter, fail of their own complexity, or make impossible demands on their operators. The current American research, development, and procurement process may simply not be able to make the transition to a militarily effective fourth generation of weapons.

## A POTENTIAL IDEA-DRIVEN FOURTH GENERATION

Technology was the primary driver of the second generation of warfare; ideas were the primary driver of the third. An idea-based fourth generation is also conceivable.

For about the last 500 years, the West has defined warfare. For a military to be effective it generally had to follow Western models. Because the West's strength is technology, it may tend to conceive of a fourth generation in technological terms.

However, the West no longer dominates the world. A fourth generation may emerge from non-Western cultural traditions, such as Islamic or Asiatic traditions. The fact that some non-Western areas, such as the Islamic world, are not strong in technology may lead them to develop a fourth generation through ideas rather than technology.

The genesis of an idea-based fourth generation may be visible in terrorism. This is not to say that terrorism is fourth generation warfare, but rather that elements of it may be signs pointing toward a fourth generation.

Some elements in terrorism appear to reflect the previously noted "carryovers" from third generation warfare. The more successful terrorists appear to operate on broad mission orders that carry down to the level of the individual terrorist. The 'battlefield' is highly dispersed and includes the whole of the enemy's society. The terrorist lives almost completely off the land and the enemy. Terrorism is very much a matter of maneuver: the terrorist's firepower is small, and where and when he applies it is critical.

Two additional carryovers must be noted as they may be useful "signposts" pointing toward the fourth generation. The first is a component of collapsing the enemy. It is a shift in focus from the enemy's front to his rear. Terrorism must seek to collapse the enemy from within as it has little capability (at least at present) to inflict widespread destruction. First generation warfare focused tactically and operationally (when operational art was practiced) on the enemy's front, his combat forces. Second generation warfare remained frontal tactically, but at least in Prussian practice it focused operationally on the enemy's rear through the emphasis on encirclement. The third generation shifted the tactical as well as the operational focus to the enemy's rear. Terrorism takes this a major step further. It attempts to bypass the enemy's military entirely and strike directly at his homeland at civilian targets. Ideally, the enemy's military is simply irrelevant to the terrorist.

The second signpost is the way terrorism seeks to use the enemy's strength against him. This "judo" concept of warfare begins to manifest itself in the second generation, in the campaign and battle of encirclement. The enemy's fortresses, such as Metz and Sedan, became fatal traps. It was pushed further in the third generation where, on the defensive, one side often tries to let the other penetrate so his own momentum makes him less able to turn and deal with a counterstroke.

Terrorists use a free society's freedom and openness, its greatest strengths, against it. They can move freely within our society while actively working to subvert it. They use our democratic rights not only to penetrate but also to defend themselves. If we treat them within our laws, they gain many protections; if we simply shoot them down, the television news can easily make them appear to be the victims. Terrorists can effectively wage their form of warfare while being protected by the society they are attacking. If we are forced to set aside our own system of legal protections to deal with terrorists, the terrorists win another sort of victory.

Terrorism also appears to represent a solution to a problem that has been generated by previous generational changes but not really addressed by any of them. It is the contradiction between the nature of the modern battlefield and the traditional military culture. That culture, embodied in ranks, saluting uniforms, drill, etc., is largely a product of first generation warfare. It is a culture of order. At the time it evolved it was consistent with the battlefield, which was itself dominated by order. The ideal army was a perfectly oiled machine, and that was what the military culture of order sought to produce.

However, each new generation has brought a major shift toward a battlefield of disorder. The military culture, which has remained a culture of order, has become contradictory to the battlefield. Even in the third generation warfare, the contradiction has not been insoluble; the *Wehrmacht* bridged it effectively, outwardly maintaining the traditional culture of order while in combat demonstrating the adaptability and fluidity a disorderly battlefield demands. But other militaries, such as the British, have been less successful at dealing with the contradiction. They have often attempted to carry the culture of order over onto the battlefield with disastrous results. At Biddulphsberg, in the Boer War, for example, a handful of Boers defeated two British Guards battalions that fought as if on parade.

The contradiction between the military culture and the nature of modern war confronts a traditional military service with a dilemma. Terrorists resolve the dilemma by eliminating the culture of order. Terrorists do not have uniforms, drill, saluting or, for the most part, ranks. Potentially, they have or could develop a military culture that is consistent with the disorderly nature of modern war. The fact that their broader culture may be non-Western may facilitate this development.

Even in equipment, terrorism may point toward signs of a change in generations. Typically, an older generation requires much greater resources to achieve a given end than does its successor. Today, the United States is spending $500 million apiece for stealth bombers. A terrorist stealth bomber is a car with a bomb in the trunk—a car that looks like every other car.

## TERRORISM, TECHNOLOGY, AND BEYOND

Again, we are not suggesting terrorism is the fourth generation. It is not a new phenomenon, and so far it has proven largely ineffective. However, what do we see if we combine terrorism with some of the new technology we have discussed?

For example, what effectiveness might the terrorist have if his car bomb were a product of genetic engineering rather than high explosives? To draw our potential fourth generation out still further, what if we combined terrorism, high technology, and the following additional elements?

- A non-national or transnational base, such as an ideology or religion. Our national security capabilities are designed to operate within a nation-state framework. Outside that framework, they have great difficulties. The drug war provides an example. Because the drug traffic has no nation-state base, it is very difficult to attack. The nation-state shields the drug lords but cannot control them. We cannot attack them without violating the sovereignty of a friendly nation. A fourth-generation attacker could well operate in a similar manner, as some Middle Eastern terrorists already do.

- A direct attack on the enemy's culture. Such an attack works from within as well as from without. It can bypass not only the enemy's military but the state itself. The United States is already suffering heavily from such a cultural attack in the form of the drug traffic. Drugs directly attack our culture. They have the support of a powerful "fifth column," the drug buyers. They bypass the entire state apparatus despite our best efforts. Some ideological elements in South America see drugs as a weapon; they call them the "poor man's intercontinental ballistic missile." They prize the drug traffic not only for the money it brings in through which we finance the war against ourselves—but also for the damage it does to the hated North Americans.

- Highly sophisticated psychological warfare, especially through *manipulation* of the media, particularly television news. Some terrorists already know how to play this game. More broadly, hostile forces could easily take advantage of a significant product of television reporting—the fact that on television the enemy's casualties can be almost as devastating on the home front as are friendly casualties. If we bomb an enemy city, the pictures of enemy civilian dead brought into every living room in the country on the evening news can easily turn what may have been a military success (assuming we also hit the military target) into a serious defeat.

All of these elements already exist. They are not the product of "futurism," of gazing into a crystal ball. We are simply asking what would we face if they were all combined? Would such a combination constitute at least the beginnings of a fourth

generation of warfare? One thought that suggests they might is that third (not to speak of second) generation militaries would seem to have little capability against such a synthesis. This is typical of generational shifts.

The purpose of this paper is to pose a question, not to answer it. The partial answers suggested here may in fact prove to be false leads. But in view of the fact that third generation warfare is now over 70 years old, we should be asking ourselves the question, what will the fourth generation be?

# From Classical Terrorism to "Global" Terrorism

MICHEL WIEVIORKA

## CLASSICAL TERRORISM

As a historical reality, terrorism is like many other social or political phenomena: it has undergone considerable transformations since the period between 1960 and 1980. To be more precise, it has moved from the classical era to the global era. Some observers challenge this image of distinct change or break. Hans Magnus Enzensberger, for example, while not minimizing the innovations brought in by radical Islamism which has, in his words, "replaced the omniscient and all powerful Central Committee by a flexible network," insists on recalling that "modern terrorism is a European invention dating from the nineteenth century. . . In recent years," he points out, "its main source of inspiration has been the extreme left terrorism of the 1960s and 1970s". He considers that the techniques of the Islamists, their symbols, the style of their communiqués, etc., borrow on a wide scale from the extreme left groups of the past. One might add, to go for a moment in his direction, that the practice of suicide is not a novelty in terrorism. The terrorists of the end of the nineteenth and beginning of the twentieth century took risks which verged on suicide in approaching their

target with a bomb, a pistol, or a knife. Bobby Sands in 1981, other members of the (Irish) IRA, Ulrike Meinhof in 1976, Andreas Baader in 1977, and other members of the (German) Red Army Fraction all committed suicide in prison—although it is true that their gestures did not involve the deaths of anyone other than themselves.

The fact remains that Enzensberger himself, a few lines later in the book quoted above, weakens the thesis of historical continuity by noting that the Islamist terrorists "are in reality pure products of the globalized world which they are fighting" and that "in comparison to their predecessors, they have gone considerably further, not only in the techniques which they use but in their use of the media". While it would be absurd to postulate an absolute break, it nevertheless does seem to us more relevant to insist on the elements of a move from one era to another, rather than those which indicate a degree of continuity. This move can be observed in material terms by analyzing the forms and the meanings which terrorism assumed yesterday and by comparing them with present-day forms and meanings. It also involves the considerable changes in the categories which we can

Reprinted with permission from the author.

now use in considering this phenomenon. In the period 1960–1980 terrorism came in the main within the province of the analytical framework of the nation-state and its extension, international relations. Within the nation-state—or, at least, the sovereign state—it corresponded to three major registers. It could be on the extreme left, the extreme right, or nationalist and in favor of independence.

By far the most widespread expression of extreme left terrorism was played out in Italy, but it was also to be found in numerous other societies in varying stages of industrialization: West Germany with the Red Army Faction and the Revolutionary Cells, France with *Action Directe,* Japan with its Red Army, Belgium with the Revolutionary Communist Cells, Greece, Portugal, etc. It was the outcome of what I termed, at the time, an *inversion* in which the perpetrators of violence, in a deviation of post-68 leftism, took over the categories of Marxism-Leninism to subvert them in the name of a working-class proletariat which they in no way represented. In each instance terrorism challenged the authority of the state, even if in some cases the state had endeavored to become international and to establish itself in a space other than national, and even if it did denounce American imperialism in no uncertain terms. Extreme right terrorism, which was less widespread, was also prompted by projects to take over the state, often associated with the presence in the machinery of the states concerned of sectors which were themselves open to projects of this type. Finally, still internal to sovereign states, terrorism could be the mode of action of nationalist movements wishing to force the independence of a nation, where it might also be a question for them of awakening by means of violence. In Europe, the Basque and Irish movements were thus characterized by their resort to the armed struggle and by comparable forms of organization with, in particular, the same type of tensions between bellicose "military" rationales and "political" rationales which were more open to negotiation.

Elsewhere, international terrorism was in the main carried out by actors claiming to adhere to the Palestinian cause, whether it be at the center—for example with the killing of Israeli athletes carried out by El Fatah in 1972 in the Olympic village in Munich—or on the periphery with, in these instance, the intervention of groups possibly manipulated by state "sponsors" (Syria, Libya, Iraq) endeavoring to weaken the central rationale of the PLO and to prevent any negotiated solution to the Israeli-Palestinian conflict. In some respects, the terrorism of the ASALA (Secret Army for the Liberation of Armenia) resembled that of the Palestinian groups on which it was modeled in particular as, like them, it found in Lebanon in crisis a territory propitious to its short-lived prosperity.

The specificity of classical terrorism, that of the period between 1960 and 1980, is that it unfolded in a "Westphalian" world, as some political analysts call it today—a world which it was possible and legitimate to approach in terms of the categories of what Ulrich Beck calls "methodological nationalism." Terrorism originated within societies which are themselves established within states; it conveyed political and ideological deviations which referred to projects for taking power at state level or for the construction of a state; and it was conveyed by an avant-garde who saw themselves as being the direction of history, the working class, and the nation. In counterpart, the campaign against terrorism was an affair in which each of the states concerned became involved for itself—which did not exclude appeals to international solidarity. Classical terrorism was conceived of and described as being primarily a danger threatening states, their order, and possibly, their territorial integrity.

## "GLOBAL" TERRORISM

The 9/11 attacks revealed what could in fact be glimpsed almost ten years previously: the entry into the "global" era of terrorism. This era had been inaugurated by various episodes bearing the mark of radical Islamism with, in particular, the first attempted Islamist attack in New York in 1993, even then aimed at the World Trade Center towers, or again the hijacking of an Air France plane in Algiers in December 1994 by Islamists who planned to crash the plane on Paris—a hijacking which was followed a few months later by a series of attacks in France falling within the same "global" rationale since international dimensions (the extension of the Algerian Islamist struggle outside Algerian national space) were combined with dimensions internal to French society (crisis in the *banlieues,* social exclusion, and the transformation of the experience of racism into violence).

It is even possible to go further back in time to find the first signs of "global" terrorism in the attacks using a suicide bomber in a delivery truck which destroyed the American Embassy in Beirut (April 1983) and then the barracks of the French contingent of the multinational force in Lebanon and the local headquarters of the United States Marines (October 1983): many believe that these were the first actions of the Hezbollah, a movement which described itself as planning an Islamist revolution throughout the region, which also intended to destroy the state of Israel and which, from then on, was capable of mobilizing people destined to kill themselves in their action.

Whatever the case may be, the "globalization" of terrorism was demonstrated in spectacular fashion by the 9/11 attacks. "Globalization" means that the phenomenon can no longer be thought of in the categories of "methodological nationalism" as it blurs the classical frontiers between rationales which are internal to sovereign states and the external or international rationales. The perpetrators of the 9/11 attack circulated in what had become a global space, their career paths took them from the society in which they were born, in this instance Saudi Arabia and Egypt, to other societies, Sudan, Pakistan and Afghanistan where they met, were formed and trained, creating links of solidarity which again fanned out to form networks all over the world and in which they had the advantage of total freedom of action in the state of the Taliban, which they subjugated. They were at ease in several countries in Europe—in Germany, where some of them attended university; in the England of "Londonistan" and its mosques, where the most radical opinions were expressed freely; and in the French *banlieues.* These players, contrary to popular opinion, were not the spokespersons of an actual, to some extent traditional, community from which

they issued forth expressing directly the expectations of the community; on the contrary, they were the products of rootlessness and were far from a community of this type; they were the products of a *transnational neo-umma,* to use the words of Farhad Khosrokhavar, of an imaginary community which tended to be constructed in the poorer areas of the major "global" cities in the modern world rather than in traditional rural areas. There were rationales in their action which mirrored the most modern possible capitalism—Bin Laden, the leader of al Qaeda, was even said to have committed the offense of "insider dealing" by speculating on the stock exchange on the consequences of the attacks which his organization was preparing.

Actors of this type are highly flexible. Functioning in networks, they know how to connect and disconnect themselves without difficulty and, instrumental rationality being to the fore, they use the most advanced communication technologies, beginning with the Internet. Their terrorism is also "global" by definition and is not restricted to a single state in which it would be a question of taking power, or separating therefrom. Their aims are indeed global and go even further than the context of the world in which we live, to be projected into the next. Having broken with the traditional forms of community life, their Islamism, inseparable from the notion of *jihad*—the holy war—transcends national frontiers and aims—including through martyrdom and therefore through sacred death—at destroying the West which at one and the same time fascinates them and excludes and despises Islam and the Muslims.

The attacks of September 11, 2001, were not the first expression of this terrorism perpetrated by transnational actors and probably to be transcended in future, but a climactic moment, an extreme case. For thereafter, numerous attacks were made in the name of al Qaeda, or at least associated with this organization, but without presenting the same transnational purity, in other words, mixing world level dimensions with others, more classically established in the context of the state targeted. Moreover it is to these hybrid expressions, which conjugate world and supranational aspects with aspects which are internal to the states concerned that the idea of globalization of terrorism best applies. Whether it be a question of the attacks in Riyadh, Casablanca, and Istanbul in 2003, of those in Madrid (March 2004), or yet again in London (July 2005), on each occasion, and along lines which vary from one experience to another, the actors combine the two dimensions which constitute "global" terrorism. On one hand at least some of them are at one and the same time to some extent immersed in the society in which they act, and are then subjected to rationales of social exclusion and contempt and express a strong sense of not finding their place in this society, or else they express their rejection of its international policies. On the other hand they are bearers of transnational, religious rationales and if need be are connected to global networks. They are therefore simultaneously part of an imaginary community of believers with no material basis and of a real community, for example of Moroccan immigrants (in Spain) or Pakistanis (in England), or yet again of the impoverished masses living in the most deprived areas of Casablanca and Istanbul. Their action is neither solely internal and classical nor solely transnational, it is both at once. This moreover is why the answers to "global" terrorism themselves combine the two dimensions, one being military ensuring defense in relation to the outside world and the other involving policing and internal security.

But is "global" terrorism really new? In the past, terrorists could have transnational trajectories and appear to be far from having solid roots in the national society they come from. For instance, the three Japanese terrorists who killed twenty-six persons at the airport in Lod, Israel, on May 30, 1972, were acting in name of the Palestinian cause—nothing to do with Japan. And the German activists belonging to terrorist organizations that joined Palestinian extremist groups or collaborated with "sponsor states" (i.e. Iraq, Syria, Libya) during the seventies did not relate their acts to Germany. There was some transnationalism, and some networking then too. But what was at stake was international support for a national cause, and not "global" action. And networks, which many

experts considered to be organized from communist countries, could exist only due to the will or tolerance of some states.

However, in some cases of "global terrorism" the transnational dimension itself is weak, even non-existent, and terrorist action is mainly restricted to its classical dimensions. The suicide attacks by the Palestinians against targets in Israel are of this type. The practice of martyrdom is an innovation in Palestinian action and the latter only recently became Islamist. But above all, this violence proceeds directly from a specific community—the populations in the territories placed under the control of the Palestinian Authority—and the references to Islam remain subordinate to the national struggle. The transnational dimensions of the action are of little import and, while it is possible to speak of terrorism, it must be clearly understood that the latter remains classical and not global.

"Global" terrorism unfolds in a space which is therefore bounded by two poles. At one extremity, it is purely transnational—this was the case with the September 11, 2001, attacks; and at the other extremity, it is classical, at least as far as its framework of reference is concerned—this is the case with the Palestinian attacks in Israeli territory.

Is this "global" terrorism the monopoly of radical Islamism? It is true that terrorist players other than Muslim do exist today in the world and that many armed movements, be they nationalist, ethnic, or the product of another religion (Hinduism, for example), do resort thereto. But radical Islamism is the only one to combine global, metapolitical aims and a possible foothold within a sovereign state in various parts of the world. As a result, this leaves less space for violent actors other than Islamist, as was seen in spectacular fashion in Spain: the terrible attacks on March 11, 2004, in Madrid (191 persons killed) were in the first instance attributed by the government to ETA before it became clear that they were the work of North African migrants. Not only did José Maria Aznar's *Partido Popular* lose the elections which took place a few days later for having wrongly accused ETA, but the Basque separatist organization found itself in a way the victim of Islamist terrorism, forced as they also were to refute such extreme violence. Henceforth their legitimacy to resort to arms or explosives was weakened. For this reason it has been said that al Qaeda, by its intervention in Spain, could signify the beginning of the historical decline of ETA.

More generally, if we consider classical terrorism, that of the 1960s and 1970s, one may have an image of a form of fragmentation. The rationales of yesteryear were indeed political, obsessed, it was said, by taking state power or by the setting up of a new state. In the present-day world terrorist action has either become more than political, overdetermined by its dimensions of sacred world-level struggle, with no possible negotiation—radical Islamism reigns here, it is metapolitical—or else less than political, concerned in these instances with economic profit, as is the case, for example, of many of the guerrilla movements in Latin America, which become infrapolitical forces. This does not prevent nationalist, or comparable, movements from continuing to exist, still liable to resort,

classically, to terrorism, but necessarily restricted and reduced to their local-level issues. . . .

The sociology of "global" terrorism thus creates a relation between what, at first sight, may seem extremely distant: on one hand, the major transformations in the world, transnational rationales and the way in which they link up with rationales which are more restricted because they are rooted within the framework of a state; and, on the other hand, the subjectivity of the actors which borders on the most intimate, their most private personal experiences, their dreams and their despair. But the creation of this relation, which is not unlike a balancing act, is possible and necessary quite simply because the subjectivity of the actors—the way in which they mentally construct themselves, produce their personal and collective imaginary world—owes a great deal to their exposure to the most "global" modernity, to their belonging but also to their peregrinations in the universe of globalization which simultaneously fascinates and rejects them.

## The Guerrilla Myth

MAX BOOT

For a student of military history, the most astonishing fact about the current international scene is that there isn't a single conflict in which two uniformed militaries are pitted against each other. The last one was a brief clash in 2008 between Russia and Georgia. In our day, the specter of conventional conflict, which has dominated the imagination of the West since the days of the Greek hoplites, has almost been lifted.

But the world is hardly at peace. Algeria fights hostage-takers at a gas plant. France fights Islamist extremists in Mali. Israel fights Hamas. The U.S. and its allies fight the Taliban in Afghanistan. Syria's Bashar al-Assad fights rebels seeking to overthrow

him. Colombia fights and negotiates with the FARC. Mexico fights drug gangs. And various African countries fight the Lord's Resistance Army.

These are wars without front lines, without neatly defined starting and end points. They are messy, bloody affairs, in which attackers, typically without uniforms, engage in hit-and-run raids and often target civilians. They are, in short, guerrilla wars, and they are deadly. In Syria alone, more than 60,000 people have died since 2011, according to the United Nations. In Mexico, nearly 50,000 have died in drug violence since 2006. Hundreds of thousands more have perished in Africa's civil wars. The past decade has also seen unprecedented terrorist attacks, ranging from 9/11 to suicide bombings in Iraq. To understand today's world, you have to understand guerrillas and the terrorist movements that are their close cousins.

Unfortunately, our ignorance of guerrilla war runs deep, even as we find ourselves increasingly entangled in such conflicts. Contrary to popular lore, guerrilla warfare wasn't invented by Che Guevara or Mao Zedong, and terrorism long predates the 1972 Munich Olympics. Nor is insurgency, as some have suggested, a distinctively "Oriental" form of warfare, difficult for Westerners to grasp.

Examining guerrilla warfare's long history not only brings to light many compelling, half-forgotten characters; it lays to rest numerous myths and allows us to come to grips with the most pressing national security issue of our time. What follows are lessons that we need to learn—but haven't—from the history of guerrilla war.

**1. Guerrilla warfare is not new.** Tribal war, pitting one guerrilla force against another, is as old as humankind. A new form of warfare, pitting guerrillas against "conventional" forces, is of only slightly more recent vintage—it arose in Mesopotamia 5,000 years ago. Calling guerrilla warfare "irregular" or "unconventional" has it backward: It is the norm of armed conflict.

Many of the world's current boundaries and forms of government were determined by battles between standing armies and insurgencies. Think of the United Kingdom, which was "united" by the success of the English in defeating centuries-old Scottish and Irish guerrilla movements. The retreat of the British Empire was partly the result of successful armed resistance, by groups ranging from the Irish Republican Army in the 1920s to the Zionists in the 1940s. Earlier still, the war waged by American colonists, some of them fighting as guerrillas, created the U.S., which reached its present borders, in turn, by waging centuries of unremitting warfare against Native American insurgents.

It is hard to think of any country in the world that has avoided the ravages of guerrilla warfare—just as it hard to think of any organized military force that hasn't spent a considerable portion of its energy fighting guerrillas.

**2. Guerrilla warfare is the form of conflict universally favored by the weak, not an "Eastern" way of war.** Thanks largely to the success of Chinese and Vietnamese Communists in seizing power in the 20th century, there has been a tendency to portray guerrilla tactics as the outgrowth of Sun Tzu and other Chinese philosophers who were supposedly at odds with the conventional tactics espoused by Western sages such as Carl von Clausewitz.

In reality, ancient Chinese and Indian armies were as massive and conventional in their orientation as the Roman legions. It wasn't the Chinese who had a cultural proclivity toward guerrilla warfare but rather their nomadic enemies in Inner Asia. For these tribesmen, as for others ranging from the Sioux to the Pashtuns, irregular warfare was a way of life.

But even tribal peoples such as the Turks, Arabs and Mongols, who employed guerrilla tactics in their rise to power, turned to conventional armies to safeguard their hard-won empires. Their experience suggests that few people have ever chosen guerrilla warfare voluntarily; it is the tactic of last resort for those too weak to create regular armies. Likewise, terrorism is the tactic of last resort for those too weak to create guerrilla forces.

**3. Guerrilla warfare has been both underestimated and overestimated.** Before 1945, the value of guerrilla campaigns was generally underestimated, leading overconfident officers such as George Armstrong Custer to disaster. Because irregulars refuse to engage in face-to-face battle, they have not gotten the respect they deserve—notwithstanding their consistent ability, ever since the barbarian assaults on Rome, to humble the world's greatest empires.

Since 1945, opinion has swung too far toward considering guerrilla movements invincible. This is largely because of the success enjoyed by a handful of rebels such as Mao Zedong, Ho Chi Minh, and Fidel Castro. But focusing on their exploits distracts from the ignominious end suffered by most insurgents, including Castro's celebrated protégé, Che Guevara, who was killed by Bolivian Rangers in 1967.

In reality, though guerrillas have often been able to fight for years and inflict great losses on their enemies, they have seldom achieved their objectives. Terrorists have been even less successful.

**4. Insurgencies have been getting more successful since 1945, but they still lose most of the time.** According to a database that I have compiled, out of 443 insurgencies since 1775, insurgents succeeded in 25.2% of the concluded wars while incumbents prevailed in 63.8%. The rest were draws.

This lack of historical success flies in the face of the widespread deification of guerrillas such as Guevara. Since 1945, the win rate for insurgents has indeed gone up, to 39.6%. But counter-insurgency campaigns still won 51.1% of post-1945 wars. And those figures overstate insurgents' odds of success because many rebel groups that are still in the field, such as the Kachin separatists in Myanmar, have scant chance of success. If ongoing uprisings are judged as failures, the win rate for insurgents would go down to 23.2% in the post-1945 period, while the counter-insurgents' winning percentage would rise to 66.1%.

Like most business startups, most insurgent organizations go bust. Yet some groups such as the Provisional IRA and Palestine Liberation Organization, which fail to achieve their ultimate objectives, can still win concessions from the other side.

**5. The most important recent development in guerrilla warfare has been the rise of public opinion.** What accounts for the fact that guerrillas have been getting more successful since 1945? Much of the explanation can be found in the growing power of public opinion, brought about by the spread of democracy, education, communications technology, mass media and international organizations—all of which have sapped the will of states to engage in protracted counter-insurgencies, especially outside their own territory, and heightened the ability of insurgents to survive even after suffering setbacks.

The term "public opinion" first appeared in print in 1776, which is fitting, since it played a major role in persuading the British to negotiate an end to their conflict with the American colonies. Greek rebels in the 1820s benefited from public opinion in the West, where sympathizers such as Lord Byron rallied their governments to oppose Ottoman abuses. A similar strategy of relying on international support was pursued by Cubans against Spain in the 1890s and Algerians against France in the 1950s; it remains a key Palestinian strategy against Israel.

A spectacular vindication of this approach occurred during the Vietnam War, when the U.S. was defeated not because it had lost on the battlefield but because public opinion had turned against the war. The same thing almost happened in Iraq in 2007, and it may yet happen in Afghanistan.

**6. Few counter-insurgency campaigns have ever succeeded by inflicting mass terror—at least in foreign lands.** When faced with elusive foes, armies often have resorted to torturing suspects for information, as the U.S. did after 9/11, and inflicting bloody reprisals on civilians, as Mr. Assad's forces are now doing in Syria. Such strategies have worked on occasion (usually when rebels were cut off from outside support), but just as often they have failed.

The armies of the French Revolution provide an example of successful brutality at home: They killed indiscriminately to suppress the revolt in the Vendée region in the 1790s. As one republican general wrote, "I have not a single prisoner to reproach myself with. I exterminated them all." But the French could not match this feat in Haiti, where they used equally brutal measures but could not put down a slave revolt led by the "Black Spartacus," Toussaint L'Ouverture.

Even in the ancient world, when there were no human-rights activists or cable news channels, empires found that pacifying restive populations usually involved carrots as well as sticks. There were considerable benefits to participating in the Pax Romana, which won over subject populations by offering "bread and circuses," roads, aqueducts and (most important) security from roving guerrillas and bandits.

**7. "Winning hearts and minds" is often successful as an anti-guerrilla strategy, but it isn't as touchy-feely as commonly supposed.** The fact that the U.S. and other liberal democratic states cannot be as brutal as dictatorial regimes—or, more precisely, choose not to be—doesn't mean they cannot succeed in putting down insurgencies. They simply have to do it in a more humane style. In Iraq in 2007–08, Gen. David Petraeus showed how successful a "population-centric" strategy could be, at least in narrow security terms, by sending troops to live in urban areas and by wooing Sunni tribes.

The best-known term for this strategy is "winning hearts and minds"—a phrase popularized by the British Gen. Gerald Templer, who saved Malaya from a communist insurgency in the 1950s. But the term is misleading, since it suggests that a counter-insurgency campaign is trying to win a popularity contest. In reality, the populace will embrace the government only if it is less dangerous to do so than to support the insurgency. That is why successful population-centric policies aim to control the people with a 24/7 deployment of security forces, not to win their love and gratitude by handing out soccer balls, medical supplies and other goodies.

**8. Most insurgencies are long-lasting; attempts to win a quick victory backfire.** The average insurgency since 1775 has lasted seven years. The figure is even longer for post-1945 insurgencies—nearly 10 years. The length of low-intensity conflicts can be a source of frustration for both sides, but attempts to short-circuit the process usually backfire. The U.S. tried to do just that in the early years of the Vietnam and Iraq wars by using its conventional might to hunt down insurgents in a push for what John Paul Vann, a legendary adviser in Vietnam, decried as "fast, superficial results." It was only when the U.S. gave up hopes of a quick victory that it started to get results.

A particularly seductive version of the "quick win" strategy is to try to eliminate the insurgency's leadership, as the U.S. and Israel regularly try to do with airstrikes against groups such as al Qaeda and Hamas. Such strategies sometimes work. The Romans, for example, stamped out a revolt in Spain by inducing some of the rebels to kill their leader, Viriathus, in 139 B.C.

But there are just as many cases where leaders were eliminated but the movement went on stronger than ever—as Hezbollah did after the loss of its secretary-general in an Israeli airstrike in 1992. Targeting leadership is most effective when integrated into a broader counter-insurgency effort designed to separate the insurgents from the population. If conducted in isolation, such raids are about as effective as mowing the lawn; the organization can usually regenerate itself.

**9. Technology has been relatively unimportant in guerrilla war—but that may be changing.** All guerrilla and terrorist tactics, from airplane hijacking and suicide bombing to hostage-taking and roadside ambushes, are designed to negate the firepower advantage of conventional forces. In this type of war, technology counts for less than in conventional conflict. Even the possession of nuclear bombs hasn't prevented the Soviet Union and the U.S. from suffering ignominious defeat at guerrilla hands. To the extent that technology has mattered in low-intensity conflicts, it has often been the non-shooting kind. As T.E. Lawrence ("Lawrence of Arabia") said, "The printing press is the greatest weapon in the armory of the modern commander." A rebel today might substitute "the Internet" for "the printing press," but the essential insight remains.

The role of destructive technology will grow in the future, however, if insurgents get their hands on chemical, biological or nuclear weapons. A terrorist cell the size of a platoon might then have more killing capacity than the entire army of a nonnuclear state like Brazil or Egypt. Cyberweapons also have the potential to wreak havoc.

That is a sobering thought on which to end. It suggests that in the future, guerrilla warfare and terrorism could pose even greater problems for the world's leading powers than they have in the past. And those problems have been substantial, varied and long-lasting.

# Section 6

# Law and International Community

# A Short History of International Law

STEPHEN C. NEFF

Indeed, the ambiguity of the term "international law" leads to various different answers to the question of when international law "began." If by "international law" is meant merely the ensemble of methods or devices which give an element of predictability to international relations (as in the silent-trading illustration), then the origin may be placed virtually as far back as recorded history itself. If by "international law" is meant a more or less comprehensive substantive code of conduct applying to nations, then the late classical period and Middle Ages was the time of its birth. If "international law" is taken to mean a set of substantive principles applying *uniquely* to States as such, then the seventeenth century would be the starting time. If "international law" is defined as the integration of the world at large into something like a single community under a rule of law, then the nineteenth century would be the earliest date (perhaps a trifle optimistically). If, finally, "international law" is understood to mean the enactments and judicial decisions of a world government, then its birth lies (if at all) somewhere in the future—and, in all likelihood, the distant future at that.

If we take the most restricted of these definitions, then we could expect to find the best evidence for a nascent international law in the three areas of ancient Eurasia that were characterized by dense networks of small, independent States sharing a more or less common religious and cultural value system: Mesopotamia (by, say, the fourth or third millennium BC), northern India (in the Vedic period after about 1600 B.C.), and classical Greece. . . .

With the advent of the great universal religions, far more broadly-based systems of world order became possible. One outstanding example was the Islamic empire of the seventh century A.D. and afterwards. Significantly, the body of law on relations between States within the Muslim world (the *Dar al-Islam*, or "House of Islam") was much richer than that regarding relations with the outside world (the *Dar al-Harb*, or "House of war"). But even with infidel States and nationals, a number of pragmatic devices evolved to permit relations to occur in predictable ways—such as "temporary" truces (in lieu of treaties) or safe-conducts issued to individuals (sometimes on a very large scale).

In Western history, the supreme exemplar of the multinational empire was Rome. But the Roman Empire was, in its formative period, a somewhat tentative and ramshackle affair, without an over-arching ethical or religious basis comparable to the Islamic religion in the later Arab empire. That began to change, however, when certain philosophical concepts were imported from Greece (from about the second century B.C.). The most important of these was the idea of a set of universal principles of justice: the belief that, amidst the welter of varying laws of different States, certain substantive rules of conduct were present in *all* human societies. This idea first surfaced in the writings of Aristotle. But it was taken much further by the philosophers of the Stoic school, who envisaged the entire world as a single "world city-State" (or *kosmopolis*) governed by the law of nature. Cicero, writing under Stoic influence, characterized this law of nature as being "spread through the whole human community, unchanging and eternal".

This concept of a universal and eternal natural law was later adopted by two other groups, the Roman lawyers and the Christian Church, and then bequeathed by them to medieval Europe. The lawyers in particular made a distinction that would have a very long life ahead of it: between a *jus naturale* (or natural law properly speaking) and a *jus gentium* (or law of peoples). The two were distinct, but at the same time so closely interconnected that the differences between them were

Michael Evans, International Law. New York: Oxford University Press often very easily ignored. Natural law was the broader concept. It was something like what we would now call a body of scientific laws, applicable not just to human beings but to the whole animal kingdom as well. The *jus gentium* was the human component, or sub-category, of it. Just as the law of nature was universal in the natural world, so was the *jus gentium* universal in the *human* world. . . .

The European Middle Ages became the great age of natural-law thought. During this period, natural-law conceptions developed under the umbrella of the Catholic Church. But it must be remembered that the idea was not specifically Christian in its inception, but rather was a legacy of the classical Stoic and Roman legal traditions. The dominant tradition—represented outstandingly by Thomas Aquinas—was rationalist in outlook, holding the content of the natural law to be susceptible of discovery and application by means of human reason rather than of revelation.

Natural law is one of the many parts of international law that have never received the systematic study that they merit. In the present context, only a few of its most salient features can be noted. Perhaps its single most outstanding feature was its all-embracing character. It encompassed and regulated the natural and social life of the universe in all its infinite variety—from the movements of the stars in their courses to the gurgling of the four humours through the veins and arteries of the human body, from the thoughts and deeds of all of the creatures of land, sea, and air, to those of human beings and the angels in the heavens. Its strictures applied universally to all cultures and civilizations, past, present, and future.

There continued to be, as in the ancient period, a distinction between the *jus naturale* and the *jus gentium*, though still without any very sharp line between the two. The *jus gentium* was much the lesser of the two, being seen largely as an application of the broader natural law to specifically human affairs. Sometimes it was regarded as comprising universal customs of purely human creation—and therefore as a sort of supplement to natural law properly speaking. . . .

Beginning in about the eleventh century, European (chiefly Italian) States began to conclude bilateral treaties that spelled out various reciprocal guarantees of fair treatment. These agreements, sometimes concluded with Muslim States, granted a range of privileges to the foreign merchants based in the contracting States, such as the right to use their own law and courts when dealing with one another. The same process was at work in the sphere of maritime trading. The seafaring community made use of the laws of Oléron (which were actually a series of court decisions from the small island of that name in the Bay of Biscay), and also of a code of rules called the *Consolato del Mare,* compiled in about the thirteenth century for the maritime community of Barcelona. These codes governed the broad range of maritime activities, including the earliest rules on the rights of neutral traders in wartime. . . .

With the European explorations of Africa and, particularly, the New World from the fourteenth century onward, questions of relations with non-European societies assumed an urgent importance—while, at the same time, posing an immense practical test for the universality of natural law. The Spanish conquest of the Indian kingdoms in the New World sparked especially vigorous legal and moral debates (even if only after the fact). The Dominican scholar, Francisco de Vitoria, in a series of lectures at the University of Salamanca, concluded that the Spanish conquest was justified, on the ground that the Indians had unlawfully attempted to exclude Spanish traders from their kingdoms, contrary to natural-law rules. But he also confessed that his blood froze in his veins at the thought of the terrible atrocities committed by the Spanish in the process. In 1550–51, there occurred one of the major legal confrontations of history, when two prominent figures—Juan Inés de Sepúlveda and Barolomé de las Casas—debated, at length, the lawfulness and legal bases of the Spanish conquest of the New World, under the judgeship of the theologian and philosopher Domingo de Soto. The result, alas, was inconclusive, as Soto declined to render a judgment. . . .

In the seventeenth and eighteenth centuries, a new spirit entered into doctrinal thought on international law. This is sometimes put in terms of a secularization of natural-law thought. That, however, is a very misleading characterization, since natural-law itself was (and had always been) primarily secular in nature. What was new in the seventeenth century was a willingness to give a degree of formal recognition to State practice as a true source of law, rather than regarding it as merely illustrative of natural-law principles. The result was a kind of dualistic outlook, with natural law and State practice maintaining a wary, and rather uneasy, form of co-existence—a state of affairs much in evidence to the present day.

The principal harbinger of this new outlook was the Dutch writer Hugo Grotius, whose major work *On the Law of War and Peace* was published in Paris in 1625—a work so dense and rich that one could easily spend a lifetime studying it (as a number of scholars have). As a natural-law writer, he was a conservative, writing squarely in the rationalist tradition inherited from the Middle Ages. In international law specifically, he had important forerunners, most notably the Italian writer, Alberico Gentili, who produced the first truly systematic study of the law of war at the end of the sixteenth century.

Where Grotius did break important new ground—and where he fully earned the renown that still attaches to his name—was in his transformation of the old *jus gentium* into something importantly different, called the *law of nations*. The distinctive feature of this law of nations was that it was regarded as something distinct from the law of *nature*, rather than as a sub-category or means of application of natural law. Furthermore, and most significantly, this law of nations was not regarded (like the old *jus gentium*) as a body of law governing human social affairs in general. Instead, it was a set rules applying specifically to one particular and distinctive category of human beings: rulers of States. Now, for the first time in history, there was a clear conception of a systematic body of law applicable specifically to the relationship between nations. Eventually, although not until the late eighteenth century, the label "international law" would be applied to this corpus of rules—with Jeremy Bentham as the coiner of the term.

It should be appreciated that Grotius's law of nations, or "voluntary law" as it was sometimes

known, was not designed to supplant or undermine traditional natural law.... The law of nature and the law of nations, in short, were seen as partners rather than as rivals. ...

There were some, however, who contended that the partnership between the law of nature and the law of nations was anything but a happy one. Foremost amongst these dissidents was the English writer Thomas Hobbes, whose master work *Leviathan* was written in 1651, shortly after Grotius's death. In sharp contrast to Grotius, Hobbes denied that the pre-political condition of human society had been orderly and law-governed. He maintained, instead, that it was a chaotic, even violent, world, with self-preservation as the only true natural right. Security could only be attained by the radical step of having all of the persons in a state of nature surrender their natural rights to a sovereign power of their own creation—with the result that, henceforth, the *only* law which they would live under would be the law promulgated by that sovereign. Natural law was not rejected in its entirety, but it was radically stripped-down, to the point of being reduced, in essence to two fundamental tenets: a right of self-preservation, and a duty to perform contracts or promises. It was this stripped-down version of natural law which, in the opinion of Hobbes, constituted the sole body of law between independent nation-states.

On this thesis, the only possible way in which States could construct a stable international system was through the painstaking process of entering into agreements whenever this proved feasible. The natural-law duty to perform promises was the fundamental basis of this system, with the detailed substantive rules being provided by the various agreements that were actually concluded. These agreements could take either of two forms: written or unwritten. The written form, of course, comprised treaties, of the sort of that States had been concluding for many centuries. The unwritten form was customary law, which in this period was seen predominantly as simply a tacit or unwritten treaty....

Instead of setting out a grand philosophical scheme, Vattel's intention was to provide a sort of handbook for lawyers and statesmen....

The writing of Grotius and Hobbes and their followers was not done in a vacuum. Various forces were at work in this period, which served to give this new law of nations a concrete reality. One of the most important of these trends was the emergence (gradual to be sure) of strong central governments, at least in Western Europe, which increasingly gained the upper hand over the older, diffused jurisdictions of the feudal age. Particularly important for this trend was the innovation of standing armies in place of the older temporary feudal levies. In addition, these centralizing Nation-States were coming to be seen as permanently existing, corporate entities in their own right, separate from the rulers who governed them at any given time—with long-term interests and political agendas of their own.

At least some of the flavour of the medieval natural law survived, however, chiefly in the form of the idea of the existence of something that has come to be called the "community of States." The clearest symbol of this—if that is the right word for it—was the peace settlement arrived at in Westphalia in 1648, at the conclusion of the Thirty Years War in Germany. It is curious that something called the "Westphalian system" is sometimes spoken of as a synonym of anarchy or of radical views of absolute State sovereignty—conceptions which actually belong (as will be seen) to the nineteenth century and not to the seventeenth. In reality, the Westphalian settlement was an arrangement reached *within* the framework of the Holy Roman Empire, with certain prerogatives of the imperial government carefully preserved—ie, with the older medieval idea of "independent" States being subject, at the same time, to certain higher norms. The Peace of Westphalia did, however, provide a sort of template for later times in the way in which it marked out a division of labour (so to speak) between national and international spheres, placing religion carefully in the realm of domestic law.

The idea of a community of States—distinct from, but also analogous to, a community of individual persons—was apparent in sundry other ways in the seventeenth and eighteenth centuries. One of these was in the concept of a balance of power. This was hardly an altogether new idea, but in this period it attained a formal articulation and recognition that it had never had before (most notably in the Peace of Utrecht in 1713, at the conclusion of the War of the Spanish Succession). In conjunction with this concept, the period was one of limited—though also of frequent—warfare. At least in Western Europe, war was largely conducted with trained professional forces, and for limited ends. As a result, European diplomacy bore more resemblance to a meticulous game of chess than to a lurid Hobbesian inferno of mayhem and turmoil. Even warfare often had a ritualistic air, with its emphasis on manoeuvre and siege rather than on pitched battle. . . .

With the definitive defeat of revolutionary and imperial France in 1815, the victorious European powers (Britain, Prussia, Russia and Austria) crafted a new kind of peace settlement, based not merely on the balance of material power between the major States but also on a set of general principles of a more substantive character. These general principles were, to be sure, of a decidedly conservative character. The goal was to craft a continent-wide set of political arrangements that would (it was hoped) keep the scourge of revolution from breaking out again.

The peace settlement was to be policed by the major powers—who were, of course, self-appointed to the task—by way of military intervention where necessary. The powers even had a grand name for their enterprise: the "public law and system of Europe." This legal order was based on faithful adherence to treaty commitments, together with respect for established laws and legitimate governments and property rights *within* the States of Europe. But it also included a duty on the part of rulers to "earn" their legitimacy by providing responsible and efficient government to their peoples and also by cooperating with movements for orderly and peaceful change. . . .

The Concert of Europe "system" (if it could really be called that) was overtly hegemonic, in modern parlance. There was little sign of any principle of equality of States. Still, the Concert of Europe did at least provide an ideal—if not always the reality—of collective, orchestrated State action for the preservation of international peace. To that extent, it foreshadowed the post-1945 United Nations. International lawyers, however, never gave it much attention. Instead, their ambitions were directed to another end: to unshackling international law from its natural-law heritage and making it something like a science in the modern sense of that term. . . .

On the conceptual front, the major feature of the nineteenth century was the dominant role of positivism. . . .

In its original form, positivism envisaged the emergence of a sort of technocratic utopia, in which the world would be governed not by clerics or politicians or lawyers (as in the past benighted ages of theology and metaphysics), but rather by engineers and industrialists and financiers. This vision had first been put forward by the eccentric French nobleman, the Comte de St-Simon, in the early nineteenth century. . . . This early vision, taken to its logical conclusion, envisaged the obsolescence of the nation-state. . . .

One of the most central aspects of positivism was its close attention to questions of the sources of international law—and, in particular, to the proposition that international law was, fundamentally, an outgrowth or feature of the will of the States of the world. Rules of law were created by the States themselves, by consent, whether express (in written treaties) or tacit (in the form of custom). International law was therefore now seen as the sum total, or aggregation, of agreements which the States of the world happen to have arrived at, at any given time. In a phrase that became proverbial amongst positivists, international law must now be seen as a law *between* States and not as a law *above* States. International law, in other words, was now regarded as a corpus of rules arising from, as it were, the bottom up, as the conscious creation of the States themselves, rather than as a pre-existing, eternal, all-enveloping framework, in the manner of the old natural law. As a consequence, the notion of a systematic, all-encompassing body of law—so striking a feature of natural law—was now discarded. International law was now seen as, so to speak, a world of fragments, an accumulation of specific, agreed rules, rather than

as a single coherent picture. In any area where agreement between States happened to be lacking, international law was, perforce, silent. . . .

The stress on the basic rights of States also gave to positivism a strongly pluralistic cast. Each nation-State possessed its own distinctive set of national interests, which it was striving to achieve in an inherently competitive, even hostile, environment. Each State was sovereign within its territory. And each State's domestic law could reflect that country's own particular history, values, aspirations, traditions, and so forth. It was in this period that the principle of "the sovereign equality of States" became the fundamental cornerstone—or even the central dogma—of international law, along with the concomitant rule of nonintervention of States into the internal affairs of one another. . . .

Positivists tended to view the rights and wrongs of a State's decision to resort to war (the *jus ad bellum*) as a political rather than a legal issue. Therefore, war was now seen as an inevitable and permanent feature of the inter-State system, in the way that friction was an inevitable and permanent feature of a mechanical system.

If positivism was by far the dominant trend in nineteenth century international law, it did fall short of having a complete monopoly. Two other schools of thought in particular should be noted. . . .

At the core of the historical school's philosophy was the thesis that each culture, or cultural unit, or nation possessed a distinctive group consciousness or ethos, which marked it off from other cultures or nations. Each of these cultural units, as a consequence, could only really be understood in its own terms. The historical school therefore rejected the universalist outlook of natural law. This opposition to universal natural law was one of the most important features that the historical school shared with the positivists.

In international law, the impact of the historical school is evident in three principal areas. The first was with regard to customary law, where its distinctive contribution was the insistence that this law was not a matter merely of consistent practice, however widespread or venerable it might be. A rule of customary law required, in addition, a mental element—a kind of group consciousness, or collective decision on the part of the actors to enact that practice into a rule of law (albeit an unwritten one). In fact, this collective mental element was seen as the most important component of custom, with material practice relegated to a clear second place. Customary law was therefore seen, on this view, as a kind of informal legislation rather than as an unwritten treaty (as the positivists tended to hold). This thesis marked the origin of the modern concept of *opinio juris* as a key component of customary international law.

The second major contribution of the historical school to international law was its theory that the fundamental unit of social and historical existence was not—or not quite—the State, as it was for the positivists, but rather the *nation*-state. In this vision, the State, when properly constituted, comprised the organization of a particular culture into a political unit. It was but a short step from this thesis to the proposition that a "people" (ie, a cultural collectivity or nation or, in the German term, *Volk*) had a moral right to organize itself politically as a State. And it was no large step from there to the assertion that such a collectivity possesses a *legal* right so to organize itself. This "nationality school" (as it was sometimes called) had the most impact in Italy, where its leading spokesman was Pasquale Mancini, who was a professor at the University of Turin (as well as an office-holder in the government of unified Italy). Although the nationality thesis did not attract significant support amongst international lawyers generally at the time, it did prefigure the later law of self-determination of peoples.

The third area where the influence of the historical school was felt was regarding imperialism—a subject that has attracted strangely little attention from international lawyers. It need only be mentioned here that the historical school inherited from the eighteenth century a fascination with "stages" of history. Under the impact of nineteenth-century anthropological thought, there came to be wide agreement on a three-fold categorization of States: as civilized, barbarian, and savage. . . .

It has been observed that positivism basically accepted the outbreak of war as an unavoidable fact of international life, and contented itself with regulating the conduct of hostilities. But that approach applied to war properly speaking. Regarding lesser measures of coercion, the legacy of just-war thought lingered on. This was the thesis that a resort to armed self-help was permissible to obtain respect for legal rights, if peaceful means proved unavailing. The most important of these forcible self-help measures were armed reprisals. . . .

It is one of history's great ironies that the natural-law tradition, which had once been so grand an expression of idealism and world brotherhood, should come to such an ignominiously blood-spattered pass. A philosophy that had once insisted so strongly on the protection of the weak against the strong was now used as a weapon of the strong against the weak. It is, of course, unfair to condemn a whole system of justice on the basis of abuses. But the abuses were many, and the power relations too naked and too ugly for the tastes of many from the developing world. Along with imperialism, forcible self-help actions left a long-lasting stain on relations between the developed and the developing worlds. . . .

The culmination of nineteenth-century international legislation—and the arrival of parliamentary-style diplomacy and treaty-drafting—came with the two Hague Peace Conferences of 1899 and 1907. The first Conference drafted two major conventions: one on the laws of war and one on the establishment of a Permanent Court of Arbitration (which was actually a roster of experts prepared to act as judges on an ad hoc basis, and not a standing court). The Second Hague Peace Conference, in 1907, was a much larger gathering than the earlier one (and hence less Europe-dominated). It produced 13 conventions on various topics, mostly on aspects of war and neutrality.

Yet another major achievement of the nineteenth century was in the area of the peaceful settlement of disputes. Although it was widely agreed that fundamental security issues were not justiciable, the nineteenth century marked a great step forward in the practice of inter-State arbitration. The trend began with the Jay Treaty of 1794, in which the United States and Britain agreed to set up two arbitration commissions (comprising nationals of each country) to resolve a range of neutrality and property-seizure issues that had arisen in the preceding years. These were followed by a number of ad hoc inter-State arbitrations in the nineteenth century, of which the most famous, again between Britain and the United States, took place in 1871–72, for the settlement of a host of neutrality-related issues arising from the American Civil War.

For all the impressiveness of these achievements, though, the state of the world was well short of utopian. Economic inequality grew steadily even as growth accelerated. The subjection of much of the world to the European imperial powers, together with the "gunboat diplomacy" that sometimes followed in the wake of legal claims, stored up a strong reservoir of ill-will between the developed and the developing worlds. . . .

The carnage of the Great War of 1914–18 concentrated many minds, in addition to squandering many lives. Many persons now held that nothing short of a permanently existing organization dedicated to the maintenance of peace would suffice to prevent future ghastly wars. Their most prominent spokesman was American President Woodrow Wilson. The fruit of their labours was the establishment of the League of Nations, whose Covenant was set out in the Versailles Treaty of 1919. This new system of public order would be of an open, parliamentary, democratic character, in contrast to the discreet great-power dealings of the Concert of Europe. The League was, however, tainted from the outset by its close association with the Versailles peace settlement, an incubus which it never managed to shake off. . . .

Although the League failed as a protector against aggressors, it would be far wrong to suppose that the inter-war period was a sterile time in international law generally. Precisely the opposite was the case. It was a time of ferment, experiment, and excitement unprecedented in the history of the discipline. A World Court (known formally, if optimistically, as the Permanent Court of International Justice) was established as a standing body, with its seat at the Hague in the Netherlands. It did not have compulsory jurisdiction over all disputes. But it decided several dozen cases, building up, for

the first time, a substantial body of international judicial practice. These cases were supplemented by a large number of claims commissions and arbitrations, whose outpourings gave international lawyers a volume of case law far richer than anything that had ever existed before.

The codification of international law was one of the ambitious projects of the period. A conference was convened for that purpose by the League of Nations in 1930, but its fruits were decidedly modest (consisting mainly of clarifications of various issues relating to nationality). But there were further initiatives by the American States in a variety of fields. These included a convention on the rights and duties of States in 1933, which included what many lawyers regard as the canonical definition of a "State" for legal purposes. The American States also concluded conventions on maritime neutrality, civil wars, asylum, and extradition.

The inter-war period also witnessed the first multilateral initiatives on human rights. A number of bilateral conventions for the protection of minorities were concluded between various newly created States and the League of Nations. In the event, these proved not to be very effective; but they set the stage for later efforts to protect minority rights after 1945, as well as human rights generally. The principle of trusteeship of dependent territories was embodied in the mandates system, in which the ex-colonies of the defeated countries were to be administered by member States of the League. But this was to be a mission of stewardship—"a sacred trust of civilization"—under the oversight of the League. Finally, the League performed heroic labours for the relief of refugees, in the face of very great obstacles—in the process virtually creating what would become one of the most important components of the law of human rights.

It was a period also of innovative thinking about international law. That the doctrinaire positivism of the nineteenth century was far from dead was made apparent by the World Court in 1927, when it reaffirmed the consensual basis of international law, in the famous (or infamous) *Lotus* case. But positivism also came under attack during this period, from several quarters. One set of attackers were the enthusiasts for collective security, as embodied in the League of Nations. . . .

In short, the inter-war period did not bring an end to war or aggression. But it was the most vibrant and exciting era in the history of the discipline up to that time (and perhaps since). . . .

The founding of the United Nations in 1945, to replace the defunct League of Nations, was a critical step in the creation of a new world order. With the UN came a new World Court (the International Court of Justice, or ICJ), though still without compulsory jurisdiction over States. The heart of the organization was the Security Council, where (it was hoped) the victorious powers from the Second World War would continue their wartime alliance in perpetuity as a collective bulwark against future aggressors. (It may be noted that "United Nations" had been the official name for the wartime alliance.) The UN therefore marked something of a return to the old Concert of Europe approach. The special status of the five major powers (the principal victors in the Second World War, of course) was formally reflected in their possession of permanent seats on the Security Council, together with the power of veto over its decisions.

The UN Charter went further than the League Covenant in restricting violence. It did this by prohibiting not only war as such, but also "the use of force" in general—thereby encompassing measures short of war, such as armed reprisals. An express exception was made for self-defence. . . .

Parallel to this security programme was another one for the promotion of global economic prosperity. The economic-integration effort of the nineteenth century, shattered by the Great War and by the Great Depression of the 1930s, was to be restructured and given institutional embodiments. The International Monetary Fund was founded to ensure currency stability, and the World Bank to protect and promote foreign investment and (in due course) economic development. Trade liberalization would be overseen by a body to be called the International Trade Organization (ITO). . . .

The euphoric atmosphere proved, alas, to be very short-lived. Scarcely had the UN begun to function than it became paralysed by Cold-War rivalry between the major power blocs—with the notable exception of the action in Korea in 1950–53 (only made possible by an ill-advised Soviet boycott of the Security Council at the relevant time). Nor did the new World Court find much effective use in its early decades. The ITO never came into being (because of a loss of interest by the United States). Plans for the establishment of a permanent international criminal court were also quietly dropped. Nor did the UN Charter's general ban against force have much apparent effect, beyond a cruelly ironic one: of propelling self-defence from a comparative legal backwater into the very forefront of international legal consciousness. Since self-defence was now the only clearly lawful category of unilateral use of force, the UN era became littered with self-defence claims of varying degrees of credibility, from the obvious to the risible. In particular, actions that previously would have been unashamedly presented as reprisals now tended to be deftly re-labelled as self-defence. . . .

Around the 1980s, a certain change of atmosphere in international law became evident, as something like the idealism of the early post-war years began, very cautiously, to return. . . . The end of the Cold War led to tangible hopes that the original vision of the UN as an effective collective-security agency might, at last, be realized. The expulsion of Iraq from Kuwait in 1991 lent strong support to this hope. Perhaps most remarkable of all was the rebirth of plans for an international criminal court, after a half-century of dormancy. A statute for a permanent International Criminal Court was drafted in 1998, entering into force in 2002 (with the first trial commencing in 2009).

In this second round of optimism, there was less in the way of euphoria than there had been in the first one, and more of a feeling that international law might be entering an age of new—and dangerous—challenge. International lawyers were now promising, or threatening, to bring international norms to bear upon States in an increasingly intrusive manner. A striking demonstration of this occurred in 1994, when the UN Security Council authorized the use of force to overthrow an unconstitutional government in Haiti. In 1999, the UN Security Council acquiesced in (although it did not actually authorize) a humanitarian intervention in Kosovo by a coalition of Western powers. It was far from clear how the world would respond to this new-found activism—in particular, whether the world would really be content to entrust its security, in perpetuity, to a Concert-of-Europe style directorate of major powers.

International legal claims were being asserted on a wide range of other fronts as well, and frequently in controversial ways and generally with results that were unwelcome to some. For example, lawyers who pressed for self-determination rights for various minority groups and indigenous peoples were accused of encouraging secession movements. Some human-rights lawyers were loudly demanding changes in the traditional practices of non-Western peoples. And newly found (or newly rejuvenated) concerns over democracy, governance, and corruption posed, potentially, a large threat to governments all over the world. Some environmental lawyers were insisting that, in the interest of protecting a fragile planet, countries should deliberately curb economic growth. (But which countries? And by how much?) Economic globalization also became intensely controversial, as the IMF's policy of "surveillance" (a somewhat ominous term to some) became increasingly detailed and intrusive, and as "structural adjustment" was seen to have potentially far-reaching consequences in volatile societies. Fears were also increasingly voiced that the globalization process was bringing an increase in economic inequality.

# The Palestine Problem: The Search for Statehood and the Benefits of International Law

ADAM G. YOFFIE

## INTRODUCTION

Palestine has had a long and checkered past in its efforts to attain statehood. Although international law failed to facilitate Palestinian statehood more than half a century ago, the legal landscape at the international level is changing. Whereas conventional wisdom assumes that international law reduces state sovereignty, this Comment argues that international political organizations and legal institutions can actually increase Palestinian chances of achieving statehood.

By the conclusion of World War II, Palestine had been ruled by Great Britain for nearly three decades. Assuming control from the Ottomans following World War I, the British never established a coherent policy for governing the disputed territory. British rule, however, did not last: on November 29, 1947—with thirty-three votes in favor, thirteen against, ten abstentions, and one absence—the U.N. General Assembly passed Resolution 181 calling for the exit of British forces and the partition of Palestine into "[i]ndependent Arab and Jewish States." The United Nations, then a nascent organization formed out of the ashes of the Second World War, recognized that "the present situation in Palestine [was] one which [was] likely to impair the general welfare and friendly relations among nations" and that the only sensible solution was "the Plan of Partition." Based on the recommendations of the U.N. Special Committee on Palestine, Resolution 181 aimed to find a peaceful solution to the problem, but instead led to regional warfare. The Arab League, which included the states neighboring Palestine, refused to accept the United Nations' creation of a Jewish State. As a result, Palestine failed to attain the statehood it so

The Yale Journal of International Law, 36, 2: 497–511

desperately craved. This failure is indicative of international law's shortcomings; international law can offer concrete steps toward statehood, but if applied too rapidly or too harshly, can also undermine stability.

Israel's road to internationally recognized statehood has been somewhat smoother. Battling its neighbors while awaiting the formal withdrawal of British forces, the State of Israel did not formally declare its independence until May 14, 1948. Yet it was not until a year after independence that Israel gained admittance to the United Nations, on May 11, 1949. As fighting continued through the first half of the year, the U.N. Security Council refrained from referring the matter to the General Assembly for a vote. After signing a series of armistice agreements with its neighbors, Israel gained majority support in the Security Council and subsequently in the General Assembly to become an official member of the United Nations. Fast-forward sixty years, and Israel—a state born out of two General Assembly resolutions with a positive recommendation from the Security Council in between—faces the prospect of bearing witness to similar action by the United Nations on behalf of the Palestinians. This time around, the Israeli government has firmly stated its opposition to what Palestinian leaders are referring to as "Plan B."

"Plan B" represents a multifaceted approach to achieving recognition of a Palestinian State from four major international bodies: the U.N. Security Council, the U.N. General Assembly, the International Court of Justice (ICJ), and the International Criminal Court (ICC). The Palestinian Authority (PA), which declared unilateral statehood more than two decades ago, is thus not restricting its push for recognition to individual nations. Following another round of collapsed peace talks brokered by the United States, Palestinian Foreign Minister Riad Malki publicly declared his intention to seek U.N. recognition of a Palestinian state in September 2011. The U.N. route, however, is not an easy process. To obtain U.N. membership, Malki would first need to gain support from the Security Council, as the General Assembly can only vote on membership based on a positive recommendation from the Security

Council. But the foreign minister has made clear that in the face of an expected Security Council veto by the United States, the Palestinians will still push for a vote in the General Assembly, where they are more likely to garner majority support. Such action would not result in membership but function as a purely symbolic measure on the part of the General Assembly.

In addition to focusing on the United Nations, the PA is also likely to appeal to the ICJ and ICC. The emergence of a nascent but rapidly expanding international judicial system over the past three decades has contributed to the perceived legitimacy and actual authority of international courts. In addition to the long tenure of the ICJ and the approaching ten-year anniversary of the ICC, the international legal system now includes a number of specialized tribunals, as well as hybrid and regional courts, charged with meting out justice outside of and across traditional national boundaries. The ICJ and ICC thus offer additional forums for focusing international attention on the issue of Palestinian statehood and influencing Israeli policy in the process—powerful tools that are part of a greater judicial system that was unavailable to the Palestinians in the mid-twentieth century.

The PA's Plan B, therefore, would invert the standard relationship between international bodies and state sovereignty, as it seeks to use the former to advance the latter. In other words, the PA intends to use international bodies that generally take a state's sovereignty as an axiom to establish that sovereignty in the first place. Palestine has been an aspiring state for sixty years, and international bodies can and should play a more direct role in helping Palestinians achieve their decades-long goal. . . .

## INTERNATIONAL LAW AS A STEP LADDER, NOT A STUMBLING BLOCK, TO STATE SOVEREIGNTY FOR ASPIRING STATES

International law, enforced through international legal institutions and political organizations, is generally considered to infringe upon state sovereignty. By signing on to any form of international agreement, states necessarily surrender some form of control over their internal affairs.

Palestine, for example, joined the Arab League in 1974, and in the event of a war with Israel, a majority vote within the League would subject the signatory to the League's mediation and arbitration decisions. Yet such external, extra-state influence is in keeping with the writing of political science professor Eric Leonard, who describes a modern shift beyond the "Westphalian Order" to a new form of "global civil society" in which a wide range of nonstate actors are able to intervene in intrastate matters. Citing the creation of the International Criminal Tribunals for the former Yugoslavia (ICTY) and Rwanda (ICTR), Leonard writes: "These Courts were given the ability, by the U.N. Security Council, to intervene in the affairs of two sovereign states, and prosecute their citizenry at an international tribunal that is held outside of their territorial boundaries." Leonard correctly states that such a mandate violates the theoretical underpinnings of Westphalian sovereignty. But he takes a far too narrow view of the world—and of the concept of sovereignty—by failing to recognize the sovereignty-enhancing potential of such international bodies, particularly for aspiring states.

According to Stanford political scientist Stephen D. Krasner, the ever-elusive concept of "sovereignty" can be broken down into four different forms: international legal sovereignty, Westphalian sovereignty, domestic sovereignty, and interdependence sovereignty. The former two "involve issues of authority and legitimacy, but not control," whereas the latter two revolve around "control." Within the Israeli/Palestinian context, international bodies have the most potential to enhance international legal sovereignty, which Krasner defines as "practices associated with mutual recognition, usually between territorial entities that have formal juridical independence." Note that Krasner's definition speaks of "territorial entities," as opposed to states, and revolves around that entity's standing in a judicial setting. Thus, international bodies tasked with carrying out international law may infringe upon the Westphalian sovereignty of current states but actually advance the international legal sovereignty of aspiring states. . . .

## THE ROLE OF INTERNATIONAL BODIES IN SECURING STATEHOOD: GARNERING INTERNATIONAL SUPPORT UNDER "PLAN B"

### The Conventional Path—The United Nations

The conventional path to statehood runs through the United Nations, and the Security Council and General Assembly have wrestled with the complicated questions of Israeli and Palestinian statehood since those bodies' founding. In an indication of the inevitable role the United Nations will play in any future agreement, former Israeli Prime Minister Ehud Olmert envisioned Palestinian statehood arising out of resolutions in the Security Council and General Assembly. Olmert, describing the two-state agreement that was nearly reached with his Palestinian counterpart Mahmoud Abbas, stated: "My idea was that, before presenting it to our own peoples, we first would go to the U.N. Security Council and get a unanimous vote for support . . . . Then we would ask the General Assembly to support us ." . . .

. . . The "conventional path," provides a plausible scenario for advancing Palestinian sovereignty, but the PA is ultimately unwilling to rely solely on an international body that has failed to deliver over the past sixty years. Therefore, the Palestinians are adopting a broader view of international law that is not restricted to the United Nations.

### The Unconventional Path— International Courts

International courts provide an unconventional path to statehood that was largely unavailable during the twentieth century. Less mired in politics, international courts are not beholden to nearly two hundred member states and thus have the capacity to "intervene" in seemingly intractable disputes. They also have the judicial independence and nonpolitical disposition to be wary of making a decision that could reignite conflict in the region. The following two Subsections explain how the two most visible international courts— the ICJ and ICC—should help advance Palestinian statehood.

## The International Court of Justice

The International Court of Justice is not a new-comer to the "Palestine Problem"; the United Nations pulled the Court into the fray seven years ago. In a highly scrutinized advisory opinion—issued at the request of the General Assembly—the ICJ held that Israel's security wall in the Occupied Palestinian Territories violated international law. Addressing American and Israeli objections to the Court's jurisdiction, the ICJ even noted its "permanent responsibility" to Palestine due to the U.N. system that has granted Palestine the "special status of observer." Building upon such earlier involvement, the PA is not restricted to asking the General Assembly to recognize a Palestinian state within the 1967 borders. The PA could also ask the General Assembly to submit a request for an advisory opinion to the ICJ. The language could be similar to that presented following Kosovo's declaration of independence: are efforts by the Palestinian people to declare a state within the internationally recognized 1967 borders in accordance with international law? An ICJ advisory opinion would serve as another crucial, falling domino in the greater push toward statehood. . . .

. . . The controversial issue of Israeli settlements offers countless opportunities for the General Assembly to submit questions to the ICJ. In the aforementioned 2004 advisory opinion regarding Israel's security wall, the Court used the opportunity to highlight earlier U.N. resolutions condemning the illegality of Israeli settlement building in the West Bank and East Jerusalem. The ICJ also allowed Palestine to submit a written statement and participate in oral arguments in spite of the Court's statute restricting such participation to states parties or intergovernmental organizations. The Court justified the decision by "taking into account the fact that the General Assembly had granted Palestine a special status of observer and that [Palestine] was co-sponsor of the draft resolution requesting the advisory opinion." Participating in advisory opinions is a significant step toward full recognition as a state party with the power to bring a contentious dispute. Unlike blanket U.N. resolutions, such participation offers a more measured approach to the advancement of Palestinian sovereignty without the same risk of a backlash or full-scale conflict.

## The International Criminal Court

Despite the relative youth of the ICC, which began operating in 2002, it is already considering engaging the Palestinian issue. The ICC has a limited jurisdiction that is still developing. Less than a decade old, the court had been criticized for undermining peace efforts in Uganda and Sudan. Yet that did not stop the ICC from considering whether it had jurisdiction to prosecute Israel for the alleged crimes it perpetrated in the Gaza Strip during its 2009 offensive. The PA has already argued its case and is awaiting chief prosecutor Luis Moreno-Ocampo's jurisdictional decision. If the ICC allows the suit to proceed, it will implicitly be recognizing Palestinian statehood. The Rome Statute states: "The Court may exercise its functions and powers, as provided in this Statute, on the territory of any State Party and, by special agreement, on the territory of any other State." Israel is not a State Party; thus Palestine would have to be a state for the court to exercise its jurisdiction. Article 12, "Preconditions to the exercise of jurisdiction," explicitly refers to "State" parties in all three paragraphs.

If the court dismisses the case, the Palestinians could petition for an investigation of ongoing Israeli "war crimes" committed in the Occupied Territories of the West Bank. By maintaining a continual presence on the court's agenda, the Palestinians would then invite the Israeli Supreme Court to respond. Less than two weeks before the ICJ handed down its decision regarding the legality of Israel's separation barrier, the Israeli Supreme Court issued its own opinion on the subject. The Court held that the separation fence's route in several areas caused disproportionate harm to Palestinian inhabitants, and ordered the government to reexamine the fence's route in those areas. If the Israeli Supreme Court responded to an anticipated ICJ decision, it will likely do the same in advance of any potential ruling by the ICC. The mere specter of a case before the ICC could thereby advance the international legal sovereignty of Palestine through the Israeli Supreme Court's judicial recognition of Palestinian grievances.

## CONCLUSION—STRIKING A BALANCE

International organizations need to strike a balance between recognizing a people's grievances by openly acknowledging their statehood ambitions and contributing to interparty warfare between existing and aspiring states. Efforts by the United Nations and international courts thus need to be carefully calibrated, as the potential for sweeping declarations by the former drives the incremental steps of the latter.

The case of East Timor independence offers a cautionary tale to other aspiring states intent on advancing their international legal sovereignty through international bodies operating out of sync with one another. Four years after Portugal, the former colonizing power, levied a complaint against Australia on behalf of East Timor, the ICJ ultimately determined that it lacked jurisdiction due to Indonesia's refusal to grant consent to the Court to adjudicate the dispute. By a vote of fourteen to two, the Court decided not to rule on Portugal's claim that Australia had violated its duty to respect the former's role as the Administering Power and the Timorese people's right to self-determination, despite recognizing that such a right existed. The drawn-out legal dispute and muddled result likely contributed to the geopolitical instability that paved the way for increasing violence in East Timor during the final years of the twentieth century. The aspiring state ultimately needed a 1999 U.N.-sponsored referendum and three years under the U.N. Transitional Authority to achieve statehood.

Further research on the advancement of international legal sovereignty is therefore necessary to examine what conditions render an aspiring state most receptive to the involvement of international political organizations and courts—and the extent to which international bodies need to coordinate their efforts under alternative scenarios. What is already clear, however, is that international law holds tremendous power to help facilitate statehood ambitions. With regard to Palestine, the cumulative impact is already evident at the international level. On April 6, 2011, the International Monetary Fund declared that the Palestinian Authority has the capability to direct the economy of an independent state.

# After *Chabad*: Enforcement in Cultural Property Disputes

GISELLE BARCIA

## INTRODUCTION

Cultural property is a unique form of property. It may be at once personal property and real property; it is non-fungible; it carries deep historical value; it educates; it is part tangible, part transient. Cultural property is property that has acquired a special social status inextricably linked to a certain group's identity. Its value to the group is unconnected to how outsiders might assess its economic worth. If, as Hegel posited, property is an extension of personhood, then cultural property, for some, is an extension of nationhood.

Perhaps because of that unique status, specialized rules have developed, both domestically and internationally, to resolve some of the legal ambiguities inherent in "owning" cultural property. The United States, for example, has passed numerous laws protecting cultural property and has joined treaties and participated in international conventions affirming cultural property's special legal status. Those rules focus primarily on conflict *prevention* and rely upon strong protections to preempt cultural property disputes. But specialized cultural property laws, in the United States

The Yale Journal of International Law, 37, 2: 463-478

and elsewhere, pay scant attention to the issues that arise when prevention fails. Specifically, those laws neglect to provide adequate guidelines for cultural property litigation and enforcement.

That legal lacuna underlies the recent developments in the cultural property case *Agudas Chasidei Chabad v. Russian Federation,* more commonly known as *Chabad v. Russia.* This Comment addresses the problem of enforcement in international cultural property law, as manifested in *Chabad v. Russia.* The Chabad organization brought litigation against Russia in U.S. federal court to recover the Schneerson Collection, held at the Russian State Library. The Collection consists of sacred Jewish texts on Chabad Chassidic tradition amassed by successive generations of Rebbes beginning in 1772. The Collection has two components: the "Library," nationalized during the Bolshevik Revolution, and the "Archive," plundered during the Second World War. The Collection, then, is simultaneously a part of Russian heritage and integral to the historical, religious, and ethnic identity of Chabad. After a decades-long diplomatic campaign to recover ownership of the Collection, Chabad challenged the legality of those two takings in U.S. federal court in 2006. In July 2010, the Court of Appeals for the D.C. Circuit ruled in Chabad's favor.

Despite that judgment for Chabad, Russia refused to return the Collection. Russia's Foreign Ministry deemed the judgment "an unlawful decision" and stipulated that "[t]he Schneerson [Collection] has never belonged to Chabad." Most importantly, the Ministry stated, "[t]here is no agreement between Russia and the U.S. on mutual recognition and enforcement of civil judgments." Chabad, in fact, had established jurisdiction in the United States under the Foreign Sovereign Immunities Act (FSIA). Chabad's lawyers, in response to Russia's nonperformance, reportedly considered asking the court to confiscate art in the United States on loan from Russia "as a kind of legal hostage." Although U.S. law indemnifies against the loss of or damage to loaned works, the threat nevertheless spread rapidly until one of Chabad's attorneys finally intervened, stating that it would not seek to enforce the judgment through attachment of any indemnified cultural work.

Such assurance notwithstanding, Russian cultural officials warned the country's museums that artwork on loan in the United States could be confiscated. In early 2011, Russian museums canceled existing art loans to American institutions and issued a lending freeze. The National Gallery of Art in Washington, the J. Paul Getty Museum, the Los Angeles County Museum of Art, and the Metropolitan Museum of Art (the Met) were all left with costly gaps to fill for long-planned exhibitions. Despite assurances from many U.S. government officials, Russia's Minister of Culture issued a "verbal force majeure" in March 2011 to the Museum of Russian Icons in Clinton, Massachusetts. The museum had thirty-seven icons and artifacts on loan for its "Treasures From Moscow" exhibit, but Russia sent a curator immediately to supervise the objects' return. In the midst of the revocation from the Museum of Russian Icons, the Russian Special Presidential Envoy for International Cultural Cooperation, Mikhail Shvydkoy, stated that the Schneerson Collection would not be moved from Moscow, and that until the conflict with Chabad was resolved, there would be no exhibition of Russian cultural property in the United States.

A sort of cultural cold war began when American museums and institutions responded in kind to Russia's cancelations. In May 2011, the Met warned Russian museums that unless and until Russia lifted the ban, the Met would not send costumes for a planned touring exhibition. Other major lending institutions followed the Met's lead, revealing that they, too, were considering discontinuing their own loans of cultural property to Russian museums and other cultural institutions. In response to the standoff, the parties returned to court, and Chabad chastised Russia's behavior in the suit: "Russia's conduct is an affront to this Court. It's a slap in the face of international and American law, let alone morality." Yet, after another year in court trying to enforce the judgment, Chabad has temporarily abandoned litigation and has again engaged Russia in negotiations outside the courtroom.

Chabad's struggle to enforce the U.S. decree escalated from a legal dispute to a political and cultural public relations battle between the two countries. The protracted conflict had a profound impact in the art world as well as the political world. It resulted in diplomatic tension between the United States and Russia, inefficiencies in the market for art loans, and, accordingly, decreased access to cultural property. The post-judgment conflict in *Chabad* also exposes a gap in cultural property law: an absence of clear guidelines on enforcement. It suggests that the existing options for enforcement are inappropriate for international cultural property disputes. Although cultural property law perhaps rightly focuses on dispute prevention, it must also provide an enforcement mechanism for international "conflicts of culture" litigation. Until then, parties in cultural property disputes should rely on an impartial, nonbinding recommendation before litigation. . . .

As *Chabad* illustrates, cultural property is not above the law—it is subject to many of the same rules and regulations governing other kinds of property. But addressing international cultural property disputes like any other right of action under the FSIA will not motivate enforcement. Without a forceful international treaty addressing those issues, perhaps independent arbitration as a precursor to litigation could help curb some of these issues. Then, both parties in the dispute might exhaust fact-finding and argumentation and receive an impartial, preliminary judgment that could provide guidance on how to approach international litigation if necessary. Without enforcement mechanisms built into cultural property law, the struggles in *Chabad* will doubtless repeat themselves in future cultural property disputes involving foreign sovereigns.

## ENFORCEMENT IN CULTURAL PROPERTY DISPUTES

. . . *Chabad* illustrates that performance itself can sometimes carry deep cultural implications for the losing party. Those effects may be just as powerful as those on the winning side: for Chabad, repatriation of cultural property, and for Russia, the cultural heritage of the Russian Revolution and the trophies of the war campaign. Cultural property laws, both domestically and internationally, do not

offer a mechanism for judicial enforcement in such conflicts.

If specific performance decrees already challenge enforcement, then cultural property specific performance decrees present an added layer of difficulty: the defining quality of cultural property—subjective valuation based on deep cultural, ethnic, or historical identification—renders enforcement even more problematic. The losing party, for example, may subjectively value keeping the cultural property (i.e., nonperformance) over returning it (i.e., complying with the specific performance decree), despite the possible legal ramifications in that calculus.

In *Chabad*, all of those obstacles to enforcement feature in the post-litigation conflict. Yet *Chabad* features other unique challenges as well. The court established jurisdiction over Russia, but Russia has refused to recognize that determination—a move that, regardless of its legal merits, further emphasizes the U.S. court's powerlessness to enforce its decisions in Russia. Russia may value nonperformance itself for reasons other than the cultural qualities of owning the Collection. Cultural property judgments amplify the difficulties already present in specific performance decrees. The uniqueness of cultural property distinguishes cultural property disputes from other kinds of litigation that also seek specific performance.

## Resolution Methods for Cultural Property Disputes: Agreements, Arbitration, and Litigation

The method of resolution chosen for resolving a cultural property dispute—ranging from a bilateral agreement to arbitration and litigation—often influences the difficulty of subsequent enforcement.

Two parties who are willing to compromise can draft a bilateral agreement. One of the most successful bilateral agreements has been the import restriction on Italian archaeological material between the United States and Italy. In 2001, the two countries signed a bilateral agreement that created import restrictions on antiquities from Italy. The Department of Homeland Security, in cooperation with museums and cultural institutions, enforces those import restrictions. Throughout the last decade, the United States has returned more than 120 objects from public and private collections, most notably the Princeton University Art Museum and the Met. The agreement was renewed in 2006 and again in 2011; that most recent iteration created a new subcategory for specific coins. But the agreement allows some flexibility for rotation and lending between Italy and the institutions that lost antiquities. That model allows for a compromise with low risk of enforcement difficulties since both parties were willing to initiate a bargain in the first place.

When the two parties disagree and fail to reach an agreement, arbitration provides a seemingly ideal alternative for resolving their cultural property dispute. Given the tense nature of such disputes, arbitration offers a relatively informal route, with "the procedures of the decision-making process . . . shaped by the parties to fit their needs." Arbitration thus allows the parties to limit the amount of time and money they spend on resolving the dispute. Moreover, with the sensitive quality of cultural property disputes, arbitration offers the advantages of privacy and confidentiality, without upsetting any art markets. . . .

Arbitration, however, is not the only way to secure a successful resolution in a cultural property dispute. Although advocates for the use of arbitration in cultural property disputes claim that litigation is "a most costly and destructive way to deal with [art-related] disputes," litigation can, in some cases, provide an effective, enforceable specific performance remedy. With public oversight of litigation, too, nonperformance can ignite media frenzy. That factor can pressure the losing party to perform. Although the challenges of specific performance will always be present, litigation of cultural property will not pose a substantially greater challenge than litigation of any other kind of property; in most circumstances, the underlying legal system will enforce the specific performance decree. Enforcing a specific performance decree in litigation becomes more challenging, however, when the suit is international—when existing conflicts of law and jurisdiction issues are more likely to complicate the cultural property dispute.

## Challenges to Enforcement in *Chabad*

The circumstances of *Chabad* reveal enforcement difficulties beyond the typical challenges characteristic of specific performance suits. First, *Chabad* presents a disconnect between the actors in the lawsuit and the trend toward repatriation in cultural property disputes. . . .

In *Chabad*, repatriation (giving the Collection to Chabad) is *also* internationalist (spreading resources beyond the borders of the source nation). Thus, the standard model of the cultural property dispute no longer applies. Usually, a foreign party from a resource-rich nation brings a suit to recover property in a resource-poor nation, where the cultural property has been bought through the black market. In the recent trend toward repatriation, the resource-poor nation applies the new, strict cultural property ownership laws of the resource-rich nation, and repatriation usually follows. That structure does not follow in *Chabad*. Instead, the foreign party (i.e., Russia, the source nation) possesses the cultural property and is forced into litigation in the resource-poor nation, which asserts ownership of the cultural property. Russia's 1919 and 1920 nationalization statutes, moreover, act as the traditional ownership statutes, but, in this case, they pose hindrances to repatriation, unlike in most cultural property cases. That odd mismatch of traditional motivations in *Chabad* led to the application of the FSIA in a cultural property dispute.

Second, *Chabad* presents unique "conflicts of culture," a fact that underscores the difficulty of enforcement. Enforcement has proved especially challenging in this case because Russia's *fulfillment* of the specific performance decree would, in a way, suggest a betrayal of its own cultural heritage. If Russia returns the Library, it undermines the legality of takings during nationalization in the Soviet Union. If Russia returns the Archive, it undermines its legal claim to all the cultural treasures it acquired during the Soviet "retrieval" of Nazi loot, jeopardizing a significant portion of its holdings in museums and cultural institutions. Meanwhile, if Russia retains the Schneerson Collection, then Chabad remains without a central piece of its cultural heritage. That tension between two cultural heritages further complicates the cultural property aspect of *Chabad*. There is no international mechanism to resolve such "conflicts of culture" that can emerge in cultural property disputes. *Chabad* represents a cultural cold war not only because of the standoff between American and Russian museums, but also because there will be a forfeiture of cultural heritage regardless of whether Russia performs. . . .

## The Foreign Sovereign Immunities Act

The FSIA became law on October 21, 1976. The purpose of the Act was to define jurisdiction in disputes involving foreign sovereigns and, especially, "[t]o define . . . the circumstances in which foreign states are immune from suit and in which execution may not be levied on their property, and for other purposes." The statute came as a reaction against complete deference to the sovereign immunity doctrine, in which U.S. courts had had to dismiss cases against foreign states when they pled sovereign immunity. The State Department's famous "Tate Letter" in 1952 first brought the problem of absolute sovereign immunity to light: with every dismissed plea also came a citizen who was denied access to litigation. As courts over the next two decades gradually moved away from absolute sovereign immunity, they granted sovereign immunity unevenly, and the FSIA sought to eliminate those inconsistent applications. Accordingly, the FSIA represents "a substantial contribution to the harmonization of international sovereign immunity law."

Given that history, the statute itself is consciously structured to favor foreign sovereigns. It assumes that foreign states are immune from the jurisdiction of U.S. courts. The law specifies that baseline assumption directly and also suggests its benefit: the assumption "serve[s] the interests of justice and would protect the rights of both foreign states and litigants in United States courts." That restrictive principle was consistent with the prevailing view on sovereign immunity in international law as well.

The statute goes on to stipulate the situations in which a foreign sovereign is *not* immune from U.S. jurisdiction. Exceptions occur when, for example, the foreign state actor (1) has waived its immunity, explicitly or implicitly; (2) has conducted commercial activity in the United States; (3) has taken property in violation of international law, and that property is connected to the commercial activity; (4) is situated in the United States; or (5) may be potentially liable for a tortious act or omission occurring in the United States.

The exception at issue in *Chabad* is the commercial activity exception to foreign immunity from U.S. jurisdiction. The Act defines "commercial activity" as "either a regular course of commercial conduct or a particular commercial transaction or act." The standard for determining commercial conduct is not by reference to its purpose, but rather "by reference to the nature of the course of conduct or particular transaction or act."

The commercial activity prong of the FSIA has a parallel in international law. However, although the Russian Federation and the United States are parties to the Hague Convention on the Service Abroad of Judicial and Extrajudicial Documents in Civil or Commercial Matters, Russia does not currently recognize this treaty relationship with the United States. In July 2003, Russia unilaterally suspended all judicial cooperation with the United States in civil and commercial matters. . . .

## Challenges to Enforcement Under the FSIA in *Chabad*

After the D.C. Circuit made its ruling in *Chabad*, Russia's Ministry of Culture released a statement on its website denying the legality of U.S. jurisdiction. "Unfortunately," the statement read, "the U.S. judge made an unlawful decision, which cannot be enforced in Russia, as a matter of fact. There is no agreement between Russia and the U.S. on mutual recognition and enforcement of civil judgments." . . .

In April 2011, Chabad filed a motion to permit attachment and execution on the default judgment. . . .

. . . Chabad's lawyers threatened that the assets they planned to attach were Russian artworks on loan in the United States. Although Chabad's lawyers denied that they ever intended that attachment, in theory it logically follows from the attachment process in many FSIA judgment enforcement strategies: attaching cultural property in cultural property disputes is analogous to attaching financial assets held in the United States in commercial disputes. In this case, the Russian Federation has not returned the Schneerson Collection to Chabad. Chabad's lawyers, in turn, threatened to hold loaned Russian artworks hostage until Russia fulfills the judgment. That threat, of course, had a weak legal basis. The FSIA acknowledges that the ability to attach property is not absolute. If property is "entitled to enjoy the privileges, exemptions, and immunities provided by the International Organizations Immunities Act," then it is not available for attachment. Works of art, moreover, are independently protected; they are immune from seizure while on loan in the United States.

Although Chabad's threat to seize Russian artworks on loan in the United States was weak from a legal perspective, it nevertheless had very concrete repercussions. First, it prompted Russia to retain all the art it had planned to loan to U.S. museum exhibits, as well as to revoke artworks already loaned to one museum. Second, diplomatic relations between Russia and the United States have frayed. With the cultural feud simmering, the State Department initially only became involved in a diplomatic capacity, in hopes of quelling the tensions between the two nations. As tensions between the two sides failed to subside, in 2011 the United States became an interested party in the lawsuit.

... The FSIA, then, served its purpose in *Chabad* in establishing U.S. federal jurisdiction over Russia's commercial activity with archival material in the United States. The purpose of the FSIA, however, is inconsistent with the structure of cultural property litigation. Although the FSIA was useful in *Chabad* in establishing jurisdiction, the problem of enforcement stubbornly remains.

## CONCLUSION

... As *Chabad* illustrates, blindly addressing international cultural property disputes under the commercial prong of the FSIA will not ensure enforcement. Cultural property law needs an international mechanism that directly addresses enforcement. Without such an enforcement mechanism built into international law, future cultural property disputes involving foreign sovereigns would stand to benefit from internationally required, nonbinding, independent arbitration. Then, perhaps, both parties to the dispute would exhaust fact-finding and argumentation and receive an impartial, preliminary judgment or recommendation for how to draft an agreement. With that recommendation, parties would be better advised on how to proceed in their dispute. It is possible that the parties would choose to limit the costs of protracted litigation and draft an agreement, according to the recommendation. If the parties choose to proceed in international litigation, then the preliminary judgment could inform future strategy. Regardless, the *Chabad* case reveals both the strength and limitation of the legal protections of cultural property: those protections require an enforcement mechanism tailored to the unique challenges of cultural property disputes.

---

# The International Court of Justice and the Irony of System-Design

JEAN D'ASPREMON

Many international lawyers like to think of international law as a system. Such a representation makes their object of study look more noble and sophisticated. It also enhances the image of international lawyers themselves, as a systemic portrayal of international law makes those having the knowledge thereof look like masterful geeks rather than unrefined sophists. The image of system

Republished with permission of Oxford University Press. From d'Aspremon, Jean (2016). "The International Court of Justice and the Irony of System-Design." *Journal of International Dispute Settlement*, Vol. 8, Issue, 2: 366–387. Permission conveyed through Copyright Clearance Center, Inc.

simultaneously sheds a rather technical veil on doc- trinal controversies, seemingly keeping them alien to the supposedly dirty normative and political choices of the law-appliers and law-interpreters.

Systemic thinking about international law eventually opens an infinite world of possibilities for international law and international lawyers. The idea of international law as a system has thus many drivers and this is why it constitutes a very popular construction in the legal academy. The idea of international law as a system is thus not in need of drivers in contemporary international legal thought. Nor does it seem in need of an ar- chitect. It is submitted here that international lawyers commonly find in the International Court of Justice (hereafter the ICJ) and its sources-based and rules-based modes of legal reasoning the support as well as the necessary components to build (and sell) their much-cher- ished idea of an international legal system. It is the aim of this article to examine how interna- tional lawyers constantly turn to the ICJ and its rules-based and sources-based modes of legal ar- gumentation to secure the necessary means for their portrayal of international law as a system. This article will particularly shed light on the irony at the heart of system-design in interna- tional legal thought, namely that the ICJ, al- though it is elevated into the main architect of the systemic features of international law, is gener- ally more concerned with the microsystematicity of its legal arguments than with the construction of an international legal system.

## THE OBJECT OF THE CONSTRUCTION: SYSTEM OF RULES VERSUS SYSTEM OF ARGUMENTS

A fundamental preliminary observation is war- ranted as to the notion of system with which this article grapples. For the sake of the discussion of- fered here, a distinction must be made between the idea of system of rules and the idea of system of arguments. Indeed, it is argued here that the ICJ generally pays heed to the systemic virtues of its arguments rather than the systemic character of international law as a whole and, yet, it is consid- ered by international lawyers as the main architect of the latter.

When international law is approached as argu- mentative practice, it is possible to claim that in- ternational legal argumentation requires an exercise of systematization that bears upon the validity of legal argumentation. From this per- spective, any legal argument about international law is supposed to be a micro offspring of a macro argumentative pattern. Said differently, if one looks at international law as an argumentative practice, legal arguments about international law are meant to be the systemic product of pre-exist- ing argumentative structures, the derivation of the former from the latter creating systematicity in legal argumentation on the basis of which the va- lidity of legal argument will be assessed. The famous doctrine of precedent, for instance, is a manifestation of this need for a systemic deriva- tion of legal argument from more general struc- tures of argumentation. In fact, the doctrine of precedent can be understood as a system of argu- mentative constraints meant to build past-based and future determinative coherence. Another manifestation of the quest for systematicity in in- ternational legal argumentation can be found in the doctrine of interpretation which tries to build predictability in content-determination on the basis of an overarching abstract set of interpretive constraints. As is illustrated by the doctrine of precedents and the doctrine of interpretation— and the amount of scholarly discussion which they generate—systemic reasoning can be said to con- stitute an intrinsic component of legal arguments. This is a form of systematicity that is ubiquitous in international law. It is important to stress, how- ever, that the systematicity of legal arguments is not at the heart of the irony with which this article is primarily grappling.

The question is how international lawyers un- derstand international law as a system of rules ir- respective of whether the argumentative practices found in international law can simultaneously constitute a system of legal arguments. At stake here is the idea that international law could con- stitute a set of rules where relations between such rules and composite orders are systematically or- ganized, possibly creating a unity of sorts. The idea of an international legal system is thus used here in a sense that presupposes a relationship between certain standards of behavior and existential mechanisms of (in)validation which govern the formation, termination and interpretation of such standards as well as the consequences of a breach thereof.

It must be acknowledged that, although this article focuses exclusively on how international lawyers build the idea of an international legal system of rules, these two types of systematicity may not be completely alien to one another. This is so even if the idea of systemic reasoning and the idea of system of rules are grounded in a different understanding of international law. Indeed, systemic legal argumentation can itself be made dependent on there being a system of rules. It may be that in order to generate systemic legal arguments one needs to claim that international law constitutes a system of rules or that the relations between rules or the relations between orders denote some form of systematicity. This seems to be the case of legal argumentation on *jus cogens* for instance. That a system of rules enhances the systematicity of arguments is not an issue that ought to be tackled here. In other words, the actual argumentative benefits (or costs) of systemic thinking about international law are not examined here. The point that needs to be made at this preliminary stage is simply that the idea of a system of rules and the idea of systemic legal argumentation, even if they are sometimes intertwined, must be distinguished.

Be that as it may, it must be stressed that the notion of system, whether pertaining to the construction of a system of rules or a system of argument, remains an operation of the mind. Systems, and especially systems of rules on which this article focuses, are not "out there" and ready to be discovered. Rather, systems are created by those systemic descriptive frameworks deployed by the observer. This is certainly the case with respect to the idea of an international system of rules. Indeed, the idea of an international legal system is the result of international lawyers' performative descriptive tools. This means that the international legal system does not exist as such but is always constructed, even in the presence of explicit references in the case law of courts. It is the main

properties of the descriptive frameworks and normative choices relied on by international lawyers which this article seeks to outline and evaluate, and especially the place reserved therein to the case law of the ICJ.

Unsurprisingly, international lawyers' understanding of what makes international law a legal system has always varied enormously. They fundamentally disagree as to what makes international law a legal system or even what a legal system is in the first place. And such disagreements fluctuate over time. There is however one aspect of system-design which seems shared by most international lawyers, that is their finding of systemic support in the case law of the ICJ.

## THE ARCHITECT: THE INTERNATIONAL COURT OF JUSTICE

When it comes to system-design, the irony which this article seeks to reveal is that the architect of the system is not necessarily interested in system-design, other than the systemic quality of its legal argumentation. In that sense, it is submitted here that the Court is an architect *malgré elle*. In other words, international lawyers rely on the Court's pronouncement to think of international law as a system but the Court itself never consciously seeks to project a systemic image of international law. The Court itself does not make an explicit use of the idea of legal system. Whilst the idea regularly permeates separate and individual opinions of judges or is echoed in statements by presidents of the Court, explicit references to the idea of an international legal system are notably absent from its judgments and opinions. The Court occasionally touches on the idea of legal system when it offers insights on its own systemic embedment in the UN structure. It also speaks in terms of legal system in relation to some specific UN mechanisms like the Mandate or trusteeship systems, the UN itself, the Permanent Court of International Justice (PCIJ), some specific treaty frameworks or specific areas of law. It is true that it often qualifies domestic legal orders as legal systems. Yet, this falls short of any qualification of international law as a legal system. It may be that the only moment the Court did not exclude that international law constitutes a legal system is when, in its Reparation for Injuries advisory opinion it stated that "[t]he subjects of law in any legal system are not necessarily identical in their nature or in the extent of their rights, and their nature depends upon the needs of the community" or when, in its Namibia opinion, it contended that "an international instrument has to be interpreted and applied within the framework of the entire legal system prevailing at the time of the interpretation." Again, this fell short of any direct and explicit acknowledgment that international law constitutes a legal system.

The same holds for some requests for advisory opinion, like the one pertaining to the Legality of the Threat or Use of Nuclear Weapons. A few—sometimes courageous—positions on the micro-systematicity were developed on these occasions but those judgments and opinions fell short of any statement on the systemic character of international law as a whole. What is more, the past resistance of the Court to acknowledge some of the legal effects of hierarchy of norms in international law (*jus cogens*)—which is often seen as the expression of some form of systematicity—could also be read as the manifestation of the Court's reluctance to engage in system-design.

It would be of no avail to speculate on the reasons of such a silence of the Court on the systemic character of international law. Probably the ICJ did not find any argumentative advantage or any source of semantic authority that would have justified that it engages in painstaking and risky discussions on the quality of international law as a legal system. After all, the ICJ, besides being an advisory organ for UN-affiliated bodies, is nothing more than a—supposedly inexpensive—bureaucratic machine providing services for the resolution of inter-states disputes in the form of authoritative decisions. It does not seem surprising that the delivery of such services does not require it to venture into convoluted discussions on the systemic nature of international law.

Claiming that ICJ is not interested in system design does not mean that the ICJ excludes any manufacturing role from its functions. Certainly, the Court sees itself as indispensable to the functioning and improvement of international law. It feels that it is not only the central magistrate of the UN dispute settlement mechanism but also the central plumber of the international legal order. Yet, the ICJ does not go as far as claiming some monopoly on the design of the systemic features of international law. In the same vein, it should be stressed that the indifference of the ICJ towards system-design does not mean the ICJ has never contributed to the design of the international legal system. The dialectical relation between the International Law Commission and the ICJ in relation to the making of secondary rules of international law is well-known and it is obvious that some specific ICJ pronouncements have been relied on to cast some specific mechanism of international law. Yet, the contribution of the ICJ to system-design has usually been piecemeal and sporadic and has never been the result of a holistic approach.

Although the work of regional courts is not the main focus of this article, it is worth noting that the attitude of the World Court in relation to the idea of legal system—and its general indifference thereto—contrasts with the use by regional courts of this idea. Indeed, regional courts have .... constantly tailored the idea of an international legal system to their needs, which is in a way that preserves their powers or give them new powers.

For instance, their recognition of an international legal system has fallen short of bringing about any hierarchy between orders or courts. They have also recognized their membership to an overarching system where the ICJ occupies a key role and whose interpretation must be reckoned with but in which they constitute "autonomous" judicial institution(s). This membership to international legal system has similarly meant the application of some of the secondary rules of that international legal system adjusted to preserve their autonomy. In particular, most of them have applied international instruments like the Vienna Convention on the Law of Treaties regarding rules on interpretation or rules on reservations but they have done so in picking and choosing those provisions of international law that would not frustrate their own powers and the application of the regime of which they are the guardian. Their invocation of international law has also been geared towards the reinforcement of the obligation to comply with the regional regime. The foregoing means that the resort to the idea of international legal system by regional courts has usually been very opportunistic. Contrary to the ICJ, they make use of the idea of an international legal system and follow argumentative moves that support the idea of international legal system. Yet, they do so as long as the idea of international legal system supports or legitimizes their own powers or the regime they monitor. When the implications of the idea of system come at the expense of their powers, they do not hesitate to tailor it. This is not without paradox, for regional courts use the idea of an international legal system to shield their own domain and their autonomy. Be that as it may, such a narrative of convenience is, as such, neither surprising nor regrettable. Courts resort to patterns of argumentative structures that are conducive to the persuasiveness of their decisions. What is noteworthy is that regional courts, contrary to the ICJ, have found that the idea of an international legal system carries some benefits, can preserve their autonomy, and can improve the persuasiveness of their decisions.

It is common among international lawyers to turn to the ICJ for support for their systemic thinking about international law. Said differently, it is very common among international lawyers to resort to the practice of the Court to "unearth" an international legal system or validate their projection of an international legal system.

This can be illustrated by the codification of the law of State responsibility, or the work of the International Law Commission on the formation and identification of customary law. The literature pertaining to the sources in general, responsibility in general, discussions on hierarchy of norms (*jus cogens*), the literature on interpretation, or the literature on universal legal standing (*erga omnes*) similarly bespeak the same reliance on the Court's case law. The systemic reading which international lawyers make of the Court's case law sometimes pertains, not to specific (in)validating mechanisms—i.e. secondary rules—but rather to

meta-structures. For instance, they find systemic materials in the case law of the ICJ which vindicate communitarian views about international law or, conversely, find communitarian materials that support a systemic vision of international law. Be that as it may, whether for specific secondary rules or meta-structures, the architect always seems to include the ICJ. Whilst this may not be surprising for questions which have a direct procedural bearing—as questions of legal standing in relation to *erga omnes* obligations—such an overall reliance by international lawyers on the Court for system-design is remarkable, especially since it seems to be witnessed across the board.

Interestingly this reliance on the case law of the ICJ to support the idea of an international legal system has not always been so entrenched in the argumentative practices of international lawyers. It may be useful to recall that, on the eve of the major codification enterprises of the second half of the 20th centuries, international lawyers would not always feel the need to turn to the PCIJ to find (support for) the development of the systemic rules of international law. This is fabulously illustrated by the candidness of Roberto Ago in his famous course on the international delict at the Hague Academy in 1938—which paved the way for the subsequent codification of the subject after the Second World War—and where he would bluntly recognize that system-design has much to do with scholarly choices. The same holds for the Committee of Jurists which prepared the Statute of the Permanent Court of International Justice which did not deem it necessary to rely on the practice of earlier—albeit less numerous—courts or arbitral tribunals during its—limited—discussion on sources. In that sense, the elevation of the ICJ in the architect of the international legal system seems to be a late 20th century and early 21st century attitude. Said differently, it has not always been the case that international lawyers—consciously or unconsciously—empower the Court with wide-ranging design powers by virtue of which international law is made an international legal system.

# International Political Economy: From the North-South Divide to Globalization

# The Old IPE and the New

ROBERT O. KEOHANE

## THE OLD IPE

When Susan Strange, Joseph Nye, Peter Katzenstein, Stephen Krasner, John Ruggie, and I started to explore IPE—Susan in the 1960s, Joe and Steve and I around 1970, Peter and John a few years later—there was no field. Very little research was being done. Most economists were ignoring politics, and international relations specialists saw political economy as "low politics," minor, boring, and incomprehensible. So our task—and opportunity—was first one of identification, then of broad interpretation. In his RIPE paper and his book, Professor Cohen provides an account that closely corresponds to my memory of these early days. Identification of IPE as a proper subject of study was inaugurated in the United Kingdom by Strange's 1970 article in *International Affairs*, "International Economics and International Relations: A Case of Mutual Neglect", followed by her book, *Sterling and British Policy*, which traced connections between politics and economically historically. The key markers in the United States were three special issues of *International Organization* during the 1970s—on transnational relations, politics and economics, and foreign economic policies of advanced industrialized states.

It would be misleading to give the impression that these new formulations were entirely original. Indeed, we responded in part to what Richard Cooper, in *The Economics of Interdependence*, defined as the central problem of international economic cooperation: how to maintain openness while enabling states to retain sufficient autonomy to pursue legitimate objectives. In 1970 Charles Kindleberger edited a volume on the multinational corporation that contained an essay by Kenneth Waltz on the "myth" of interdependence that presented an important challenge for Nye and me, and in 1973 Kindleberger published *The World in Depression*, which made a great impact on all of us. In 1971 Raymond Vernon, who was at the Center for International Affairs at Harvard, published his book on multinational corporations, *Sovereignty at Bay*, as the culmination of years of work on this subject. Finally, Nye's work, and mine, were influenced by the contributions of Ernst B. Haas, particularly to the study of regional integration.

Nye and I contrasted what we called the "politics of interdependence" with then-dominant statist and security-oriented conceptions of international relations. We sketched out broad concepts—such as transnational relations, transgovernmental relations, and connections between asymmetrical interdependence and power. We characterized what Realists viewed as "reality" in world politics as an ideal type, and contrasted it with another ideal type, that of "complex interdependence." In situations of complex interdependence, we argued, there were multiple actors (rather than just states), multiple issues that were not necessarily hierarchically ordered, and force and the threat of force were not valuable tools of policy. In our view, neither the Realist model nor complex interdependence fully described world politics; but regional politics, and issue areas, varied in how close they were to one pole or the other.

Nye and I also elaborated a concept first brought to the IPE literature in another special issue of *International Organization* by Ruggie: that of *international regimes*. In *Power and Interdependence* we sought to describe and explain regime change, not merely theoretically but also with systematic empirical work on the politics of money and oceans, and on US relations with Australia and Canada. In his edited volume on foreign economic policies, which also appeared in 1977, Katzenstein demonstrated that our international relations analysis of what was now called "international political

"The Old IPE and the New", Robert Keohane, Review of International Political Economy, 2009, Taylor & Francis Ltd, repritned by permission of publisher

economy," or IPE, was too one-dimensional. Genuinely comparative analysis was required, since there was no single template of state responses to interdependence. Peter Gourevitch brilliantly pursued a related theme in his notable 1978 article on "the second image reversed", and Ruggie followed several years later with his creative concept of "embedded liberalism". During the 1970s this cluster of challenges to Realism was itself challenged most cogently by Robert Gilpin, most notably in his 1975 book on *U.S. Power and the Multinational Corporation*; and by Krasner, in a major article on "State Power and the Structure of International Trade".

We were young, exuberant, and friends with one another, neither expecting nor wanting general agreement. In her brilliant paper in this symposium, Kathleen McNamara captures well the richness—I would say, "joyous contestation"—of these debates. To us, the under-explored area of political economy offered irresistible territory for intellectual adventure and, one might say, conquest. To paraphrase the words of a famous Tammany Hall boss, "we seen our chance and we 'tuk' it." But in the context of contemporary political science, our empiricism was loose and sketchy, and we did not engage in sophisticated causal inference to support our grand theories. . . .

## FIVE BIG QUESTIONS ABOUT CHANGE

Suppose we asked, as Nye, Strange and I did in 1970: what are the big changes going on in the world political economy? Surely one could make a longer list, including such issues as outsourcing and migration, but I will mention five major changes:

**1.** *For the first time in human history, genuine economic development is taking place for much of the world's population.* East Asia (excluding China) led the way with four decades of high sustained growth, and growth has for over two decades been rapid in India and extremely fast in China. In more recent years, there have been indications that sustained rates of high growth may be emerging in parts of Latin America, although the situation in most of sub-Saharan Africa remains bleak. Our theories of IPE were constructed in a very different world: of "developed" and "developing" countries—the latter

identified mostly by the fact that they were *not* developing. Indeed, for this reason perhaps, Gourevitch, Katzenstein, Nye, and I paid most of our attention to developed countries. Dependency theory, of course, emphasized—and it now seems, exaggerated—the structural differences between countries in the center and in the periphery. It is perhaps less obvious that the assumption of political as well as economic hierarchy between rich and poor is also deeply embedded in the theories of asymmetrical interdependence that Nye and I, and others developed, and in realist or quasi-realist theories of American hegemony and western dominance such as those of Krasner. I expect that our implicit hegemonic assumptions will continue to hamper our vision until scholars from Brazil, India and China, and other emerging great powers, become more prominent in the field.

**2.** *China in particular has become a huge player in international trade and finance,* as the manufacturing center of the world for a huge number of products in ordinary life. China was the largest economic power for centuries, before the industrial revolution, although in those times economic interdependence was much lower than now. China's re-entry into the world political economy since 1978 has been a huge shock to the system—it would seem to be at least comparable to the opening up of the North Atlantic grain trade in the 1870s so memorably studied by Gourevitch. An appropriate metaphor is that of an elephant jumping into a small pond. The effects are already evident in trade, and will increasingly be apparent on financial issues, since China's foreign reserves of well over $1 trillion constitute a political as well as an economic resource. In the West, scholars have been slow to take China sufficiently into account, although there are signs of change. Without China, we would be staging *Hamlet* without the Prince.

**3.** *Volatility in financial and energy markets has been extreme.* Kindleberger long ago emphasized the tendency of capitalism toward "manias, panics, and crashes," and his insight was borne out again in 2008. At the same time, oil price shifts have again been driving shifts in power and asymmetrical interdependence. The sharp rise in oil prices up until mid-2008 contributed to policy changes such as the resistance of oil producers, from Venezuela to Russia and even to Saudi Arabia, to American demands; Brazil's leadership in ethanol production and technologies to use ethanol in automobiles; and China's drive for energy resources in Africa, which is undercutting "good governance" initiatives, and the influence of the international organizations like the World Bank, on that continent. In the 1970s, rising oil prices, and greater leverage for producers, had major effects on world politics, reflected in the creation and persistence of OPEC and the Arab oil embargo of 1973, which led to the creation of the International Energy Agency, associated with the OECD. But OPEC turned out to be ineffective and prices declined sharply in the mid-1980s and stayed well below late 1970s prices, in real terms, throughout the twentieth century. What will happen to them now is a great unknown. There is some discussion now of how oil affects democracy, civil conflict, and aggressive foreign policy, but the demand for analysis of the causes and consequences of oil price fluctuations surely exceeds by far the supply of serious scholarship on the subject.

4. *Truly global actors are now important in world politics.* Global corporations and NGOs such as Human Rights Watch, Oxfam, or Greenpeace are exemplary. As John Ruggie comments, "This isn't 'IPE' any more, and it certainly isn't 'CPE.' Global actors demand global rules." There is some work on this aspect of globalization, but we still have relatively little systematic knowledge about the implications of global civil society for political outcomes. Law faculties have paid attention: one of the most important research programs on this topic focuses on the new field of "global administrative law". Anne-Marie Slaughter has written about a "new world order," in which the state is disaggregated and networks of governmental subunits, NGOs, private corporations, and a variety of regulatory and coordinating bodies become prominent participants in rule-making. John Ruggie has played an important policy role in this emerging global society and has also commented on the politics that ensues. It would be good if some IPE scholars could turn their attention, and

their analytical tools, toward what might be called "GPE," or "Global Political Economy."

5. *Electronic technologies have become the basis for global communications.* We are aware of how such technologies have affected commerce, finance, and investment, but what about their effects on political power? To exercise influence, sets of individuals with common values or interests need to be able to communicate with one another, to form groups, and to act collectively. Indeed, Hannah Arendt once defined power as "the ability to act in common." Historically, such communication has been very difficult except through formal organizations, including the state, and all but impossible across state boundaries except with the aid of states. This formerly constant reality has been changing with incredible speed during the last two decades, but we have hardly begun to understand the implications of this momentous fact. One implication may be that collective action on a global scale, for good or ill, is easier than it has ever been before. In this sense, there is *more power* in the system than in the past. Since variations in power are crucial to world politics, the changes in electronic technology have to be important, but I have not seen recent work addressing these issues of communication and power.

In discussing these big questions, innovative scholars may discover rigorous and quantitative methods that can illuminate them. If so, more power to them. But we cannot afford to wait to address these questions for such methods, if they are not available now. As Finnemore and Farrell, and McNamara argue, more attention needs to be paid in graduate programs to rigorous qualitative methods, which have undergone a renaissance during the last 15 years; and as Katzenstein argues, more problem-oriented research is needed to maintain a focus on really important questions. I would urge scholars now active in the IPE field to spend more of their time pondering the big questions about change, and asking not only what the best existing research tells us about them, but what interpretive leaps may be necessary to point the way to more profound and relevant scholarship.

I offer this admonition particularly to those scholars who have attained reputations for science and can therefore afford to let the wings of imagination spread.

*Study major changes in world politics using a diverse portfolio of methods*: this is the message of my brief essay. The best insights of the British school and contemporary American IPE are both valuable—so are contributions from historical and economic sociology, and from the "ideational turn" in much international relations scholarship. Our standards should be high; but a monoculture, as McNamara implies, depletes the soil from which it grows.

Normatively, I value the critical spirit of British IPE, and of Susan Strange and Robert Cox, because, like them, I am unwilling to accept the contemporary political-economic system as either natural or good. Injustice and inequality are endemic to IPE. But I also value the discipline of social science, as reflected in American IPE, which seeks to separate value judgments from positive analysis. I believe that in the long run, social scientists can have a more positive impact on the human condition through rigorous, persuasive analysis than through subjective criticism. But for us to help improve the human condition, we need to reflect on the big questions.

# The General Theory of Employment, Interest and Money

JOHN MAYNARD KEYNES

## I

The outstanding faults of the economic society in which we live are its failure to provide for full employment and its arbitrary and inequitable distribution of wealth and incomes. The bearing of the foregoing theory on the first of these is obvious. But there are also two important respects in which it is relevant to the second.

Since the end of the nineteenth century significant progress towards the removal of very great disparities of wealth and income has been achieved through the instrument of direct taxation—income tax and surtax and death duties—especially in Great Britain. Many people would wish to see this process carried much further, but they are deterred by two considerations; partly by the fear of making skilful evasions too much worth while and also of diminishing unduly the motive towards risk-taking, but mainly, I think, by the belief that the growth of capital depends upon the strength of the motive towards individual saving and that for a large proportion of this growth we are dependent on the savings of the rich out of their superfluity. Our argument does not affect the first of these considerations. But it may considerably modify our attitude towards the second. For we have seen that, up to the point where full employment prevails, the growth of capital depends not at all on a low propensity to consume but is, on the contrary, held back by it; and only in conditions of full employment is a low propensity to consume conducive to the growth of capital. Moreover, experience suggests that in existing conditions saving by institutions and through sinking funds is more than adequate, and that measures for the redistribution of incomes in a way likely to raise the propensity to consume may prove positively favourable to the growth of capital.

The existing confusion of the public mind on the matter is well illustrated by the very common belief

Keynes, John Maynard (1965). Concluding Notes on the Social Philosophy Towards which the General Theory Might Lead. In *The General Theory of Employment, Interest and Money*. New York: Harcourt, Brace & World.

that the death duties are responsible for a reduction in the capital wealth of the country. Assuming that the State applies the proceeds of these duties to its ordinary outgoings so that taxes on incomes and consumption are correspondingly reduced or avoided, it is, of course, true that a fiscal policy of heavy death duties has the effect of increasing the community's propensity to consume. But inasmuch as an increase in the habitual propensity to consume will in general (i.e. except in conditions of full employment) serve to increase at the same time the inducement to invest, the inference commonly drawn is the exact opposite of the truth.

Thus our argument leads towards the conclusion that in contemporary conditions the growth of wealth, so far from being dependent on the abstinence of the rich, as is commonly supposed, is more likely to be impeded by it. One of the chief social justifications of great inequality of wealth is, therefore, removed. I am not saying that there are no other reasons, unaffected by our theory, capable of justifying some measure of inequality in some circumstances. But it does dispose of the most important of the reasons why hitherto we have thought it prudent to move carefully. This particularly affects our attitude towards death duties: for there are certain justifications for inequality of incomes which do not apply equally to inequality of inheritances.

For my own part, I believe that there is social and psychological justification for significant inequalities of incomes and wealth, but not for such large disparities as exist today. There are valuable human activities which require the motive of money-making and the environment of private wealth-ownership for their full fruition. Moreover, dangerous human proclivities can be canalised into comparatively harmless channels by the existence of opportunities for money-making and private wealth, which, if they cannot be satisfied in this way, may find their outlet in cruelty, the reckless pursuit of personal power and authority, and other forms of self-aggrandisement. It is better that a man should tyrannise over his bank balance than over his fellow-citizens; and whilst the former is sometimes denounced as being but a means to the latter, sometimes at least it is an alternative. But it is not necessary for the stimulation of these activities and the satisfaction of these proclivities that the game should be played for such high stakes as at present. Much lower stakes will serve the purpose equally well, as soon as the players are accustomed to them. The task of transmuting human nature must not be confused with the task of managing it. Though in the ideal commonwealth men may have been taught or inspired or bred to take no interest in the stakes, it may still be wise and prudent statesmanship to allow the game to be played, subject to rules and limitations, so long as the average man, or even a significant section of the community, is in fact strongly addicted to the money-making passion.

## II

There is, however, a second, much more fundamental inference from our argument which has a bearing on the future of inequalities of wealth; namely, our theory of the rate of interest. The justification for a moderately high rate of interest has been found hitherto in the necessity of providing a sufficient inducement to save. But we have shown that the extent of effective saving is necessarily determined by the scale of investment and that the scale of investment is promoted by a low rate of interest, provided that we do not attempt to stimulate it in this way beyond the point which corresponds to full employment. Thus it is to our best advantage to reduce the rate of interest to that point relative to the schedule of the marginal efficiency of capital at which there is full employment.

There can be no doubt that this criterion will lead to a much lower rate of interest than has ruled hitherto; and, so far as one can guess at the schedules of the marginal efficiency of capital corresponding to increasing amounts of capital, the rate of interest is likely to fall steadily, if it should be practicable to maintain conditions of more or less continuous full employment unless, indeed, there is an excessive change in the aggregate propensity to consume (including the State).

I feel sure that the demand for capital is strictly limited in the sense that it would not be difficult to increase the stock of capital up to a point where its marginal efficiency had fallen to a very low figure. This would not mean that the use of capital instruments would cost almost nothing, but only that the return from them would have to cover little more than their exhaustion by wastage and obsolescence together with some margin to cover risk and the exercise of skill and judgment. In short, the aggregate return from durable goods in the course of their life would, as in the case of short-lived goods, just cover their labour costs of production *plus* an allowance for risk and the costs of skill and supervision.

Now, though this state of affairs would be quite compatible with some measure of individualism, yet it would mean the euthanasia of the rentier, and, consequently, the euthanasia of the cumulative oppressive power of the capitalist to exploit the scarcity-value of capital. Interest today rewards no genuine sacrifice, any more than does the rent of land. The owner of capital can obtain interest because capital is scarce, just as the owner of land can obtain rent because land is scarce. But whilst there may be intrinsic reasons for the scarcity of land, there are no intrinsic reasons for the scarcity of capital. An intrinsic reason for such scarcity, in the sense of a genuine sacrifice which could only be called forth by the offer of a reward in the shape of interest, would not exist, in the long run, except in the event of the individual propensity to consume proving to be of such a character that net saving in conditions of full employment comes to an end before capital has become sufficiently abundant. But even so, it will still be possible for communal saving through the agency of the State to be maintained at a level which will allow the growth of capital up to the point where it ceases to be scarce.

I see, therefore, the rentier aspect of capitalism as a transitional phase which will disappear when it has done its work. And with the disappearance of its rentier aspect much else in it besides will suffer a sea-change. It will be, moreover, a great advantage of the order of events which I am advocating, that the euthanasia of the rentier, of the functionless investor, will be nothing sudden, merely a gradual but prolonged continuance of what we have seen recently in Great Britain, and will need no revolution.

Thus we might aim in practice (there being nothing in this which is unattainable) at an increase

in the volume of capital until it ceases to be scarce, so that the functionless investor will no longer receive a bonus; and at a scheme of direct taxation which allows the intelligence and determination and executive skill of the financier, the entrepreneur *et hoc genus omne* (who are certainly so fond of their craft that their labour could be obtained much cheaper than at present), to be harnessed to the service of the community on reasonable terms of reward.

At the same time we must recognise that only experience can show how far the common will, embodied in the policy of the State, ought to be directed to increasing and supplementing the inducement to invest; and how far it is safe to stimulate the average propensity to consume, without foregoing our aim of depriving capital of its scarcity-value within one or two generations. It may turn out that the propensity to consume will be so easily strengthened by the effects of a falling rate of interest, that full employment can be reached with a rate of accumulation little greater than at present. In this event a scheme for the higher taxation of large incomes and inheritances might be open to the objection that it would lead to full employment with a rate of accumulation which was reduced considerably below the current level. I must not be supposed to deny the possibility, or even the probability, of this outcome. For in such matters it is rash to predict how the average man will react to a changed environment. If, however, it should prove easy to secure an approximation to full employment with a rate of accumulation not much greater than at present, an outstanding problem will at least have been solved. And it would remain for separate decision on what scale and by what means it is right and reasonable to call on the living generation to restrict their consumption, so as to establish in course of time, a state of full investment for their successors.

## III

In some other respects the foregoing theory is moderately conservative in its implications. For whilst it indicates the vital importance of establishing certain central controls in matters which are now left in the main to individual initiative, there are wide fields of activity which are unaffected. The State will have to exercise a guiding influence on the propensity to consume partly through its scheme of taxation, partly by fixing the rate of interest, and partly, perhaps, in other ways. Furthermore, it seems unlikely that the influence of banking policy on the rate of interest will be sufficient by itself to determine an optimum rate of investment. I conceive, therefore, that a somewhat comprehensive socialisation of investment will prove the only means of securing an approximation to full employment; though this need not exclude all manner of compromises and of devices by which public authority will co-operate with private initiative. But beyond this no obvious case is made out for a system of State Socialism which would embrace most of the economic life of the community. It is not the ownership of the instruments of production which it is important for the State to assume. If the State is able to determine the aggregate amount of resources devoted to augmenting the instruments and the basic rate of reward to those who own them, it will have accomplished all that is necessary. Moreover, the necessary measures of socialisation can be introduced gradually and without a break in the general traditions of society.

Our criticism of the accepted classical theory of economics has consisted not so much in finding logical flaws in its analysis as in pointing out that its tacit assumptions are seldom or never satisfied, with the result that it cannot solve the economic problems of the actual world. But if our central controls succeed in establishing an aggregate volume of output corresponding to full employment as nearly as is practicable, the classical theory comes into its own again from this point onwards. If we suppose the volume of output to be given, i.e. to be determined by forces outside the classical scheme of thought, then there is no objection to be raised against the classical analysis of the manner in which private self-interest will determine what in particular is produced, in what proportions the factors of production will be combined to produce it, and how the value of the final product will be distributed between them. Again, if we have dealt otherwise with the problem of thrift, there is no

objection to be raised against the modern classical theory as to the degree of consilience between private and public advantage in conditions of perfect and imperfect competition respectively. Thus, apart from the necessity of central controls to bring about an adjustment between the propensity to consume and the inducement to invest, there is no more reason to socialise economic life than there was before.

To put the point concretely, I see no reason to suppose that the existing system seriously misemploys the factors of production which are in use. There are, of course, errors of foresight; but these would not be avoided by centralising decisions. When 9,000,000 men are employed out of 10,000,000 willing and able to work, there is no evidence that the labour of these 9,000,000 men is misdirected. The complaint against the present system is not that these 9,000,000 men ought to be employed on different tasks, but that tasks should be available for the remaining 1,000,000 men. It is in determining the volume, not the direction, of actual employment that the existing system has broken down.

Thus I agree with Gesell that the result of filling in the gaps in the classical theory is not to dispose of the "Manchester System," but to indicate the nature of the environment which the free play of economic forces requires if it is to realise the full potentialities of production. The central controls necessary to ensure full employment will, of course, involve a large extension of the traditional functions of government. Furthermore, the modern classical theory has itself called attention to various conditions in which the free play of economic forces may need to be curbed or guided. But there will still remain a wide field for the exercise of private initiative and responsibility. Within this field the traditional advantages of individualism will still hold good.

Let us stop for a moment to remind ourselves what these advantages are. They are partly advantages of efficiency—the advantages of decentralisation and of the play of self-interest. The advantage to efficiency of the decentralisation of decisions and of individual responsibility is even greater, perhaps, than the nineteenth century supposed;

and the reaction against the appeal to self-interest may have gone too far. But, above all, individualism, if it can be purged of its defects and its abuses, is the best safeguard of personal liberty in the sense that, compared with any other system, it greatly widens the field for the exercise of personal choice. It is also the best safeguard of the variety of life, which emerges precisely from this extended field of personal choice, and the loss of which is the greatest of all the losses of the homogeneous or totalitarian state. For this variety preserves the traditions which embody the most secure and successful choices of former generations; it colours the present with the diversification of its fancy; and, being the handmaid of experiment as well as of tradition and of fancy, it is the most powerful instrument to better the future.

Whilst, therefore, the enlargement of the functions of government, involved in the task of adjusting to one another the propensity to consume and the inducement to invest, would seem to a nineteenth-century publicist or to a contemporary American financier to be a terrific encroachment on individualism. I defend it, on the contrary, both as the only practicable means of avoiding the destruction of existing economic forms in their entirety and as the condition of the successful functioning of individual initiative.

For if effective demand is deficient, not only is the public scandal of wasted resources intolerable, but the individual enterpriser who seeks to bring these resources into action is operating with the odds loaded against him. The game of hazard which he plays is furnished with many zeros, so that the players *as a whole* will lose if they have the energy and hope to deal all the cards. Hitherto the increment of the world's wealth has fallen short of the aggregate of positive individual savings; and the difference has been made up by the losses of those whose courage and initiative have not been supplemented by exceptional skill or unusual good fortune. But if effective demand is adequate, average skill and average good fortune will be enough.

The authoritarian state systems of today seem to solve the problem of unemployment at the expense of efficiency and of freedom. It is certain that the world will not much longer tolerate the

unemployment which, apart from brief intervals of excitement, is associated and in my opinion, inevitably associated with present-day capitalistic individualism. But it may be possible by a right analysis of the problem to cure the disease whilst preserving efficiency and freedom.

## IV

I have mentioned in passing that the new system might be more favourable to peace than the old has been. It is worth while to repeat and emphasise that aspect.

War has several causes. Dictators and others such, to whom war offers, in expectation at least, a pleasurable excitement, find it easy to work on the natural bellicosity of their peoples. But, over and above this, facilitating their task of fanning the popular flame, are the economic causes of war, namely, the pressure of population and the competitive struggle for markets. It is the second factor, which probably played a predominant part in the nineteenth century, and might again, that is germane to this discussion.

I have pointed out in the preceding chapter that, under the system of domestic laissez-faire and an international gold standard such as was orthodox in the latter half of the nineteenth century, there was no means open to a government whereby to mitigate economic distress at home except through the competitive struggle for markets. For all measures helpful to a state of chronic or intermittent under-employment were ruled out, except measures to improve the balance of trade on income account.

Thus, whilst economists were accustomed to applaud the prevailing international system as furnishing the fruits of the international division of labour and harmonising at the same time the interests of different nations, there lay concealed a less benign influence; and those statesmen were moved by common sense and a correct apprehension of the true course of events, who believed that if a rich, old country were to neglect the struggle for markets its prosperity would droop and fail. But if nations can learn to provide themselves with full employment by their domestic policy (and, we must add, if they can also attain equilibrium in the trend of their population), there need be no important economic forces calculated to set the interest of one country against that of its neighbours. There would still be room for the international division of labour and for international lending in appropriate conditions. But there would no longer be a pressing motive why one country need force its wares on another or repulse the offerings of its neighbour, not because this was necessary to enable it to pay for what it wished to purchase, but with the express object of upsetting the equilibrium of payments so as to develop a balance of trade in its own favour. International trade would cease to be what it is, namely, a desperate expedient to maintain employment at home by forcing sales on foreign markets and restricting purchases, which, if successful, will merely shift the problem of unemployment to the neighbour which is worsted in the struggle, but a willing and unimpeded exchange of goods and services in conditions of mutual advantage.

## V

Is the fulfilment of these ideas a visionary hope? Have they insufficient roots in the motives which govern the evolution of political society? Are the interests which they will thwart stronger and more obvious than those which they will serve?

I do not attempt an answer in this place. It would need a volume of a different character from this one to indicate even in outline the practical measures in which they might be gradually clothed. But if the ideas are correct—an hypothesis on which the author himself must necessarily base what he writes—it would be a mistake, I predict, to dispute their potency over a period of time. At the present moment people are unusually expectant of a more fundamental diagnosis; more particularly ready to receive it; eager to try it out, if it should be even plausible. But apart from this contemporary mood, the ideas of economists and political philosophers, both when they are right and when they are wrong, are more powerful than is commonly understood. Indeed the world is ruled by little else. Practical men, who believe themselves to be quite exempt from any intellectual influences, are usually the slaves of some defunct economist. Madmen in authority, who hear voices in the air, are distilling their frenzy from some academic scribbler of a few years back. I am sure that the power of vested interests is vastly exaggerated compared with the gradual encroachment of ideas. Not, indeed, immediately, but after a certain interval; for in the field of economic and political philosophy there are not many who are influenced by new theories after they are twenty-five or thirty years of age, so that the ideas which civil servants and politicians and even agitators apply to current events are not likely to be the newest. But, soon or late, it is ideas, not vested interests, which are dangerous for good or evil.

# The Great Transformation: The Political and Economic Origins of Our Time (1944)

KARL POLANYI

Nineteenth-century civilization was not destroyed by the external or internal attack of barbarians; its vitality was not sapped by the devastations of World War I nor by the revolt of a socialist proletariat or a fascist lower middle class. Its failure was not the outcome of some alleged laws of economics such as that of the falling rate of profit or of underconsumption or overproduction. It disintegrated as the result of an entirely different set of causes: the measures which society adopted in order not to be, in its turn, annihilated by the action of the self-regulating market. Apart from exceptional circumstances such as existed in North America in the age of the open frontier, the conflict between the market and the elementary requirements of an organized social life provided the century with its dynamics and produced the typical strains and stresses which ultimately destroyed that society. External wars merely hastened its destruction.

After a century of blind "improvement" man is restoring his "habitation." If industrialism is not to extinguish the race, it must be subordinated to the requirements of man's nature. The true criticism of market society is not that it was based on economics—in a sense, every and any society must be based on it—but that its economy was based on self-interest. Such an organization of economic life is entirely unnatural, in the strictly empirical sense oi exceptional. Nineteenth-century thinkers assumed that in his economic activity man strove for profit, that his materialistic propensities would induce him to choose the lesser instead of the greater effort and to expect payment for his labor; in short, that in his economic activity he would tend to abide by what they described as economic rationality, and that all contrary behavior was the result of outside interference. It followed that markets were natural institutions, that they would spontaneously arise if only men were let alone. Thus, nothing could be more normal than an economic system consisting of markets and under the sole control of market prices, and a human society based on such markets appeared, therefore, as the goal of all progress. Whatever the desirability or undesirability of such a society on moral grounds, its practicability—this was axiomatic—was grounded in the immutable characteristics of the race.

Actually, as we now know, the behavior of man both in his primitive state and right through the course of history has been almost the opposite from that implied in this view. Frank H. Knight's "no specifically human motive is economic" applies not only to social life in general, but even to economic life itself. The tendency to barter, on which Adam Smith so confidently relied for his picture of primitive man, is not a common tendency of the human being in his economic activities, but a most infrequent one. Not only does the evidence of modern anthropology give the lie to these rationalistic constructs, but the history of trade and markets also has been completely different from that assumed in the harmonistic teachings of nineteenth century sociologists. Economic

history reveals that the emergence of national markets was in no way the result of the gradual and spontaneous emancipation of the economic sphere from governmental control. On the contrary, the market has been the outcome of a conscious and often violent intervention on the part of government which imposed the market organization on society for noneconomic ends. And the self-regulating market of the nineteenth century turns out on closer inspection to be radically different from even its immediate predecessor in that it relied for its regulation on economic selfinterest. The congenital weakness of nineteenth-century society was not that it was industrial but that it was a market society. Industrial civilization will continue to exist when the Utopian experiment of a selfregulating market will be no more than a memory.

Yet the shifting of industrial civilization onto a new nonmarketing basis seems to many a task too desperate to contemplate. They fear an institutional vacuum or, even worse, the loss of freedom. Need these perils prevail?

Much of the massive suffering inseparable from a period of transition is already behind us. In the social and economic dislocation of our age, in the tragic vicissitudes of the depression, fluctuations of currency, mass unemployment, shiftings of social status, spectacular destruction of historical states, we have experienced the worst. Unwittingly we have been paying the price of the change. Far as mankind still is from having adapted itself to the use of machines, and great as the pending changes are, the restoration of the past is as impossible as the transferring of our troubles to another planet. Instead of eliminating the demonic forces of aggression and conquest, such a futile attempt would actually ensure the survival of those forces, even after their utter military defeat. The cause of evil would become endowed with the advantage, decisive in politics, of representing the possible, in opposition to that which is impossible of achievement however good it may be of intention.

Nor does the collapse of the traditional system leave us in the void. Not for the first time in history may makeshifts contain the germs of great and permanent institutions.

Within the nations we are witnessing a development under which the economic system ceases to lay down the law to society and the primacy of society over that system is secured. This may happen in a great variety of ways, democratic and aristocratic, constitutionalist and authoritarian, perhaps even in a fashion yet utterly unforeseen. The future in some countries may be already the present in others, while some may still embody the past of the rest. But the outcome is common with them all: the market system will no longer be self-regulating, even in principle, since it will not comprise labor, land, and money.

To take labor out of the market means a transformation as radical as was the establishment of a competitive labor market. The wage contract ceases to be a private contract except on subordinate and accessory points. Not only conditions in the factory, hours of work, and modalities of contract, but the basic wage itself, are determined outside the market; what role accrues thereby to trade unions, state, and other public bodies depends not only on the character of these institutions but also on the actual organization of the management of production. Though in the nature of things wage differentials must (and should) continue to play an essential part in the economic system, other motives than those directly involved in money incomes may outweigh by far the financial aspect of labor.

To remove land from the market is synonymous with the incorporation of land with definite institutions such as the homestead, the cooperative, the factory, the township, the school, the church, parks, wild life preserves, and so on. However widespread individual ownership of farms will continue to be, contracts in respect to land tenure need deal with accessories only, since the essentials are removed from the jurisdiction of the market. The same applies to staple foods and organic raw materials, since the fixing of prices in respect to them is not left to the market. That for an infinite variety of products competitive markets continue to function need not interfere with the constitution of society any more than the fixing of prices outside the market for labor, land, and money interferes with the costing-function of prices in respect to the various products. The

nature of property, of course, undergoes a deep change in consequence of such measures since there is no longer any need to allow incomes from the title of property to grow without bounds, merely in order to ensure employment, production, and the use of resources in society.

The removal of the control of money from the market is being accomplished in all countries in our day. Unconsciously, the creation of deposits effected this to a large extent, but the crisis of the gold standard in the 1920s proved that the link between commodity money and token money had by no means been severed. Since the introduction of "functional finance" in all-important states, the directing of investments and the regulation of the rate of saving have become government tasks.

To remove the elements of production—land, labor, and money—from the market is thus a uniform act only from the viewpoint of the market, which was dealing with them as if they were commodities. From the viewpoint of human reality that which is restored by the disestablishment of the commodity fiction lies in all directions of the social compass. In effect, the disintegration of a uniform market economy is already giving rise to a variety of new societies. Also, the end of market society means in no way the absence of markets. These continue, in various fashions, to ensure the freedom of the consumer, to indicate the shifting of demand, to influence producers' income, and to serve as an instrument of accountancy, while ceasing altogether to be an organ of economic self-regulation.

In its international methods, as in these internal methods, nineteenth-century society was constricted by economics. The realm of fixed foreign exchanges was coincident with civilization. As long as the gold standard and—what became almost its corollary—constitutional regimes were in operation, the balance of power was a vehicle of peace. The system worked through the instrumentality of those Great Powers, first and foremost Great Britain, who were the center of world finance, and pressed for the establishment of representative government in less-advanced countries. This was required as a check on the finances and currencies of debtor countries with the consequent need for controlled budgets, such as only responsible bodies can provide. Though, as a rule, such considerations were not consciously present in the minds of statesmen, this was the case only because the requirements of the gold standard ranked as axiomatic. The uniform world pattern of monetary and representative institutions was the result of the rigid economy of the period.

Two principles of nineteenth-century international life derived their relevance from this situation: anarchistic sovereignty and "justified" intervention in the affairs of other countries. Though apparently contradictory, the two were interrelated. Sovereignty, of course, was a purely political term, for under unregulated foreign trade and the gold standard governments possessed no powers in respect to international economics. They neither could nor would bind their countries in respect to monetary matters—this was the legal position. Actually, only countries which possessed a monetary system controlled by central banks were reckoned sovereign states. With the powerful Western countries this unlimited and unrestricted national monetary sovereignty was combined with its complete opposite, an unrelenting pressure to spread the fabric of market economy and market society elsewhere. Consequently, by the end of the nineteenth century the peoples of the world were institutionally standardized to a degree unknown before.

This system was hampering both on account of its elaborateness and its universality. Anarchic sovereignty was a hindrance to all effective forms of international cooperation, as the history of the League of Nations strikingly proved; and enforced uniformity of domestic systems hovered as a permanent threat over the freedom of national development, especially in backward countries and sometimes even in advanced, but financially weak countries. Economic cooperation was limited to private institutions as rambling and ineffective as free trade, while actual collaboration between peoples, that is, between governments, could never even be envisaged.

The situation may well make two apparently incompatible demands on foreign policy: it will require closer cooperation between friendly countries than could even be contemplated under nineteenth-century sovereignty, while at the same time

the existence of regulated markets will make national governments more jealous of outside interference than ever before. However, with the disappearance of the automatic mechanism of the gold standard, governments will find it possible to drop the most obstructive feature of absolute sovereignty, the refusal to collaborate in international economics. At the same time it will become possible to tolerate willingly that other nations shape their domestic institutions according to their inclinations, thus transcending the pernicious nineteenth-century dogma of the necessary uniformity of domestic regimes within the orbit of world economy. Out of the ruins of the Old World, cornerstones of the New can be seen to emerge: economic collaboration of governments and the liberty to organize national life at will. Under the constrictive system of free trade neither of these possibilities could have been conceived of, thus excluding a variety of methods of cooperation between nations. While under market economy and the gold standard the idea of federation was justly deemed a nightmare of centralization and uniformity, the end of market economy may well mean effective cooperation with domestic freedom.

The problem of freedom arises on two different levels: the institutional and the moral or religious. On the institutional level it is a matter of balancing increased against diminished freedoms; no radically new questions are encountered. On the more fundamental level the very possibility of freedom is in doubt. It appears that the means of maintaining freedom are themselves adulterating and destroying it. The key to the problem of freedom in our age must be sought on this latter plane. Institutions are embodiments of human meaning and purpose. We cannot achieve the freedom we seek, unless we comprehend the true significance of freedom in a complex society.

On the institutional level, regulation both extends and restricts freedom; only the balance of the freedoms lost and won is significant. This is true of juridical and actual freedoms alike. The comfortable classes enjoy the freedom provided by leisure in security; they are naturally less anxious to extend freedom in society than those who for lack of income must rest content with a minimum of it. This becomes apparent as soon as compulsion is suggested in order to more justly spread out income, leisure and security. Though restriction applies to all, the privileged tend to resent it, as if it were directed solely against themselves. They talk of slavery, while in effect only an extension to the others of the vested freedom they themselves enjoy is intended. Initially, there may have to be reduction in their own leisure and security, and, consequently, their freedom so that the level of freedom throughout the land shall be raised. But such a shifting, reshaping and enlarging of freedoms should offer no ground whatsoever for the assertion that the new condition must necessarily be less free than was the old.

Yet there are freedoms the maintenance of which is of paramount importance. They were, like peace, a by-product of nineteenthcentury economy, and we have come to cherish them for their own sake. The institutional separation of politics and economics, which proved a deadly danger to the substance of society, almost automatically produced freedom at the cost of justice and security. Civic liberties, private enterprise and wage-system fused into a pattern of life which favored moral freedom and independence of mind. Here again, juridical and actual freedoms merged into a common fund, the elements of which cannot be neatly separated. Some were the corollary of evils like unemployment and speculator's profits; some belonged to the most precious traditions of Renaissance and Reformation. We must try to maintain by all means in our power these high values inherited from the market-economy which collapsed. This, assuredly, is a great task. Neither freedom nor peace could be institutionalized under that economy, since its purpose was to create profits and welfare, not peace and freedom. We will have consciously to strive for them in the future if we are to possess them at all; they must become chosen aims of the societies toward which we are moving. This may well be the true purport of the present world effort to make peace and freedom secure. How far the will to peace can assert itself once the interest in peace which sprang from nineteenth-century economy has ceased to operate will depend upon our success in establishing an international order.

As to personal liberty, it will exist to the degree in which we will deliberately create new safeguards for its maintenance and, indeed, extension. In an established society the right to nonconformity must be institutionally protected. The individual must be free to follow his conscience without fear of the powers that happen to be entrusted with administrative tasks in some of the fields of social life. Science and the arts should always be under the guardianship of the republic of letters. Compulsion should never be absolute; the "objector" should be offered a niche to which he can retire, the choice of a "second-best" that leaves him a life to live. Thus will be secured the right to nonconformity as the hallmark of a free society.

Every move toward integration in society should thus be accompanied by an increase of freedom; moves toward planning should comprise the strengthening of the rights of the individual in society. His indefeasible rights must be enforceable under the law even against the supreme powers, whether they be personal or anonymous. The true answer to the threat of bureaucracy as a source of abuse of power is to create spheres of arbitrary freedom protected by unbreakable rules. For however generously devolution of power is practiced, there will be strengthening of power at the center, and, therefore, danger to individual freedom. This is true even in respect to the organs of democratic communities themselves, as well as the professional and trade unions whose function it is to protect the rights of each individual member. Their very size might make him feel helpless, even though he had no reason to suspect ill-will on their part. The more so, if his views or actions were such as to offend the susceptibilities of those who wield power. No mere declaration of rights can suffice: institutions are required to make the rights effective. Habeas corpus need not be the last constitutional device by which personal freedom was anchored in law. Rights of the citizen hitherto unacknowledged must be added to the Bill of Rights. They must be made to prevail against all authorities, whether state, municipal, or professional. The list should be headed by the right of the individual to a job under approved conditions, irrespective of his or her political or religious views, or of color and race. This implies guarantees against victimization however subtle it be. Industrial tribunals have been known to protect the individual member of the public even from such agglomerations of arbitrary power as were represented by the early railway companies. Another instance of possible abuse of power squarely met by tribunals was the Essential Works Order in England, or the "freezing of labor" in the United States, during the emergency, with their almost unlimited opportunities for discrimination. Wherever public opinion was solid in upholding civic liberties, tribunals or courts have always been found capable of vindicating personal freedom. It should be upheld at all cost—even that of efficiency in production, economy in consumption or rationality in administration. An industrial society can afford to be free.

The passing of market-economy can become the beginning of an era of unprecedented freedom. Juridical and actual freedom can be made wider and more general than ever before; regulation and control can achieve freedom not only for the few, but for all. Freedom not as an appurtenance of privilege, tainted at the source, but as a prescriptive right extending far beyond the narrow confines of the political sphere into the intimate organization of society itself. Thus will old freedoms and civic rights be added to the fund of new freedom generated by the leisure and security that industrial society offers to all. Such a society can afford to be both just and free.

Yet we find the path blocked by a moral obstacle. Planning and control are being attacked as a denial of freedom. Free enterprise and private ownership are declared to be essentials of freedom. No society built on other foundations is said to deserve to be called free. The freedom that regulation creates is denounced as unfreedom; the justice, liberty and welfare it offers are decried as a camouflage of slavery. In vain did socialists promise a realm of freedom, for means determine ends: the U.S.S.R., which used planning, regulation and control as its instruments, has not yet put the liberties promised in her Constitution into practice, and, probably, the critics add, never will.... But to turn against regulation means to turn against reform. With the liberal the idea of freedom thus degenerates into a mere

advocacy of free enterprise—which is today reduced to a fiction by the hard reality of giant trusts and princely monopolies. This means the fullness of freedom for those whose income, leisure, and security need no enhancing, and a mere pittance of liberty for the people, who may in vain attempt to make use of their democratic rights to gain shelter from the power of the owners of property. Nor is that all. Nowhere did the liberals in fact succeed in reestablishing free enterprise, which was doomed to fail for intrinsic reasons. It was as a result of their efforts that big business was installed in several European countries and, incidentally, also various brands of fascism, as in Austria. Planning, regulation, and control, which they wanted to see banned as dangers to freedom, were then employed by the confessed enemies of freedom to abolish it altogether. Yet the victory of fascism was made practically unavoidable by the liberals' obstruction of any reform involving planning, regulation, or control.

Freedom's utter frustration in fascism is, indeed, the inevitable result of the liberal philosophy, which claims that power and compulsion are evil, that freedom demands their absence from a human community.

No such thing is possible; in a complex society this becomes apparent. This leaves no alternative but either to remain faithful to an illusionary idea of freedom and deny the reality of society, or to accept that reality and reject the idea of freedom. The first is the liberal's conclusion; the latter the fascist's. No other seems possible.

Inescapably we reach the conclusion that the very possibility of freedom is in question. If regulation is the only means of spreading and strengthening freedom in a complex society, and yet to make use of this means is contrary to freedom per se, then such a society cannot be free.

Clearly, at the root of the dilemma there is the meaning of freedom itself. Liberal economy gave a false direction to our ideals. It seemed to approximate the fulfillment of intrinsically Utopian expectations. No society is possible in which power and compulsion are absent, nor a world in which force has no function. It was an illusion to assume a society shaped by man's will and wish alone. Yet this was the result of a market view of society which equated economics with contractual relationships, and contractual relations with freedom. The radical illusion was fostered that there is nothing in human society that is not derived from the volition of individuals and that could not, therefore, be removed again by their volition. Vision was limited by the market which "fragmentated" life into the producers' sector that ended when his product reached the market, and the sector of the consumer for whom all goods sprang from the market. The one derived his income "freely" from the market, the other spent it "freely" there. Society as a whole remained invisible. The power of the state was of no account, since the less its power, the smoother the market mechanism would function. Neither voters, nor owners, neither producers, nor consumers could be held responsible for such brutal restrictions of freedom as were involved in the occurrence of unemployment and destitution. Any decent individual could imagine himself free from all responsibility for acts of compulsion on the part of a state which he, personally, rejected; or for economic suffering in society from which he, personally, had not benefited. He was "paying his way," was "in nobody's debt," and was unentangled in the evil of power and economic value. His lack of responsibility for them seemed so evident that he denied their reality in the name of his freedom.

But power and economic value are a paradigm of social reality. They do not spring from human volition; noncooperation is impossible in regard to them. The function of power is to ensure that measure of conformity which is needed for the survival of the group; its ultimate source is opinion—and who could help holding opinions of some sort or other? Economic value ensures the usefulness of the goods produced; it must exist prior to the decision to produce them; it is a seal set on the division of labor. Its source is human wants and scarcity—and how could we be expected not to desire one thing more than another? Any opinion or desire will make us participants in the creation of power and in the constituting of economic value. No freedom to do otherwise is conceivable.

We have reached the final stage of our argument.

The discarding of the market Utopia brings us face to face with the reality of society. It is the dividing line between liberalism on the one hand, fascism and socialism on the other. The difference between these two is not primarily economic. It is moral and religious. Even where they profess identical economics, they are not only different but are, indeed, embodiments of opposite principles. And the ultimate on which they separate is again freedom. By fascists and socialists alike the reality of society is accepted with the finality with which the knowledge of death has molded human consciousness. Power and compulsion are a part of that reality; an ideal that would ban them from society must be invalid. The issue on which they divide is whether in the light of this knowledge the idea of freedom can be upheld or not; is freedom an empty word, a temptation, designed to ruin man and his works, or can man reassert his freedom in the face of that knowledge and strive for its fulfillment in society without lapsing into moral illusionism?

This anxious question sums up the condition of man. The spirit and content of this study should indicate an answer.

We invoked what we believed to be the three constitutive facts in the consciousness of Western man: knowledge of death, knowledge of freedom, knowledge of society. The first, according to Jewish legend, was revealed in the Old Testament story. The second was revealed through the discovery of the uniqueness of the person in the teachings of Jesus as recorded in the New Testament. The third revelation came to us through living in an industrial society. No one great name attaches to it; perhaps Robert Owen came nearest to becoming its vehicle. It is the constitutive element in modern man's consciousness.

The fascist answer to the recognition of the reality of society is the rejection of the postulate of freedom. The Christian discovery of the uniqueness of the individual and of the oneness of mankind is negated by fascism. Here lies the root of its degenerative bent.

Robert Owen was the first to recognize that the Gospels ignored the reality of society. He called this the "individualization" of man on the part of Christianity and appeared to believe that only in a cooperative commonwealth could "all that is truly valuable in Christianity" cease to be separated from man. Owen recognized that the freedom we gained through the teachings of Jesus was inapplicable to a complex society. His socialism was the upholding of man's claim to freedom in such a society. The post-Christian era of Western civilization had begun, in which the Gospels did not any more suffice, and yet remained the basis of our civilization.

The discovery of society is thus either the end or the rebirth of freedom. While the fascist resigns himself to relinquishing freedom and glorifies power which is the reality of society, the socialist resigns himself to that reality and upholds the claim to freedom, in spite of it. Man becomes mature and able to exist as a human being in a complex society. To quote once more Robert Owen's inspired words: "Should any causes of evil be irremovable by the new powers which men are about to acquire, they will know that they are necessary and unavoidable evils; and childish, unavailing complaints will cease to be made."

Resignation was ever the fount of man's strength and new hope. Man accepted the reality of death and built the meaning of his bodily life upon it. He resigned himself to the truth that he had a soul to lose and that there was worse than death, and founded his freedom upon it. He resigns himself, in our time, to the reality of society which means the end of that freedom. But, again, life springs from ultimate resignation. Uncomplaining acceptance of the reality of society gives man indomitable courage and strength to remove all removable injustice and unfreedom. As long as he is true to his task of creating more abundant freedom for all, he need not fear that either power or planning will turn against him and destroy the freedom he is building by their instrumentality. This is the meaning of freedom in a complex society; it gives us all the certainty that we need.

# Critical Thinking and Discussion Questions for Part II (Sections 5–7)

## SECTION 5

1. **There are twenty-eight arguments used in the piece selected from von Clausewitz (on the companion website) to describe and explain war. Apply Arguments 3–9 to the following:**
   - The US military actions in Afghanistan begun in 2001
   - The US military actions in Iraq begun in 2003
   - The conflict in Ukraine in 2014
   - A military conflict of your choice

2. **Explain the "political object of war" according to Von Clausewitz.**
   - Has this objective been achieved in the war in Afghanistan that started in 2001?
   - Has this objective been achieved in the war in Iraq that started in 2003?
   - Has this objective been achieved in the conflict in Ukraine that started in 2014?

3. **Explain the polarity principle offered by von Clausewitz.**
   - Apply this principle to modern US–China relations.
   - Apply this principle to modern US–Iran relations.
   - Apply this principle to modern US–Russia relations.
   - Apply this principle to modern North Korea–South Korea relations.

4. **McMaster describes the "conditions of uncertainty" in modern warfare. (See this article on the companion website.) What are they?**
   - Suggest other uncertainties that, in your view, have not been mentioned in the article.

5. **What were the mistakes of the Israeli military strategists in the 2006 war in Lebanon, according to McMaster? What lessons do you think Israel learned from these mistakes today? (See this article on the companion website.)**

6. **Examine the Web to see what is being commonly called today the *collateral damage* in war.**
   - What is your personal view of the collateral damage concept in warfare?
   - If you were president, what would you do to reduce the collateral damage in a military conflict?

7. **Michel Wieviorka distinguishes between classical and contemporary forms of terrorism. Describe both.**
   - Describe the most significant differences between the two forms. Suggest examples.
   - Discuss the similarities between these two forms. Suggest examples.

8. Could the demands of modern global terrorist groups be largely satisfied to avoid global, continuous violence? If yes, which demands? Which demands cannot be addressed? Explain your point of view.

9. Terrorist actions can be effective not only because they instill fear in target populations, but also because they cause governments and individuals to respond in ways that aid the terrorists' cause.
   - Look for examples (different from those used in the article) or illustrations supporting this statement.
   - Look for examples that disprove the previous statement about the effectiveness of terrorist actions.

10. As Max Boot suggests, because mass media in democratic countries report heavily on casualties and destruction caused by insurgency's actions, public opinion in such countries may develop a "war fatigue" faster.
    - What is war fatigue and how does it develop?
    - War fatigue can come and go, which means it may increase or diminish. Do you think that war fatigue in the United States is increasing or decreasing today? Explain your view.

11. Imagine that the United States becomes energy independent in 2025. However, as many argue, the United States' forthcoming energy independence does not necessarily guarantee security.
    - In your view, will the energy independence significantly improve the security of the United States and why?
    - Will the impact of energy independence be significant or insignificant?
    - What other resources-driven conflicts may emerge in your view in five years and where?
    - What other resources-driven conflicts may emerge in fifteen years?

12. Apply David Lake's argument (see the article on the companion website) that security policies still depend on the balance of gains and losses to specific policies of the United States:
    - toward China and Taiwan;
    - toward North and South Korea;
    - toward Russia and its neighbors; and
    - toward Israel, Saudi Arabia, and its neighbors.

13. Judith Stiehm claims (on the companion website) that there should be *gender-mainstreamed* foreign policy, meaning that more women must be involved in countries' institutional security and defense policies.
    - Using open sources on the Web, find out how many female defense secretaries there are in the world today.
    - See if the number of women admirals and generals increased in the United States' armed forces over the past ten years. Discuss the findings.

14. **In your opinion, which moral dilemmas would new technologies bring to current and future military conflicts?**
   - How do drones change the nature of a conflict?
   - How do software-based weapons change the nature of war?

# SECTION 6

1. **Hugo Grotius, in his writings (on the companion website), refers a number of times to God. Underline all these references.**
   - Compare these references. What other topics are discussed or mentioned in these statements?
   - Is there a main theme or an underlying idea that can summarize these references to divine power in the context of law (or references to law in the religious context)?

2. **The Hague Peace Conferences of 1899 and 1907 (see the companion website) were inspired by the desire of several of the world leaders to establish a set of common rules to reduce the risk of war and diminish its cruelties. However, wars and atrocities did not stop after the conferences.**
   - Do you think that the Hague agreements were generally useful or useless in the context of history? Explain your view.

3. **Identify and discuss the strengths and weaknesses of the Treaty on the Non-Proliferation of Nuclear Weapons. (See the companion website.)**
   - What steps should be taken to make this treaty more effective by 2025?
   - Discuss the argument that if all countries possessed nuclear weapons, the world would be a safer place simply because governments would start acting very carefully out of fear of provoking nuclear war.

4. **We know that sovereign countries (states) are solely responsible for the decisions they make. In this case, what is your personal view on the need to have international law?**

5. **What are the main weaknesses of international law?**
   - Use the League of Nations case to illustrate.
   - Use the record of the United Nations' decisions and actions to illustrate.
   - Use recent examples to illustrate.

6. **According to Neff, what is the role of natural law in international law?**

7. **Using the Neff article, ask your professor to suggest examples from the past of successful applications or functioning of international law. Discuss them.**
   - Find and discuss other, more contemporary examples (from the past or this year) to underline international law's success.

8. **Discuss several reasons why distribution problems are central to territorial disputes.**
   - Use the dispute in South China as an example.
   - Use the dispute in Kashmir, involving India and Pakistan, as an example.
   - Use the 2014 conflict in Ukraine.

9. **Suggest two or three potential territorial disputes that could emerge by 2023.**
   - What legal measures should be taken now to prevent these conflicts from growing?

10. **Yoffie writes that international law can offer concrete steps toward statehood, but if applied too rapidly or too harshly, it can also undermine international stability. In addition to the Palestinian problem discussed in the article, could you provide other examples supporting this statement?**

11. **Which legal steps does a country have to take to obtain UN membership?**
    - Why were Palestinian authorities unable to obtain UN membership by applying through the conventional path, such as UN institutions?

12. **What is an unconventional path to statehood that was largely unavailable during the twentieth century but may be available today, according to Yoffie?**

13. **Explain the essence of the *cultural cold war* that broke out between American and Russian museums in 2010–11 (and the legal authorities that represented them).**

14. **How did Barcia explain the biggest problem (or problems) in international culture property disputes?**

15. **Two parties who are willing to compromise can draft a bilateral agreement (according to Barcia). Give an example of such successful bilateral agreements.**

16. **Would you like to see an international legal system (Jean d'Aspremont) formally established by 2025? What aspects of law should it be concerned with?**

# SECTION 7

1. **Why were most economists in the 1970s ignoring politics? Why were specialists in international relations dismissing political economy, according to Robert Keohane?**
   - What has changed in the international environment since the 1970s to bring attention to international political economy?

2. **How do new communication technologies affect international trade?**
   - How would these technological changes affect international relations in the future?

3. **What is mercantilism's view about the best route to national prosperity? (See the article on mercantilism on the companion website.)**
   - Imagine that every country has turned to mercantilist policies. What impact would this switch have on international relations?

4. **Discuss why China's economic policies may be considered partly mercantilist.**
   - Do you think that China will soon change some of its mercantilist policies?
   - What liberal elements exist in China's economic policies?

5. **Discuss the argument that the global financial and economic crisis that began in 2008 was overcome (around 2012) because the principles of *Keynesian economics* were successfully applied by the United States and its European allies.**

6. **Should the United States or the European Union borrow a few elements from the Chinese model of economic and political development or not? Discuss your opinion.**

7. **Explain the meaning of *internationalization of production* by Susan Strange (on the companion website).**
   - What consequences to international relations has this phenomenon had so far?

8. **Which groups should receive the most attention in contemporary global economic policies, according to Susan Strange?**

9. **Critics of globalization argue today that the free trade has "destroyed" millions of local jobs: small businesses cannot compete with large international corporations or with countries, such as China or Indonesia, where labor is very cheap. If you were president, how would you address this problem of preserving local jobs and embracing the free trade?**

10. **TransFair USA, a nonprofit organization, certifies and labels products manufactured under fair trade principles, which guarantee a certain decent price for the farmer for her or his product regardless of the market's fluctuations. Would you support the application of fair trade principles to all food imports to the United States? Critics argue that you must then pay a higher price for food. Proponents of fair trade reply that in Norway and Germany, for example, higher food prices do not seem to devastate family budgets. Conduct an experiment. Would a 10 percent price increase be acceptable given *your* financial situation? Think of the food products that you purchased in the last week and try to find out where they came from. If they are foreign, add 10 percent to their price tag. How much more would you pay each month? Is it a significant increase in your budget? How have these calculations affected your views of fair trade?**

# PART III

# TWENTY-FIRST-CENTURY CHALLENGES

## Environmental Challenges, Human Rights Protection and Development, Culture and Nationalism, and Forecasting the World of 2025 (Editorial Introduction)

When we compiled this reader, we assumed it would be very important to discuss the issues that have been historically at the center of the debates about international relations. Yet the developments since the turn of the twenty-first century have brought new challenges and generated new concerns for theorists and decision-makers. Among these concerns is the renewed and increased attention of the world community to environmental problems and policies, to human rights and related humanitarian issues, and to factors in world politics such as nationalism and its new manifestations. These topics reflect on the challenges that are likely to remain very important today and tomorrow. Do these encounters compel us to rethink the classical approaches to international relations and reconsider their applications? Do these problems involving environmental and humanitarian challenges eclipse many so-called traditional issues of international politics including war, diplomacy, and military and economic security? Do these problems require dramatic new solutions or do we still have to focus on the most successful strategies of the past? These questions evoke much debate. Only in open and informed dialogue do new and effective solutions to international challenges occur.

It is an understatement to say that the world is facing overwhelming environmental problems. Coal and oil remain key sources of energy contributing to dangerous atmospheric pollution. These dangers are acknowledged not only by scientists and activists but also by the vast majority of governments around the world. The international community encouraged and launched new programs and initiatives to address environmental problems. A whole new dimension of international relations has emerged. Just several decades ago, it was essentially enough for a group of economically advanced countries to coordinate their policies to address environmental issues. For example, several countries agreed about thirty years ago to coordinate their efforts related to the diminishing ozone layer; then the countries acted together and the problem was, for the most part, addressed. A different effort is required today. It must be persistent and it must be global. Can the current international system generate policies to address the environmental problems of a global magnitude (see Figure 8)?

International environmental policies can be understood as a continuum. On one side of this continuum is environmentalism, the movement that stands for urgent and comprehensive actions to protect the environment. Environmentalists support conservation of natural resources, push for sustained measures against contamination, and endorse sustainable development: economic growth coupled with environmental protection. They believe that many environmental problems are urgent and that the earth's natural resources are limited. Environmentalists do not form a unitary actor; they are a community of actors that agree on many things, yet disagree among themselves on methods, tactics, and the scope of environmental policies. This should not be surprising: Historians and political scientists have many examples reflecting a common tendency in almost any political and social movement. On the one hand, there are those who demand a radical and decisive action now. They need no compromises with the opposition and prefer risky strategies to win the support of the undecided. On the other hand, there are those who believe in consensus, gradual changes, and reasoning with the opposition. They warn that radical political demands are likely to cause resistance from the undecided, rather than their support. Moreover, radical

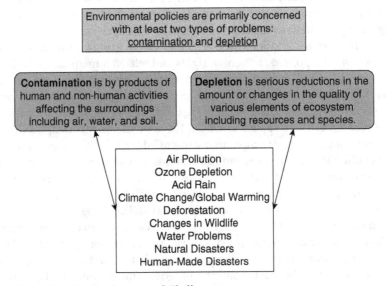

Figure 8.   Key Environmental Challenges

policies, as far as the argument goes, could invigorate the opposition, whose views represent the other side of the continuum.

Indeed, the developments of the past twenty years show that vigorous and passionate environmental ideas and policies created a formidable opposition: the skeptics, who question the sincerity, scientific foundations, and political wisdom of environmentalism. Bjørn Lomborg, a Danish activist and author (you can easily Google his name and his online essays) and one of these well-known skeptics, does not deny the need for global environmental policies. Yet he doubts the efficiency of costly international environmental efforts and questions many strict forms of conservation and environmental regulations. Environmentalists argue back and claim that people like Lomborg serve the interests of big business, corrupt politicians, and transnational corporations that seek to avoid policies of conservation and protection of nature. Environmentalists must acknowledge that the environmental enthusiasm has had its ups and downs since the beginning of the heated climate change debates in the early 2000s. Therefore, the importance of environmental education and open discussion of environmental challenges is hard to overestimate.

Thomas Homer-Dixon warned in the 1990s about emerging environmental changes as causes of acute conflict. These environmental changes can shift the balance of power between states, thus creating instability. Warmer temperatures, for example, are likely to increase contention over ice-free zones of accessible resources. In rich countries, environmental problems may widen social inequality: The wealthy would move to environmentally safe areas and invest in their own security, while the poor would remain in environmentally dangerous zones. The gap between the global North and the global South should also increase, thus inevitably causing tensions between wealthy and poor countries. Food supplies may become very tight and many jobs may be lost. As a result, new waves of environmental refugees will occur and may affect cross-border tensions. Poor countries, however, will be more susceptible to environmental change than rich ones, and tensions are more likely to occur in the developing world as a result of decreased agricultural production, economic decline, population displacement, and disruption of social order. How plausible have been such warnings? The debates are relentless.

Joshua Goldstein, for example, agrees that climate is a security factor because it definitely affects how and where military forces operate in today's world. Potential population displacements, infectious disease outbreaks, and natural disasters such as catastrophic floods and droughts should require massive troop deployments and international cooperation, which will demand many changes in military and security policies. However, little evidence is found in support of the suggestion that climate change should significantly increase violence at the state and substate levels. Overall, as Goldstein continues, droughts, floods, and crop failures in recent times have contributed to poverty but not particularly to war. Refugees are frequently the effect of armed conflicts, but seldom their cause. Nevertheless, it is wrong to deny that the risk of a new wave of population displacement, hunger, disease, destruction of infrastructure, and economic recession—caused by the increasing severity of weather-related disasters—remains real.

Recent developments in the Arctic region can illustrate how today's changing environment affects international affairs and vice versa. The continued melting of the

Arctic ice should pose economic, military, and environmental challenges to all countries in this region and beyond. Many experts believe that the melting of the ice gives countries more opportunities to explore and extract oil, gas, and minerals and to seek greater access for commercial shipping and fishing. These opportunities are likely to create competition and even international tensions. In terms of international law, it is crucial for all "Arctic states," including yet not limited to Russia, Canada, the United States, Denmark, and Norway, to agree on the codes of conduct and avoid rivalries that may aggravate detrimental environmental changes. New international agreements will be needed. The record of the developments after 2010 mixed: On the positive side, there is a Russian–Norwegian agreement that delineated both countries' zones in the Arctic. However, and this is a negative trend, the United States and Russia have been increasingly seeing each other as rivals in the Arctic area and no diplomatic solution has been accepted yet.

Some experts believe that the threat of conflict has been reduced and energetic environmental policies have already paid off. Fossil fuels—like coal, oil, and natural gas—that contribute to pollution should soon, in this view, become obsolete because of technological innovations and the appearance of reliable substitutes for petroleum. Getting the United States off fossil fuels (by developing alternative sources of energy) would inevitably affect this country's foreign policy. A world where the United States and other developed countries depend less on oil would have fewer oil-sponsored dictatorships and less corruption, terrorism, conflict, and war. Phasing out fossil fuels would stimulate global economic development and reduce the gap between the global South and North, which is also in the United States' interest. How plausible are such expectations? Recent breakthroughs in fracking (hydraulic fracturing) technology and the extraction of large quantities of relatively inexpensive natural gas and oil will certainly affect global politics as well as the optimistic forecasts about the lessening importance of fossil fuels. Yet fracking presents a new challenge to the environment.

History shows that a collective effort and mutual compromises have solved several serious environmental problems in the past. Are countries today ready to cooperate and sacrifice for the sake of everyone's future? The countries of the European Union have had problems in developing a common policy on energy, so that it would satisfy environmental concerns and security issues. Germany, for instance, turned away from coal and nuclear energy, but its dependence on Russian gas has increased as a result. This led to Germany's disagreement with the United States on the construction of a new gas pipeline from Russia across the Baltic Sea. Some analysts suggest that so long as Europe remains heavily dependent on the import of oil and gas from the Middle East and Russia, a threat to these countries' security would exist. The debates about global environment and environmental policies, as well as the tensions between these policies and other aspects of international relations, will continue to divide countries in the years to come.

Yet political scientists tend to believe that a collective and coordinated international action is urgently needed. As Joana Pereira suggests, in today's increasingly multipolar world, with several new centers of power emerging, there is a strong necessity to create and develop effective global governance institutions to maintain international dialogue and agree on joint policies. Cooperation is the most appropriate way to meet present and future environmental challenges, and climate change may be one of the catalysts of how countries are likely to manage a new global order.

More experts believe today that environmental policies should focus on individuals, their well-being, and security and not only on traditional state-centric threats and national defense. Therefore, environmental problems are becoming humanitarian problems as well.

Years ago, humanitarian problems were not considered a special subfield of international relations, but rather a part of a big discussion on violence, war, and peace. Today, foreign policy in many countries increasingly includes humanitarian issues. Indeed, a few military interventions in the past were justified by humanitarian considerations. The study of international relations is no longer focusing exclusively on sovereign states, but increasingly on the individual and the individual's rights. Nowadays, governments and nongovernmental organizations pay significantly more attention to the means and ways to alleviate the suffering of millions of people, particularly in developing and economically poor countries. These people too often become victims of political and ethnic violence, natural disasters, acute infectious diseases, abusive policies, and forceful migration. In some countries, especially Western ones, politicians, nongovernment organizations, and the media argue that consequences of human-made political actions (usually involving violence) and natural disasters are so significant that they require other countries to act in advance and more vigorously than ever before. Ideally, the proponents of this view argue, the whole international community should be involved in addressing humanitarian crises—incidents or continuing problems threatening the health, safety, security, and well-being of many, usually in a distinct geographic area (see Figure 9).

Humanitarian policies today are based on three fundamental principles: humanity, impartiality, and independence. Humanity means that policies, first, must save lives and alleviate suffering. Impartiality means no preference for any political leader,

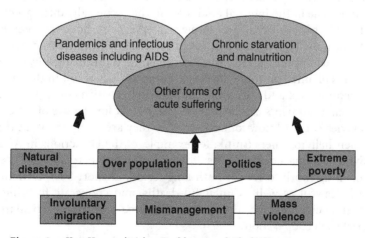

Figure 9.  Key Humanitarian Problems and Their Causes

country, or group. Independence means that humanitarian policies are conducted independent of political, economic, or military objectives of participating states. One of the means of humanitarian policies is effective communication. According to the *naming and shaming* strategy, placing certain countries in a spotlight for human rights violations and openly criticizing their governments in the media may prompt some leaders to begin addressing humanitarian problems for which they are criticized. However, the words of shame are frequently not enough to make a difference. Too often, governments (especially in failing states) have no means or motivation to address a humanitarian crisis that causes or threatens to cause massive suffering or loss of life. Therefore, there is a need for humanitarian interventions, which are the actions of international community, guided by the United Nations, nongovernmental organizations, or some sovereign countries to prevent or alleviate a humanitarian crisis. Such humanitarian interventions may take place with or without the approval of a legal authority controlling the area.

There is an ongoing debate about the legality and effectiveness of humanitarian interventions. One of the objections against them is that such interventions, in fact, violate sovereignty of countries and often involve the use of the military to enforce humanitarian policies. The critics of humanitarian interventions argue that, according to international law, all governments have the ultimate right (as a feature of their sovereignty) to accept or reject humanitarian interventions on their territories. The advocates of humanitarian interventions disagree and argue that the humanitarian tradition, or humanitarianism, should provide a necessary moral justification for such interventions: people who suffer at the hand of their government or, because of this government's neglect, have no other sources of help. Applied to international relations, this means that governments have the responsibility to protect their citizens from the consequences of natural disasters, mass violence, starvation, or infectious diseases. If they do not fulfill their responsibility, other countries should.

Both critics and supporters of humanitarian interventions draw on a rich intellectual and legal tradition. The British philosopher John Stuart Mill (1806–73) argued in the nineteenth century that the British Empire should set limits on when one country should intervene in the internal affairs of another, especially during a civil war in that country. He believed that any foreign intervention, however benign its proclaimed intent, must be judged as an act of violence driven by cynical self-interest. This view remains important today. It is accepted that, unfortunately, any intervention, even if it is planned on sound ethical arguments, may result in the suffering and death of human beings and have other unintended negative consequences. Second, although ethical arguments can be offered as a pretext for the use of violence, intervening countries cannot know for sure whether they are doing the right thing when they offer their help to others (think, for example, of the US actions in Afghanistan, Iraq, and Syria in the past decade). Despite disagreements, it is generally accepted that governments must work to reduce both long-term and short-term civilian harm in war, atone for lawful as well as unlawful deaths, and cooperate to bring nonstate actors that target civilians to justice. But what if some countries, particularly nuclear powers, reject such cooperation?

The humanitarian tradition claims that countries have the moral right to intervene in affairs of other countries for humanitarian reasons and not just out of strategic or security considerations. The responsibility to protect (often known as R2P or RtoP) is a new legal concept stating that if a sovereign country does not protect its own people from identifiable causes of death and acute suffering, then the international community must act. First appearing in scholarly publications and political discussions in the early 2000s, this concept was embraced at the UN World Summit in 2005.

The events that the world has been witnessing since the 1990s demonstrate that R2P has gained support in some countries but not in others. Russia and China argue, for instance, that in Yugoslavia in 1999 and in Libya in 2011, the use of NATO forces was not justified. Supporters of R2P argue back that interventions should be used with caution and only if a government is manifestly failing to protect its own people. Only then should international protection be provided in accordance with the UN Charter.

The concept of R2P is evolving. It is based on politics, values, identity, current political and social contexts, and many other factors. Values often shape diplomatic priorities, and sometimes they affect the political will to use force. On the one hand, studies have shown both that peacekeepers, when properly mandated and equipped, can offer protection from atrocious crimes and that international engagement has already helped to prevent genocidal acts in troubled societies. On the other hand, there is a very delicate balance between a country's sovereignty and international humanitarian activism. In 1999, the United States and other NATO countries started a military campaign against Yugoslavia as a humanitarian intervention to stop the *ethnic cleansing* of ethnic Albanians living in Kosovo. Russia disagreed and protested the war, citing the absence of UN resolutions to use force in Kosovo. In most recent years, Russian diplomats mentioned the Kosovo case when they portrayed the consequences of the Ukrainian government's actions against separatists in Eastern Ukraine as a humanitarian crisis. The western courtiers rejected this claim. As you will remember from Part II, in international relations, perceptions of other states' actions matter. Such perceptions often affect institutional policies.

Moral principles are often mentioned as justification for humanitarian actions. In reality, implementation of humanitarian activism runs into many practical dilemmas and difficult impasses. Among the most significant are the evolving contradictions between moral values and legal rules: We may believe that we are right, yet are our actions legal? Another issue is a conflict between the genuine desire to help, on the one hand, and the lack of knowledge about a country's local conditions on the other. This often makes international aid unproductive. Yet another problem is that some countries, particularly those with authoritarian governments, often claim that humanitarian interventionism is just another excuse for the dominant Western countries to impose their will and shape the international system according to their interests.

Humanitarian actions and the use of force to implement them will be discussed for years to come. Besides the moral aspect of such actions, there is also concern about the effectiveness of some humanitarian policies. Some researchers (such as Jacob Mchangama and Guglielmo Verdirame) discuss *human rights proliferation*. They argue that even the most resourceful governments and nongovernment organizations cannot do too many things in too many places. Liberal democracies, in their view, should not weaken their effort by overextending their humanitarian efforts. Instead, they should pay the most serious attention to the most egregious violations of human rights and focus on the most significant threats before turning to others.

Humanitarian policies certainly have roots in domestic politics. Take immigration, for instance. As Immanuel Wallerstein argues, the basic argument in European public debate about immigration has been one between the advocates of compassion and morality, on the one hand, and the advocates of self-protection and cultural preservation on the other. Wealthy countries, such as those in Europe, as well the United States and Canada to South Africa, Australia, Indonesia, and Japan, will be in the spotlight for some time to display the policies their government would adopt toward immigration—especially on humanitarian grounds. As Philip Alston argues, a trend has emerged in the second decade of this century, when the nationalistic, xenophobic, and anti-human rights agenda started to dominate the minds and actions of many political leaders and parties in various countries. Therefore, there is a need, in his view, to re-evaluate domestic strategies and broaden outreach, while reaffirming the basic principles of the human rights movement rooted in care, humanism, and impartiality. A new level of coordination is necessary between international and local human rights movements.

Humanitarian policies involve healthcare, especially in poor regions in which people have little or no access to doctors and medication. Studies show that subsidies, proper management, and activists' support can make a difference in the lives of millions of people. The number of deaths from malaria—a dangerous infectious disease that killed almost one million people a year in the beginning of this century, mostly children, mostly in Africa—has been reduced to about four hundred thousand by 2020. This was possible because of a massive effort by governments and nongovernmental organizations. Studies also suggest the benefits of government-sponsored health programs. Such programs not only save millions of lives, but also improve countries' health conditions, children's academic performance, and people's well-being.

International peace and lasting cooperation cannot be ensured by military and economic domination alone. Peace and cooperation require an informed consent of diverse groups of people, the consent of *hearts and minds*. In today's world, however, there are regions where such consent is difficult to reach. We know that some ideas and symbols are shared globally and some are not. Look, for instance, at the success of European soccer or American college and professional basketball: They are winning the hearts of hundreds of millions of followers globally. However, the values of liberal democracy (associated with key economic, political, and personal freedoms), for example, evoke resistance in many places across the globe. Western commentators, for instance, acknowledge the failure to spread liberal values to China, which remains undemocratic, despite its large and growing middle class. Nationalist sentiments and religious passions can shape and change international politics as profoundly as the issues related to economic inequality and military security.

The very nature of values and ideas in international relations is a disputed issue, with many perspectives competing. Feminists, for example, emphasize the urgent importance of *gendering* international relations, arguing that most concepts and doctrines in this field have been drawn from the male perspective. Feminism as a political movement influenced academic feminism in the theory of international relations and this has, in turn, affected our understanding of international politics.

Another perspective comes from research in social psychology. Holger Mölder, a prominent Estonian scholar, introduces an important psychological dimension to the discussion of international politics: He calls it *a culture of fear*. Fear, as an emotion, is an individual's response to a threat, as well as to uncertainty and instability. Political leaders can provoke fear in their citizens. They can even cultivate a culture of fear in their countries using media and social networks available to them. Social problems, ethnic tensions, and diplomatic disputes may strengthen the culture of fear. Where such a culture exists, interstate negotiations and compromises become more difficult and the risk of war significantly increases. Cultural factors become a major aspect in managing relations between international allies. Values, identities, and beliefs are also important to study because they help explain the worldview and motivations of potential adversaries.

Nationalism is one of the most intriguing phenomena in the study of international relations, the arena where interests, identities, and values mesh. Nationalism is also a powerful political force. Nationalist ideas capture the imagination of individuals and large groups easily and often rapidly. Nationalism is not exclusively rooted in psychological factors. Jerry Muller sees the core of nationalism as a shared cultural heritage, which usually includes a common language, a common faith, and often (but not always) a common ethnic ancestry. In Europe in the late nineteenth century the growth of nationalism coexisted with the rise of political representation, industrial capitalism, bureaucratic state, modern communications, universal literacy, and urbanization. As railroads and public schools undermined local identities as the power of the clan, the guild, and the church was diminishing, Europeans developed allegiance to *nation-states*. In other countries, this process was different.

The formation of nation-states is not over. The collapse of the Soviet Union in 1991, for instance, gave birth to independent Baltic States, Ukraine, Moldova, and many other sovereign countries that used to be in the union. Ukraine and Russia historically shared very close cultural and linguistic ties. Igor Torbakov in *History, Memory, and National Identity* shows how the national identities of these two countries have been under attack from nationalist historians and politicians. In 2014 and later, the clash of identities (in addition to other factors) contributed to open hostilities between the people of Ukraine and Russia. Nationalist arguments on both sides have been fueled by state-sponsored propaganda in the media. Several years later, Russia and Ukraine remain on a collision course, and the language of nationalism that permeated the media of both countries makes any political compromises unlikely.

There are almost one billion people on earth who claim no religious identity. Will this trend weaken nationalism and intolerance? Secularization, as some believe, goes hand in hand with modernization, the spread of education, science, technology, prosperity, and tolerance. The trend toward secularization has also given way to religious resurgence, including the rise of religious fundamentalism. Religion is increasingly often a matter of individual choice, not tradition. Religion spreads among educated urban professionals. Globalization and global migration facilitate the detachment of religion from traditional ethnic and national roots. There are new, virtual, web-based communities that know no borders and reach out across ethnic and national groups. This new religious revival spawns new forms of nationalist extremism and has already changed the nature of international relations. During the Cold War, the West had a strong political but also faith-based consensus on its foreign actions regarding the atheist Soviet Union. Today, there is no longer consensus in Western countries regarding how to deal with individuals and groups driven by a combination of extreme nationalism and religious fundamentalism.

The concluding section introduces several important ideas about the future of international relations. No single theory has the power to predict the future because there are too many factors that influence world politics. Predictions have always been difficult in this field. For example, experts did not anticipate the quick implosion of Communism in Eastern Europe in 1989 and the collapse of the Soviet Union in 1991. Very few predicted a global financial meltdown in 2008 in the United States. Very few could foresee the revolutionary turmoil in the Arab world in 2011. Even fewer anticipated people in the United Kingdom voting for Brexit in 2016 and the election of Donald Trump in the same year. Most experts have been surprised by China's turn toward authoritarianism in domestic politics after 2018, instead of an increasingly liberal type of democracy, the turn that most anticipated. This list can be easily expanded.

Why are there so few good forecasts in international relations? In part, the problem is in what we call *intellectual conformism*: The majority of experts, as well as journalists, tend to have a *pack mentality*. This means that they rarely dissent from the majority opinion, even when facts and other indicators urge them to abandon the consensus or at least question it. Therefore, to battle intellectual conformism, we think that it is more important to compare different, sharply diverging views on the future of international relations. Some of them are presented for you to judge.

The American scholar Jack Goldstone points to the changing demographics as a vital indicator to watch. He argues that the relative demographic weight of the richest countries will drop; the developed countries' labor forces will substantially age; most of the world's expected population growth will increasingly be concentrated in today's poorest countries; and most people in the world will become urbanized. He shows that, because of low birth rates in the West, economic power will shift to the developing nations. There are other consequences of demographic decline for Western countries. As its indigenous population continues to age and decline, the demand for immigrant workers will grow. At the same time, the world's youngest population will be increasingly concentrated in today's poorest countries, which have a dangerous lack of quality education, investments, and jobs. Moreover, most of the world's population will become urbanized, with the largest urban centers in the world's poorest countries, where decent living conditions are scarce. This could lead to a deepening global polarization, increased political instability, and social unrest.

Will the demographic, social, and economic problems undermine the spread of democracy? Could these problems push the world into new authoritarianism? Almost seven decades ago, George Orwell published *1984*. This widely acclaimed novel described the world of 1984 in which three empires divide the world and are constantly engaged in megawars among themselves. All power belongs to an "inner party," an authoritarian and well-organized clique. The masses are obedient, terrorized, and distracted by propaganda and cheap entertainment. All facts are manipulated, extorted beyond recognition, and simply exchanged for lies. Although the novel has never been considered a scholarly analysis of the future, today's experts from different fields use it as an allegory for pessimistic scenarios of international relations.

Today, however, deeply pessimistic forecasts alluding to a global revival of authoritarianism are rare. In fact, an opposite trend—many forecasts filled with optimism and confidence—has emerged in scholarly analyses of the future of international relations. Alexander Wendt proposes a global state, a non-authoritarian one, which in his view is inevitable in one hundred years or so. He predicts a gradual evolution of the international order, which will move from a congregation of states to a society of states and, finally, to a world state, which will be nonauthoritarian and peaceful. He further explains why and how countries will support the gradual reduction of their sovereignty in favor of international institutions and international norms.

G. John Ikenberry provides another example of an optimistic forecast against the increasingly gloomy settings. He sees no viable alternative to a global democratic project. Even authoritarian countries have no choice but to play by the rules set by economic and political liberalism. China, they argue, would not challenge the liberal order because the Chinese leaders want to benefit from its policies, practices, and institutions while being in the center of the global liberal system. Ikenberry acknowledges in *The Illusion of Geopolitics* that some "backsliding" from the liberal order has occurred. Indeed, it continues today. Based on his optimistic assessment, only two countries, Brazil and Turkey, have turned against liberalism and toward autocracy. Will they continue to stay on this path and for how long?

Which countries are likely to play the key economic role in the world of tomorrow? There is one argument that any country that hopes to become an economic superpower must be large, vibrant, and globally integrated. It cannot be isolated. Most experts agree today that the future will be decided by the competition between the United States and China. The European Union is a third candidate, but because of its integrated nature, it cannot effectively project political and economic leadership globally, at least not now.

What about the role of the United States in the global world? A body of research shows that the United States since the early 2000s was in decline relative to China. Some even say that the United States, because of its liberal democratic system, is likely to lose its competition with China, where the state spends billions on innovative infrastructure and technology. Other experts believe that this outlook is wrong. The United States, in their view, will remain wealthier, more innovative, and more militarily powerful than China. Furthermore, globalization or anti-globalization will reinforce US power, not erode it. The United States will continue to set the rules, norms, and values of the international system—all much to its benefit.

Overall, a key question remains: Will globalization continue or has this process seriously slowed down? Facts from the end of the second decade of the twenty-first century suggest that international investment, trade, bank loans, and supply chains have all been decreasing for a few years or stagnating relative to world gross domestic product. Globalization has given way to a new period of resistance. Some authors, as you should remember, call it *slowbalization*. Will this global trend continue in the 2020s? Will the world find itself divided in regional blocks dominated by Russia, China, and the United States, among others? Time will tell which of these predictions were most accurate. But it is never too late to think about the future and make educated decisions about it now.

# GENERAL DISCUSSION QUESTIONS RELATED TO THE READING MATERIALS ON ENVIRONMENTAL CHALLENGES, HUMANITARIAN PROBLEMS, IDENTITY AND CULTURE FACTORS, AND FORECASTS

These general questions are for class discussions as well as individual assignments. The discussion of these questions should help students think critically and better understand the materials in this section. Other, more specific critical-thinking and practice questions related to the reading materials appear at the end of Part III.

- Do any of the global environmental problems directly affect you or people you know personally? If yes, in what way? Suggest an example.
- Using a case of your choice, analyze a *depletion* problem that has led or might lead to an international conflict. Consider water or other resources (and access to them) as an illustration.
- Contemporary environmental discussions resemble the longtime debate between cornucopians (a reference to the cornucopia, or horn of plenty), who believed that natural resources are practically limitless, and neo-Malthusians, the followers of the nineteenth-century British scholar Thomas Robert Malthus, who predicted that the inevitable depletion of natural resources would generate conflict. Would you consider yourself a cornucopian, a neo-Malthusian, somewhere in between, or neither of these two choices? Discuss your position.
- Despite their differences, environmentalists and skeptics may agree on a few issues. Which ones, and why?
- Imagine that affordable alternative energy sources have finally emerged and fossil fuels such as oil and coil have become too expensive and thus obsolete.

    - How would this new energy situation affect international relations?
    - If oil no longer is a top commodity on the global market, will this new development affect (a) Washington's policies toward Saudi Arabia and (b) the European Union's policies toward Russia?

- Will it be possible, in your opinion, to eradicate global poverty during your lifetime? What should be done in terms of international policies to eradicate global poverty?
- Investigate and suggest the conditions under which a restrictive migration (immigration) policy—within one country as well as between two or more countries—becomes a humanitarian problem.
- In most countries today, children's education is mandatory and paid for by the government. A child's access to education is considered a basic right. Do you think that every person by 2025 should have guaranteed access to healthcare and employment regardless of where the person lives? Should the right to receive healthcare be a universal human right? Will it be achievable in ten years? Explain your view.
- Why are values and identities important in international relations? How might a leader's cultural identity affect his or her decisions in foreign policy? Give one example.

- We know about negative consequences of religious intolerance and fundamentalism. Suggest examples of how religious values can positively affect international relations by promoting peace, tolerance, and care.
- We all know that perceptions matter in politics. What factors (such as specific policies), in your view, should diminish anti-American stereotypes among some people in the non-Western world?
- Global fertility rates are declining, which means that today, on average, women tend to have fewer children than they had in 2000. In many countries (including Latin America, Turkey, and Iran) the fertility rate is at a record low, about two children per woman. Discuss how falling fertility rates may affect cultural values involving the family, traditions, and interpersonal communications. Discuss how ongoing demographic changes could affect countries' polices and, ultimately, international relations by 2025
- Does China have economic and financial incentives to challenge the global liberal order today? Will China, in your opinion, challenge this order for any other reason? Explain your view.

# Section 8

# Environmental Challenges and Policies

# Environmental Issues and International Relations, a New Global (Dis)Order—The Role of International Relations in Promoting a Concerted International System

JOANA CASTRO PEREIRA

## NATURAL RESOURCES IN A GLOBALIZED WORLD

In 2014, the world has seen an abrupt fall of oil prices, due to a slowdown in the emerging countries and Europe's demand, and mostly due to the huge increase in the US production of non-conventional oil. Saudi Arabia reacted in a strategic long-term approach for avoiding the depletion of its oil reserve assets in face of a rapid development of non-conventional oil and renewable energy. The country's bet is to keep the oil price below the cost of production of a significant part of the producers of shale oil in the US. This reduction in oil prices is producing major effects in oil exporters dependent on a high price for keeping their national budget on balance—Russia, Venezuela, Iran, Iraq, Nigeria, Ecuador, etc.—; therefore, in most of these countries domestic social unrest is a significant threat. On the contrary, the US seems to be winning, since the country is benefiting from a large increase in its production and from being a major consumer (the country is importing cheaper oil). Some may interpret this development in prices as an aggression from the US against Russia, but howsoever there is an evident geostrategic tension in the international system, which constitutes a security risk.

With regard to exporting states, the existence of valuable natural resources heightens competition for control of the state and postpones the development of other sectors of economic life, given that, in most cases, these states have very weak political institutions, something that increases the likelihood of political authoritarianism and civil strife. It is important to underline that these conflicts begin as national security risks, but can quickly turn into international or global problems. Le Billon (2012) argues that resource allocations, operating practices, social rights and the discursive representations contribute to shape vulnerabilities and opportunities for the emergence of armed conflicts, which means that, in many cases, security problems are originated within a state, but have a large potential to surpass national borders and affect regional and international security. The idea of future conflicts over scarce resources and anthropogenic environmental change needs to be considered in terms of particular geographies of vulnerability, threat and insecurity, as well as the new dynamics associated with globalization. So, traditional geopolitics perspectives over natural resources conflicts seem to be increasingly obsolete, inasmuch as they focus on resource supply for rich countries, pointing towards military invasions and national autarky, regarding natural resources as strategic imperatives based on state-centric perspectives which stress conflict risks fueled by ideas of shrinking resources and difficulties in supply. Given that one needs to study potential conflicts over resources in light of geographies of vulnerability, threat and insecurity, one also should be careful when analyzing geopolitical narratives about the threat of interstate resource wars due to the growing economies of Asia, for example, since they can promote them instead of avoiding them, simply because this is a simplistic view on the issue, which neglects the multidimensional nature of environmental issues and the need for global cooperation. As Frerks et al. (2014) argue, mono-causal approaches underlining the environment as the reason for war in the 21st century have given way to

Pereira, Joana Castro. 2015. "Environmental Issues and International Relations, a New Global (Dis)Order—The Role of International Relations in Promoting a Concerted International System." *Revista Brasileira de Política Internacional* 58 (1): 191–209. http://dx.doi.org/10.1590/0034-7329201500110.

a more modest approach in which environmental factors are not discarded as a conflict factor, but positioned into a broader and more complex framework (surpassing simple neo-Malthusian approaches) where scarcity directly leads to conflict.

One cannot assert the decay of geopolitics, one must admit that geopolitics is still relevant and important, but geopolitics cannot be the only perspective on environmental issues and natural resources in particular, since globalization itself has made the environment a global problem. Globalization and its global issues challenge the orthodox vision that emphasizes traditional geopolitics and the struggle for power among states, pointing to the importance of a new perspective, one which focus its attention on a geocentric perspective (in the politics of global social relations) or in a new geopolitics, given the increasing importance of soft power in international relations. Howsoever, this is another aspect that proves globalization is a "double-edged sword."

In the core of geopolitical thinking lies the realistic notion of the importance of achieving world order by means of a balance of power that seeks to prevent regional and global hegemony of rising powers, and some supporters of globalization suggest that world order can be achieved through greater economic and cultural interaction. So, according to this view, the Arab Spring events can be viewed both from the perspective of globalization and from the perspective of geopolitics. Globalization was important in disseminating ideas (through social networks, especially) and in spreading weapons through state borders, which challenged dictators across the Arab world. Also, external powers were asked to intervene either directly or indirectly, in order to establish a balance of power in a critical region of the world, one that can serve their interests (Heywood 2014). It was in Libya, where the ores and fuels account for 97 percent of exports and more than half of GDP, that the Arab Spring became, for the first time, violent, leading to NATO's intervention. One must keep in mind that outsiders have to deal with the problems associated with national conflicts over resources—problems such as illegal migration, terrorism, human or drug trafficking—becoming entangled

in weak states trying to control these events, but that great power involvement may be aggressive and selfish, instead of defensive or altruistic (Hendrix and Noland 2014). The more assertive example of this is the US invasion of Iraq.

Thus, there are many narratives about competition over resources between the US and China (Klare 2013): they mention the effects of this competition for US–China relations, as well as possible tensions between China and countries such as Japan, India and Southeast Asian countries. As Reed (2014) emphasizes, "Chinese and US economies are intimately connected, while the two countries also compete for geostrategic influence at regional and global levels." Given its rise in economic, political and military terms, China may exert critical influence in countries full of valuable natural resources. Chinese influence in Africa is already a reality, because the country has surpassed the United States as the single largest provider of aid to the continent, and Chinese outward foreign direct investment is deeply targeted at the extractive sector. This resource boom can occasion a geopolitical confrontation between the United States and China (Hendrix and Noland 2014).

The question is: can China rise peacefully? So, China's rise is one of the reasons why the environment and natural resources are becoming more and more important in international relations. The other reasons encompass, for example, India, which is about to be the world's most populous country, having an emerging economy and being a political force stabilizing the South and Southeast regions of the Asian continent; Brazil, a major provider of commodities on world markets and an extremely important player in terms of global food security; or the Russian Arctic, destined to be the heart of an enormous struggle of extractive industries and commercial and shipping centers. Besides, these are regions of high priority to the US; all of them are vulnerable to natural resource shocks and to the effects of climate change. "Small" events can have very significant effects across regions and the entire globe. According to Reed (2014), illegal trade in natural resources runs in the hundreds of billions of dollars annually. This illegal resource trade distorts international trade, weakens rules governing international commerce, and causes economic loss to producers and consumers in the United States.

Garrett and Piccinni (2012, 5) also mention this fact, focusing on war economies, "a fertile business environment for international criminal networks and arms traffickers, who seek to exchange arms and other inputs in return for access to natural resource revenues or commercialization opportunities provided by high-value commodities."

Another risk encompasses the fact that natural resource exporting states are empowered by higher prices, which makes them less amenable to international norms, namely those associated with global environmental governance and human rights, two global issues. In fact, these states tend to be economically highly integrated and they are associated with a low degree of political integration, in other words, they are very weakly linked to the global governance system. This fact can be explained by the fear of loss of sovereignty and autonomy, which reveals that we are living in "an international system under conservative hegemony" (Viola et al. 2013).[1] Its smaller political integration complicates efforts to deal with issues that require collective global action, particularly those related to the environment. This dynamic is very clear in the negotiations to manage climate change, where the material interests of oil-exporting countries are at stake (Pereira 2013). Economic integration tends to reduce the likelihood of international environmental treaties ratification, while political globalization increases this probability. Therefore, energy exporting countries will hardly participate in the global governance of the environment. Additionally, since these countries are poorly integrated in political institutions, they are less likely to adhere to international norms associated with the use of force, both nationally and across borders, so their behavior is not constrained as it should be. Moreover, their weak political institutional links mean that especially energy resource exporters have fewer forums in which to peacefully solve their tensions with other countries. Consequently, these states are also isolated regarding conflict behavior.

However, despite the aggressive behavior of most exporting states, the truth is that their belligerence rarely culminates in armed conflict, something related to the post-Westphalian characteristics of war in the twenty-first century system, given that about 95 percent of armed conflicts since the second half of the 1980s occurred within states and not among states (Heywood 2014), which reveals that, whilst international organizations are not designed to integrate the new powers' aspirations and natural resource exporters tend not to join political institutions, the embryonic global governance system of the twenty-first century has influenced states and its behavior in international arenas.

> because oil is a strategic resource, major powers invest significant resources in securing global supply lines and have incentives to prevent large-scale conflict in oil-producing countries that might result in global price spikes. [. . .] As a result of both domestic spending on defense in energy-exporting countries and their strategic significance for major powers, oil producers are less likely to experience wars. (Hendrix and Noland 2014, 60)

Power and wealth have always been associated to warfare and cooperation, but since the environment belongs to the entire humankind and globalization gave birth to a number of global environmental challenges, which can only be addressed by all, cooperation will have to prevail in an effort to keep order in the international system. In fact, as Reed (2014) underlines, resource scarcities have obliged the governments of many countries to develop bilateral and regional resource management systems to prevent conflicts among neighbors while providing citizens with access to needed resources, which proves that environmental issues have the ability to promote cooperation.

> the emergence of conflicts is now often seen as related to the management of natural resources or more widely to the nature of resource governance regimes. (. . .) When managed properly, resource issues may help to foster a culture of environmental cooperation (. . .). Proper resource governance could not only help resolve resource conflicts, but also prevent them and lead to peaceful mutual relations.

Thereby, geopolitics and globalization are not two incompatible concepts, inasmuch as globalization opens many doors for international conflict, which should be considered in the light of geopolitics, but it also calls for unprecedented cooperation. Thus, the world may be heading for a new order or a new disorder. The growing interdependence among states and the global governance system "have borne fruit," but the international community is not free from the triggering of conflicts and wars. And here is where International Relations come in.

## THE PATH FOR COOPERATION: WHY GLOBAL ENVIRONMENTAL ISSUES "BELONG" TO INTERNATIONAL RELATIONS

The environment is perhaps the most global and multidimensional issue in the international system and International Relations is a scientific field which benefits from a number of sciences and intends to combine knowledge from other disciplines with which the discipline itself develops, so it is the perfect field of study to analyze and build up a better understanding of the contemporary world. "Understanding the present world and its future evolution requires interdisciplinary knowledge. It requires an understanding of each of the drivers of change" (Calouste Gulbenkian Foundation 2014, 1), which means that, concerning a multidimensional and global issue such as the environment, International Relations seems to be the most appropriate discipline to develop and provide to local, regional and international stakeholders a framework to understand global dynamics and its implications for the international community, as well as underline risks and find paths for cooperation. In the hybrid international system of the twenty-first century, where the world faces geopolitical challenges and the need to cooperate on a global scale, International Relations emerges as a highly relevant discipline. As we have seen, the world seems to be heading for a new global order or a new global disorder, deeply linked to the environment, which makes it extremely important to study this new global context, in order not to fall in global disorder.

Since International Relations study the diplomatic and strategic relations between or among states, cross-border transactions of all types and the multiple dimensions of contemporary globalization, it can contribute to building solutions for the new challenges of the twenty-first century, in other words, it can help promoting collective responses for problems that affect us all and for which there is no solution unless the international community joins forces, because the discipline has the potential to develop new knowledge about the political, economic and social dynamics of the present world. What happens inside of a state influences the global sphere and what happens globally affects the domestic domain: that is what globalization has created and has been exacerbating, and that is what we need to understand with the view to adapt to these new circumstances, avoiding conflicts and benefiting from the existence of common issues to promote a cooperative and concerted international system.

Nevertheless, there are some obstacles which have to be surpassed. Given that International Relations is a recent discipline, created after the end of the First World War, there is a very significant number of countries where this scientific field is still underdeveloped and underestimated, struggling to emancipate itself and conquer its very own place. Therefore, it seems fair to assert that, in International Relations, in many countries, there is still a very inadequate and insufficient body of knowledge, as well as inappropriate methodologies and scarce resources. Wherefore, scholars of International Relations need to work hard with the aim of developing the discipline, as well as proving its value and importance for a changing and interconnected world. This would be extremely important not only to develop a discipline which emerges as fundamental for understanding the present world, but also to promote scientific studies and its conclusions among elites (decision makers, stakeholders, etc.)—inasmuch as it would provide them with very relevant data to think up new policies or even propone these new policies—and the general public, because an informed population has greater power and greater capacity to influence decisions, as well as the direction their countries will follow, and consequently the international system, fostering and developing the idea of global citizenship.

With respect to the environment, all of the challenges already exposed in this article require, firstly, a holistic perspective on environmental insecurity, one that focuses on cause (global, economic, political, modernity), context (history, culture) and effects (health, natural disasters, slow cumulative changes, accidents, conflict) (Schnurr and Swatuk 2012)—International Relations has tools for developing this holistic perspective—and then a new way of living, a new philosophy of life. In other words, extremely efficient life styles in terms of resource use and global responses, something that asks for a global mindset change. This is another challenge for International Relations' scholars, given that, in this discipline, one finds the prevalence of a paradigm that does not link human society with its biological basis (the exception is traditional geopolitics), which is considered infinite. The truth is that the essential holistic paradigm still lies in the sideline of the discipline. However, because the protection of the environment constitutes a civilizational imperative, this paradigm must become predominant, in other words, International Relations' scholars have to develop this area towards a view which takes into account planetary boundaries. It is impossible to develop this scientific field without transforming it towards a total perception of the unbreakable link between social and natural spheres. We need to find a new way of articulating the local and global environmental insecurities and injustices that affects us all, but unequally so (Schnurr and Swatuk 2012). This requires a new approach to national interest. The international community must act keeping in mind global problems and, consequently, global interest, which is not contrary to national interest. We must face national interest in a new way, different from the traditional one: we have to build a concept of national interest which is strictly related to global interest, in the sense that it is impossible to achieve the most important domestic goals without thinking globally, without achieving the interest of humankind, and the environment seems to corroborate this fact. Thus, national and global interests are two sides of the same coin and not two incompatible realities, simply because globalization, one way or another, links our destinies.

Concerning water, for instance, we need to associate water management to global governance, in order to improve governance of the drivers causing pressures on water (climate change, population growth, economic development). Thirty to fifty percent of the food produced in the world is wasted, lost or converted (Calouste Gulbenkian Foundation 2014) and the production of energy is the second largest user of water, activities that put pressure on this vital resource and make it very difficult to fight against poverty in the most vulnerable regions of the globe and promote human rights. Taking into account the great civilizational challenge of climate change, the international community needs to "re-engineer the energy of nations" (Leggett 2013), international leaders and citizens must converge and commit to provide a fair and efficient use of fundamental resources, as well as to develop the path for a green economy, which should be a priority in a globalizing world. Although the international community is aware of the existence of global commons, global responsibilities and common goals, the truth is that, in practice, responses are based on narrow and simplistic approaches to the problems. There are neo-Malthusian assumptions of the future, but they seem to be insufficient to trigger effective action, hence the importance of promoting the prevalence of a holistic paradigm in International Relations. Current constraints can be broken and there is no need to be Malthusian, since trends are not destiny. Changing contexts must be explored and it is vital to highlight that new opportunities are also emerging (Calouste Gulbenkian Foundation 2014).

This is what Klare (2013, 227) calls "the race to adapt," which is "a contest to become among the first to adopt new materials, methods, and devices that will free the world from its dependence on finite resource supplies. (. . .) Power and wealth will come (. . .) from mastery of the new technologies." The disregard for the development of technology was one of the biggest mistakes in Malthus' theory. However, one may not forget that the creation of an effective environmental global governance regime and the move towards a green and sustainable economy will require political will and action from the greatest powers of the international system, both with regard to its internal contexts, as for the transition to sustainability in the poorest countries. The international community can start with a global governance regime for the resource sector which levels the playing field for populations, governments, and businesses and encourages greater transparency and improved management of natural resource wealth (Le Billon 2012). Thereby, scholars of International Relations have the potential and the duty to seek and propose new ways of global organization, holistic ones, because, as Hendrix and Noland (2014, 56) argue, membership in international organizations and political globalization have powerful implications for reducing international conflict behavior and increasing respect for human rights, since international institutions can be important shapers and transmitters of international norms. Furthermore, by renewing our sense of unity with the rest of Nature, we can imagine new ways of being and through cooperation and innovation we can achieve them (Calouste Gulbenkian Foundation 2014).

As we have seen, globalization and the emergence of new powers can create a climate of tension and conflict in the international system, but these processes also create a great opportunity to develop a regime of unprecedented multilateral co-operation. For this to happen, researchers of International Relations must study new ways of political integration, new institutions designed to face global long-term challenges and to embrace new emerging powers, inasmuch as the Western world cannot solve the twenty-first century problems alone and the Global South cannot achieve its most prominent goals without joining forces with developed countries of the North. Ultimately, this may pressure world leaders to rethink the very basis of capitalism (Leggett 2013)—in other words, to develop a "sustainable capitalism"—which will affect our political and social structures. In a much more distant horizon, this could lead to a cosmopolitan perception of the international system, which would beat the current nationalist division of the world.

The capacity of International Relations to make use of a plethora of data and knowledge from other disciplines makes it the right area to study global,

international, national, community and individual perspectives, with the aim of revealing the complexity behind environmental insecurity, prevent wars in the international system and create a new global order based on multilateral cooperation, promoted by the need to preserve our common environment.

## BIBLIOGRAPHIC REFERENCES

Calouste Gulbenkian Foundation. *Water and the Future of Humanity. Revisiting Water Security.* London: Springer, 2014.

Frerks, Georg, Ton Dietz and Pieter van der Zaag. "Conflict and Cooperation on Natural Resources: Justifying the CoCooN Programme." In *Conflicts over Natural Resources in the Global South. Conceptual Approaches*, edited by Maarten Bavinck and Lorenzo Pellegrini, 13–34. CRC Press, Taylor & Francis Group: London, 2014.

Garrett, Nicholas and Anna Piccinni. *Natural Resources and Conflict. A New Security Challenge for the European Union.* Resource Consulting Services: London, 2012.

*Geopolitics of Natural Resource Governance.* Washington, DC: Peterson Institute for International Economics, 2014.

Heywood, Andrew. *Global Politics.* London: Palgrave Macmillan, 2014.

Klare, Michael T. *The Race for What's Left. The Global Scramble for the World's Last Resources.* New York: Picador, 2013.

Le Billon, Philippe. *Wars of Plunder. Conflicts, Profits and the Politics of Resources.* London: Hurst, 2012.

Leggett, Jeremy. *The Energy of Nations: Risk Blindness and the Road to Renaissance.* Routledge: New York, 2013.

Mildner, Stormy-Annika, Solveig Richter and Gitta Lauster. *Resource Scarcity—A Global Security Threat?* SWP: Berlin, 2011.

Pereira, Joana Castro. "Segurança e Governação Climáticas: O Brasil na Cena Internacional." PhD diss., New University of Lisbon, 2013.

Reed, David. *In Pursuit of Prosperity: U.S. Foreign Policy in an Era of Natural Resources Scarcity.* Routledge: New York, 2014.

Schnurr, Matthew A. and Larry A. Swatuk. "Towards Critical Environmental Security." In *Natural Resources and Social Conflict. Towards Critical Environmental Security*, edited by Matthew A. Schnurr and Larry A. Swatuk, 1–14. London: Palgrave Macmillan, 2012.

Viola, Eduardo, Matías Franchini and Thais Lemos Ribeiro. *Sistema Internacional de Hegemonia Conservadora. Governança Global e Democracia na Era da Crise Climática*. São Paulo: Annablume, 2013.

**Notes**

[1] According to the authors, climate change is the main civilizational vector of the present, which requires deep global governance, and it reflects the inability of international institutions to respond to the challenges of the twenty-first century. The system is defined as being "under conservative hegemony" due to the low degree of commitment to global governance and, above all, the climate commitment, since climate change requires a great level of cooperation.

# Climate Change as a Global Security Issue

JOSHUA GOLDSTEIN

Is climate change a global security issue? The answer depends on one's concept of security, but in three ways, the answer could be "yes."

First, and least controversially, a changing climate will affect how and where military forces operate. The US administration has laid out the parameters of these effects in several recent policy documents (White House 2015). Perhaps most interesting from an International Relations (IR) perspective is the opening of the Arctic region as sea ice melts, requiring the adaptation of military forces to operate effectively there, especially if new shipping routes require protection or if conflicts develop over natural resources in this previously inaccessible area (White House 2013).

An obvious example is the question of additional US heavy icebreakers, which currently number just two (lagging behind Russia with twenty-seven as well as Canada, Finland, and Sweden). The navy relies on the coast guard for icebreaking, but even one new heavy icebreaker at a billion dollars would consume the entire annual coast guard acquisition budget.

The likelihood of sea-level rise, storm surges, and widespread extreme weather at home and abroad also affects military planning. Naval bases tend to be located on the coast (!) and are especially vulnerable. Threats to critical infrastructure such as electricity and water systems, roads, runways, and communications also challenge military forces with a more demanding operating environment. Weapons systems must be redesigned for a world of higher temperatures and more moisture and sand.

Humanitarian operations by military forces will also evolve as climate change leads to potential population displacements, infectious disease outbreaks, and response to natural disasters. All these adaptations in military planning, affecting all major military powers, matter greatly for policy decisions but are not particularly interesting from an IR perspective.

The second and more IR-relevant question is whether climate change will lead to increasing armed conflict. The upturn in global violence over the past four years, reversing decades of decline, largely results from the civil war in Syria. Drought has been cited as a contributing factor in that war (Fountain 2015), so it can be argued that this climate effect is already upon us. Homer-Dixon (2001) argued that scarcity of resources—such as water, land, and forests—would increase violent conflict. Many others since (e.g., Klare 2012) have followed similar reasoning, which now seems to be conventional wisdom.

The truth, however, is more ambiguous. Little evidence actually supports a major effect of climate change on intergroup violence at the state and substate levels (Linke et al. 2015; Williams 2015). The situation does vary from country to country (Moran 2011), but in general, effects such as droughts, floods, and crop failures produce poverty but not particularly war. Refugee populations are frequently the effect of armed conflicts but seldom their cause (although there are exceptions, such as the impact of refugees from Rwanda after 1994 on the subsequent civil war in the Democratic Republic of the Congo). Some research suggests that resource scarcity may actually sometimes stimulate international cooperation (Dinar 2011).

One way to assess future climate impacts is to study past natural disasters, which even if not related to climate change produce many of the same results. For example, the 2015 earthquake in Nepal did not reignite the serious civil war there but rather triggered a political breakthrough, ending years of deadlock over the country's postwar governance (Sharma and Barry 2015). Similarly, the devastating tsunami that hit Aceh province in Indonesia in 2004 seems to have strongly contributed to ending the long-standing civil war there the following year.

More fundamentally, and often overlooked in environmental discussions, hundreds of millions of people in the world's poorest countries have been rising up from abject poverty in recent decades, powered by coal and other fossil fuels. Since poverty is the single best predictor of civil war risk (Doyle and Sambanis 2006, 34; Fearon 2008, 293), these rising incomes very likely have contributed to the worldwide decline of armed conflict following the Cold War. Thus, burning coal probably *both* leads to catastrophic climate change and reduces the risks

of armed conflict. (More broadly, economist William Nordhaus [2013] argues that economic growth today in poor countries will better equip them to adapt to climate change in future decades, so the trade-offs are not simple.) Those who blame capitalism and globalization for both climate change and war (e.g., Klein 2014) generally miss these points.

Nuclear power presents a special dilemma. It potentially offers one of the very few scalable carbon-free energy sources that could bring about necessary "deep decarbonization" of the global economy by mid-century. But it also presents risks of proliferation that could lead to scenarios of international violence (e.g., a terrorist nuclear weapon) far more severe than anything seen in recent years. The *Bulletin of the Atomic Scientists'* "doomsday clock" now reflects both nuclear weapons threats and climate threats (which actually are moving in opposite directions over the past thirty years), and the clock-keepers reject increased nuclear risk as a price of solving climate risk (Benedict 2015).

Ironically, few if any of the 15,000 people killed in the 2011 earthquake and tsunami in Japan died from the Fukushima nuclear plant meltdown. Yet, the decisions of Japan and Germany to phase out nuclear power in the wake of that incident, forcing them back onto coal, have caused thousands of deaths from air pollution in the short term and caused Germany to fall off its climate-change targets (Kharecha and Hansen 2013; Eddy 2015). Obviously, this calculus would completely shift if the downside of nuclear energy consisted of nuclear weapons blowing up cities rather than the occasional meltdown forcing long-term evacuations nearby. Thus, the nexus of energy, security, technology, and politics in the nuclear power industry is complex.

The third aspect of climate change that implicates global security is the concept of global warming itself *as* a security threat. If "global security" encompasses human security and economic security rather than strictly military security, then humanity seems likely to face its greatest threats not from the weapons of war but from the inexorable and devastating effects of climate change. Many of the effects of war on society—death and injury, population displacement, hunger, disease, destruction of infrastructure, and economic recession—will result from the increasing severity of weather-related disasters such as droughts, fires, and storms. Most importantly, "tipping point" scenarios of climate change, such as the onset of a new ice age, could pose threats to civilization potentially comparable to the nuclear war fears of earlier times, yet these scenarios remain highly uncertain as of today. The danger is real but not present.

The best analogy, perhaps, would be a meteor discovered to be on a probable collision course with Earth years in the future, with catastrophic but uncertain effects. A costly response now to avoid a bad outcome years in the future would be problematic and entail various collective-goods problems and intergenerational conflicts. Yet, the longer we waited to shoot off some rockets at the thing, the harder it would be to knock it off course. The timing of the disaster would be key: a collision predicted for three years in the future would provoke a massive international response with great-power military forces no doubt mobilized into the effort to Stop the Rock. However, for a likely collision in thirty years—with our lives unaffected meanwhile—the response would be far less certain. The latter is what we face with climate change.

The scholarly IR community will need to adapt if it is to engage a global threat that is not derivative of armed conflict. As Keohane (2015) has cogently argued, climate change poses a new and severe challenge to the adequacy of political institutions. He notes that the complexity of international negotiations, and the difficulty of enacting domestic policies that "require increased payments by the median voter in the current generation," have led to a "malign politics of too little action." International efforts to manage the problem through global governance, such as in the 1997 Kyoto protocol and other comprehensive regimes, have failed. (The 2015 Paris negotiations saw the latest and perhaps more successful efforts to set targets through the United Nations, a process that Victor [2011] criticizes for focusing on getting politically feasible agreements rather than ones that actually make a difference.) Authoritarian governments such as Russia and China have a poor record, but also some major developed democracies—Australia, Canada, and Japan—have backtracked substantially since Kyoto, Keohane observes.

The daunting governance challenges that Keohane identifies should sound familiar to IR scholars. They parallel the big, collective-goods issues in international security such as arms races, nuclear proliferation, and the potential militarization of outer space (as well as nonsecurity issues such as trade deals and fishing conflicts). A major factor of interest to IR scholars, the global North–South divide, has proven fundamental in the breakdown of global governance when it comes to dividing up the costs of preventing catastrophic climate change. Under the Kyoto protocol, poor countries—which after all did not contribute much to the carbon already in the atmosphere—had few obligations. Yet, China is now by far the world's largest carbon polluter (in absolute, not per capita, terms) and countries such as India and Brazil are coming along right behind.

Political scientists face here the perennial question of explaining how to reach cooperation in the absence of a world government. We have many things to say on that subject, but have not done very much when it comes to climate change. Javeline (2014) argues that adaptation to climate change is "fundamentally political," as even the most technical issues in such areas as energy innovation and coastal protection depend on political action that is now stymied both internationally and domestically. Yet, she notes, few political scientists are studying adaptation to climate change.

IR has gone wrong, in my view, by subsuming climate change under "environmental politics." The topics do overlap, since pro-environmental policies and lifestyles tend to use less energy. Furthermore, some work on narrower environmental issues such as watershed pollution has produced concepts relevant to the large climate issue, such as the roles of scientific and technical communities in framing political discourse (Haas 1989)—a major element in UN negotiations guided by scientists on the Intergovernmental Panel on Climate Change.

But a great deal of work on environmental politics has little bearing on climate change. Such topics as the law of the sea, the flow of water and air pollution across national borders, fisheries, biodiversity, and the uses of Antarctica and other global commons all provide fertile ground for studying the international politics of environmental management. Yet, they relate only tangentially to climate change. (Indeed, environmentalism can sometimes even cover for climate inaction, as when someone feels smug about recycling while mindlessly wasting electricity and gasoline.) The widespread notion that climate action is about saving attractive animals such as polar bears makes political solutions all the harder.

Carbon pollution differs from the gamut of more technical and narrow environmental concerns because it results from absolutely fundamental economic processes that powered industrialization and continue to do so in poorer countries just getting a leg up. Climate would seem in many ways more an economic issue than an environmental one. (Of course, it is both and more.)

Furthermore, the "climate movement" today mixes in so many environmental and social justice issues that political discourse has become hopelessly muddled. The key mass demonstration for climate action, in New York in 2014, was led off by some giant sunflowers, had no speeches to provide substantive content, featured many signs mostly opposing various pipelines, and used the slogan "To Change Everything, We Need Everyone."

Perhaps, by recasting climate change as a global security issue, political scientists could make a valuable contribution by redirecting this conversation. Responding to a *security* threat, we would stop trying to "change everything" but rather head off a calamity through practical, focused solutions such as energy innovation, carbon pricing, treaty commitments, and so forth. Our job as political scientists would be to analyze how what we know about politics can make such solutions politically feasible.

If, indeed, a meteor were heading our way, IR scholars would not focus on polar bears or changing everything. We would dive directly into what we do best—studying how weak global norms and institutions can nonetheless resolve the collective-goods problems entailed by the emergence of catastrophic global threats in a world still divided into sovereign states.

## REFERENCES

Benedict Kennette. 2015. "Doomsday Clockwork." *Bulletin of the Atomic Scientists.* Accessed December 18, 2015. http://thebulletin.org/doomsday-clockwork8052.

Dinar Shlomi. 2011. *Beyond Resource Wars: Scarcity, Environmental Degradation, and International Co-operation.* Cambridge, MA: MIT Press.

Doyle Michael W., Sambanis Nicholas. 2006. *Making War and Building Peace: United Nations Peace Operations.* Princeton, NJ: Princeton University Press.

Eddy Melissa. 2015. "Europe Unlikely to Meet Climate Goal, Study Finds." *New York Times*, March 2.

Fearon James D. 2008. "Economic Development, Insurgency, and Civil War." In *Institutions and Economic Performance*, edited by Helpman Ethanan. Cambridge, MA: Harvard University Press.

Fountain Henry. 2015. "Researchers Link Syrian Conflict to a Drought Made Worse by Climate Change." *New York Times*, March 2.

Haas, Peter M. 1989. "Do Regimes Matter? Epistemic Communities and Mediterranean Pollution Control." *International Organization* 43: 377–403.

Homer-Dixon Thomas F. 2001. *Environment, Scarcity, and Conflict.* Princeton, NJ: Princeton University Press.

Javeline Debra. 2014. "The Most Important Topic Political Scientists Are Not Studying: Adapting to Climate Change." *Perspectives on Politics* 12: 420–434.

Keohane Robert O. 2015. "The Global Politics of Climate Change: Challenge for Political Science." *PS: Political Science & Politics* 48: 19–26.

Kharecha Pushker A., Hansen James E. 2013. "Prevented Mortality and Greenhouse Gas Emissions from Historical and Projected Nuclear Power." *Environmental Science and Technology* 47: 4889–4995.

Klare Michael L. 2012. *The Race for What's Left: The Global Scramble for the World's Last Natural Resource.* London: Picador.

Klein Naomi. 2014. *This Changes Everything: Capitalism vs. the Climate.* New York: Simon and Schuster.

Linke Andrew M., Mccabe J. Terrence, O'Loughlin John, Tir Jaroslav, Witmer Frank. 2015. "Rainfall

Variability and Violence in Rural Kenya: Investigating the Effects of Drought and the Role of Local Institutions with Survey Data." *Global Environmental Change* 34: 35–47.

Moran Daniel, ed. 2011. *Climate Change and National Security: A Country-Level Analysis.* Washington, DC: Georgetown University Press.

Nordhaus William. 2013. *The Climate Casino: Risk, Economics, and Uncertainty for a Warming World.* New Haven, CT: Yale University Press.

Sharma Bhadra, Barry Ellen. 2015. "Earthquake Prods Nepal Parties to Make Constitutional Deal." *New York Times*, June 9, A6.

Victor David G. 2011. *Global Warming Gridlock: Creating More Effective Strategies for Protecting the Planet.* New York: Cambridge University Press.

White House. 2015. "Findings from Select Federal Reports: The National Security Implications of a Changing Climate." Accessed December 18, 2015. https://www.whitehouse.gov/sites/default/files/docs/national_security_implications_of_changing_climate_final_051915_embargo.pdf.

White House. 2013. "National Strategy for the Arctic Region." Accessed December 8, 2015. https://www.whitehouse.gov/sites/default/files/docs/nat_arctic_strategy.pdf.

Williams David O. 2015. "Conflict Experts Dispute Impact of Global Climate Change on National Security." *Real Vail*, March 11. Accessed December 18, 2015. http://www.realvail.com/conflict-experts-dispute-impact-of-global-climate-change-on-national-security/a1812.

Section 9

# Human Rights in the World:
# Their Protection and Development

# When Should Governments Subsidize Health?
# The Case of Mass Deworming

AMRITA AHUJA, SARAH BAIRD, JOAN HAMORY HICKS, MICHAEL KREMER, EDWARD MIGUEL, AND SHAWN POWERS

## I. INTRODUCTION

In this paper, we discuss how evidence and theory might be combined to provide insight on appropriate subsidies for the prevention and treatment of communicable diseases, focusing on the case of deworming. Intestinal worm infections are among the most widespread diseases globally, affecting over a billion people mainly in low income countries. Safe, low-cost drugs are available to treat intestinal worm infections and are the standard of medical care. In fact, because treatment is inexpensive and safe but diagnosis is relatively expensive, the World Health Organization (WHO) recommends periodic mass treatments in areas where worm infections are above certain thresholds. However, some have challenged this WHO policy, accepting that those who are known to be infected should be treated, but questioning whether the existing evidence base is strong enough to support mass treatment.

What evidence could one gather to shed light on the question of what public policy is appropriate? That may depend in part on one's normative theoretical perspective, and one could imagine a range of such perspectives. For example: Note that under the first approach, there may not be any evidence that would make deworming subsidies appropriate, and under a strong enough form of the final perspective, subsidies for mass deworming might be appropriate under any evidence that does not challenge the medical appropriateness of deworming for infected individuals and its safety for those without infections. In this article we will review the evidence on deworming to try to shed light on what might be normatively appropriate under perspectives 2 through 4.

1.   A strong *libertarian view* might be that families have different needs and that parents should decide how to spend resources themselves, so that it is inappropriate for the state to take their money in taxes and then decide to subsidize one particular type of expenditure over another.

2.   In a *welfare economics/public finance approach*, individuals are presumed to make decisions that maximize their own welfare, but government intervention may be justified in cases where individual actions create externalities for others. In particular, subsidies may be appropriate if use of the good creates positive externalities. This could include health externalities from reductions in the transmission of infectious disease, as well as fiscal externalities if treatment of children increases their long-run earnings and tax payments.

3.   A third approach focuses on *cost effectiveness in achieving policy maker goals* (and need not assume that the policy maker's goal is to maximize a weighted sum of household utilities). For example, policy makers may seek to achieve universal primary education (as in the Millennium Development Goals) or to maximize GNP growth subject to constraints, which in turn will lead them to undertake investments with high rates of return. The standard welfare economics/public finance approach assumes that consumers will maximize their own welfare, treats them as rational and informed, and abstracts from conflicts within the household (e.g., between parents and children).

This cost effectiveness approach does not do that, but of course it potentially risks efficiently achieving goals that are not those of most citizens.

4. From a *human rights perspective*, individuals might be seen as having a right to good health care. Under this approach, one might argue that children have a basic right to treatment for easily and cheaply treated medical conditions.

We will argue first that deworming is highly responsive to price. Second, we will review evidence showing that mass school-based deworming is a highly cost-effective educational investment and a high-return economic investment even in the absence of any other health benefits from deworming. We will discuss evidence suggesting that the epidemiological and fiscal externalities associated with deworming are large enough to support the WHO's position advocating mass presumptive deworming treatment of children in endemic regions, even under a relatively restrictive welfare economics/public finance perspective. Finally, we will compare the costs associated with the two leading policy options in endemic areas, namely, mass treatment versus the screening and treatment of those found to be infected.

## II. BACKGROUND ON INTESTINAL WORMS

Roughly one in four people are infected with soil transmitted helminthes (STH) in endemic countries (Pullan et al. 2014), and a further 187 million individuals are infected with schistosomiasis, mostly in Africa (Hotez et al. 2006). These two types of worms follow different modes of disease transmission. STH (which include hookworm, whipworm, and roundworm) are transmitted via eggs deposited in the local environment when individuals defecate in their surroundings or do not practice proper hygiene after defecating, while the schistosomiasis parasite is spread through contact with infected fresh water. Due to their transmission mechanisms, school-aged children are especially vulnerable to these worm infections (Hotez et al. 2006).

The potential health consequences of worm infections are generally agreed to depend on the number of worms in the body, rather than a simple binary indicator of infection status, but there is no scientific consensus on the functional form of this relationship. Some have argued that treating worm infections once or twice per year can improve child appetite, growth, and physical fitness (Stephenson et al. 1993), and reduce anemia (Stoltzfus et al. 1997; Guyatt et al. 2001). Deworming may also strengthen the immunological response to other infections, such as malaria (Kirwan et al. 2010) and human immunodeficiency virus (HIV; Kjetland et al. 2006). Furthermore, chronic parasitic infections in childhood generate inflammatory (immune defense) responses and elevated cortisol levels that lead energy to be diverted from growth, and this may produce adverse health consequences throughout the life course, including organ damage, atherosclerosis, impaired intestinal transport of nutrients, and cardiovascular disease (Crimmins and Finch 2005).

Safe, low-cost drugs are available to treat worm infections and are the standard of medical care (Horton 2000; Keiser and Utzinger 2008; Perez et al. 2012). Because treatment is inexpensive and safe but diagnosis is relatively expensive (requiring lab analysis of a stool sample), the WHO recommends periodic mass school-based treatments in areas where worm infections are above certain thresholds (WHO 2014). Mass school-based deworming involves administering deworming drugs to all children at a school in an area where worms are endemic, without individual diagnosis. The Copenhagen Consensus, the Disease Control Priorities Project, Givewell, and the Abdul Latif Jameel Poverty Action Lab (J-PAL) have reviewed the evidence for, and comparative cost-effectiveness of, a wide range of development interventions and have consistently ranked deworming as a priority for investment.

Despite this recommendation, some have challenged the view that mass deworming of schoolchildren should be a policy priority, contending that the evidence on mass treatment programs is of poor quality or inconclusive and is therefore insufficient to justify these programs (Taylor-Robinson et al. 2012; Hawkes 2013), although they do not dispute that those known to be infected with worms should be treated.

By randomizing at the individual level, most studies on deworming in the public health literature fail to consider the potential for epidemiological externalities from treatment, where treatment can improve outcomes not only for the person treated but also others by reducing the chance of disease transmission (Bundy et al. 2009). The underlying biological mechanisms suggest that treating infected people can prevent them from spreading infection, and existing evidence suggests that such externalities can be substantial.

## III. IMPACT OF PRICING ON TAKE-UP

Before turning to the evidence on the educational and economic impacts of deworming, we first discuss evidence on the impact of pricing on take-up. Under standard welfare economics, the ratio of intramarginal to marginal consumers will be important in determining optimal tax and subsidy policy, since the fiscal costs of increasing subsidies are proportional to the number of inframarginal consumers, while the benefits of any positive epidemiological or fiscal externalities depend on the number of marginal consumers who will be induced to deworm by subsidies. Such considerations will also be important from a cost effectiveness perspective. From a human rights perspective, if parents are not willing to pay for treatment, then the larger society may have an obligation to make treatment free and convenient so children can be treated.

Kremer and Miguel (2007) study the behavioral response to a change in the price of deworming treatment in the context of the Kenyan school-based deworming program. The implementing NGO had a policy of using community cost-recovery in its projects to promote sustainability and confer project ownership on its beneficiaries. Thus, starting in 2001, a random subset of participating schools were allocated to pay user fees for the deworming treatment, with the average cost of deworming per child set at US$0.30 (about one-fifth of the cost of drug purchase and delivery through this program). The authors find that this cost-sharing reduced take up by 80 percent, from 75 percent to 19 percent. This result is consistent with findings observed for other products for disease prevention and treatment of nonacute conditions such as bednets for malaria and water treatment.

A more detailed examination of the data on the observed price elasticity of demand suggests that insights from behavioral economics may be important in explaining these results. Cost-sharing came in the form of a per-family fee, so that families with more children effectively faced a lower per-child price. Kremer and Miguel (2007) find no evidence that adoption is sensitive to these variations in positive price, despite the high sensitivity to there being a positive price at all. Moreover, the authors find that user fees did not help target treatment to the sickest students: students with moderate to heavy worm infections were not more likely to pay for the drugs in the cost-sharing schools. In standard models of human capital investment, people weigh the opportunity costs of an investment against the discounted value of returns (Becker 1993). Small fees should not make much difference unless people happen to be right at the margin of whether or not to make the investment. In fact, relatively small short-run costs (e.g., $0.30 per deworming pill) appear to generate large movements in adoption, consistent with models of time inconsistent preferences (Laibson 1997). To the extent that people are subject to behavioral biases, there may be a stronger rationale for policymakers basing decisions on deworming programs on their educational and economic cost-effectiveness rather than on conventional public finance criteria.

## IV. EDUCATION AND LABOR MARKET IMPACTS OF DEWORMING

In this section we summarize the existing evidence on the impact of deworming on education and labor market outcomes. These direct benefits will help inform the cost-effectiveness perspective, while the fiscal externalities resulting from labor market impacts will be important from a welfare economics perspective. The combination of the findings that many parents will not purchase deworming medication for their children and that deworming affects children's educational and economic outcomes raises concerns from the perspective of the human rights of the child. To the extent that governments are committed to ensuring that the rights of children are protected, there may be a stronger case for free mass deworming.

## School Participation

Early work on the links between deworming and education focuses on simple correlations between worm infection levels and school participation, and finds a significant positive relationship between infection rates and school absenteeism ($P$ <.001; Nokes and Bundy 1993). More recently, clustered evaluations have tried to carefully identify the causal effect of deworming on school participation, and avoid issues of confounding that may underlie simple correlations (Bundy, Walson, and Watkins 2013).

In his difference-in-difference study of the US South, Bleakley (2007) finds that between 1910 and 1920 counties characterized by higher worm prevalence prior to the deworming campaign saw substantial increases in school enrollment, both in absolute terms and relative to areas with lower infection rates. The author estimates that a child infected with hookworm would have been 20 percentage points less likely to be enrolled in school than a noninfected child and was also 13 percentage points less likely to be literate. His estimates suggest that due to the deworming campaign, a county with a 1910 infection rate of 50 percent would experience an increase in school enrolment of 3–5 percentage points and an increase in attendance of 6–8 percentage points, relative to a county with no infection problem. Because his analysis is performed at the county (and state) level, these results encompass any within-county (state) externality effects but not spillovers across counties (states).

Since Bleakley (2007) is not randomized, one concern is that something other than deworming is driving the difference in outcomes detected for children. However, the finding remains significant when controlling for a number of potentially confounding factors, such as state-level policy changes during that period and the demographic composition of high- and low-worm load areas. In addition, Bleakley (2007) finds no significant differences in adult outcomes, including literacy and labor force participation, across counties with higher and lower prevalence over the period of the deworming campaign. Since adults had much lower infection rates and hence were unlikely to benefit as much from deworming, the lack of a difference in adult outcomes bolsters the case that deworming, and not something else, was driving the enrollment surge in areas that previously had high hookworm prevalence.

Miguel and Kremer (2004) also provide evidence on the impact of deworming on school participation through their cluster-randomized evaluation of the school-based deworming program in Busia, Kenya. The authors find substantially greater school participation in schools that had been assigned to receive deworming than in those that had not yet been phased in to the program. Participation increased not only among treated children but also among untreated children in the treatment schools (e.g., girls of reproductive age, who at that time were not approved for mass drug administration) and among pupils in schools located near treatment schools. The total increase in school participation, including these externality benefits, was 8.5 percentage points (Miguel and Kremer 2004). As discussed in Dhaliwal et al. (2012), these results imply that deworming is one of the most cost-effective ways of increasing school participation.

## Academic Test Scores

In their study of the Kenyan deworming program, Miguel and Kremer (2004) do not find effects on cognition or a short-run effect on academic test scores. However, the long-run follow-up evaluation of the same intervention (Baird et al. 2014) finds that among females, deworming increased the rate of passing the national primary school exit exam, by almost 25 percent (9.6 percentage points on a base of 40 percent). One hypothesis is that the children receiving treatment were too old for any potential gains in cognitive function but learned more simply through increased school participation.

In the long-run follow-up of the cluster-randomized Uganda deworming program, Croke (2014) analyzes the English, math, and combined test scores comparing treatment and control, as well as looking at whether the impact is greater for those who received multiple deworming treatments as compared to those who were dewormed once. The study finds that children in treatment villages have significantly higher scores as compared to those in control villages, with effect sizes ranging from 0.15 to 0.36 standard deviations.

Effect sizes also more than double for children who were dewormed more than once, but the difference in coefficients is only significant for math scores.

## Employment and Income

Bleakley (2007) uses data from the 1940 US census to compare adult outcomes among birth cohorts who entered the labor force before and after the deworming campaign in the US South. Adults who had more "exposure" to deworming as children were significantly more likely to be literate and had higher earnings as adults. He finds a 43 percent increase in adult wages among those infected as children. This effect is large enough to suggest that hookworm infections could have explained as much as 22 percent of the income gap between the US North and South at the time. Given initial infection rates of 30 percent–40 percent, hookworm eradication would therefore imply a long-run income gain of 17 percent (based on 43 percent increase in wages and a 40 percent infection rate) (Bleakley 2010).

Children who were treated for worms in Kenya also had better outcomes later in life. Baird et al. (2014) consider females and males separately, given the different set of family and labor market choices they face in this context (Pitt, Rosenzweig, and Hassan 2012). They find that Kenyan females who received more deworming treatment have higher school enrollment and are more likely to pass the national primary school exit exam. They are also more likely to grow cash crops and reallocate labor time from agriculture to entrepreneurship. Treated males work 3.5 more hours per week, spend more time in entrepreneurial activities, and are more likely to work in higher-wage manufacturing jobs.

The increases in earnings allow Baird et al. (2014) to compute an annualized internal rate of return (IRR) of 32 percent–52 percent to deworming, depending on whether health spillovers are included. This is high relative to other investments, implying deworming is cost effective on economic grounds, even without counting any health benefits.

Furthermore, because deworming increases labor supply, it creates a fiscal externality though its impact on tax revenue. In fact, Baird et al. (2014) estimate that the net present value (NPV) of increases in tax revenues greatly exceeds the cost of the program. The fiscal externalities are thus sufficiently strong that a government could potentially reduce tax rates by instituting free mass deworming. Deworming thus easily satisfies the weaker conditions required for the benefit to exceed the costs to taxpayers.

## V. THE COST OF MASS TREATMENT PROGRAMS VERSUS SCREENED TREATMENT

The WHO recommends mass treatment once or twice a year in regions where worm prevalence is above certain thresholds (WHO 2014). Screening followed by treatment of those testing positive for worms is far less practical and more costly than mass treatment of infected and uninfected children without diagnostic testing. From a practical perspective, screening programs are also logistically difficult, requiring collection of stool samples, and more than 20 minutes of health worker time per sample collected (Speich et al. 2010). For a national program like the current one in Kenya, this would result in the need for approximately 1,200 health workers focused full time on such testing each year.

Turning attention to costs, delivering deworming medicine for soil-transmitted helminths through school-based programs is estimated to cost approximately US$0.35 per child per round of treatment, including delivery costs (Givewell 2014). Diagnosis of worm infections, on the other hand, is far more expensive and complicated, requiring skilled staff. Taylor-Robinson et al. (2012) state that screening for worm infections is not recommended by the WHO because the cost of screening is 4–10 times that of the treatment itself. Speich et al. (2010) estimate that the cost per child of testing via the Kato–Katz test, the most commonly used method for testing for worms in the field, is US$1.88 in 2013 dollars. Assuming that the test has a specificity of 100 percent (i.e., identifies 100 percent of infections) and that all the children who are screened are also present on the day that treatment is provided, the cost per infection treated would be more than six times higher with treatment following screening as compared to mass treatment without screening. Mass treatment is hence clearly preferred on cost-effectiveness and public finance grounds.

The numbers above, however, ultimately underestimate the cost of screening. First, tests for worms do not identify all infections. Estimates of the specificity for the Kato–Katz method range from about 91 percent to about 52 percent (Barda et al. 2013; Assefa et al. 2014). With a specificity of 52 percent, the cost per infection treated would be about 12 times higher for screened treatment as compared to mass treatment. Second, a large number of infections would remain untreated. The fact that screened treatment programs need to reach infected children a second time to treat them, and that it is unlikely they can reach each child who was tested, makes screening even less cost-effective and leaves even more infections untreated.

The vast majority of the 870 million children at risk of worm infections (Uniting to Combat Neglect Tropical Diseases 2014) could be treated each year via mass deworming programs at a cost of approximately 300 million dollars a year, which is feasible given current health budgets. The cost of treating them via screened programs would likely be closer to 2 billion dollars annually, if not higher.

## VI. CONCLUSION

The WHO recommends mass treatment once or twice a year in regions where worm prevalence is above 20 percent and above 50 percent, respectively (WHO 2014). Deworming is currently being implemented as policy in many parts of the developing world, with recent estimates suggesting that 280 million children (out of 870 million in need) are treated for worms, many via school-based and community-based integrated neglected tropical disease programs (Uniting to Combat Neglect Tropical Diseases 2014).

Our analysis suggests that the WHO recommendations are justified on human rights, welfare economics, and cost-effectiveness grounds. Of course, more evidence would be useful and some uncertainty remains. Although our conclusions are based on evidence from two radically different contexts (East Africa at the turn of the 21st century and the US South at the turn of the 20th century), the impact of deworming will of course vary to some degree with the local context, including circumstances such as type of worm, worm prevalence and intensity, comorbidity, the extent of school participation in the community, and labor market factors.

The most commonly used deworming drugs— albendazole, mebendazole and praziquantel—have all been through clinical trials, have been approved for use by the appropriate regulatory bodies in multiple countries, and have shown to be efficacious against a variety of worm infections and also to have minimal side effects (Horton 2000; Fenwick et al. 2003; Keiser and Utzinger 2008; Perez del Villar et al. 2012). This means that the decision of whether to expend resources on deworming is one that can be made based on comparing expected benefits and costs, given the available evidence.

It is worth noting that deworming would be highly cost effective in many settings on educational and economic grounds alone, even if its benefits were to be only a fraction of those estimated in Kenya, Uganda, and the southern United States. Thus, policy makers would be warranted in moving ahead with deworming even if they thought its benefits were likely to be substantially smaller in their own context, or even if they had some uncertainty about whether benefits would be realized at all. In particular, even if the impact of deworming on school participation is only 1/10th of that estimated in Miguel and Kremer (2004), it would still be among the most highly cost effective ways of boosting school participation. Furthermore, labor markets effects half as large as those estimated in Baird et al. (2014) would be sufficient for deworming to generate enough tax revenue to fully cover its costs. A sophisticated welfare analysis would be explicitly Bayesian, taking into account policy makers' priors and their assessment of their specific context, and we believe that under a Bayesian analysis that placed even modest weight on evidence discussed here, mass school-based deworming would be justified in areas with worm prevalence above the WHO cutoffs.

# REFERENCES

Alderman, Harold, Joseph Konde-Lule, Isaac Sebuliba, Donald Bundy, and Andrew Hall (2006). "Increased Weight Gain in Preschool Children Due to Mass Albendazole Treatment Given During 'Child Health Days' in Uganda: A Cluster Randomized Controlled Trial." *British Medical Journal*, 333, 122-6.

Assefa L.M., T. Crellen, S. Kepha, J.H. Kihara, S.M. Njenga, R.L. Pullan, and S.J. Brooker (2014). "Diagnostic Accuracy and Cost-Effectiveness of Alternative Methods for Detection of Soil- Transmitted Helminths in a Post-Treatment Setting in Western Kenya." *PLoS Neglected Tropical Diseases*, 8(5): e2843.

Baird, Sarah, Joan Hamory Hicks, Michael Kremer, and Edward Miguel (2014). "Worms at Work: Long-Run Impacts of Child Health Gains." *Unpublished Manuscript.*

Banerjee, Abhijit Vinayak, Esther Duflo, Rachel Glennerster, and Dhruva Kothari (2010). "Improving Immunisation Coverage in Rural India: Clustered Randomised Controlled Evaluation of Immunisation Campaigns with and without Incentives." *British Medical Journal*, 340(7759): 1291.

Barda, Beatrice, Henry Zepherine, Laura Rinaldi, Giussepi Cringoli, Roberto Burioni, Massimmo Clementi, and Marco Albonico (2013). "Mini-FLOTAC and Kato-Katz: helminth eggs watching on the shore of lake Victoria." *Parasites & Vectors*, 6: 220.

Becker, Gary (1993). *Human Capital: A Theoretical and Empirical Analysis, with Special Reference to Education*. The University of Chicago Press, Chicago.

Bleakley, Hoyt (2007). "Disease and Development: Evidence from Hookworm Eradication in the American South." *Quarterly Journal of Economics.* 122(1):73-117.

Bleakley, Hoyt (2010). "Health, Human Capital, and Development". *Annual Review of Economics*, 2: 283-310.

Bundy, D.A.P., Michael Kremer, Hoyt Bleakley, Matthew C. Jukes, and Edward Miguel (2009). "Deworming and Development: Asking the Right Questions, Asking the Questions Right." *PLoS Neglected Tropical Diseases*, 3(1), e362.

Bundy, Donald A.P., Judd L. Walson and Kristie L. Watkins (2013). "Worms, wisdom and wealth: why deworming can make economic sense." *Trends in Parasitology*, 29(3): 142-148.

Bundy, D.A.P, M.S. Wong, L.L. Lewis and J. Jorton (1990). "Control of geohelminths by delivery of targeted chemotherapy through schools." *Transactions of the Royal Society of Tropical Medicine and Hygiene.* 84:115-120.

Crimmins, Eileen M., and Caleb E. Finch (2005). "Infection, inflammation, height, and longevity", *Proceedings of the National Academy of Sciences*, 103(2): 498-503.

Croke, Kevin (2014). "The long run effects of early childhood deworming on literacy and numeracy: Evidence from Uganda." *Unpublished Manuscript.*

de Silva, NR, S Brooker, PJ Hotez, A Montresor, D Engels, and L Savioli (2003). "Soil-transmitted helminth infections: updating the global picture." *Trends in Parasitology*, 19(12): 547-51.

Dhaliwal, Iqbal, Esther Duflo, Rachel Glennerster, and Caitlin Tulloch (2012). *"Comparative cost- effectiveness analysis to inform policy in developing countries: a general framework with applications for education."* Cambridge, MA: Abdul Latif Jameel Poverty Action Lab.

Disease Control Priorities Project (2008). *"Deworming Children Brings Huge Health and Development Gains in Low-Income Countries."* Available at www.dcp2.org, accessed October 14, 2014.

Dupas, Pascaline (2014). "Getting essential health products to their end users: Subsidize, but how much?" *Science*, 345: 1279-1281.

Fenwick, Alan, Lorenzo Savioli, Dirk Engels, N. Robert Bergquist, and Matthew H. Todd (2003). "Drugs for the control of parasitic diseases: current status and development in schistosomiasis." *Trends in Parasitology*, 19(11): 509-515.

Givewell (2013). http://www.givewell.org/charities/top-charities. Accessed October 14, 2014.

Givewell (2014). http://www.givewell.org/international/top-charities/deworm-world-initiative. Accessed October 14, 2014.

Guyatt, H.L., A. Brooker, C.M. Kihamia, A. Hall, and D.A. Bundy (2001). "Evaluation of efficacy of school-based anthelmintic treatments against anaemia in children in the United Republic of Tanzania." *Bulletin of the World Health Organization*, 79(8): 695-703.

Hall, Andrew and Sue Horton (2008). *"Best Practice Paper: Deworming."* Copenhagen Consensus Center, Denmark.

Hawkes, Nigel (2013). "Deworming debunked." *British Medical Journal*, 346:e8558.

Horton, J (2000). "Albendazole: a review of anthelmintic efficacy and safety in humans." *Parasitology*, 121 Suppl: S113-32.

Hotez, Peter J, Donald A. P. Bundy, Kathleen Beegle, Simon Brooker, Lesley Drake, Nilanthi de Silva, Lorenzo Savioli (2006). *"Helminth Infections: Soil-transmitted Helminth Infections and Schistosomiasis"* in Disease Control Priorities in Developing Countries (2nd edition), (eds.) Dean T Jamison, Joel G Breman, Anthony R Measham, George Alleyne, Mariam Claeson, David B Evans, Philip Musgrove. Washington DC: World Bank.

J-PAL Policy Bulletin (2011). *"The Price is Wrong."* Cambridge, MA: Abdul Latif Jameel Poverty Action Lab.

J-PAL Policy Bulletin (2012). *"Deworming: A Best Buy for Development."* Cambridge, MA: Abdul Latif Jameel Poverty Action Lab.

Kabatereine N, Tukahebwa E. Brooker S, Alderman H, Hall A (2001). "Epidemiology of intestinal helminth infections among schoolchildren in southern Uganda." *East African Medical Journal*, 78: 283-6.

Keiser, J. and J. Utzinger (2008). "Efficacy of current drugs against soil-transmitted helminth infections: systematic review and meta-analysis." *Journal of the American Medical Association*, 299(16): 1937-48.

Kirwan, Patrick, Andrew L Jackson, Samuel O Asaolu, Sile F Molloy, Titilayo C Abiona, Marian C Bruce, . . . and Celia V Holland (2010). "Impact of repeated four-monthly anthelmintic treatment on Plasmodium infection in preschool children: a double-blind placebo-controlled randomized trial." *BMC Infectious Diseases*, 10: 277.

Kjetland EF, Ndhlovu PD, Gomo E, Mduluza T, Midzi N, Gwanzura L, Mason PR, . . . and Gundersen SG (2006). "Association between genital schistosomiasis and HIV in rural Zimbabwean women." *AIDS*, 20(4): 593-600.

Kremer, Michael, and Rachel Glennerster. (2011). *"Improving Health in Developing Countries: Evidence from Randomized Evaluations"* in Handbook of Health Economics (Vol. 2), (eds.) Mark V. Pauly, Thomas G. Mcguire and Pedro P. Barros, Elsevier Press.

Kremer, Michael, and Alaka Holla (2009). *"Pricing and Access: Lessons from Randomized Evaluations in Education and Health"* in What Works in Development: Thinking Big and Thinking Small, eds. W. Easterly and J. Cohen. Washington: Brookings Institution Press.

Kremer, Michael, and Edward Miguel (2007). "The Illusion of Sustainability." *Quarterly Journal of Economics*, 112(3): 1007-1065.

Laibson, David (1997). "Golden Eggs and Hyperbolic Discounting." *Quarterly Journal of Economics*, 102(2): 443-477.

Miguel, Edward and Michael Kremer (2004). "Worms: Identifying Impacts on Education and Health in the Presence of Treatment Externalities." *Econometrica*, 72(1): 159-217.

Miguel, Edward and Michael Kremer (2014). "Guide to Replication of Miguel and Kremer (2004)." Accessible at http://emiguel.econ.berkeley.edu/research/worms-identifying-impacts-on-education-and-health-in-the-presence-of-treatment-externalities.

Nokes, C. and D.A.P. Bundy (1993). "Compliance and absenteeism in school children: implications for helminth control." *Transactions of the Royal Society of Tropical Medicine and Hygiene*, 87: 148-152.

Ozier, Owen (2014). *"Exploiting Externalities to Estimate the Long-Term Effects of Early Childhood Deworming."* World Bank Policy Research Working Paper #7052.

Perez del Villar L, Burguillo FJ, Lopez-Aban J, Muro A. 2012. "Systematic Review and Meta- Analysis of Artemisinin Based Therapies for the Treatment and Prevention of Schistosomiasis." *PLoS ONE*, 7(9): e45867.

Pitt, Mark M., Mark R. Rosenzweig, and Nazmul Hassan (2012). "Human Capital Investment and the Gender Division of Labor in a Brawn-Based Economy." *American Economic Review*. 102(7): 3531-3560.

Pullan, R.L., J.L. Smith, R. Jasrasaria, S.J. Brooker (2014). "Global numbers of infection and disease burden of soil transmitted helminth infections in 2010." *Parasites and Vectors*, 7: 37.

Simeon, Donald T., Sally M. Grantham-McGregor, Joy E. Callender and Michael S. Wong (1995). "Treatment of Trichuris trichiura Infections Improves Growth, Spelling Scores and School Attendance in Some Children." *The Journal of Nutrition*, 125(7): 1875-1883.

Speich, Benjamin, Stefanie Knopp, Khalfan A Mohammed, I Simba Khamis, Laura Rinaldi,

Giuseppe Cringoli, David Rollinson and Jürg Utzinger (2010). *Parasites & Vectors*, 3(71): 1-11.

Stephenson, L.S., MC Latham, EJ Adams, SN Kinoti and A Pertet (1993). "Physical fitness, growth and appetite of Kenyan school boys with hookworm, Trichuris trichiura and Ascaris lumbricoides infections are improved four months after a single dose of albendazole." *The Journal of Nutrition*, 123(6): 1036-1046.

Stoltzfus, R.J., Chwaya HM, Tielsch JM, Schulze KJ, Albonico M, and Savioli L (1997). "Epidemiology of iron deficiency anemia in Zanzibari schoolchildren: the importance of hookworms", *American Journal of Clinical Nutrition*, 65(1): 153-9.

Taylor-Robinson, David C., Nicola Maayan, Karla Soares-Weiser, Sarah Donegan, and Paul Garner (2012). "Deworming drugs for soil-transmitted intestinal worms in children: effects on nutritional indicators, haemoglobin and school performance." *Cochrane Database of Systematic Reviews*, Issue 11. Art. No.: CD000371.

Uniting to Combat Neglected Tropical Diseases. 2014. "Delivering on Promises and Driving Progress". Available at http://unitingtocombatntds.org/sites/default/files/document/NTD_report_04102014_v4_sing les.pdf. Accessed October 14, 2014.

Watkins WE, Cruz JR, and Pollitt E (1996). "The effects of deworming on indicators of school performance in Guatemala." *Transactions of the Royal Society of Tropical Medicine and Hygiene*, 90(2): 156-61.

World Health Organization (2014). "Soil-transmitted helminth infections" Fact Sheet N°366. http://www.who.int/mediacentre/factsheets/fs366/en/, accessed October 17, 2014.

# Passions about Migrants

IMMANUEL WALLERSTEIN

In a world in which almost any subject seems to arouse deep cleavages within and among countries, arguably the one that has today the deepest and geographically widest resonance is migrants. At the moment, the most acute locus of attention is Europe, where there is a vociferous debate concerning how European countries should respond to the flight to Europe of refugees, especially those from Syria but also those from Iraq and Eritrea.

The basic argument in European public debate has been one between the advocates of compassion and morality who wish to welcome additional migrants and the advocates of self-protection and cultural preservation who wish to close the door against the entry of any more. Europe is in the spotlight for the moment, but parallel debates have long been going on across the world—from the United States and Canada to South Africa, Australia, Indonesia, and Japan.

The immediate precipitant of the European debate is the massive outflow from Syria, where the deterioration of the conflict has created an acute state of personal danger for a very large percentage of the population. Syria has become a country to which it is considered against international law to return emigrants. The debate has been about what therefore to do.

There are three different ways in which one can analyze the underlying issues: in terms of the consequences of migrants for the world and national economies, for local and regional cultural identities, and for the national and world political arenas. A good part of the confusion stems from a failure to distinguish these three perspectives.

If one starts with the economic consequences, the principal question is whether taking in migrants is a plus or minus for the receiving country. The answer is that it depends on which country.

Immanuel Wallerstein, "Passion about Migrants." *Commentary* No. 409, Sept. 15, 2015. http://iwallerstein.com/articles/. Reprinted with permission of Immanuel Wallerstein.

We are now familiar with the demographic transition in which the wealthier the country, the more likely it is that families with middle-level incomes will have fewer children. This is basically because reproducing for one's child the same or higher income prospects requires a considerable investment in formal and informal education. This is financially burdensome if one does it for more than one child. In addition, improved health facilities result in longer-lived populations.

The consequence over time of a lowered birth-rate and longer lives is that the demographic profile of a country becomes tilted to a higher percentage of older persons and a lengthening of the period in which a child is kept out of the active labor market. It follows that fewer persons in the active work range are supporting an increased number of persons at the older and younger age ranges.

One solution for this is to accept migrants, who can expand the proportion of the active work force and thereby ease the problem of financial support for the older and younger populations of the country. Against this argument is the assertion that the immigrants tap welfare resources and are therefore costly. But the welfare outputs seem to cost far less than the income from the active work inputs plus the additional taxes from working immigrants.

The situation is of course quite different in less wealthy countries, where the major impact of accepting migrants would be precisely to threaten the jobs of a population still willing to agree to do onerous work because of the country's overall demographic profile.

As for the world-economy as a whole, migration merely shifts the location of individuals and probably changes very little. Migrants do however pose a global cost because of the necessity to limit the negative humanitarian consequences of enormous numbers of migrants. Just think of paying for rescuing drowning migrants who have fallen off shaky boats in the Mediterranean.

If one looks at the question from the perspective of cultural identity, the arguments are quite different. All states promote a national identity as a necessary mechanism of ensuring the primacy of allegiance. But of what national identity are we talking? Is it French-ness or Chinese-ness? Or is it Christian-ness or Buddhist-ness? This is precisely the question that differentiates the position of Germany's Chancellor Angela Merkel and Hungary's President Viktor Orban. Merkel asserts that new migrants of whatever ethnic or religious origin can be integrated as German citizens. Orban sees Muslim migrants as invaders that threaten the permanence of Hungary's Christian identity.

The debate extends beyond national boundaries. For Merkel, the migrant's integration is not only to Germany but to Europe. For Orban, the migrant's threat is not only to Hungary, the state, but to all of "Christian Europe." But see the comparable debate in France about Muslim garb for women. For some, the question is not relevant if the migrants give their loyalty to France as a citizen. But for defenders of an absolute version of laïcité, Muslim garb for women is totally unacceptable, violating the cultural identity of France.

There is no middle path in this kind of cultural debate. It creates an absolute impasse. And precisely because it creates an impasse, this pushes the discussion to the political arena. The ability to prevail in implementing a cultural priority depends on being able to control the political structures. Merkel and Orban, as every other politician, must obtain political support (including of course votes) or they are removed from the decision-making process. In order to maintain themselves in office, they often have to make concessions to strong currents of opinion that they do not like. This may also involve adjustments in economic policy. So, if on one day they lay out a clear line of policy, the next day they may seem to be less firm. The actors have to maneuver in a national, regional, and world political arena.

Where will Europe be ten years from now in terms of feelings about migrants? Where will the world be? It is an open question. Given the chaotic realities of a world in transition to a new historical system, we can only say that it depends on the moment-by-moment changing strengths of the contesting programs for the future. Migrants are one locus of the debate, but the debate is much wider.

# Hearts and Minds: Culture and Nationalism

# The Populist Challenge to Human Rights

PHILIP ALSTON

## 1. THE SHAPE OF THINGS TO COME

The world as we in the human rights movement have known it in recent years is no longer. The populist agenda that has made such dramatic inroads recently is often avowedly nationalistic, xenophobic, misogynistic, and explicitly antagonistic to all or much of the human rights agenda. As a result, the challenges the human rights movement now faces are fundamentally different from much of what has gone before. This does not mean, as scholars have told us, that these are "the endtimes of human rights" (Hopgood 2013), that human rights are so compromised by their liberal elite association that they are of little use in the fight against populism (Hopgood 2016), or that we have entered "the post-human rights era" (Wuerth 2016). Nor does it mean that we should all despair and move on, or that there is a "desperate need" to find tools other than human rights with which to combat the many challenges brought by the new populism combined with an old authoritarianism with which we are all too familiar (Moyn 2016).

But it does mean that human rights proponents need to rethink many of their assumptions, re-evaluate their strategies, and broaden their outreach, while not giving up on the basic principles. As each new wave of bad news sweeps in, most of us are now suffering from commentary and analysis fatigue. But there has not been enough reflection by human rights advocates on the innovative thinking and creative strategizing that are urgently needed.

One justification for the absence of such analysis is that it is too soon. We need to wait and see what will happen before we can know how to respond. Sadly, it's not true. We might not yet know exactly what policies the new Trump Administration will adopt either bilaterally or in multilateral forums, or how exactly the political chemistry among the leaders of the new world disorder will work, but we know the basics in terms of the challenges that will confront human rights advocates.

Assuming then that the general thrust of the future policy on rights is what Donald Rumsfeld would call a "known known," the other important variable is that an increasingly diverse array of governments have all expressed a desire to push back against key pillars of the international human rights regime. While it is certainly true that the nature and extent of the challenges differ greatly from one country to the next, it also seems that they have much in common. For the purposes of considering the implications for the international regime I would foresee, with considerable confidence, the emergence of a powerful and energetic "coalition of the willing," to reprise an infamous phrase from the not so distant past. The coalition will consist of governments of many different stripes which are keen to challenge and dilute existing human rights standards and especially to undermine existing institutional arrangements which threaten to constrain them in any way.

There have always been coalitions of would-be wreckers, but in the past they have met with at least some pushback from the United States and other leading Western and Latin American governments. The prospect of effective pushback in the future is now evaporating before our eyes. We will soon know what sorts of coalitions from hell will emerge in the context of the UN Human Rights Council, the International Criminal Court, the Inter-American human rights system, and so on. Unpredictability is certain, but few targets will be off limits. In contrast to the past, the coalitions will be more diverse, less focused on particular issues, more willing to depart from established understandings and conventions, and less constrained by appeals to behave responsibly or in line with their legal obligations.

## 2. MINDSET

Before reflecting on how best the international human rights community can respond to challenges that will undoubtedly be more severe and sustained than anything we have witnessed since the depths of the cold war, it is useful to keep some general principles in mind.

First, we need to maintain perspective, despite the magnitude of the challenges. Defending human rights has never been a consensus project. It has almost always been the product of struggle. The modern human rights regime emerged out of the ashes of the deepest authoritarian dysfunction and the greatest conflagration the world had ever seen. It has duelled with and been shaped by the eras of reluctant decolonization, the cold war, neoliberalism, and now populism. Dejection and despair are pointless and self-defeating. It's assuredly not a lost cause, but we should not be fooled into thinking that it's ever going to be a winning cause; it's an ongoing struggle.

Second, this is the start of a long-term effort; it won't be over in four years. I don't need to read out the "honour" roll of recently triumphant populists, nor the list of those waiting in the wings, shortly to gain their moment of glory. But there are many, and no continent is immune—unless we count Antarctica, but even there I suspect that there are some very alienated and angry penguins! The main characteristic of the new populist–authoritarian era is disdain for social conventions, a currency on which respect for human rights norms has long been heavily dependent. The devaluation of that currency opens up immense horizons for the enemies of human rights.

Third, the human rights movement needs to develop a spirit of introspection and openness. Historically, it has not responded well to criticism. As long as the critics were mainly governments seeking to defend themselves or despairing deconstructionist scholars, it was not difficult to continue with business as usual. Going forward, it will be highly desirable for the movement to be open to reflecting on its past shortcomings and to involve a broader range of interlocutors in its reflections than has been the case in the past. Most "lessons learned" exercises seem to have been solely or largely internal affairs, and it is most unclear how many lessons have actually been learned. Perhaps the starting point is greater transparency in acknowledging what lessons we think we need to learn.

## 3. SOME KEY ISSUES

In terms of specifics, there are a great many issues that will demand our attention in the years ahead. I want to focus on just five, all of which seem to me to be central to the challenges that we now confront.

The first is the populist threat to democracy. While this is a complex phenomenon, much of the problem is linked to post-9/11 era security concerns, some of which have blended seamlessly into an actual or constructed fear and hatred of foreigners or minorities. The resulting concerns have been exploited to justify huge trade-offs. This is not only a strategy pursued by governments of many different stripes, but one that has been sold with remarkable success to the broader public. People are now widely convinced that security can only be achieved through making enormous trade-offs, whether in terms of freedom of movement, privacy, non-discrimination norms, or even personal integrity guarantees. The new era of internal threats, which have dramatically increased in recent years, is bringing with it a move to normalize states of emergency. For example, remarkably little attention has been paid as the French government continues to extend and enthusiastically implement a rather draconian state of emergency. This is not for a moment to suggest that the seriousness of the threats that may have been identified, and the horrors that have taken place, should be downplayed, but the fact that the depth and scope of the emergency provisions have been so little debated is both stunning and instructive.

And it is not just in countries that are already in turmoil that there is a declining faith in democracy. Foa and Mounk (2016), building on their earlier work, have recently suggested three tests that should be applied in order to assess the robustness of democracy. The first is the extent of public support. In other words, how important is it for people that their country remains democratic. The second is the openness of the public to the possibility of a non-democratic government, gauged in terms of whether individuals would countenance military rule "if needs be." If things went really wrong, would we countenance a role for the military in the governance of the UK? Would we countenance that in Australia? The third test is the extent to which anti-system parties and movements have grown in the society. Based on these criteria, the authors argue that there has in fact already been a radical diminution in the support for democracy in many of the established democracies. In other words, there is a growing openness to considering alternatives which might be seen to offer a happier future.

The second major issue is the role of civil society. It is now fashionable among human rights proponents to decry the fact that the "space for civil society is shrinking." But this phrase is all too often a euphemism, when the reality is that the space has already closed in a great many countries. The opportunities for civil society to operate are being closed down, and very effectively so in many countries. I was in Mauritania earlier this year in my capacity as UN Special Rapporteur on extreme poverty and human rights. In principle, one can set up a human rights NGO in Mauritania. All that is needed is prior authorization from the Ministry of Interior, which takes a very, very long time to get; and if you are serious about human rights, it is unlikely ever to come. Many organizations thus have to operate without authorization, which brings the possibility of being arrested and imprisoned at any moment. The one sector that is absolutely thriving is that of government-sponsored NGOs. I have had meetings in Geneva with NGO representatives who flew over to Geneva just to meet me. They let me know that I had completely misunderstood all that was going on in the country and that in fact the government was totally dedicated to promoting respect for human rights and was the best chance there is in this regard; this was the NGO sector. A month or so after my visit to the country, during which I met with some of the most prominent and respected activists, four

of them from the *Initiative pour la Résurgence du Mouvement Abolitionniste*, the leading NGO fighting against the rather considerable "remnants of slavery," were arrested on charges that are widely considered to have been trumped up. They were charged with participating in a demonstration at which they claim they were not present, but which turned violent. For their troubles, they and several others were sentenced to terms of between three and fifteen years in prison. So much for civil society's shrinking space. In many countries it has shrunk to the size of a prison cell.

I also visited China, in August 2016. It was appropriate for the government to have invited a rapporteur dealing with poverty given the immense and certainly admirable progress it has made towards eliminating extreme poverty. But a visit by an independent expert to China was an interesting experience, if I can put it that way. Through research and suggestions, I obtained the names of a range of distinguished scholars, some of whom worked on human rights issues but most of whom were in development-related fields. I contacted them by phone, email, text, or whatever and sought meetings. But almost to a person, they informed me that my visit would coincide with time they had set aside to visit their parents in the countryside. Now I know that the values of familial loyalty are highly prized in China, and indeed are enforceable by law, but this seemed like a very strange coincidence. The reality was much more likely that a loud and clear message had been sent by the authorities that none of them was to speak to a UN Special Rapporteur. One of those who did manage to meet with me, a well known human rights lawyer named Jiang Tianyong, was subsequently arrested and has been charged with crimes that are sure to bring very severe penalties. Others were subsequently harassed systematically immediately after meeting with me. And in case the powers of the security services prove insufficient, the government has adopted a law making it virtually impossible for any but entirely innocuous foreign NGOs to work in China, and a separate law regulating charities which leaves funding for human rights work entirely at the government's discretion. Between them these new laws and regulations have basically succeeded in closing all space for any groups that consider themselves to be working on human rights. As I noted in my end of mission statement, the overall strategy involves "a carefully designed law and order Pincer Movement" (UN OHCHR 2016).

The third issue is the linkage between inequality and exclusion. Populism is driven in part by fear and resentment. To the extent that economic policies are thus critical, it is noteworthy that mainstream human rights advocacy addresses economic and social rights issues in a tokenistic manner at best, and the issue of inequality almost not at all. Similarly, the focus of most human rights advocacy is on marginal and oppressed individuals and minority groups. From our traditional perspective, that is how it should be—they are the ones who most need the help. People like me do not need help—elderly white males are fine thank you, we are doing well. But the reality is that the majority in society feel that they have no stake in the human rights enterprise, and that human rights groups really are just working for "asylum seekers," "felons," "terrorists," and the like. This societal majority seems far less likely today than it might have been in the past to be supportive of the rights of the most disadvantaged merely out of some disappearing ethos of solidarity. I believe that a renewed focus on social rights and on diminishing inequality must be part of a new human rights agenda which promises to take into account the concerns, indeed the human rights, of those who feel badly done by as a result of what we loosely call globalization-driven economic change.

The fourth issue that I want to highlight is the undermining of the international rule of law. This is a potentially huge area and I will focus on just two aspects of it. The first is the systematic undermining of the rules governing the international use of force. Western countries, and particularly the United States through the global operations of the Central Intelligence Agency (CIA) and the Joint Strategic Operations Command (JSOC) and its ever-supportive, never-questioning allies such as the United Kingdom and Australia, have set us up very nicely for the era of Syria, Crimea and Yemen in which countries wishing to use force can more or less write their own rules. Having stood

by and let those different agencies operate around the world carrying out targeted killings and other dubious acts, we are not well placed to then turn around and say that some of the tactics used by countries we do not like are in violation of international rules. The assiduous efforts of government legal advisers in countries like the United States, the United Kingdom, and Australia to rationalize these incursions are now reaping the rewards that they so richly deserve. It's tragic. When I was involved in my capacity as UN Special Rapporteur on extrajudicial executions in the debate over targeted killings, I warned that the countries justifying these practices were setting precedents that would inevitably be invoked by much less well-meaning forces in the future, and by administrations that had even fewer qualms about legality (UN Human Rights Council 2010). Those practices are now coming back to haunt us.

The second aspect of the international rule of law concerns the shocking breakdown in respect for the principles of international humanitarian law. In a 2016 opinion poll undertaken by the International Committee of the Red Cross (ICRC), a mere 30 percent of American respondents considered it to be unacceptable to torture a captured enemy combatant "to obtain important military information." In the same poll, taken in 1999, the figure had been 65 percent. In Nigeria, 70 percent supported such torture and in Israel 50 percent did (ICRC 2016: 10). Systematic targeted attacks on medical facilities, on operations by *Médecins Sans Frontières* and other humanitarian groups are commonplace and barely remarked upon. The United States did apologize for one very direct and inexplicably precisely targeted attack, but its denials are not credible in the absence of any independent inquiry. At the same time, the UK Prime Minister is promising to liberate British forces from the constraints imposed upon them if they have to respect the European Convention on Human Rights. And during his campaign, President Trump made similar noises about how US troops had fought "very politically correct" wars implying that they should not be constrained by laws and standards that their enemies don't fully respect. His most specific proposal for dealing with terrorists was the insight that "you have to take out their families." International humanitarian law is in for a rough ride.

The fifth and final issue concerns the fragility of international institutions. The International Criminal Court (ICC) is under sustained attack with various African states announcing their planned withdrawals. And the announcement by the Office of the Prosecutor that she is actively investigating the activities of the CIA and other forces in Afghanistan and related countries will also further endear the court to the Trump Administration. We are in for an extremely tough ride in terms of trying to withstand and protect what has been achieved by the ICC and its immense potential.

## 4. TOWARDS AN AGENDA

Perhaps that is enough gloom and doom, so let me try to be a little bit more constructive. What sort of strategies does the human rights community need to start considering in response to the fundamentally new circumstances that we are now confronting?

### 4.1 Local/International Synergies

We need to reflect on how better to ensure effective synergies between international and local human rights movements. The large NGOs have still not achieved the right balance. Human Rights Watch is perhaps the classic example, but it is by no means alone. Its original model relied heavily on the assumption that the US government or congress or both would be responsive to reporting and lobbying, at least in response to significant violations in a reasonable range of countries. It then broadened its template so that recommendations were also addressed to as many other entities as possible, but the basic assumptions remained. As it became more apparent that there is no substitute for (also) advocating at the country level, it made a huge effort to establish national offices at the country level. But it is not clear that the fundamental model has changed significantly, even if the geographical scope has expanded. The deeper challenge is to see how the activities of international NGOs can have less of an extractive character (extracting information and

leaving) and focus more on building or complementing national capacity. Of course, this is not always possible, but where it is, it is the key to sustainability. For its part, Amnesty International has undergone dramatic decentralization, but it is far from clear that it has yet found the best formula for strengthening local and national capacities. And it is increasingly clear that we can no longer rely on one level or the other operating in isolation. There will be times when only international groups can function effectively; but there will also be situations in which exclusively international advocacy will be ineffective and perhaps counterproductive.

### 4.2 The Economics of Rights

Economic and social rights must be an important and authentic part of the overall agenda. In a recent report to the Human Rights Council I argued that a surprisingly small proportion of self-described human rights NGOs do anything much on economic and social rights (UN Human Rights Council 2016, on the marginality of economic and social rights). Is that a problem? The United States government and many others have argued that this is how it should be because if people enjoy political freedoms they can stand up for their social rights. But empirically, the argument does not stand up. The enjoyment of civil rights has not brought social rights to a great many residents of the United States; and it has not on its own brought them to most other countries. We need to start insisting, in fidelity to the Universal Declaration of Human Rights, that the catalogue of human rights includes equally both categories of rights. That does not mean that every human rights group must suddenly devote itself to economic and social rights, but all groups should reflect on ways in which they can constructively contribute to both sides of the agenda. Amnesty International has tried, but they have not yet succeeded. They have been reluctant to grasp the real nettle which is the need to treat economic and social rights as full-fledged human rights. What is not needed is to move the focus to the blight of poverty, or to denials of dignity, or even to the need for more resources for development.

What is needed, in broad outline, is to follow the recipe that we have developed for civil and political rights promotion at the domestic level. Take the fight against torture, for example. The first thing we say to a state is that we do not just want blind assurances that it will not torture; rather we want legislation in place to ban the practice. We then ask for institutions that are able to follow up by promoting good practices and monitoring. And finally, we insist upon accountability, so that torturers can be prosecuted and governments held to account.

A great many human rights proponents still resist this sort of analysis by insisting that economic and social rights are fundamentally different because of the resources they require for their full implementation. But this distinction has long ago been discredited. All rights cost money and society is always called upon to make choices. The current choice whereby civil and political rights are privileged and economic and social rights are all but ignored works fine for the elites. It suits me, for example. As an older white male, I suffer no discrimination, I have a generous pension and excellent health insurance, my children's schooling is provided for. All I really need is that my civil and political rights are protected so that I am not arbitrarily arrested, nor prevented from expressing my views, and that I am secure in public. But that list of priorities does little to capture the principal threats facing the great majority of the population. If the concept of human rights is to have strong universal appeal, the other side of the balance sheet also needs to be promoted.

## 4.3 Broadening the Base
The next challenge is for the human rights community to start expanding its horizons in terms of thinking about which other actors it can work with. The renewed push for privatization, along with the continuing abdication of governmental responsibility for various functions, guarantees that the huge role already played by corporate actors will only grow in the years ahead. I must confess that while I think engagement with corporate actors is necessary and indispensable, I have always retained a fundamental scepticism about the proposition

that businesses are going to be persuaded to act as great proponents of human rights. While the Guiding Principles on Business and Human Rights and other such initiatives have achieved a breakthrough in some respects, we also need to begin more of a big-picture conversation with the larger corporations about whether an authoritarian, anti-rights, and anti-welfare future is really in their interests. They, but also we, need to start thinking about where, how and when they can legitimately and constructively stand up to policies that cross certain lines and how they can use their influence and power to make the case for more human rights–friendly approaches. And it is not just corporations. We need to start thinking more creatively about other potential allies with whom the human rights movement can cooperate.

## 4.4 Persuasion
Next, we need to acknowledge the need to devote more time and effort to being persuasive and convincing, rather than simply annunciating our principles as though they were self-evidently correct and applicable. By way of example, I recently wrote a report on the responsibility of the United Nations for bringing cholera to Haiti. In that report I started by observing that "arguments based on human rights or international law often do not suffice to convince Member States, or even the United Nations, to take the necessary steps." I added that those "in authority also need to be convinced of the unsustainability and costliness of existing policies, and of the feasibility of change" (UN General Assembly 2016). A human rights defender, for whom I have immense respect, and who saw the draft, suggested that the statement be taken out on the grounds that the role of human rights proponents is to state principles and remind actors of their responsibilities, not to acknowledge that they might need more broad-based encouragement as well. I demurred because I strongly believe that we need to be much more instrumentalist than we have been in the past. I think we need to start thinking why the other side is not doing what we consider to be the right thing. While there are egregious violations to which this doesn't apply, a

great many human rights issues are quite complex and a concerted effort to understand the other side, to address their formal as well as their real concerns, and to seek to identify constructive ways forward, will bring much greater results.

Linked to this approach of seeking to be more persuasive, I think we need to take a step back from the absolutism that sometimes manifests itself. We pride ourselves, sometimes rightly and unavoidably, on being uncompromising. We fear that if we make any concessions along the way we are selling out on the basics of human rights. As an antidote to this type of thinking, it behooves us to recall a lecture given some 25 years ago by José ("Pepe") Zalaquett. He is a very distinguished human rights defender, former head of Amnesty International's International Executive Committee, and a member of the Chilean National Commission for Truth and Reconciliation. In it he explained the choice that the commission had made in giving priority to truth over justice (Zalaquett 1992). His lecture conveyed in a thoughtful and nuanced manner a number of messages that today's human rights movement needs to keep very much in mind. First, the path forward in strongly contested situations is rarely straightforward. There are many dilemmas to be confronted and choices to be made. There are, as Pepe said, "no hard and fast rules on how to proceed." Second, the politics of absolutism and ideological purity can easily be self-defeating:

> In the face of a disaster brought about by their own misguided actions, politicians cannot invoke as a justification that they never yielded on matters of conviction. That would be as haughty as it would be futile. . . .

Third, there is a need to strike a balance between the principles involved and the "actual political opportunities and constraints." And fourth, while none of this should involve compromising on fundamental principles, it requires a creative exploration of the art of the possible.

Adopting a more calibrated approach that acknowledges the times in which we live and the context in which we function might also mean breaking with some of the old certainties. Let me give an example which I expect will be highly controversial within the human rights community. It concerns the potentially existential threat to the International Criminal Court. In championing opposition to the Court a number of African governments in particular have been motivated by their opposition to the principle that sitting Heads of State are subject to the Court's jurisdiction. A number of states that are planning to leave, or contemplating the possibility, claim that it is because they consider it to be unacceptable that a Head of State can have charges brought against him or her, and then be required to appear before the Tribunal at The Hague. Let me note immediately that one of the great achievements of the Rome Statute is precisely the principle that no one is immune, and that everyone is subject to the Court's jurisdiction, if they are alleged to have committed any of the grave crimes listed in the statute. In principle, it seems clear to the human rights community that few individuals could be more deserving of such an indictment than a president who is in office and who is undertaking such criminal acts. But we might also need to step back for a moment and acknowledge the extraordinary importance of the ICC enterprise in historical, legal, cultural and other terms and the fact that there is a huge amount at stake which goes far beyond the principle of Head of State immunity. The fact is that in a great many countries sitting Heads of State are not able to be prosecuted. France is a well-known example in this regard. And in some such contexts, there even continues to be a deep reluctance or unwillingness to bring the full force of domestic law to bear against a former President. So the question is whether supporters of the ICC should not contemplate making some sort of concession. It would not and should not involve an amendment to the Statute, but it could well involve a readiness to consider agreeing that the Security Council can use its existing authority to defer the commencement of any proceedings in such circumstances. This can only be done on a year to year basis, but it would respond to the concerns that many states have that international practice has moved dramatically ahead of what many countries are prepared to accept. I don't want to exaggerate the importance of this particular example, but I do think that we need to start thinking more creatively about what it is that might take some of the wind out of the sails of the principal opponents to some key initiatives. As Pepe Zalaquett's comments suggest, this does not mean a surrender. We cannot give up on fundamental principles but there are strategies for moving in the right direction and they might not be all or nothing approaches.

## 4.5 The Role of Scholars

What role do scholars have in all of this? As teachers, as researchers, as publicists, we have obligations to our students and to our readers. It has become fashionable, especially at elite universities in the West, to disparage human rights by accentuating in dramatic and sometimes destructive ways the undoubted shortcomings of international human rights norms and institutions. At a range of law schools that I have visited I have encountered students who have become deeply disillusioned or cynical because they have been taught that the human rights enterprise is largely an illusion, that it is not something that they really should be putting their time into, that it is built on sand, and that it has no future. I remember a talk given at New York University by one of the world's leading international legal scholars which was essentially about the illusion of human rights; why there can be no such thing as a valid meta-norm and why there could not reasonably be universal rights to strive for; that there could be no way of proving or justifying any particular rights; and that most are heavily contingent and subjective. A student stood up and explained that she found the lecture rather distressing and was seeking a solution because she had come to law school hoping to make a career working to defend and promote human rights. The professor responded that he was sorry she felt that way, but that his role was only to show the audience that there was an abyss in front of anyone seeking to take human rights seriously; it was not to suggest alternative strategies but simply to ensure that students were aware that the abyss was there.

Now I do not underestimate the extent to which the best of critical scholarship in this field has taught us important lessons. Some of those are doubtless reflected in my earlier remarks. But I also do not underestimate how much of critical scholarship is formulaic, and unfocused in meaningful or instructive ways on the real challenges that confront us and on the challenges that are becoming more and more real by the day in our world. I am not suggesting that all human rights scholars should become activists, or cheerleaders. But I do think that all scholars should take responsibility for what many of the critical scholars warn others about, which is the problem of unintended consequences. It is a common and sometimes relentless refrain that human rights proponents do not take account of the unintended consequences of the positions they advocate. I suggest that critical scholars too need to take account of the "unintended consequences" of a lot of the work that they do. This is not for a moment an attempt to diminish the importance of critical scholarship. As I have noted, many of my own ideas have drawn from some of the best of that scholarship. But there is a great deal of unenlightening dead-end scholarship which simply leads us to despair and does no favours to our students, let alone our fellow humans.

## 4.6 What Each of Us Can Do

A crucial element in responding to the populists and autocrats is for each one of us to reflect carefully on what contributions we can make. All of us can stand up for human rights, but each in our own way. In my travels around the world as a UN Special Rapporteur one of the most instructive questions that regularly pops up about half way through my time in the country concerned is something along the lines of "Who invited this bastard?" It is usually a very good question and the answer informative. An invitation rarely comes on the personal initiative of the Foreign Minister; it is almost certainly not the presidency. Eventually it emerges that a less prominent minister or a behind the scenes bureaucrat has taken the initiative because he or she believes that it will be beneficial to have the scrutiny that comes with such a visit. The simple point is that each one of us is in a position to make a difference if we want to do so. Despondency or defeat is not the answer, because there is always something we can do. It might be a rather minor gesture in the overall scheme of things, but it makes a difference. It might be merely a financial contribution. It does now seem time to be contributing to human rights groups and advocates in ways that most of us probably have not been in the past. It is absolutely essential for us to strengthen the frontline organizations that are going to be best placed to stand up and defend human rights against the threats posed by the new populism.

I want to finish by adapting the old admonition by Pastor Martin Niemöller made during the period between the two world wars. Today's version, at least for a New York resident like myself, would be simply:

First they came for the Hispanics, and I did not speak out—because I was not a Hispanic.
Then they came for the Muslims, and I did not speak out—because I was not a Muslim.
Then they came for the Black Lives Matter activists, and I did not speak out—because I am not Black.
Then they degraded and belittled women, and I did not speak out—because I am not a woman.
Then they came for me and there was no one left to speak for me.

The point is simply that we cannot wait, we need to start acting; we need to do whatever we can to strengthen respect for international human rights. We need to commit to the principles in our own lives, in our own areas. We are going to need to operate in a much more creative fashion both internationally and locally. There is going to be a complex relationship between these two levels but there are always places where we can make a difference. These are extraordinarily dangerous times, unprecedentedly so in my lifetime. Even during most of the cold war there was a degree of certainty, but today we have lost much of that and almost anything seems possible. The response is really up to us.

## REFERENCES

Foa, R. S., and Y. Mounk. 2016. The Democratic Disconnect. *Journal of Democracy* 27(3): 5–17.
Foa, R. S., and Y. Mounk. 2016. Fascism Rising. *Open Democracy*. 9 November. https://www.

opendemocracy.net/openglobalrights/stephen-hopgood/fascism-rising (referenced 26 February 2017).
Hopgood, S. 2013. *The Endtimes of Human Rights*. Ithaca, NY: Cornell University Press.
Hopgood, S. 2016. Fascism Rising. *Open Democracy*. 9 November. https://www.opendemocracy.net/open-globalrights/stephen-hopgood/fascism-rising (Referenced August 11, 2019).
International Committee of the Red Cross (ICRC). 2016. People on War: Perspectives from 16 Countries. https://www.icrc.org/en/document/people-on-war (referenced 26 February 2017).
Moyn, S. 2016. Trump and the Limits of Human Rights. *Open Democracy*. 14 November, https://www.opendemocracy.net/openglobalrights/samuel-moyn/trump-and-limits-of-human-rights (referenced 26 February 2017).
UN, Office of the High Commissioner for Human Rights (OHCHR). 2016. End-of-Mission Statement on China, by Professor Philip Alston, United Nations Special Rapporteur on extreme poverty and human rights. http://www.ohchr.org/en/NewsEvents/Pages/DisplayNews.aspx?NewsID=20402&LangID=E (referenced 26 February 2017).
UN General Assembly. 2016. Report of the Special Rapporteur on Extreme Poverty and Human Rights. A/71/367.
UN Human Rights Council. 2010. Report of the UN Special Rapporteur on Extrajudicial, Summary or Arbitrary Executions, Philip Alston: Study on Targeted Killings. A/HRC/14/24/Add.6.
UN Human Rights Council. 2016. Report of the Special Rapporteur on Extreme Poverty and Human Rights, Philip Alston. A/HRC/32/31.
Wuerth, I. 2016. International Law in the Age of Trump: A Post-Human Rights Agenda. *Lawfare blog*. 14 November. https://www.lawfareblog.com/international-law-age-trump-post-human-rights-agenda (referenced 26 February 2017).
Zalaquett, J. 1992. Balancing Ethical Imperatives and Political Constraints: The Dilemma of New Democracies Confronting Past Human Rights Violations (The Mathew O. Tobriner Memorial Lecture). *Hastings Law Journal* 43: 1425–1438.

# The Culture of Fear in International Politics—A Western-Dominated International System and Its Extremist Challenges

HOLGER MÖLDER

## THE CULTURE OF INTERNATIONAL SYSTEMS

Hedley Bull stated that an international system comes into force "when two or more states have sufficient contact between them, and have sufficient impact on one another's decisions to cause them to behave as parts of a whole."[1] Although since the 1990s the role and importance of other actors (e.g. international institutions, transnational networks, etc.) has notably grown, states have still maintained a status of principal international actors within the international system.

An international system is a governing body that has an ability to arrange relations between different political, social, and cultural entities and operates by using various international regimes for this purpose. It is a self-regulative structure, not a cultural entity, but various political cultures can influence the development of a system. In its turn, the system has an ability to shape its cultural environment. Modern and post-modern international systems have been predominantly influenced by the Western political cultures, and therefore can be identified as Hobbesian, Lockean and Kantian systems depending on which political culture prevails within the system.[2] The international actors will normally accept mutually recognized norms, which support interactions within the system.

Various social forces may intervene for the transformation of anxious emotions into fear.[3] The extremist actors and ideologies may force the culture of fear facilitating their political gains. The culture of fear is also influenced by the concept of security dilemma, which refers to a situation in which actors provoke an increase of mutual tensions in order to improve their own security.[4] There will emerge a 'moral panic'—that occurs when a "condition, episode, person or group of persons emerges to become defined as a threat to societal values and interests."[5] If the culture of fear

is empowered by populist politicians from both sides, it may lead to the non-solvable security dilemma transferred into the sphere of emotions and irrational narratives powered by fear. Such dilemmas are most complicated to manage.

The culture of fear, practiced by powerful international actors, can destabilize international systems. Which is important, certain ideologies, particularly Nationalism and Marxism in their extreme representations, tend to play an important role in producing system-related security dilemmas. Eric Hobsbawm called the 20th century the age of extremes with two global wars and the rise and fall of the messianic faith of Communism.[6] The ideological societies, which emerged rapidly after the World War I, promoted the culture of fear not regionally as it happened in the 19th century but already in global terms. The Marxist revolution in Russia set up an ideological alternative to the world society and positioned Russia as a deviant actor, similarly to North Korea or Iran within the current international system, having only a limited access to mainstream international politics. Systemic confrontations between the international system and deviant actors continued through the activities of Fascist Italy from 1922, Nazi Germany from 1933 or Shōwa Nationalist Japan from 1920s-1930s. These three ideologies founded common paradigms in uniting nationalism, socialism and militarism together for creating an alternative subsystem to the post-World War I Versailles system.[7]

The Westphalian concept of national sovereignty is based on two general principles: recognition of territorial integrity of states and recognition of the rule that external actors have no right to interfere into the domestic matters of states.[8] These principles have prevailed throughout modern society, until the last modern international system, the Cold War's bipolarity, ended. The end of the

ENDC Proceedings, Volume 14, 2011, pp. 241–263.

Cold War marks another breakthrough from the overwhelmingly Hobbesian/Lockean modern international systems to the Kantian post-modern one. The transition was accompanied by a cultural clash, which stems from different cultural practices and narratives used by modern and post-modern actors within the system.

Since the 1990s, a liberal democracy has been the main incentive for stimulating cooperative international regimes in the Euro-Atlantic security environment, which is shifting towards a global community of democratic states. The majority of European states started to follow the principles of the Kantian political culture, which helped to end the emergence of violent international conflicts in most parts of Europe. However, the introduction of the Kantian international system did not exclude the co-existence of the Hobbesian actors and environments with the Kantian trend of the system. The cultural differences between the Hobbesian/Lockean actors and the Kantian actors reflect the ideological clash between the Western liberal democracy and the rest of the world, where the modern ideologies like Nationalism or Marxism retained their influential positions in many countries and regions.

The logic of postmodern society recognizes supranational principles (e.g. human rights, liberal democracy), which do not entirely fit with the concept of national sovereignty prevailing in the modern society. The conflict between the logic of modern society and the logic of post-modern society may produce cultural security dilemmas between actors and environments representing different cultures and values. Several powerful countries, first of all China and Russia, prefer to keep alive modern principles of the international system, which complicates the involvement of international society in stabilizing the whole system by emphasizing peace, stability, and human rights.

International systems existentially depend on two dependant paradigms: polarity and stability. Polarity implies that there are competing antagonistic subsystems within a system. The Hobbesian and Lockean systems are polarized international systems, while the Kantian system intends to avoid the polarization and if any actor will find itself in opposition with the Kantian system, it may be identified as a deviant actor, outside of the system. The stability within the system may be changed by actions usually taken by major powers. In the long-run, the Soviet invasion to Afghanistan in 1979 caused the crash of the Cold War system. The invasion of the US-led coalition to Iraq in 2003 destabilized the post-modern Kantian system.

Societies stemming from the Hobbesian and Lockean political cultures tend to treat polarity as a natural behavior of the international system. This would indeed describe the 19th century society wherein the ideological differences had a minor influence on the international society and the motives of actors manifested quite similar characteristics. A century later, major powers under the auspices of the Western democracy were forced to find consolidating factors and curb their national interests in standing against the competing extremist ideologies from German National Socialism to Soviet Communism. Lebow explains that, contrary to the realist assumptions, within a non-polar system powerful actors attempt to conform to the rules of the system as the system would help them to use their power capabilities in the most efficient and effective manner.[9] In return, they should limit their national goals to those which others consider as legitimate and the interests of the community as a whole.

## EXTREMISM IN INTERNATIONAL POLITICS

The culture of fear polarizes and destabilizes international systems as it is able to force emotional motives, which are able to avoid rational calculations and lead to a political extremism. In their extreme manifestations,[10] Nationalism, Marxism and certain religion-affiliated ideologies may produce ideological states and ideological societies. Lebow explains fear as one of the general motives shaping international relations, which settles security as a primary goal for fear-based societies and uses power as an instrument to achieve more security in eternal competition for increasing security-related capabilities.[11]

Organic ideologies may attribute a certain status of ideal to the community—*we are going the right way, and all those who behave differently, are trying to hinder the achievement of the desired ideal.* Consequently, it would be necessary to provide for all those who as renegade deviate from these ideals. In extreme cases, it may lead to the use of violence in order to bring the renegades back to the "right track." The ideological societies, which are based on a strong sense of identity with Us and Others contrasted and polarized, would impact their positioning towards the system related to some other cultural environment. "As a general rule, individuals, groups, organizations and political units attempt to create, sustain and affirm identities in their interactions with other actors."[12]

In interstate relations, a fear is an emotion, which demands that security is guaranteed through the direct acquisition of military power and economic well-being is a tool for establishing such a power requirement. Brian Frederking includes interactions that produce mistrust and hostilities between actors (traditional nation-state warfare, Israeli-Palestinian relations, imperialism, and Global War on Terrorism) as manifestations of the Hobbesian security culture,[13] which is traditionally characterized by producing uncertainty and misperceptions between actors. The Lockean culture in its turn intends to create some collective actions in balancing security-related fears (i.e. doctrines increasing state security under the circumstances of international anarchy like power balancing, bandwagoning or neutrality).

The Kantian culture of the post-Cold War international society looked for opportunities to produce a more stable non-polarized environment. In Europe, Kantian principles progressed significantly through the European Union and the transforming of NATO. The post-Communist societies of Eastern Europe could fall under the influence of extremist ideologies, if they did not succeed in the transition to consolidated liberal democracies. State extremism can more easily emerge in illiberal democracies and non-democracies than in consolidated democracies.[14] The experience of the former Yugoslavia and the Soviet Union, which in many cases were not able to avoid violent post-dissolution conflicts, confirms this assessment. Therefore, the immediate objective of the European institutions after the Cold War required the engagement of the Central European countries with the rest of Europe.

The Gulf War, the Yugoslavian conflicts, the Afghanistan operation and many others manifest violent interactions between the Kantian and the Hobbesian environments in the post-modern international system. Some environments in the European neighborhood and beyond are mistrustful of the Kantian security culture and hold cultural security dilemmas to be actual. The Greater Middle East, which includes vast areas from Morocco and Mauritania in West Africa to Afghanistan and Pakistan in Central Asia, represents a foremost security concern for the Kantian international system in the near future, as the region is marked by recurrent violence and instability. Despite some progress in the peace processes, the Middle-East remains to be an unstable and polarized region. Besides the Middle-East, Africa poses another serious concern for Europe, as it is still an unstable continent with huge amounts of potential global and regional security risks, including civil wars, ethnic clashes, political, economic and social instability, poverty and famine among others.

The Self-Other binary draws support from Foucault's assertion[15] that order and identity are created and maintained through discourses of deviance (Lebow 2008, 476).[16] If the self-identification of a particular actor contrasts with the culture used by the international system, it may cause the appearance of extremist behavior in the actor-system relationship. There are countries on the world map, which submit challenges to the valid Kantian international system, while practicing the Hobbesian culture towards the system—i.e. North Korea, Iran, Sudan, and Venezuela among others. The extremist stance in international politics may directly or indirectly force deviant countries to support illegitimate actions, international terrorism among others. The Global War on Terrorism has been regarded as a manifestation of the culture of fear in the post-Cold War society,[17] which was able to evoke challenges to the prevailing Kantian political culture and thus destabilize the whole international system.

Lebow notes that deviant actors "attempt to gain attention and recognition by violating norms of the system."[18] Countries like North Korea, Cuba, Libya, Sudan, Iran, Syria, Iraq of Saddam Hussein, Yugoslavia of Milosevic, or Afghanistan of the

Taliban have taken actions that did not fit with the general principles of the international society. . . .

## ASYMMETRIC AXIS

The post-Cold War arrangement in international relations favors globalization and an enhanced interdependence between nations. Collective punitive actions against Iraq in 1991 and against Serbia in Bosnia and Kosovo some years later symbolize the cooperative goals of the international society, which corresponded to the principles fixed within the UN Charter, chapters VI and VII. Even while the states have remained as main actors in the international arena, the role and importance of non-governmental entities has rapidly grown. These trends have been accompanied by the increasing importance of asymmetric risks and threats. These are risks and threats with possible international influence, which can emerge at some other level than states, from global risks to domestic risks as well. Asymmetric actors may include international interest groups, non-governmental organizations, transnational companies, individuals—which all may go beyond a particular citizenship.

After 2001, the international societal environment fostered the emergence of a culture of fear, while terrorism, which has never been a "mainstream political tool," has been promoted to the next level by a small and relatively little-known Islamic fundamentalist group Al-Qaeda. Al-Qaeda succeeded in increasing the amount of uncertainty, which produced instability within the whole international system and caused political risks to be taken by actors.[19] As follows, the international society was confronted "with an increased awareness of risks because more decisions are taken in an atmosphere of uncertainty."[20] International terrorism has often been mentioned among the most important manifestations of a new asymmetric axis, which involves transnational networks and therefore comes into conflict with the traditional approaches to international systems based on national interests performed by states. Jessica Stern, while analyzing the effectiveness of Al-Qaeda, notes its capability for change, which makes Al-Qaeda more attractive for new recruits and allies.[21] Colin Wight notes that Al-Qaeda followed a structural form without clear lines of hierarchy and channels of control over the cells, which makes it harder to detect and destroy it.[22]

A global transnational network corresponds to the timely principles of the post-modern society. It is somehow symbolic as NATO for the first time throughout its history used its article V against the asymmetric threat, terrorism, and on behalf of its major military power, the United States. The attacks organized against international terrorism are justified in that they are not against states but terrorist organizations, the United States fought in Afghanistan against the Taliban and Al-Qaeda, and in 2006 Israel fought against a Lebanese Shia extremist militant group Hezbollah, not Lebanon, which moves asymmetric groups to the level comparable with states.[23] Notably, the United Nations performed sanctions against Al-Qaeda and the Taliban in 1998 and against Hezbollah in 2006.[24]

In 1990s Samuel Huntington invented a descriptive theory that prescribes general trends in international politics while emphasizing a possible cultural conflict between opposing civilizations.[25] The attack of September 11, 2001 led to the Global War on Terrorism with the world divided between "good" and "evil" once again and polarity-based policies started gradually to return. The offensive strategy characterizing the counterterrorist policies carried through the western world during the GWoT, which frequently demonized the Muslim faith and the Islamic civilization, fitted more with the Hobbesian security culture practicing enmities between different entities and has evidently promoted the direction towards the clash of civilizations, once predicted by Huntington and damaged hopes for the end of history as described ten years ago by Francis Fukuyama.[26]

Although the defensive actions against international terrorism, including military operations in Afghanistan, have been widely approved by the international society, the Kantian world favoring democratic peace, multiculturalism and international cooperation did not satisfy apologists of power policies. Extremist movements were successful in splitting a still fragile Western unity. The emerging culture of fear could be observed as a counterideology to the rising Islamic fundamentalism especially in the

United States, where the neo-conservative ideological movement strengthened with Bush's presidency of the United States.

During the Cold War, the Islamists were often treated as natural allies of the Western bloc because of their fighting against the spread of Communist ideologies. Their opposition to Atheism practiced by the Communist regimes made Islamism a powerful competing ideology especially in the Third World countries. Huntington mentioned that "at one time or another during the Cold War many governments, including those of Algeria, Turkey, Jordan, Egypt, and Israel, encouraged and supported Islamists as a counter to communist and hostile nationalist movements."[27] Pro-Western countries provided massive funding to the Islamists groups in various parts of the world. The United States often saw Islamists as an opposition to the Soviet influence under the circumstances of the bipolar competition of the Cold War.

At the same time, secular movements in Islamic countries, contrariwise, often flirted with Marxism and thus gained support from the Soviet Union. The Pan-Arabist leaders of Egypt, Syria, Iraq and Algeria shared the anti-American and anti-Imperialist views of the Soviet ideological establishment. From 1979, the situation gradually started to change with the Islamic revolution in Iran and the Soviet occupation of Afghanistan, which strengthened Islamic solidarity instead of socialist and nationalist sentiments. Whilst pan-Arabism followed the structure of Western ideologies and settled it into the specific Nationalist environment with Socialist influences, the contemporary Islamic Fundamentalism is a direct challenge to the Western model of the state and politics, and constitutes a form of political resistance.[28]

In 1980s, the Western governments supported the Sunni resistance in the Afghanistan conflict and only a smaller Shia community of Islam was mostly involved in the anti-Western confrontation. The revolution in Iran established a new regime that was simultaneously anti-Western and anti-Soviet and did not suit with the Cold War's bipolarity. Sunnis remained silent and used Western support in Afghanistan and other conflict areas, whereby they fought for their values and identities. Paradoxically, in the course of the Iraqi-Iran war 1980–1988, the East and the West both supported the leftist Arab nationalist regime of Saddam Hussein against Iran.

The post-Cold War era produced some regrouping between international powers and groups of interests. The Islamic militants started to stand against the spread of western liberal democracy, which did not fit with their ideological goals. In the 1990s, the clash between western liberal democracy and Islamic fundamentalism developed rapidly. The Sunni fundamentalist Taliban movement established their control over Afghanistan in 1996. More serious signs of ideological clash emerged in 1998, when Al-Qaeda terrorists attacked the US embassies in East-Africa. With the GWoT, cultural conflicts became indeed more visible. The confrontation between Western liberal democracy and Islamic fundamentalism verified that Huntington was right in predicting a clash of civilizations.

The transnational character of asymmetric actors allows them to introduce non-traditional methods effectively (e.g. international terrorism) as they have no territoriality or sovereignty to defend, which makes it more efficient in balancing the possible sanctions from the valid international system. Legally, there is a difference between asymmetric transnational terrorism and symmetric state terrorism—terrorist organizations have no legitimate right to kill, contrariwise to political communities, though they may apply to some form of revolutionary vanguard the term, "good people" who destroy "bad people."[29] The promotion of a culture of fear would be one of the most important challenges caused by international terrorism. Strategies of terrorist groups aim to produce chaos and political, economic, social and military damage, hoping that the destabilization of existing societies following the terrorist attack may help them to validate their ideological goals. . . .

## CONCLUSIONS

A culture of fear most effectively supports the logic of the Hobbesian culture, which emphasizes a state of war between international actors. It may provoke extremist challenges against peace and stability and conflicting ideologies compose a powerful agenda for initiating fear-based polarizations. Fear in the hands of ideologies has an enormous capability to provoke irrational decisions and security dilemmas. At first glance, the rise of Islamic fundamentalism and the culture of fear seem to be depending on each other. The Hollywood-like scenario of September 11, 2001, by which the charismatic leader of Al-Qaeda Osama Bin Laden recorded himself in the history of the world, caused the worldwide diffusion of fear, which in its turn opened the door for the extremist neo-conservative reaction in the United States. Recent news about the liquidation of the protean enemy hardly makes the world safer.

The post-modern Kantian international system continually includes multiple Hobbesian security environments. The variety of cultural environments makes the whole international system conflict-prone and it is able to produce a culture of fear involving different civilizations, identities or ideologies. Deviant actors often find themselves manipulating the culture of fear in justifying their legitimacy within the international system. The axis-building policies between good and evil can destabilize the international system by introducing new polarizations. Various factors reproducing a culture of fear (e.g. social problems, ethnic tensions with strengthening national sentiments, nuclear dilemmas) may inflict the emergence of most problematic security dilemmas into the Kantian international system. The successful alternative to fear-based political incentives largely depends on maintaining a non-polarized cooperative framework within the valid international system. A less ideologized world tends to be a safer world.

## Notes

[1] Hedley Bull. The Anarchical Society: A Study of Order in World Politics. New York: Columbia University Press, 1977, pp. 9–13.
[2] See also Holger Mölder. Cooperative Security Dilemma—practicing the Hobbesian security culture in the Kantian security environment. Tartu: Tartu University Press, 2010, pp. 94–100.
[3] See also Frank Furedi. The Politics of Fear. Beyond Left and Right. Continuum International Publishing Group, 2005.
[4] Ken Booth and Nicholas J. Wheeler. The Security Dilemma. Fear, Cooperation and Trust in World Politics. New York: Palgrave MacMillan, 2008, p. 9.
[5] Stanley Cohen. Folk Devils and Moral Panics. St Albans: Paladin, 1973, p. 9.
[6] Eric Hobsbawm. The Age of Extremes. A History of World, 1914–1991. London: Michael Joseph and Pelham Books, 1994.
[7] The Versailles system may be identified as the first Kantian international system, see Mölder 2010, pp. 94–100.
[8] See also Stephen D. Krasner. Sovereignty: organized hypocrisy. Princeton: Princeton University Press, 1999.
[9] Lebow 2008, p. 497.
[10] If ideologies are capable of forcing conflict within societies, their behavior can be identified as extremist. For example, Chauvinism is an extreme manifestation of Nationalism and Communism respectively refers to Marxist extremism.
[11] Lebow 2008, p. 90.
[12] Lebow 2008, p. 497.
[13] Brian Frederking. Constructing Post-cold War Collective Security. – American Political Science Review, 3/2003, p. 368.
[14] This does not refer to other formations of extremism.
[15] Reference is made to Michel Foucault's book: The Archaelogy of Knowledge and the Discourse on Language. New York: Pantheon Books, 1972.
[16] Richard Ned Lebow. Identity and International Relations. – International Relations, 4/2008 (a), p. 476.
[17] Lebow 2008, p. 544.
[18] Lebow 2008, p. 488.
[19] See Mary Douglas; Aaron Wildavsky. Risk and Culture: An essay on the selection of technical and environmental dangers. Berkeley: University of California Press, 1982.
[20] Frank Furedi. Culture of Fear: Risk Taking and the Morality of Low Expectation. Continuum International Publishing Group, 2002, p. 8.
[21] Jessica Stern. A1 Qaeda: the Protean Enemy. – Foreign Affairs, 4/2003.
[22] Colin Wight. Theorising terrorism: The State, Structure, and History. – International Relations 1/2009, p. 105.

[23]Daren Bowyer. The moral dimension of asymmetrical warfare: accountability, culpability and military effectiveness. – Baarda, Th. A. van; Verweij, D. E. M. (eds.). The moral dimension of asymmetrical warfare: counter-terrorism, democratic values and military ethics. Leiden: Martinus Njihoff, 2009, p. 139.
[24]UN Security Council Sanctions Committees. Available online at: <http://www.un.org/sc/committees/>, (accessed 06.05.2011).
[25]Samuel P. Huntington. The Clash of Civilizations. Remaking World Order. New York: Touchstone Book, 1997.

[26]In his book: Francis Fukuyama. The End of History and the Last Man. New York: Free Press, 1992.
[27]Huntington 1997, p. 115.
[28]Wight 2009, p. 104.
[29]Carl Ceulemans. Asymmetric warfare and morality: from moral asymmetry to amoral symmetry?— Baarda, Th. A. van; Verweij, D. E. M. (eds.). The moral dimension of asymmetrical warfare: counter-terrorism, democratic values and military ethics. Leiden: Martinus Njihoff, 2009.

# Us and Them: The Enduring Power of Ethnic Nationalism

JERRY Z. MULLER

Projecting their own experience onto the rest of the world, Americans generally belittle the role of ethnic nationalism in politics. After all, in the United States people of varying ethnic origins live cheek by jowl in relative peace. Within two or three generations of immigration, their ethnic identities are attenuated by cultural assimilation and intermarriage. Surely, things cannot be so different elsewhere.

Americans also find ethnonationalism discomfiting both intellectually and morally. Social scientists go to great lengths to demonstrate that it is a product not of nature but of culture, often deliberately constructed. And ethicists scorn value systems based on narrow group identities rather than cosmopolitanism.

But none of this will make ethnonationalism go away. Immigrants to the United States usually arrive with a willingness to fit into their new country and reshape their identities accordingly. But for those who remain behind in lands where their ancestors have lived for generations, if not centuries, political identities often take ethnic form, producing competing communal claims to political power. The creation of a peaceful regional order of nation-states has usually been the product of a violent process of ethnic separation. In areas where that separation has not yet occurred, politics is apt to remain ugly.

A familiar and influential narrative of twentieth-century European history argues that nationalism twice led to war, in 1914 and then again in 1939. Thereafter, the story goes, Europeans concluded that nationalism was a danger and gradually abandoned it. In the postwar decades, western Europeans enmeshed themselves in a web of transnational institutions, culminating in the European Union (EU). After the fall of the Soviet empire, that transnational framework spread eastward to encompass most of the continent. Europeans entered a postnational era, which was not only a good thing in itself but also a model for other regions. Nationalism, in this view, had been a tragic detour on the road to a peaceful liberal democratic order.

This story is widely believed by educated Europeans and even more so, perhaps, by educated Americans. Recently, for example, in the course of arguing that Israel ought to give up its claim to be a Jewish state and dissolve itself into some sort of binational entity with the Palestinians, the prominent historian Tony Judt informed the readers of The New York Review of Books that "the problem with Israel ... [is that] it has imported a characteristically late-nineteenth-century separatist project into a world that has moved on, a world of individual rights, open frontiers, and international law. The very idea of a 'Jewish state' ... is an anachronism."

Yet the experience of the hundreds of Africans and Asians who perish each year trying to get into Europe by landing on the coast of Spain or Italy reveals that Europe's frontiers are not so open. And a survey would show that whereas in 1900 there were many states in Europe without a single overwhelmingly dominant nationality, by 2007 there were only two, and one of those, Belgium, was close to breaking up. Aside from Switzerland, in other words—where the domestic ethnic balance of power is protected by strict citizenship laws—in Europe the "separatist project" has not so much vanished as triumphed.

Far from having been superannuated in 1945, in many respects ethnonationalism was at its apogee in the years immediately after World War II. European stability during the Cold War era was in fact due partly to the widespread fulfillment of the ethnonationalist project. And since the end of the Cold War, ethnonationalism has continued to reshape European borders.

In short, ethnonationalism has played a more profound and lasting role in modern history than is commonly understood, and the processes that led to the dominance of the ethnonational state and the separation of ethnic groups in Europe are likely to reoccur elsewhere. Increased urbanization, literacy, and political mobilization; differences in the fertility rates and economic performance of various ethnic groups; and immigration will challenge the internal structure of states as well as their borders. Whether politically correct or not, ethnonationalism will continue to shape the world in the twenty-first century. . . .

## THE RISE OF ETHNONATIONALISM

Today, people tend to take the nation-state for granted as the natural form of political association and regard empires as anomalies. But over the broad sweep of recorded history, the opposite is closer to the truth. Most people at most times have lived in empires, with the nation-state the exception rather than the rule. So what triggered the change?

*The rise of ethnonationalism, as the sociologist Ernest Gellner has explained, was not some strange historical mistake; rather, it was propelled by some of the deepest currents of modernity.* Military competition between states created a demand for expanded state resources and hence continual economic growth. Economic growth, in turn, depended on mass literacy and easy communication, spurring policies to promote education and a common language—which led directly to conflicts over language and communal opportunities.

Modern societies are premised on the egalitarian notion that in theory, at least, anyone can aspire to any economic position. But in practice, everyone does not have an equal likelihood of upward economic mobility, and not simply because individuals have different innate capabilities. For such advances depend in part on what economists call "cultural capital," the skills and behavioral patterns that help individuals and groups succeed. Groups with traditions of literacy and engagement in commerce tend to excel, for example, whereas those without such traditions tend to lag behind.

As they moved into cities and got more education during the nineteenth and early twentieth centuries, ethnic groups with largely peasant backgrounds, such as the Czechs, the Poles, the Slovaks, and the Ukrainians found that key positions in the government and the economy were already occupied—often by ethnic Armenians, Germans, Greeks, or Jews. Speakers of the same language came to share a sense that they belonged together and to define themselves in contrast to other communities. And eventually they came to demand a nation state of their own, in which they would be the masters, dominating politics, staffing the civil service, and controlling commerce.

Ethnonationalism had a psychological basis as well as an economic one. By creating a new and direct relationship between individuals and the government, the rise of the modern state weakened individuals' traditional bonds to intermediate social units, such as the family, the clan, the guild, and the church. And by spurring social and geographic mobility and a self-help mentality, the rise of market-based economies did the same. The result was an emotional vacuum that was often filled by new forms of identification, often along ethnic lines.

Ethnonationalist ideology called for a congruence between the state and the ethnically defined nation, with explosive results. As Lord Acton recognized in 1862, "By making the state and the nation commensurate with each other in theory, [nationalism] reduces practically to a subject condition all other nationalities that may be within the boundary. . . . According, therefore, to the degree of humanity and civilization in that dominant body which claims all the rights of the community, the inferior races are exterminated, or reduced to servitude, or outlawed, or put in a condition of dependence." And that is just what happened.

## THE GREAT TRANSFORMATION

Nineteenth century liberals, like many proponents of globalization today, believed that the spread of international commerce would lead people to recognize the mutual benefits that could come from peace and trade, both within polities and between them. Socialists agreed, although they believed that harmony would come only after the arrival of socialism. Yet that was not the course that twentieth-century history was destined to follow. The process of "making the state and the nation commensurate" took a variety of forms, from voluntary emigration (often motivated by governmental discrimination against minority ethnicities) to forced deportation (also known as "population transfer") to genocide. Although the term "ethnic cleansing" has come into English usage only recently, its verbal correlates in Czech, French, German, and Polish go back much further. Much of the history of twentieth-century Europe, in fact, has been a painful, drawn-out process of ethnic disaggregation.

Massive ethnic disaggregation began on Europe's frontiers. In the ethnically mixed Balkans, wars to expand the nation-states of Bulgaria, Greece, and Serbia at the expense of the ailing Ottoman Empire were accompanied by ferocious inter-ethnic violence. During the Balkan Wars of 1912–13, almost half a million people left their traditional homelands, either voluntarily or by force. Muslims

left regions under the control of Bulgarians, Greeks, and Serbs; Bulgarians abandoned Greek-controlled areas of Macedonia; Greeks fled from regions of Macedonia ceded to Bulgaria and Serbia.

World War I led to the demise of the three great turn-of-the-century empires, unleashing an explosion of ethnonationalism in the process. In the Ottoman Empire, mass deportations and murder during the war took the lives of a million members of the local Armenian minority in an early attempt at ethnic cleansing, if not genocide. In 1919, the Greek government invaded the area that would become Turkey, seeking to carve out a "greater Greece" stretching all the way to Constantinople. Meeting with initial success, the Greek forces looted and burned villages in an effort to drive out the region's ethnic Turks. But Turkish forces eventually regrouped and pushed the Greek army back, engaging in their own ethnic cleansing against local Greeks along the way. Then the process of population transfers was formalized in the 1923 Treaty of Lausanne: all ethnic Greeks were to go to Greece, all Greek Muslims to Turkey. In the end, Turkey expelled almost 1.5 million people, and Greece expelled almost 400,000.

Out of the breakup of the Hapsburg and Romanov empires emerged a multitude of new countries. Many conceived of themselves as ethnonational polities, in which the state existed to protect and promote the dominant ethnic group. Yet of central and eastern Europe's roughly 60 million people, 25 million continued to be part of ethnic minorities in the countries in which they lived. In most cases, the ethnic majority did not believe in trying to help minorities assimilate, nor were the minorities always eager to do so themselves. Nationalist governments openly discriminated in favor of the dominant community. Government activities were conducted solely in the language of the majority, and the civil service was reserved for those who spoke it.

In much of central and eastern Europe, Jews had long played an important role in trade and commerce. When they were given civil rights in the late nineteenth century, they tended to excel in professions requiring higher education, such as medicine and law, and soon Jews or people of Jewish descent made up almost half the doctors and lawyers in cities such as Budapest, Vienna, and Warsaw. By the 1930s, many governments adopted policies to try to check and reverse these advances, denying Jews credit and limiting their access to higher education. In other words, the National Socialists who came to power in Germany in 1933 and based their movement around a "Germanness" they defined in contrast to "Jewishness" were an extreme version of a more common ethnonationalist trend.

The politics of ethnonationalism took an even deadlier turn during World War II. The Nazi regime tried to reorder the ethnic map of the continent by force. Its most radical act was an attempt to rid Europe of Jews by killing them all—an attempt that largely succeeded. The Nazis also used ethnic German minorities in Czechoslovakia, Poland, and elsewhere to enforce Nazi domination, and many of the regimes allied with Germany engaged in their own campaigns against internal ethnic enemies. The Romanian regime, for example, murdered hundreds of thousands of Jews on its own, without orders from Germany, and the government of Croatia murdered not only its Jews but hundreds of thousands of Serbs and Romany as well.

## POSTWAR BUT NOT POSTNATIONAL

One might have expected that the Nazi regime's deadly policies and crushing defeat would mark the end of the ethnonationalist era. But in fact they set the stage for another massive round of ethnonational transformation. The political settlement in central Europe after World War I had been achieved primarily by moving borders to align them with populations. After World War II, it was the populations that moved instead. Millions of people were expelled from their homes and countries, with at least the tacit support of the victorious Allies.

Winston Churchill, Franklin Roosevelt, and Joseph Stalin all concluded that the expulsion of ethnic Germans from non-German countries was a prerequisite to a stable postwar order. As Churchill put it in a speech to the British parliament in December 1944, "Expulsion is the method which, so far as we have been able to see, will be the most satisfactory and lasting. There will be no mixture of populations to cause endless trouble. . . . A clean sweep will be made. I am not alarmed at the prospect of the disentanglement of population, nor am I alarmed by these large transferences." He cited the Treaty of Lausanne as a precedent, showing how even the leaders of liberal democracies had concluded that only radically illiberal measures would eliminate the causes of ethnonational aspirations and aggression.

Between 1944 and 1945, five million ethnic Germans from the eastern parts of the German Reich fled westward to escape the conquering Red Army, which was energetically raping and massacring its way to Berlin. Then, between 1945 and 1947, the new postliberation regimes in Czechoslovakia, Hungary, Poland, and Yugoslavia expelled another seven million Germans in response to their collaboration with the Nazis. Together, these measures constituted the largest forced population movement in European history, with hundreds of thousands of people dying along the way.

The handful of Jews who survived the war and returned to their homes in eastern Europe met with so much anti-Semitism that most chose to leave for good. About 220,000 of them made their way into the American-occupied zone of Germany, from which most eventually went to Israel or the United States. Jews thus essentially vanished from central and eastern Europe, which had been the center of Jewish life since the sixteenth century.

Millions of refugees from other ethnic groups were also evicted from their homes and resettled after the war. This was due partly to the fact that the borders of the Soviet Union had moved westward, into what had once been Poland, while the borders of Poland also moved westward, into what had once been Germany. To make populations correspond to the new borders, 1.5 million Poles living in areas that were now part of the Soviet Union were deported to Poland, and 500,000 ethnic Ukrainians who had been living in Poland were sent to the Ukrainian Soviet Socialist Republic. Yet another exchange of populations took place between Czechoslovakia and Hungary, with Slovaks transferred out of Hungary and Magyars sent away from Czechoslovakia. A smaller number of Magyars also moved to Hungary from Yugoslavia, with Serbs and Croats moving in the opposite direction.

As a result of this massive process of ethnic un-mixing, the ethnonationalist ideal was largely re-alized: for the most part, each nation in Europe had its own state, and each state was made up almost exclusively of a single ethnic nationality. During the Cold War, the few exceptions to this rule included Czechoslovakia, the Soviet Union, and Yugoslavia. But these countries' subsequent fate only demonstrated the ongoing vitality of eth-nonationalism. After the fall of communism, East and West Germany were unified with remarkable rapidity, Czechoslovakia split peacefully into Czech and Slovak republics, and the Soviet Union broke apart into a variety of different national units. Since then, ethnic Russian minorities in many of the post-Soviet states have gradually immigrated to Russia, Magyars in Romania have moved to Hungary, and the few remaining ethnic Germans in Russia have largely gone to Germany. A million people of Jewish origin from the former Soviet Union have made their way to Israel. Yugoslavia saw the secession of Croatia and Slovenia and then descended into ethnonational wars over Bosnia and Kosovo.

The breakup of Yugoslavia was simply the last act of a long play. But the plot of that play—the dis-aggregation of peoples and the triumph of ethnon-ationalism in modern Europe—is rarely recognized, and so a story whose significance is comparable to the spread of democracy or capitalism remains largely unknown and unappreciated.

## DECOLONIZATION AND AFTER

The effects of ethnonationalism, of course, have hardly been confined to Europe. For much of the developing world, decolonization has meant ethnic disaggregation through the exchange or expulsion of local minorities.

The end of the British Raj in 1947 brought about the partition of the subcontinent into India and Pakistan, along with an orgy of violence that took hundreds of thousands of lives. Fifteen million people became refugees, including Muslims who went to Pakistan and Hindus who went to India. Then, in 1971, Pakistan itself, originally unified on the basis of religion, dissolved into Urdu-speaking Pakistan and Bengali-speaking Bangladesh.

In the former British mandate of Palestine, a Jewish state was established in 1948 and was promptly greeted by the revolt of the indigenous Arab community and an invasion from the sur-rounding Arab states. In the war that resulted, re-gions that fell under Arab control were cleansed of their Jewish populations, and Arabs fled or were forced out of areas that came under Jewish control. Some 750,000 Arabs left, primarily for the sur-rounding Arab countries, and the remaining 150,000 constituted only about a sixth of the popu-lation of the new Jewish state. In the years after-ward, nationalist-inspired violence against Jews in Arab countries propelled almost all of the more than 500,000 Jews there to leave their lands of origin and immigrate to Israel. Likewise, in 1962 the end of French control in Algeria led to the forced emigration of Algerians of European origin (the so-called pieds-noirs), most of whom immigrated to France. Shortly thereafter, ethnic minorities of Asian origin were forced out of post-colonial Uganda. The legacy of the colonial era, moreover, is hardly finished. When the European overseas empires dissolved, they left behind a patchwork of states whose boundaries often cut across ethnic patterns of settlement and whose in-ternal populations were ethnically mixed. It is wishful thinking to suppose that these boundaries will be permanent. As societies in the former colo-nial world modernize, becoming more urban, lit-erate, and politically mobilized, the forces that gave rise to ethnonationalism and ethnic disaggre-gation in Europe are apt to drive events there, too.

## THE BALANCE SHEET

Analysts of ethnic disaggregation typically focus on its destructive effects, which is understandable given the direct human suffering it has often en-tailed. But such attitudes can yield a distorted per-spective by overlooking the less obvious costs and also the important benefits that ethnic separation has brought.

Economists from Adam Smith onward, for ex-ample, have argued that the efficiencies of com-petitive markets tend to increase with the markets' size. The dissolution of the Austro-Hungarian Empire into smaller nation-states, each with its own barriers to trade, was thus economically irrational and contributed to the region's travails in the interwar period. Much of subsequent European history has involved attempts to overcome this and other economic fragmentation, culminating in the EU.

Ethnic disaggregation also seems to have deleterious effects on cultural vitality. Precisely because most of their citizens share a common cultural and linguistic heritage, the homogenized states of postwar Europe have tended to be more culturally insular than their demographically diverse predecessors. With few Jews in Europe and few Germans in Prague, that is, there are fewer Franz Kafkas.

Forced migrations generally penalize the expelling countries and reward the receiving ones. Expulsion is often driven by a majority group's resentment of a minority group's success, on the mistaken assumption that achievement is a zero-sum game. But countries that got rid of their Armenians, Germans, Greeks, Jews, and other successful minorities deprived themselves of some of their most talented citizens, who simply took their skills and knowledge elsewhere. And in many places, the triumph of ethnonational politics has meant the victory of traditionally rural groups over more urbanized ones, which possess just those skills desirable in an advanced industrial economy.

But if ethnonationalism has frequently led to tension and conflict, it has also proved to be a source of cohesion and stability. When French textbooks began with "Our ancestors the Gauls" or when Churchill spoke to wartime audiences of "this island race," they appealed to ethnonationalist sensibilities as a source of mutual trust and sacrifice. Liberal democracy and ethnic homogeneity are not only compatible; they can be complementary.

One could argue that Europe has been so harmonious since World War II not because of the failure of ethnic nationalism but because of its success, which removed some of the greatest sources of conflict both within and between countries. The fact that ethnic and state boundaries now largely coincide has meant that there are fewer disputes over borders or expatriate communities, leading to the most stable territorial configuration in European history.

These ethnically homogeneous polities have displayed a great deal of internal solidarity, moreover, facilitating government programs, including domestic transfer payments, of various kinds. When the Swedish Social Democrats were developing plans for Europe's most extensive welfare state during the interwar period, the political scientist Sheri Berman has noted, they conceived of and sold them as the construction of a folkhemmet, or "people's home."

Several decades of life in consolidated, ethnically homogeneous states may even have worked to sap ethnonationalism's own emotional power. Many Europeans are now prepared, and even eager, to participate in transnational frameworks such as the EU, in part because their perceived need for collective self-determination has largely been satisfied.

## NEW ETHNIC MIXING

Along with the process of forced ethnic disaggregation over the last two centuries, there has also been a process of ethnic mixing brought about by voluntary emigration. The general pattern has been one of emigration from poor, stagnant areas to richer and more dynamic ones.

In Europe, this has meant primarily movement west and north, leading above all to France and the United Kingdom. This pattern has continued into the present: as a result of recent migration, for example, there are now half a million Poles in Great Britain and 200,000 in Ireland. Immigrants from one part of Europe who have moved to another and ended up staying there have tended to assimilate and, despite some grumbling about a supposed invasion of "Polish plumbers," have created few significant problems.

The most dramatic transformation of European ethnic balances in recent decades has come from the immigration of people of Asian, African, and Middle Eastern origin, and here the results have been mixed. Some of these groups have achieved remarkable success, such as the Indian Hindus who have come to the United Kingdom. But in Belgium, France, Germany, the Netherlands, Sweden, the United Kingdom, and elsewhere, on balance the educational and economic progress of

Muslim immigrants has been more limited and their cultural alienation greater.

How much of the problem can be traced to discrimination, how much to the cultural patterns of the immigrants themselves, and how much to the policies of European governments is difficult to determine. But a number of factors, from official multiculturalism to generous welfare states to the ease of contact with ethnic homelands, seem to have made it possible to create ethnic islands where assimilation into the larger culture and economy is limited.

As a result, some of the traditional contours of European politics have been upended. The left, for example, has tended to embrace immigration in the name of egalitarianism and multiculturalism. But if there is indeed a link between ethnic homogeneity and a population's willingness to support generous income-redistribution programs, the encouragement of a more heterogeneous society may end up undermining the left's broader political agenda. And some of Europe's libertarian cultural propensities have already clashed with the cultural illiberalism of some of the new immigrant communities.

Should Muslim immigrants not assimilate and instead develop a strong communal identification along religious lines, one consequence might be a resurgence of traditional ethnonational identities in some states—or the development of a new European identity defined partly in contradistinction to Islam (with the widespread resistance to the extension of full EU membership to Turkey being a possible harbinger of such a shift).

## FUTURE IMPLICATIONS

Since ethnonationalism is a direct consequence of key elements of modernization, it is likely to gain ground in societies undergoing such a process. It is hardly surprising, therefore, that it remains among the most vital—and most disruptive—forces in many parts of the contemporary world.

More or less subtle forms of ethnonationalism, for example, are ubiquitous in immigration policy around the globe. Many countries—including Armenia, Bulgaria, Croatia, Finland, Germany, Hungary, Ireland, Israel, Serbia, and Turkey—provide automatic or rapid citizenship to the members of diasporas of their own dominant ethnic group, if desired. Chinese immigration law gives priority and benefits to overseas Chinese. Portugal and Spain have immigration policies that favor applicants from their former colonies in the New World. Still other states, such as Japan and Slovakia, provide official forms of identification to members of the dominant national ethnic group who are noncitizens that permit them to live and work in the country. Americans, accustomed by the U.S. government's official practices to regard differential treatment on the basis of ethnicity to be a violation of universalist norms, often consider such policies exceptional, if not abhorrent. Yet in a global context, it is the insistence on universalist criteria that seems provincial.

Increasing communal consciousness and shifting ethnic balances are bound to have a variety of consequences, both within and between states, in the years to come. As economic globalization brings more states into the global economy, for example, the first fruits of that process will often fall to those ethnic groups best positioned by history or culture to take advantage of the new opportunities for enrichment, deepening social cleavages rather than filling them in. Wealthier and higher-achieving regions might try to separate themselves from poorer and lower-achieving ones, and distinctive homogeneous areas might try to acquire sovereignty—courses of action that might provoke violent responses from defenders of the status quo.

Of course, there are multiethnic societies in which ethnic consciousness remains weak, and even a more strongly developed sense of ethnicity may lead to political claims short of sovereignty. Sometimes, demands for ethnic autonomy or self-determination can be met within an existing state. The claims of the Catalans in Spain, the Flemish in Belgium, and the Scots in the United Kingdom have been met in this manner, at least for now. But such arrangements remain precarious and are subject to recurrent renegotiation. In the developing world, accordingly, where states are more recent creations and where the borders often cut across ethnic boundaries, there is likely to be further ethnic disaggregation and communal conflict. And as scholars such as Chaim Kaufmann have noted, once ethnic antagonism has crossed a certain threshold of violence, maintaining the rival groups within a single polity becomes far more difficult.

This unfortunate reality creates dilemmas for advocates of humanitarian intervention in such conflicts, because making and keeping peace between groups that have come to hate and fear one another is likely to require costly ongoing military missions rather than relatively cheap temporary ones. When communal violence escalates to ethnic cleansing, moreover, the return of large numbers of refugees to their place of origin after a ceasefire has been reached is often impractical and even undesirable, for it merely sets the stage for a further round of conflict down the road.

Partition may thus be the most humane lasting solution to such intense communal conflicts. It inevitably creates new flows of refugees, but at least it deals with the problem at issue. The challenge for the international community in such cases is to separate communities in the most humane manner possible: by aiding in transport, assuring citizenship rights in the new homeland, and providing financial aid for resettlement and economic absorption. The bill for all of this will be huge, but it will rarely be greater than the material costs of interjecting and maintaining a foreign military presence large enough to pacify the rival ethnic combatants or the moral cost of doing nothing.

Contemporary social scientists who write about nationalism tend to stress the contingent elements of group identity—the extent to which national consciousness is culturally and politically manufactured by ideologists and politicians. They regularly invoke Benedict Anderson's concept of "imagined communities," as if demonstrating that nationalism is constructed will rob the concept of its power. It is true, of course, that ethnonational identity is never as natural or ineluctable as nationalists claim. Yet it would be a mistake to think that because nationalism is partly constructed it is therefore fragile or infinitely malleable. Ethnonationalism was not a chance detour in European history: it corresponds to some enduring propensities of the human spirit that are heightened by the process of modern state creation, it is a crucial source of both solidarity and enmity, and in one form or another, it will remain for many generations to come. One can only profit from facing it directly.

# History, Memory and National Identity: Understanding the Politics of History and Memory Wars in Post-Soviet Lands

IGOR TORBAKOV

> Tell me what you remember and I'll diagnose your condition.
>
> —ALEKSANDR KUSTARYOV

At the end of June 2010, a remarkable text appeared on the website of the Russian liberal radio station *Ekho Moskvy*. Its author, the prominent Russian lawmaker Konstantin Kosachev, suggested that it was time for Russia to elaborate upon what he called a comprehensive "set of principles, an 'historical doctrine' of sorts" that would help Moscow to disclaim, once and for all, any political, financial, legal or moral responsibility for the policies and actions of the Soviet authorities on the territories of the former USSR and the states of Eastern Europe. Kosachev's proposal is simple,

"History, Memory and National Identity: Understanding the Politics of History and Memory Wars in Post-Soviet Lands." Igor Torbakov, first published in Demokratizatsiya, 2011, reprinted with permission of the publisher.

blunt and seemingly effective. In a nutshell, it boils down to the two key points: (1) Russia fulfills all international obligations of the USSR as its successor state; however, Russia does not recognize any moral responsibility or any legal obligations for the actions and crimes committed by the Soviet authorities; and (2) Russia does not accept any political, legal or financial claims against it for violations by the Soviet authorities of international or domestic laws enforced during the Soviet period.

To be sure, Kosachev's proposal didn't emerge out of the thin air. His idea should be placed into the broader context of Russia's attempts at crafting and pursuing the robust "politics of history." Like other members of the country's ruling elite, Kosachev appears to perceive memory and history as an important ideological and political battleground: Russia's detractors—both foreign and domestic—allegedly seek to spread interpretations of past events that are detrimental to Russia's interests, and there is an urgent need to resolutely counter these unfriendly moves. Several elements of such politics of history have already been introduced in Russia: a set of officially sponsored and centrally approved textbooks with the highly pronounced statist interpretation of 20th-century Russian history; the attempts to establish the "regime of truth" using legislative means; and the creation of a bureaucratic institution to fight the "falsification of history." . . .

There appears to be a consensus among professional historians and political analysts that over the past several decades, the "politics of history" has become a significant aspect of domestic politics and international relations, both within Europe and in the world at large. One could thus suggest that Russia's latest moves should be seen in perspective and perceived as a manifestation of a Europe-wide trend, their clumsiness and cartoonish character notwithstanding. This trend toward politicizing and instrumentalizing of history might take on various shapes and forms in different countries, but there are basically two main objectives that are usually pursued. First is the construction of a maximally cohesive national identity and rallying the society around the powers that be. Second is eschewing the problem of guilt. The two are clearly interlinked: having liberated oneself of the

sense of historical, political, or moral responsibility, it is arguably much easier to take pride in one's newly minted "unblemished" identity based on the celebratory interpretation of one's country's "glorious past," which is habitually regarded as "more a source of comfort than a source of truth." I would thus argue that it is extremely important to investigate the vital links between history, memory and national identity. The main objective of this article, then, is to explore how the memories of some momentous developments in the tumultuous 20th century (above all, the experience of totalitarian dictatorships, World War II, the "division" and "reunification" of Europe, the collapse of the Soviet Union) and their historical interpretations relate to concepts of national identity in the post-Soviet lands. Identities are understood here not as something immutable; by contrast, I proceed from the premise that identities are constantly being constructed and reconstructed in the course of historical process. "As communities and individuals interpret and reinterpret their [historical] experiences . . . they create their own constantly shifting national identities in the process."

I will begin with the analysis of the reasons underlying the intensification of "history wars" between Russia and its neighbors. I will then discuss the prominent role that the reinterpretation of the history of World War II plays in the politics and geopolitics of identity in post-Soviet Eurasia. The analysis of Russia's symbolic politics will come next. I will conclude with exploring possible ways of reconciling national memories and historical narratives.

## WHY ESCALATION?

The past two decades following the collapse of the Soviet Union have witnessed an escalation of memory wars in which Russia has largely found itself on the defensive, its official historical narrative being vigorously assaulted by the number of the newly independent ex-Soviet states. Suffice it to recall just the most important episodes of this monumental "battle over history." Following the Soviet collapse, Museums of Occupation were set up in Latvia and Estonia; one of the museums' main objectives is to highlight the political symmetry between the two totalitarian regimes that occupied the Baltics in the 20th century—German national socialism and Soviet Communism. In May 2006, a Museum of Soviet Occupation opened in Tbilisi, Georgia, following the Baltic States' example. That same month, the Institute of National Memory was established in Ukraine, inspired by the Polish model. . . . That same year also saw the adoption of two international documents that couldn't fail to rile official Moscow—a resolution of the European Parliament entitled "On European Conscience and Totalitarianism" and a resolution passed by the Parliamentary Assembly of the Organization for Security and Cooperation in Europe entitled "Divided Europe Reunited: Promoting Human Rights and Civil Liberties in the OSCE Region in the 21st Century." Both resolutions branded Nazism and Stalinism as similar totalitarian regimes, bearing equal responsibility for the outbreak of World War II and the crimes against humanity committed during that period. The resolutions strongly called for the unconditional international condemnation of European totalitarianism. Moscow's reaction to all of this was unambiguously negative; in particular, Russian lawmakers, incensed at Stalinism and Nazism being lumped together, called the OSCE resolution an "offensive anti-Russian provocation" and "violence over history." . . .

There appear to be two sets of reasons behind the increasingly acrimonious disputes over history in which Russia is pitted against the former imperial borderlands. First is what might be called the "classical" politics of identity following the collapse of a multinational empire. Second, there is a specific geopolitical conjuncture primarily connected with the expansion of the European Union and the growing rivalry between the EU and Russia over their overlapping neighborhoods. An important subplot linked with both the Soviet Union's unravelling and the EU's eastward thrust is the struggle over the contested issue of Russia's own shifting identity.

Students of anthropology, political science and postcolonialism have long explored history writing (and mythmaking) as part of an overarching problem of nationalism, national identity and nation-building. Their key premise has been that (re)writing history and (re)making myths is what

nation-states generally do, history being a principal tool to construct national identity. It has also been argued (particularly forcefully within the field of postcolonial studies) that any regime change inevitably entails a confrontation with the past: "a new future requires a new past." In cases when regime change, state-creation and nation-building coincide, the confrontation with the past becomes particularly acute. This is precisely the situation in which the countries that emerged from under the rubble of the Soviet Union found themselves.

The key problem here is this: new states have emerged from the debris of the Soviet Union, but in many cases they exist without clear-cut identities or links to logically conceived "nations." Yet, identity, as some scholars argue, is decisively a question of empowerment. As Jonathan Friedman has perceptively noted, "The people without history . . . are the people who have been prevented from identifying themselves for others." So what were, realistically, the available strategies that the newly independent ex-Soviet countries could resort to?

Under Communism, studies of nationalism or national identities were not a terribly popular topic. "National question" in the Soviet Union was routinely explored as an aspect of class paradigm. As it has famously been postulated, liquidation of class distinctions (creation of classless society) would automatically lead toward the solution of national problem—through the creation of the "new historical entity" (the "Soviet people") in which national/ethnic differences would be preserved in their harmless (i.e., non-political) ethnographic form. National histories of the Soviet Union's multifarious peoples were secondary (and highly controlled) narratives—the component parts of the Soviet grand narrative.

Following the demise of Communism and the Soviet Union's unraveling, the incipient nation-states either returned to national historiographic tradition (where it existed) or hastily set about creating one. One common feature has been the "nationalization of history" whereby the history of a newly born post-Soviet state is conceptualized as the history of a titular nation, the latter being associated with the titular ethic group.

Yet this strategy of nationalizing history inevitably leads to strains, both internally and externally. As Clifford Geertz noted, defining the national particularism may be fraught with inherent difficulties because "new states tend to be bundles of competing traditions gathered accidentally into concocted political frameworks rather than organically evolving civilizations." Thus, "nationalization" of history centered on a titular nation cannot help but produce what can be called "mutually exclusive" histories, whereby national minorities are excluded and/or designated as *Others*. In the situation when all post-Soviet states are multiethnic and multicultural, the exclusivist narrative is counterproductive at best and outright dangerous at worst. . . .

*Following the demise of Communism and the Soviet Union's unraveling, the incipient nation-states either returned to national historiographic tradition . . . or hastily set about creating one.*

A recent Russian study based on the examination of nearly 200 school history textbooks and teacher guides from Russia's 12 post-Soviet neighbors demonstrated that the trends toward nationalizing history and "othering" are gaining momentum in most new independent states. The report, released in Moscow in the end of 2009 and entitled "The Treatment of the Common History of Russia and the Peoples of the Post-Soviet Countries in the History Textbooks of the New Independent States," argues that Russia's neighbors are now using textbooks that present Russia in all its historical incarnations as the enemy of the peoples of these countries. . . .

Some Russian historians appear to have been unpleasantly surprised, even hurt, by what they called the blatantly nationalistic and viciously anti-Russian interpretations of Russian imperial and Soviet history by non-Russian scholars from neighboring states. "It is a revisiting, at a new level, of the theory of 'absolute evil' which used to be popular during the early Soviet period," contends Moscow University Professor Aleksandr Vdovin. "Back then, this nefarious role in Soviet historiography was played by the [Russian] Tsarism that 'oppressed the peoples of the empire.' Now it is

Russia that is painted as the 'absolute evil.'" But more perceptive Russian and international commentators seem to agree that a certain degree of anti-Russian bias in the new independent countries' historiographies was all but inevitable. It should not be treated as an "unexpected phenomenon," argues one Russian analyst; rather, it should be understood as a "norm." In their efforts to assert their still shaky and fragile national identities and root them in the (re)invented national traditions, the new countries were bound to "push against" Russia's official historical narrative. "The shaping of an image of the ethnic or cultural Other has become an inalienable part of the cultural and political mobilization as well as of the politics of memory pursued by the newly independent states," writes the prominent Ukrainian historian Georgiy Kasyanov. It should come as no surprise, adds Kasyanov, that in the post-Soviet space it was "Russia and the Russians" who ended up being the "absolute champions" as far as the forming of negative ethnic stereotypes and "othering" are concerned. Thus the ground for "history wars" was in fact inherent in the post-imperial situation. These conflicts could have been somewhat attenuated had Russia—a former imperial overlord—had at least a modest success in what Germans call *Vergangenheitsbewältigung*, meaning coming to terms with the past. But it hadn't. I will address Russia's stance in greater detail below.

## GEOPOLITICS OF IDENTITY

. . . Why this sudden spike in the politicization of history? It would appear that the EU enlargement has undermined a historical consensus that used to exist within and among the Western European countries with regard to World War II and postwar experiences. As some scholars have pointed out recently, three main narratives of war and dictatorship exist in regard to Europe: a Western European story, a Soviet/Russian story, and an Eastern European story. Interestingly, the first two are somewhat similar in that both tend to highlight the glorious victory over Nazi Germany, successful postwar reconstruction, and the long period of postwar peace and economic development. By contrast, Eastern Europeans were largely focusing not so much on "liberation" as on the dark years of Soviet occupation and dreaming of their eventual "return to Europe."

The leading Western historians of Eastern Europe, such as Norman Davies and Timothy Snyder, long argued that the West badly misunderstood the East European experience. "What seems to have happened is that western opinion was only gradually informed about the war in Eastern Europe over forty to fifty years and that the drip-feeding was insufficient to inspire radical adjustments to the overall conceptual framework," Davies argued several years ago. But it is precisely Eastern Europe's devastating war experience that needs to be "recovered" and reintegrated into a European historical narrative. One has to remember that arguably the most awful acts of carnage and violence in Europe in the 20th century occurred in what Snyder calls the "bloodlands": the territories of Poland, Lithuania, Belarus and Ukraine. The sad irony, though, is that because after the war's end these countries found themselves behind the Iron Curtain and under Stalinist rule, their histories were marginalized or expelled altogether from a general European account. This "postwar exorcism," to use Michael Geyer's term, was carried out through a particular organization of knowledge about Europe. The latter, neatly following the postwar division of Europe, was split into *national histories* of Western Europe and *area studies* for Eastern Europe. Thus, "historiographic elision" was firmly institutionalized. Curiously, it appears to linger on, even more than twenty years after the Wall fell. As Snyder contends, "[E]ven as East Europeans gained the freedom to write and speak of their own histories as they chose after 1989 or 1991, and even as many East European countries acceded to the European Union in 2004 and 2007, their national histories have somehow failed to become accepted as European. Their histories have failed to flow into a larger European history that all, in East and West, can recognize as such."

But now the enlargement has made the accommodation of the Eastern European perspective inevitable—as a necessary precondition for the solidarity of the extended EU. Pushing aside "the other half" of European history runs the risk of

undermining the project of Europeanizing national histories. Furthermore, "it thwarts an assessment of Europe as a whole."

But as Eastern Europeans are pushing for the reintegration of their disastrous war experience into a (pan-)European narrative, they rarely manage to resist the temptation to turn the reinterpretation of World War II into the key element of their countries' politics of history. The reason behind this is simple. Most Eastern European nations now view the wartime and postwar period as a "useable past"—crucial for strengthening separate identity, giving a boost to populist nationalism, externalizing the Communist past, and casting their particular nation as a hapless victim of two bloodthirsty totalitarian dictatorships. The German historian Wilfried Jilge specifically points to the tendency of Eastern European intellectuals to construct what he terms the "national Holocausts" and thus confer on their nations a status of victim—and the perceived moral high ground that goes along with it. "From this position of moral superiority, the crimes of one's own nation are justified as defensive actions," writes Jilge in an article tellingly titled "The Competition of Victims"—the phrase he borrowed from the former Polish Foreign Minister Wladyslaw Bartoszewski. "In this context," Jilge goes on, "national stereotypes serve to distance 'one's own' national history from 'false' Soviet history and thus to 'cleanse' 'one's own' nation of everything that is Soviet."

This is yet another example of how Russia's Eastern European neighbors, while reinterpreting their most dramatic 20th-century experiences, are also reshaping their identities. They craft their historical narratives in such a way as to reposition themselves in Europe, seeking to strengthen their own sense of Europeanness and distinguish themselves from Russia, which is often cast as a non-European, Eurasian power—in a word, as Europe's constitutive *Other*. This is, of course, a problematic historiographical strategy. A number of Eastern European intellectuals note that almost everywhere in Eastern Europe, the new ruling elites chose to base—in varying degrees and shapes—their ideological legitimization on the conservative counterrevolutionary tradition that was dominant in the region during the interwar period, as well as on the mythology of the "national resistance" whose multifarious forms also included the collaboration with Nazi Germany, perceived as a suitable ally in the struggle against "Russian Communism." For this purpose, the Eastern European elites seek to (re)construct their countries' wartime histories as a story of the "national liberation struggle." In these new historical narratives, says Tamas Krausz, one of the leading Hungarian specialists in Eastern European history, "Russia is made a scapegoat." Another negative consequence of this historical reinterpretation, Krausz and other like-minded Eastern European intellectuals argue, is that it is being accompanied by the rehabilitation of the ethnic nationalist thinking. . . .

I would argue that the Eastern Europeans' lingering wariness of Russia is directly linked to the present-day Russia's ambiguous international identity. On the one hand, Russia claims legitimacy in Europe as a post-Soviet *European* state; on the other, it presents itself as the legal continuation of the Soviet Union. The latter stance entails two important implications: Russia's claim to a status of great power with a sphere of "privileged interests," and its reluctance to fully recognize Soviet/Stalinist crimes.

## RUSSIA'S PREDICAMENT: FACING UP TO THE DIFFICULT PAST WHILE COMING TO TERMS WITH THE GREAT LOSS

There is no question that Russia is seriously affected by this new historiographic situation stemming from the confluence of the post-imperial controversies and the history debates born of the recent geopolitical changes in Europe. It should not then come as a surprise that Moscow responds, sometimes very harshly, to what it perceives as a challenge to its national interests. The latter are believed to be particularly gravely threatened by the "hostile interpretations" of World War II (or what is better known in Russia as the "Great Patriotic War"). My key point here is that, similar to its Eastern European neighbors, Moscow's conduct, too, can only be properly understood within the context of Russian identity politics. After all, what is at stake—as it is perceived by the Russian elites—in the ongoing

history wars with the former Eastern Bloc satellites and ex-Soviet republics is no less than Russia's status as a "European nation."

So long as the erstwhile historical consensus remained intact, Russia's victory over Nazism legitimized its "great power" status in Europe and its sphere of influence in the eastern part of the continent. The new historical controversies over the nature of the Soviet "liberation" of Eastern Europe effectively undermine Russia's status as the "liberator of Europe" and erode whatever symbolic capital it might claim to prop up its "Europeanness." What we are witnessing is basically a "clash" of two very different notions of "liberation." In today's Europe (and, for that matter, the United States), the liberation of Europe in World War II is inseparably welded with the idea of democracy—the restoration of democratic order in that part Europe which was cleansed by the Western Allies of the "brown plague." Such interpretation presupposes that whatever the Soviet Union did in the eastern half of Europe that fell under Stalin's control could be called anything but "liberation."

Nowhere was the Russian official narrative—and the identity based upon it—challenged so vigorously of late as at the 2009 Vilnius Conference on "European Histories." Addressing the gathering, Valdas Adamkus, the outgoing president of Lithuania, reminded his audience that for Eastern Europeans, it is not just the defeat of Nazi Germany that comes to mind on May 8, 1945. "For Lithuania, like many other eastern European nations, May 8 of 1945 did not bring victory over violence, but simply change of oppressor," Adamkus has forcefully stated. "Once again, history was turned into the handmaiden of politics and ideology and thrust upon Lithuania and its people to cover up injustice and crime, distort facts, slander independence and freedom fighters." Yale historian Timothy Snyder would completely concur. Attacking in a 2005 article what he called a "common European narrative"—which is largely shared by Moscow—Snyder asserted that 1945 "means something entirely different in most of Eastern Europe—for most citizens of the states admitted to the Union in May 2004. For them, 1945 means a transition from one occupation to another; from Nazi rule to Soviet rule." Now, participating in the Vilnius gathering, Snyder offered his reinterpretation of Europe's tragic 20th-century experience that, according to one observer, "in key respects threw into question the established historical consensus."

Such treatment of the wartime and postwar developments is regarded in Moscow as a direct attack on Russia's image as a great *European* power—a status that the Kremlin leadership values highly. To get a better sense of the true extent of Moscow's wrath, one has to understand that 1945 represents the absolute pinnacle of Russia's geopolitical might: some scholars have argued that following its defeat in the Crimean war in 1856 and until the Soviet victory in WWII Russian power has been in a relative decline. "Don't forget," Tony Judt reminded us,

> that as seen from a historian's perspective, a historian of contemporary Europe, Stalin was in many ways the natural successor to Catherine the Great, and the tsars of the 19th century, expanding into the Russian near west, and to the Russian southwest in particular—territories that Catherine began her expansion into, which have always been regarded as crucial by Russian strategists, both because of access to resources, access to warm water ports, and because it gives Russia a role in Europe, as well as in Asia.

Just consider two plain historical facts: Russia was among the biggest losers in World War I, and saw its statehood crumbling and the borderlands seceding, while World War II results confirmed at Yalta and Potsdam turned Russia (in the form of the Soviet Union) into the world's second superpower—a status that included Moscow's immense geopolitical clout in Europe. However, Russia's four-decades-long dominance over Eastern Europe was brought down in a series of "velvet revolutions" in 1989. As one pithy comment put it, "Russia was the main victor in WWII and the main loser in 1989."

But what is particularly important for my discussion here is that, unlike most of its Eastern European neighbors, the post-Soviet Russia has refused to view the EU as a norm-maker and is reluctant to accept its standards and values. At the same time, Russian leadership adamantly insists that its country is inherently European—as European as any other major European state. One cannot find a better expression of this attitude than a defiant passage in Vladimir Putin's 2005 Annual Address to the Federal Assembly. As if reiterating Catherine the Great's famous dictum, Putin forcefully asserted that "Above all else Russia was, is and will, of course, be a major European power":

> Achieved through much suffering by European culture, the ideals of freedom, human rights, justice and democracy have for many centuries been our society's determining values. For three centuries, we—together with the other European nations—passed hand in hand through reforms of Enlightenment, the difficulties of emerging parliamentarianism, municipal and judiciary branches, and the establishment of similar legal systems . . . I repeat we did this together, sometimes behind and sometimes ahead of European standards.

Such a stance, naturally, implies that Europe should be held to *Russian* standards of Europeanness, too. So when Moscow castigates the "rehabilitation of fascism" in certain parts of Europe or lashes out at the "glorification of Nazi collaborators" in some Baltic states or in Ukraine, it claims it protects *European* values—the ones that the EU itself allegedly chose to ignore. Thus Russian leadership's jeremiads against the "inadmissible revision of WWII results" should be read as an element of its strategic ideological ambition to advance an alternative interpretation of what *Europe* means.

There is also a very important domestic dimension of Russian leadership's struggle against the "revision of World War II history." Here, a myth of the "Great Patriotic War" or, more precisely, a myth of the "great Victory" plays a pivotal role. Created in the 1960s, this myth—in which the memory of *war,* with all its unbearable everyday hardships, untold number of victims, millions of POWs, chaos of evacuation, etc., had been replaced by the memory of *victory*—was successfully exploited by the Soviet Communist rulers. First, it provided an effective means of legitimization for the political power. Second, it was a powerful instrument of identity politics as it told an uplifting story of a "birth of the Soviet people in the crucible of the total war." . . .

The official commemoration of the "Great Patriotic War" also appears to be the sole ideological mechanism that can be employed to foster Russia's social cohesion. According to Carnegie Moscow Center analyst Nikolai Petrov, "There is absolutely nothing else in the whole of Russian history that can be used to unite the nation." Petrov's remark is significant in that it reveals what arguably constitutes Russia's most formidable "historiographical" problem—namely, the lack of even a minimal consensus within the Russian society as to the interpretation of the country's turbulent past, following the century of violent political upheavals. To achieve a healthy degree of cohesion, within any society there should be a certain public agreement as to the basic values system upon which rests the whole edifice of historical memory of the given society. After all, any "memorial construct" is a system of values; the "memory as such" simply does not exist. As the Russians fail to agree on how to treat the most significant episodes of their country's past, the "victory myth" is being used by the ruling elites as a kind of "social glue."

Treating the "Great Patriotic War" as a "usable past" also fits into a broader strategy of "normalizing" Soviet history which has been vigorously pursued under Putin. "Normalization" of the Soviet past as a "part of our glorious thousand year old history" contributes to the revived ideology of statism as a perennial source of Russian identity.

Integrating the Stalin period into a greater Russian story is not just an elite project—the polls demonstrate that it is generally supported by the masses. For the West in general and Russia's Eastern European neighbors in particular, the process appears both puzzling and menacing; increasingly, there is talk about Moscow's backlash and imperial comeback. There is, however, a compelling psychological reason for the rise of such public attitudes, and some more astute commentators contended that a backlash in one form or another was inevitable. One has to understand, notes Judt, that for the majority of Russians, the demise of the Soviet Union involved the loss of not just territory and status but also of a *history* that they could live

with. "Everything has been unraveled before their eyes," says he, adding that any other nation would have been morally devastated by such an experience.

> If this had happened to Americans, or Brits, it would have been culturally catastrophic; to lose the equivalent of, say Texas and California, to be told that all the founding fathers right down to FDR were a bunch of criminals, to discover that you are regarded as on the par with Hitler, in terms of the accepted description of 20th-century evils that we have since overcome.

No wonder, then, that the "trope of loss," as Serguei Oushakine demonstrates so well in his *The Patriotism of Despair,* has become the most effective and widely used symbolic device which Russians employ to make sense of their Soviet experience in the post-Soviet context.

There is, of course, a vexed question about the interrelation between the glory of the "Great Patriotic War" and the horrors of Stalinist terror. Some liberal Russian scholars have skillfully demonstrated how the memory of the war is being (ab)used to construct a kind of "blocking myth" in order to suppress the memories of the totalitarian regime's terror, of the Gulag and other crimes of the period. If the atrocities perpetrated by the Soviet regime do occasionally pop up in the official narrative, they are presented as some insignificant episode in the otherwise heroic and glorious Soviet history. But one also must bear in mind the existence of significant differences in the ways the trauma of the Soviet collapse affected public perceptions and memories of Russians and those of their neighbors in Eastern Europe: "In Russia itself, the disintegration of the USSR was linked much more closely with the painful immediacy of everyday survival than with archived horrors of the Great Terror . . . The need to equate the Soviet Union with the Stalinist regime, which was so crucial for many Western [and East European] commentators, was less obvious in the midst of [Russia's] post-Soviet changes."

And yet, the ambiguity of a Russian official position, rooted in the inability of making a comprehensive and honest assessment of the nature of the

Soviet regime, makes it extremely difficult for Moscow to approach the crucial issue of responsibility that appears to be at the heart of history wars in the post-Soviet space. . . .

## CONCLUSION

Is it realistic to believe that post-Soviet states will ever do without politics of history and that the memory wars between them will eventually end? I would begin discussion of this question by suggesting that while national images of the past will never fully coincide, it appears feasible to reach some reconciliation between them and thus avoid creating negative identities. Such reconciliation can be achieved in the course of a broad and mutually respectful dialogue between national memories and historical narratives. All the participants of this dialogue would agree that while national memories are not congruent and historical narratives might diverge, one's image of the past could only be enriched through the knowledge of alternative interpretations.

Such dialogue, however, will only be possible if three formidable obstacles are overcome. The most important obstacle is authoritarian political culture. As Karl Schlögel argues, "Authoritarian conditions are hostile to memory. A mature historical culture and a civil culture belong together." Indeed, scholars have noted the close correlation between regime type and the degree of regime's reliance on historical myths. True, all regimes resort to and rely on myth-making. But in liberal democracies, political legitimacy is much less dependent on the unifying historical narrative that would foster compliance with government policies than it is in authoritarian regimes. Genuine democracies are thus much more tolerant of dissent, controversy, competing ideas and can afford the luxury of treating history that challenges habitual assumptions with relative equanimity. This trait, in the words of the eminent British historian Michael Howard, is a mark of maturity. By contrast, authoritarian leaders prefer to feed their subjects with what Howard calls "nursery history." In his view, "[A] good definition of the difference between a Western liberal society

and a totalitarian one—whether it is Communist, Fascist, or Catholic authoritarian—is that in the former the government treats its citizens as responsible adults and in the latter it cannot."

The second problem is the widespread perceptions that mass publics hold about what history actually is. Sociological surveys demonstrate that in most post-Soviet states, people are largely unaware of one fundamental thing—that studying history is a complex and continuous process in the course of which what used to be perceived as "historical truth" can (and should) be refuted as new evidence emerge or new interpretations are advanced. According to the recent data provided by VTsIOM, a Russian pollster, 60 percent of the respondents hold that history should not be revised, that past events should be studied in such a way which would exclude "repeat research" leading to new approaches and interpretations. Only 31 percent of those polled believe that the study of history is a continuous and open-ended process. Furthermore, 79 percent spoke in favor of using one single textbook when teaching history course in schools—lest the young minds get confused by alternative interpretations. Symptomatically, 78 percent supported the creation of the presidential commission charged with fighting "falsification of history," and 60 percent said the passing of a "memory law" criminalizing the "revision of WWII results" would be a good thing. Ironically, when 61 percent of Russians say that "national interpretations" of the past are inadmissible, they appear to be oblivious of the fact that their own interpretation is no less "national."

This picture of public attitudes should correct an oversimplified perception of symbolic politics in the post-Soviet lands as basically a one-way street whereby the discourse that serves the interests of ruling elites is being imposed upon society. In more ways than one, the prevalent attitudes toward history and memory demonstrate the meeting of the minds between the rulers and the ruled in Eurasia.

It would appear that these attitudes can be changed only slowly through the changes in the way national histories are written in Russia and other ex-Soviet republics. And this is the third big problem that needs to be tackled. It would be naive to believe that national governments (or die-hard nationalists, for that matter) will one day stop regarding (and exploiting) historical narrative as a useful means of nationalist mobilization. After all, common history is what holds the imagined community together. So an ethnic-centric, "nationalized" history is likely to persist. But what is needed, assert some leading historians, is to supplement a traditional national narrative by *multiethnic* or, better still, *transnational* approach. "Transnational" or "transcultural" history, argues Andreas Kappeler, would be based on "multiperspectivity and comparison, investigate interactions, communications and overlapping phenomena and entanglements between states, nations, societies, economies, regions, and cultures."

These new approaches would probably still not help overcome the divide between memories in the post-Soviet world. But as I have stated above, there is no need to try bridging the gap between national memories. This goal is unattainable. The objective to be pursued is much more modest: to promote understanding of other perspectives and interpretations.

# Section 11

## Global Forecasting: The World of 2025

# Can We Predict Politics? Toward What End?

MICHAEL D. WARD

## SHIPWRECKS AND SECURITY STUDIES

In 1901, off the Greek island of Antikythera, a ship pulled into a bay to wait out a storm. After the storm was over, its divers discovered an ancient shipwreck containing many valuable antiquities, including jewelry, coins, statues, and pottery. One item was a lump of corroded bronze and wood. Everything was carted off to the National Museum of Archeology in Athens. In 1902, an archeologist noticed that the corroded lump had what appeared to be gears in it. He assumed that it was some sort of astrological clock, but it appeared to be too far advanced given the dating of the other items it was found with, which were initially dated to about 150 BCE, and it was ignored for five decades. Several years later, it was X and $y$ rayed, resulting in images of eighty-two different fragments of the device.

By the end of 2014, it had been established that the mechanism dated back further, to about 250 BCE. Many consider it to be the first computing machine (Freeth et al. 2006). This device was able to calculate and display celestial cycles, including phases of the moon, as well as a solar calendar. Perhaps more importantly, it was able to predict eclipses—seen at the time as omens. In fact, many think of the Antikythera Mechanism as an *omen prediction device*, with all the other predictions it makes simply by-products of its true purpose.

The main purpose of this mechanism was to generate accurate predictions, and whoever used it could do so without a detailed theoretical knowledge of Hipparchosian astronomy as applied to irregular phases of ellipsoid orbits. Thus, it was pure prediction and did not "explain" anything. At the same time, it embodied detailed engineering that was based on a theoretical mechanism that provided exquisite details of planetary orbits in general as well as specifically. For some, that might suffice

as explanation. It seems clear that this accurate prediction device was possible only because it was based on a deep understanding of celestial orbits. What is particularly surprising is that this level of astronomical prediction was apparently lost in the shipwreck and did not reappear in Europe for over a millennium. In retrospect, it seems unlikely that this device would simply disappear, given how powerful it must have been in 250 BCE. Yet, as far as we know, this is exactly what happened.

Jumping ahead a thousand years, we see that prediction is deeply embedded in the philosophy of science. Although in hiding in the aftermath of the French Revolution, Marie Jean Antoine Nicolas de Caritat, marquis de Condorcet, wrote in *Historical View of the Progress of the Human Mind* (1795, translated):

> If man can, with almost complete assurance, predict phenomena when he knows their laws, and if, even when he does not, he can still, with great expectation of success, forecast the future on the basis of his experience of the past, why, then, should it be regarded as a fantastic undertaking to sketch, with some pretense to the truth, the future destiny of man on the basis of his history. The sole foundation for belief in the natural sciences is this idea, and the general laws directing the phenomena of the universe, known or unknown, are necessary and constant.

This theme continues to the current day through Auguste Comte (1846), John Stuart Mill (1843), A. J. Ayer (1936), Carl Hempel (1935), Karl Popper (1935), Thomas Kuhn (1962), and even Jon Elster (1989, 2007), who notes:

> To predict that less of a good will be bought when its price goes up, there is no need to form a hypothesis about human behavior. Whatever the

springs of individual action—ration, traditional, or simply random—we can predict that people will buy less of a good simply because they can afford less of it. Here there are several mechanisms that are constrained to lead to the same outcome, so that for predictive purposes there is no need to decide among them. Yet for explanatory purposes the mechanism is what matters. It provides understanding whereas prediction at most offers control. (1989, 9)

The argument is that if you can develop models that provide an understanding—without a teleology of why things happen—you should be able to generate predictions that will not only be accurate, but may also be useful in a larger societal context. The basic argument is essentially that it should be possible to develop a predictive science of human behavior. It is debatable whether the so-called regularities are constant or changing.

During the height of the war in Vietnam, in the mid-1960s, a graduate student at Stanford began to systematically study the details of the war, down to the level of troop numbers on all sides, number of bombing sorties, casualties, troop attrition, kill ratios (then a big indicator in McNamara's Defense Department), and political support in the United States and South Vietnam for the incumbent administration and the war itself, along with the number of Viet Cong and North Vietnamese defectors. Statistical models of the relationships among these variables were constructed and validated toward the goal of generating predictions (from computer simulations) about the escalation of the war. Jeffrey S. Milstein published his efforts in *Dynamics of the Vietnam War: A Quantitative Analysis and Predictive Computer Simulation* in 1974, and his working papers on this topic were widely read in the academic and policy communities. This was one of the first uses of prediction in the study of international relations (IR) and security studies. By 1974, articles were starting to promote forecasting in the realm of world politics (Choucri 1974), and a few years later, there was a volume devoted to the topic (Choucri and Robinson 1978).

There have been a number of scholarly efforts at prediction in the realm of international and domestic conflict. (Ironically, the Vietnam War was considered international by many comparativists, but a civil conflict by many IR scholars). One of the first calls for greater attention was by Herman Weil (1974), then working in the defense-consulting sector. After a few efforts in the later 1970s, an article by Gurr and Lichbach (1986) took Gurr's model of *Why Men Rebel* (1970) and used it to make out-of-sample forecasts of where there would be future conflicts. It did so explicitly to test the theoretical model of conflict that had been initially developed by Ted Robert Gurr. It forecasts the number of days of protests as well as the number of deaths in protests in ten countries. But this study generated forecasts that used data measured in five-year periods, and the period from 1971 to 1975 was forecast based on data for about 1970. Nonetheless, it was one of the first empirically oriented studies to focus explicitly on forecasts. Until very recently, most of this thread of work in security studies had been lost, or if not lost, at least abandoned.

Cioffi-Revilla (1996) provided a published prediction of what was likely to happen in the first Iraq War. It was the only published prediction that I can find, or remember, though it took a while to get published. By now, there is a bevy of recent efforts that include a forecasting component (Gleditsch and Ward 2000, 2010, 2013; King and Zeng 2001; Ward and Gleditsch 2002; Hegre 2008; Weidmann and Ward 2010; de Mesquita 2011; Metternich et al. 2013; Ward et al. 2013; Koubi and Böhmelt 2014; Pilster and Böhmelt 2014; Schutte 2014). Why has this thread been so sparse in security studies? Two words: Kenneth Waltz.

Many social scientists see a sharp distinction between *explanation* on the one hand and *prediction* on the other. Indeed, this distinction is often sharp enough that it is argued that doing one of these things cuts you out of doing the other. Kenneth Waltz (1997) is a good example of this belief. A long-standing, but incorrect, example has been the weather, about which it has been famously argued that while you can understand the various components of the weather system—the evaporation of water, its collection in clouds, the changing temperatures that result in lightning, and the like—having this explanation does not enable you to make actual predictions about the weather. It is argued that because the contexts are sufficiently varied and numerous, they would defeat our ability to predict the weather. Mill argued against this idea, the then-prevailing opinion that tidology would never be a precise endeavor. He proposed that weather prediction could, in principle, be successful and become an exact science. Guess what? Against all the naysayers, he was right.

Nonetheless, the idea that prediction and understanding are different has persisted and in fact is widespread in the realm of security studies. In a simple way this is true, because you can develop a predictive system without necessarily understanding all the details that are in play. A classic example often offered is that an individual can be an excellent pool player without being able to explain the basic equations of motion. But this example seems disingenuous, and solutions to the equations may take different forms. Perhaps, a kind of "intuitive" understanding may supplant a more "analytic" understanding. We know that analytic knowledge is harder to communicate to others than is intuitive information, but it may be that both types of knowledge are useful and even accurate. Moreover, who knows exactly what is going on in the nervous system of an excellent pool player at a level below cognition?

We need these predictions for four reasons. First, we need these predictions to help us make relevant statements about the world around us. We also need these predictions to help us throw out the bad "theories" that continue to flourish. These predictions will help drive our research into new areas, away from moribund approaches that have been followed for many decades. Finally, and perhaps most important, predictions will force us to keep on track. It is hard to imagine that in ten years hence, the theories I have highlighted above will have been evaluated in terms of their accuracy. It is easy to go back in the literature ten years and find similar pronouncements that were left hanging out there in the realm of JSTOR alone. At the end of the last century, John Vasquez and Kenneth Waltz debated the value of predictions in terms of their implications for theory (Vasquez 1997; Waltz 1997). As it turns out, this debate, while interesting, is not relevant for our discussion because neither Vasquez nor Waltz mean predictions in the sense of a forecast, but rather in the sense of an empirical regularity or fact that can be induced or deduced by the theoretical framework. Indeed, most of the "predictions" in this debate relate to events in the early twentieth century.

## PREDICTIONS IN THE LARGER WORLD

In the 1980s, Philip Tetlock was concerned—like many—about the possibility of a nuclear conflict between the United States and Soviet Union. Indeed, this was the main focus of most security studies during the Cold War. Popular movies and scholarly journals highlighted what time it was on the so-called "doomsday" clock. Tetlock wanted to understand why the pundits made statements about the future that were all over the place. Frustrated by the fact that pundits justified their inaccuracies with revisions of history, timing, and other excuses, he collected forecasts—an amazing number of them (~25,000)—and started to keep track and grade their accuracy. Tetlock's book, *Expert Political Judgment* (2005, 2010), showed that pundits as well as social scientists making predictions were equally and totally bad at it. An oft-cited refrain from the book is that "dart throwing chimps" were equally accurate to experts. Indeed, the most well qualified of experts often turned out to be the worst forecasters. Unlike Bill Ascher (1979), who made similar points earlier, Philip Tetlock (2005) undertook to improve forecasting methodology.

With his team of statisticians and social scientists—including Barbara Mellers and Don Moore—Tetlock was able to propose an adventurous and ambitious program of research for the then newly formed IARPA (Intelligence Research Advanced Projects Agency), a research arm of the US intelligence community focused on addressing hard problems with open-source efforts between scientists and those in the intelligence community. The Good Judgment Project (goodjudgmentproject.org) was the result. Essentially, the effort is to provide specific forecasting questions that (a) have a discernible outcome (e.g., Will Kim Jung Un preside at the May 1 parade in Pyongyang in 2014?) and (b) have a precise time of resolution. These two characteristics of the forecast can be judged independently from the forecast itself (a problem when forecasts are self-evaluated). About 4,000 people have signed up for this tournament. They are also trained to use the computing platform. Each individual is made part of a group, and these groups as well as the individuals compete in terms of their accuracy (measured largely by Brier scores).

Two major lessons are gleaned from the experiments that are embedded in these tournaments. One is that understanding the base rates at which some phenomena occur is very important. Without an understanding of what the base rate is, it becomes difficult to tell whether an event is "normal" or exceptional. Is a protest of 1,000 people in Tahrir Square in Cairo something that is unusual, or does it happen on a monthly basis, for example? The second lesson follows from the first: How do you identify an exception? Just these two skills, which can be easily taught, cause a change in thinking about what is likely to happen. And it turns out, they also help individuals make more accurate forecasts. Two other things are important. One of them is the simple act of keeping track of your successes and failures, something that is unlikely to receive widespread assent by media stars and pundits. The second is more prosaic: Aggregations help reduce bias and uncertainty. The classic example of this is the 1906 livestock fair in which 800 individuals guessed the weight of an ox on display. No single individual got the right answer, but according to Galton, both the mean and the median of these 800 estimates were within one percent of the correct weight (Galton 1907).

This leads to four points:

1. Base rates are important contexts for predictions.
2. Exceptions to base rates are important to identify; however, what an exception is remains complicated.
3. Keeping track of successes and failures is important.
4. Having a lot of answers may be the only way to get the right answer, but doing so may require some aggregation from a variety of perspectives.

How are Tetlock's forecasters doing in this competition with prediction markets, subject matter experts, and other unspecified "work products" of the intelligence community? So far, there are five independent research teams, of which Tetlock's group is one. This experiment involves over one million judgments from over 10,000 participants. This is based on about one hundred real events each year, for example "Will Iran sign an IAEA Structured Approach document before June 1, 2014?" A systematic comparison of the various approaches is underway. In short:

- Aggregations of trained forecasters beat subject matter experts by about fifty percent, and they also beat prediction markets.
- Prediction markets significantly out-perform subject matter experts. Domain expertise is less important than problem solving and belief updating.
- The top forecasters—the so-called super forecasters—tend to be the same individuals each year.

Another IARPA project is also interesting to examine. It is known as the OSI, Open Source Indicators, project, in which the basic idea is that classified information is possibly inferior to open-source materials for making important predictions. Thus, an attempt has been made to undertake detailed, precise forecasts of the type often engaged in within the intelligence community, while only using materials found in the unclassified world. The goal is to develop and test methods for the automated analysis of publicly available data to anticipate or detect significant social events. Such events include disease outbreaks, political instability, and elections. The goal is kind of a version of Google FluTrends on steroids: beat the news by fusing early indicators of events from diverse data (Ramakrishnan et al. 2014). They are less interested in theory, but do base their predictions on exactly the kind of data that are widely used in the social sciences.

Some recent predictive successes include:

1. Riots after impeachment of Paraguay's president (2012)
2. The so-called "Brazilian Spring" (June 2013)

3. Hantavirus outbreaks in Argentina and Chile (2013)
4. Venezuelan student uprising (Feb 2014)

What is remarkable here is that these predictions are graded by independent subject matter experts reading the local, non-English text. This suggests that not just trained individuals, but also trained statistical models might be able to generate accurate and useful predictions.

## DATA CONSTRAINTS

One of the difficulties of doing predictions is that data are often hard to obtain for the future. More practically, all quantitative and quality investigations are limited to information about the past. The typical response to this kind of approach is to employ all the available information, because more information is always better. In the quantitative world, this results in an undesirable dependence between the data collected and the model posited. This dependence typically results in overfitting in which the model has been sculpted to the available data but might not characterize additional data (such as the future or different cases). The same can happen qualitatively wherein new cases are sought to fit different aspects of the theory being examined or constructed.

Even if we do not have time to wait for data on the future to appear as a way of examining the external validity of our explanations, we still have the past. Ideally, we should divide our cases and samples into different groups, one of which we use to estimate the model and evaluate its characteristics as we refine or estimate it statistically. These cases are known as the training cases. A second set of observations, known as the test data, can be then examined to see if they also conform to the theory/model. This procedure, by now a gold standard in most of science, is known as cross-validation and serves as a way to anneal one's investigations against being too tied to the data at hand.

## WHAT ARE THE PROS AND CONS OF A PREDICTIVE APPROACH TO SOCIAL SCIENCE?

The main pro is that the predictive enterprise helps us evaluate how well we are doing so that we can improve our understanding of the world. It is the gold standard of a scientific approach. We do not yet have an experimental framework for many important subjects. As a result, it is important to make sure we can get the same kind of results with new information that we got with the data we began investigating. That means we have to either save some data back (a great idea), use the future to see how well our modeled understandings perform, or preferably both. There are only nascent traditions of this in the social sciences at present. Keeping track of your success is not collecting significant coefficients. *Keeping track matters.* One consequence is that we cannot just keep using the same data over and over. And over. One reason that many hate predictions is that talking heads make many predictions in the media, but few of them ever keep track of how well they are doing. Their goal is somewhat akin to a venture capitalist's: make enough bets that eventually one of them is correct enough that you get to make a lot more bets. Ascher (1979) long ago showed that the talking heads were most often wrong. This is still true. You would think that they would get better over time, but there is little evidence that this is the case.

We also will be driven into making more precise investigations once we start to predict. We will not be satisfied with annual data for most things. Nor will we necessarily be satisfied with national-level information because it becomes even more apparent in the predictive domain that the world is neither flat nor homogeneous. As a result, we should get more precise understandings of how things play out in our social world. At the same time, we have to recognize that our predictions are probabilistic and contain a large amount of uncertainty, more so than in other endeavors.

As a result of these two aspects, better and more precise understandings of our social world, it is possible to be more relevant to decision makers at all levels. This does not mean just inside the beltway. It also means decision makers at CDC (Centers for Disease Control) as well as those in non-governmental organizations around the world.

What are the cons? Several arguments are usually brought to the fore.

1. *The world is inherently unpredictable.* But we are studying it anyway. Go figure. The refrain to this litany is often "but I know what

is going to happen in this instance." Maybe, but let us keep track and find out if you are right. This is the talking heads premise, and it is demonstrably false. Making cause and effect statements about politics does imply that politics is in part, at least, predictable.

2. *This will empower the establishment and impoverish those without power.* Actually, it might. But at the same time, it provides ways in which those outside the capitals can also affect the future. Why will prediction be more valuable to the establishment than it is to the rest of society? Is the same thing true of explanation and substantive knowledge? Western society is based in part on the idea that knowledge is a valuable thing for all. It is true that some take more advantage of it than others. But having open and available knowledge can be important for many diverse groups. As an example, we might think that clandestine organizations can benefit from open knowledge, even precise actionable knowledge, but as we think these thoughts, most of us might not be thinking about transnational activist networks but rather large governmental organizations. However, it is clear that non-governmental actors are also consumers of knowledge.

3. *It is possible to predict things without true understanding or knowledge.* Sure, but rarely is this true for any but the simplest of systems. I am reminded of the wonderful essay by Calvin Trillin describing the chicken on Mott Street in New York's Chinatown that played and always won Tic-Tac-Toe. The chicken did not understand the game. But the chicken always won. It is ridiculous to suggest that we have models that predict as accurately as the (now gone) Mott Street chicken but have the same understanding of the "chicken" game. Even if it were the case (and I repeat it is not), could the opposite really be true? If you have deep understanding of the world, should you not be able to generate accurate predictions of how it will work in situations you have not seen before? Will proximate effects lead us toward distant causes much like proximate causes can lead us to distant effects?

4. *We will disrupt the space–time continuum.* If we can predict conflict, for example, we will be able to prevent it. Or start it where we want. And then we will no longer be able to predict conflict. One of my models attempts to predict where there will be coups de état and other types of irregular regime changes on a monthly level. Maybe if Muhammadu Buhari, who assumed the presidency of Nigeria at the end of May 2015, sees our manuscript, he might be able to prevent any irregular leadership change from occurring in the next six months. And maybe that would be bad. Or good. But in any case, I am pretty sure that the Nigerian president is already aware of the fragility of the Nigerian political landscape. This is a frequent type of criticism of forecasting. I think we can wait for this to become a real problem before we stop trying to develop better understandings of the world.

5. *Real social effects occur glacially. Predictions will be focused on epiphenomenal changes that won't matter in the long run.* How do you know?

In summary, we need less theory because most theory is an attempt to rescue or adapt extant theory. We need more predictions in order to keep track of how well we understand the world around us. They will tell us how good our theories are and where we need better explanations. Predictions are like cell phones. First, they seem arcane and bizarre. Then, in a few short years, there is no one around who remembers life without cell phones and your kids use them in ways you don't understand. The 2012 US presidential election was the first that was famously and accurately predicted. But it will be the first of many. All future voters will vote in an era in which accurately predicting the election will be the norm, not the exception, though as in the UK in 2015, there will be exceptions. This will have consequences for democracy. In the same way that having a product recommended to us on the web is now normal, this will become the new normal. Data science (and more data) will guide us to a better understanding of our future than we have now. Whether you are involved with commercial organizations, local government, non-governmental organizations (NGOs), the federal government, or international organizations, prediction will be part of the daily ebb and flow of information, and we shall become used to seeing accurate predictions about a wide variety of political phenomena.

But, as we get more accurate, will we be able to begin manipulating outcomes? Engineer results? It may not seem like it to everyone, but political beliefs are malleable. In fact, survey researchers are feigning shock at discovering that political surveys tend to politicize respondents. Republicans can turn into Democrats, and vice versa. Will we get equally adept at predicting what kinds of information, interactions, and initiatives will turn the tide in a particular election? Facebook and Google—and many other less famous firms—think so, and are gearing up for the 2016 election with tools that go way beyond surveys that can be used for that purpose.

What do we expect to see in the global security system? First, we know that a wider variety of actors will be consuming and generating data on their activities. Indeed, we know that a wider variety of national and non-state actors are using predictive models of behavior that might broadly be considered in the realm of political violence, ranging from strikes and protests to attacks and casualties. China, Russia, the European Union, and the UK, as well as the United States and the United Nations and the North Atlantic Treaty Organization, all have substantial forecasting capabilities in the global realm. Some of these forecasts are made on a weekly basis, and others are more long term, looking out a couple of decades. But the fact that predictive heuristics are now part and parcel of normal statecraft is important and recent. Moreover, non-state actors are not to be left out and are beginning to evolve toward greater foresight. Consider that an International Red Cross that is able to predict domestic conflicts will be better able to pre-position supplies and expertise to deal with the human toll of such conflicts. A monitoring of violent government actions that can predict the safest time to remove NGO personnel in conflict zones is another example of a predictive tool that can affect the global security system in new and beneficial ways.

The global security system is complicated, multilayered, unknown, and changing. In some ways, it is exactly like the solar system. However, it may change more quickly but maybe less dramatically. By developing explanations and subjecting them to critical evaluations, we learned more. We can learn more again. We can build Antikythera Mechanisms. Though they may or may not tell us about the next sociopolitical eclipse in the international security system, they are likely to help us get rid of bad ideas.

## REFERENCES

Ayer, Alfred Jules. 1936. *Language, Truth, and Logic*. London: Gollancz.

Choucri, Nazli. 1974. "Forecasting in International Relations: Problems and Prospects." *International Interactions* 1(2): 63–68.

Choucri, Nazli, and Thomas W. Robinson. 1978. *Forecasting in International Relations: Theory, Methods, Problems, Prospects*. San Francisco: W. H. Freeman.

Cioffi-Revilla, Claudio. 1996. "On the Likely Magnitude, Extent, and Duration of an Iraq–UN War." *Journal of Conflict Resolution* 35(3): 387–411.

Comte, Auguste. 1846. *General View of Positivism*. London: Trubner.

de Caritat (Marquis de Condorcet), Marie Jean Antoine Nicolas. 1795. *Creation de Esquisse d'un tableau historique des progres de l'esprit humain*. Translated and edited by de Caritat (Marquis de Condorcet), Marie Jean Antoine Nicolas. Philadelphia: Lang and Uttick.

de Mesquita, Bruce Bueno. 2011. "A New Model for Predicting Policy Choices: Preliminary Tests." *Conflict Management and Peace Science* 28(1): 65–87.

Elster, Jon. 2007. *Explaining Social Behavior: More Nuts and Bolts for the Social Sciences*. Cambridge: Cambridge University Press.

Elster, Jon. 1989. *Nuts and Bolts for the Social Sciences*. Cambridge: Cambridge University Press.

Freeth, Tony, Yanis Bitsakis, Xenophon Moussas, John H. Seiradakis, A. Tselikas, H. Mangou, M. Zafeiropouou, R. Hadland, D. Bate, A. Ramsey, M. Allen, A. Crawley, P. Hockley, T. Malzbender, D. Gelb, W. Ambrisco, and M. G. Edmunds. 2006.

"Decoding the Ancient Greek Astronomical Calculator Known as the Antikythera Mechanism." *Nature* 444(Supplement 7119): 587–591.

Galton, Francis. 1907. "Vox populi." *Nature* 75(1949): 450–451.

Gleditsch, Kristian Skrede, and Michael D. Ward. 2010. "Contentious Issues and Forecasting Interstate Disputes." Presented at the 2010 Annual Meeting of the International Studies Association. New Orleans.

Gleditsch, Kristian Skrede, and Michael D. Ward. 2013. "Forecasting Is Difficult, Especially the Future: Using Contentious Issues to Forecast Interstate Disputes." *Journal of Peace Research* 50(1): 17–31.

Gleditsch, Kristian Skrede, and Michael D. Ward. 2000. "War and Peace in Space and Time: The Role of Democratization." *International Studies Quarterly* 44(1): 1–29.

Gurr, Ted Robert. 1970. *Why Men Rebel*. Princeton, NJ: Princeton University Press.

Gurr, Ted Robert, and Mark Irving Lichbach. 1986. "Forecasting Internal Conflict: A Competitive Evaluation of Empirical Theories." *Comparative Political Studies* 19(3): 3–38.

Hegre, Havard. 2008. "Gravitating toward War: Preponderance May Pacify, but Power Kills." *Journal of Conflict Resolution* 52(4): 566–589.

Hempel, Carl G. 1935. "Uber den Gehalt von Wahrscheinli chkeitsaussagen." *Erkenntnis* 5: 228–260.

King, Gary, and Langche Zeng. 2001. "Improving Forecasts of State Failure." *World Politics* 53(4): 623–658.

Koubi, Vally, and Tobias Bohmelt. 2014. "Grievances, Economic Wealth, and Civil Conflict." *Journal of Peace Research* 51(1): 19–33.

Kuhn, Thomas S. 1962. *The Structure of Scientific Revolutions*. Chicago: University of Chicago Press.

Metternich, Nils W., Cassy Dorff, Max Gallop, Simon Weschle, and Michael D. Ward. 2013. "Anti-Government Networks in Civil Conflicts: How Network Structures Affect Conflictual Behavior." *American Journal of Political Science* 57(3): 892–911.

Mill, John Stuart. 1843. *A System of Logic*. London: John W. Parker, West Strand.

Milstein, Jeffery S. 1974. *Dynamics of the Vietnam War: A Quantitative Analysis and Predictive Computer Simulation*. Columbus: Ohio State University Press.

Pilster, Ulrich, and Tobias Bohmelt. 2014. "Predicting the Duration of the Syrian Insurgency." *Research & Politics* 1(2). doi: 10.1177/2053168014544586.

Popper, Karl. 1935. *Logik der Forschung: Zur Erkenntnistheorie der Modernen Naturwissenschaft*. Number Band 9. Berlin: Springer Verlag.

Ramakrishnan, Naren, Patrick Butler, Sathappan Muthiah, Nathan Self, Rupinder Paul Khandpur, Parang Saraf, Wei Wang, Jose Cadena, Anil Vullikanti, Gizem Korkmaz, Chris J. Kuhlman, Achla Marathe, Liang Zhao, Ting Hua, Feng Chen, Chang-Tien Lu, Bert Huang, Aravind Srinivasan, Khoa Trinh, Lise Getoor, Graham Katz, Andy Doyle, Chris Ackermann, Ilya Zavorin, Jim Ford, Kristen Maria Summers, Youssef Fayed, Jaime Arredondo, Dipak Gupta, and David Mares. 2014. "'Beating the News' with EMBERS: Forecasting Civil Unrest Using Open Source Indicators." *CoRR* abs/1402.7035. http://arxiv.org/abs/1402.7035.

Schutte, Sebastian. 2014. "Geography, Outcome, and Casualties: A Unified Model of Insurgency." *Journal of Conflict Resolution* 59(6): 1101–1128.

Tetlock, Philip. 2005. *Expert Political Judgment: How Good Is It? How Can We Know?* Princeton, NJ: Princeton University Press.

Tetlock, Philip. 2010. "Second Thoughts about *Expert Political Judgment*: Reply to the Symposium." *Critical Review* 22(4): 467–488.

Waltz, Kenneth N. 1997. "Evaluating Theories." *American Political Science Review* 91(4): 913–917.

Ward, Michael D., and Kristian Skrede Gleditsch. 2002. "Location, Location, Location: An MCMC Approach to Modeling the Spatial Context of War and Peace." *Political Analysis* 10(3): 244–260.

Ward, Michael D., Nils W. Metternich, Cassy L. Dorff, Max Gallop, Florian M. Hollenbach, Anna Schultz, and Simon Weschle. 2013. "Learning from the Past and Stepping into the Future: Toward a New Generation of Conflict Prediction." *International Studies Review* 16(4): 473–644.

Weidmann, Nils B., and Michael D. Ward. 2010. "Predicting Conflict in Space and Time." *Journal of Conflict Resolution* 54(6): 883–901.

Weil, Herman M. 1974. "Domestic and International Violence: A forecasting approach." *Futures* 6(6): 477–485.

# The Illusion of Geopolitics: The Enduring Power of the Liberal Order

G. JOHN IKENBERRY

Walter Russell Mead paints a disturbing portrait of the United States' geopolitical predicament. As he sees it, an increasingly formidable coalition of illiberal powers—China, Iran, and Russia—is determined to undo the post–Cold War settlement and the U.S.-led global order that stands behind it. Across Eurasia, he argues, these aggrieved states are bent on building spheres of influence to threaten the foundations of U.S. leadership and the global order. So the United States must rethink its optimism, including its post–Cold War belief that rising non-Western states can be persuaded to join the West and play by its rules. For Mead, the time has come to confront the threats from these increasingly dangerous geopolitical foes.

But Mead's alarmism is based on a colossal misreading of modern power realities. It is a misreading of the logic and character of the existing world order, which is more stable and expansive than Mead depicts, leading him to overestimate the ability of the "axis of weevils" to undermine it. And it is a misreading of China and Russia, which are not full-scale revisionist powers but part-time spoilers at best, as suspicious of each other as they are of the outside world. True, they look for opportunities to resist the United States' global leadership, and recently, as in the past, they have pushed back against it, particularly when confronted in their own neighborhoods. But even these conflicts are fueled more by weakness—their leaders' and regimes'—than by strength. They have no appealing brand. And when it comes to their overriding interests, Russia and, especially, China are deeply integrated into the world economy and its governing institutions.

Mead also mischaracterizes the thrust of U.S. foreign policy. Since the end of the Cold War, he argues, the United States has ignored geopolitical issues involving territory and spheres of influence and instead adopted a Pollyannaish emphasis on building the global order. But this is a false dichotomy. The United States does not focus on issues of global order, such as arms control and trade, because it assumes that geopolitical conflict is gone forever; it undertakes such efforts precisely because it wants to manage great-power competition. Order building is not premised on the end of geopolitics; it is about how to answer the big questions of geopolitics.

Indeed, the construction of a U.S.-led global order did not begin with the end of the Cold War; it won the Cold War. In the nearly 70 years since World War II, Washington has undertaken sustained efforts to build a far-flung system of multilateral institutions, alliances, trade agreements, and political partnerships. This project has helped draw countries into the United States' orbit. It has helped strengthen global norms and rules that undercut the legitimacy of nineteenth-century-style spheres of influence, bids for regional domination, and territorial grabs. And it has given the United States the capacities, partnerships, and principles to confront today's great-power spoilers and revisionists, such as they are. Alliances, partnerships, multilateralism, democracy—these are the tools of U.S. leadership, and they are winning, not losing, the twenty-first-century struggles over geopolitics and the world order.

## THE GENTLE GIANT

In 1904, the English geographer Halford Mackinder wrote that the great power that controlled the heartland of Eurasia would command "the World-Island" and thus the world itself. For Mead, Eurasia has returned as the great prize of geopolitics. Across the far reaches of this supercontinent, he argues, China, Iran, and Russia are seeking to establish their spheres of influence and challenge U.S. interests, slowly but relentlessly attempting to dominate Eurasia and thereby threaten the United States and the rest of the world.

This vision misses a deeper reality. In matters of geopolitics (not to mention demographics, politics, and ideas), the United States has a decisive advantage over China, Iran, and Russia. Although the United States will no doubt come down from the peak of hegemony that it occupied during the unipolar era, its power is still unrivaled. Its wealth and technological advantages remain far out of the reach of China and Russia, to say nothing of Iran. Its recovering economy, now bolstered by massive new natural gas resources, allows it to maintain a global military presence and credible security commitments.

Indeed, Washington enjoys a unique ability to win friends and influence states. According to a study led by the political scientist Brett Ashley Leeds, the United States boasts military partnerships with more than 60 countries, whereas Russia counts eight formal allies and China has just one (North Korea). As one British diplomat told me several years ago, "China doesn't seem to do alliances." But the United States does, and they pay a double dividend: not only do alliances provide a global platform for the projection of U.S. power, but they also distribute the burden of providing security. The military capabilities aggregated in this U.S.-led alliance system outweigh anything China or Russia might generate for decades to come.

Then there are the nuclear weapons. These arms, which the United States, China, and Russia all possess (and Iran is seeking), help the United States in two ways. First, thanks to the logic of mutual assured destruction, they radically reduce the likelihood of great-power war. Such upheavals have provided opportunities for past great powers, including the United States in World War II, to entrench their own international orders. The atomic age has robbed China and Russia of this opportunity. Second,

nuclear weapons also make China and Russia more secure, giving them assurance that the United States will never invade. That's a good thing, because it reduces the likelihood that they will resort to desperate moves, born of insecurity, that risk war and undermine the liberal order.

Geography reinforces the United States' other advantages. As the only great power not surrounded by other great powers, the country has appeared less threatening to other states and was able to rise dramatically over the course of the last century without triggering a war. After the Cold War, when the United States was the world's sole superpower, other global powers, oceans away, did not even attempt to balance against it. In fact, the United States' geographic position has led other countries to worry more about abandonment than domination. Allies in Europe, Asia, and the Middle East have sought to draw the United States into playing a greater role in their regions. The result is what the historian Geir Lundestad has called an "empire by invitation."

The United States' geographic advantage is on full display in Asia. Most countries there see China as a greater potential danger—due to its proximity, if nothing else—than the United States. Except for the United States, every major power in the world lives in a crowded geopolitical neighborhood where shifts in power routinely provoke counterbalancing—including by one another. China is discovering this dynamic today as surrounding states react to its rise by modernizing their militaries and reinforcing their alliances. Russia has known it for decades, and has faced it most recently in Ukraine, which in recent years has increased its military spending and sought closer ties to the EU.

Geographic isolation has also given the United States reason to champion universal principles that allow it to access various regions of the world. The country has long promoted the open-door policy and the principle of self-determination and opposed colonialism—less out of a sense of idealism than due to the practical realities of keeping Europe, Asia, and the Middle East open for trade and diplomacy. In the late 1930s, the main question facing the United States was how large a geopolitical space, or "grand area," it would need to exist as a great power in a world of empires, regional blocs, and spheres of influence. World War II made the answer clear: the country's prosperity and security depended on access to every region. And in the ensuing decades, with some important and damaging exceptions, such as Vietnam, the United States has embraced postimperial principles.

It was during these postwar years that geopolitics and order building converged. A liberal international framework was the answer that statesmen such as Dean Acheson, George Kennan, and George Marshall offered to the challenge of Soviet expansionism. The system they built strengthened and enriched the United States and its allies, to the detriment of its illiberal opponents. It also stabilized the world economy and established mechanisms for tackling global problems. The end of the Cold War has not changed the logic behind this project.

Fortunately, the liberal principles that Washington has pushed enjoy near-universal appeal, because they have tended to be a good fit with the modernizing forces of economic growth and social advancement. As the historian Charles Maier has put it, the United States surfed the wave of twentieth-century modernization. But some have argued that this congruence between the American project and the forces of modernity has weakened in recent years. The 2008 financial crisis, the thinking goes, marked a world-historical turning point, at which the United States lost its vanguard role in facilitating economic advancement.

Yet even if that were true, it hardly follows that China and Russia have replaced the United States as the standard-bearers of the global economy. Even Mead does not argue that China, Iran, or Russia offers the world a new model of modernity. If these illiberal powers really do threaten Washington and the rest of the liberal capitalist world, then they will need to find and ride the next great wave of modernization. They are unlikely to do that.

## THE RISE OF DEMOCRACY

Mead's vision of a contest over Eurasia between the United States and China, Iran, and Russia misses the more profound power transition under way: the increasing ascendancy of liberal capitalist democracy.

To be sure, many liberal democracies are struggling at the moment with slow economic growth, social inequality, and political instability. But the spread of liberal democracy throughout the world, beginning in the late 1970s and accelerating after the Cold War, has dramatically strengthened the United States' position and tightened the geopolitical circle around China and Russia.

It's easy to forget how rare liberal democracy once was. Until the twentieth century, it was confined to the West and parts of Latin America. After World War II, however, it began to reach beyond those realms, as newly independent states established self-rule. During the 1950s, 1960s, and early 1970s, military coups and new dictators put the brakes on democratic transitions. But in the late 1970s, what the political scientist Samuel Huntington termed "the third wave" of democratization washed over southern Europe, Latin America, and East Asia. Then the Cold War ended, and a cohort of former communist states in eastern Europe were brought into the democratic fold. By the late 1990s, 60 percent of all countries had become democracies.

Although some backsliding has occurred, the more significant trend has been the emergence of a group of democratic middle powers, including Australia, Brazil, India, Indonesia, Mexico, South Korea, and Turkey. These rising democracies are acting as stakeholders in the international system: pushing for multilateral cooperation, seeking greater rights and responsibilities, and exercising influence through peaceful means.

Such countries lend the liberal world order new geopolitical heft. As the political scientist Larry Diamond has noted, if Argentina, Brazil, India, Indonesia, South Africa, and Turkey regain their economic footing and strengthen their democratic rule, the G-20, which also includes the United States and European countries, "will have become a strong 'club of democracies,' with only Russia, China, and Saudi Arabia holding out." The rise of a global middle class of democratic states has turned China and Russia into outliers—not, as Mead fears, legitimate contestants for global leadership.

In fact, the democratic upsurge has been deeply problematic for both countries. In eastern Europe, former Soviet states and satellites have gone democratic and joined the West. As worrisome as Russian President Vladimir Putin's moves in Crimea have been, they reflect Russia's geopolitical vulnerability, not its strength. Over the last two decades, the West has crept closer to Russia's borders. In 1999, the Czech Republic, Hungary, and Poland entered NATO. They were joined in 2004 by seven more former members of the Soviet bloc, and in 2009, by Albania and Croatia. In the meantime, six former Soviet republics have headed down the path to membership by joining NATO's Partnership for Peace program. Mead makes much of Putin's achievements in Georgia, Armenia, and Crimea. Yet even though Putin is winning some small battles, he is losing the war. Russia is not on the rise; to the contrary, it is experiencing one of the greatest geopolitical contractions of any major power in the modern era.

Democracy is encircling China, too. In the mid-1980s, India and Japan were the only Asian democracies, but since then, Indonesia, Mongolia, the Philippines, South Korea, Taiwan, and Thailand have joined the club. Myanmar (also called Burma) has made cautious steps toward multiparty rule—steps that have come, as China has not failed to notice, in conjunction with warming relations with the United States. China now lives in a decidedly democratic neighborhood.

These political transformations have put China and Russia on the defensive. Consider the recent developments in Ukraine. The economic and political currents in most of the country are inexorably flowing westward, a trend that terrifies Putin. His only recourse has been to strong-arm Ukraine into resisting the EU and remaining in Russia's orbit. Although he may be able to keep Crimea under Russian control, his grip on the rest of the country is slipping. As the EU diplomat Robert Cooper has noted, Putin can try to delay the moment when Ukraine "affiliates with the EU, but he can't stop it." Indeed, Putin might not even be able to accomplish that, since his provocative moves may serve only to speed Ukraine's move toward Europe.

China faces a similar predicament in Taiwan. Chinese leaders sincerely believe that Taiwan is part of China, but the Taiwanese do not. The democratic transition on the island has made its inhabitants' claims to nationhood more deeply felt and legitimate. A 2011 survey found that if the Taiwanese could be assured that China would not attack Taiwan, 80 percent of them would support declaring independence. Like Russia, China wants geopolitical control over its neighborhood. But the spread of democracy to all corners of Asia has made old-fashioned domination the only way to achieve that, and that option is costly and self-defeating.

While the rise of democratic states makes life more difficult for China and Russia, it makes the world safer for the United States. Those two powers may count as U.S. rivals, but the rivalry takes place on a very uneven playing field: the United States has the most friends, and the most capable ones, too. Washington and its allies account for 75 percent of global military spending. Democratization has put China and Russia in a geopolitical box.

Iran is not surrounded by democracies, but it is threatened by a restive pro-democracy movement at home. More important, Iran is the weakest member of Mead's axis, with a much smaller economy and military than the United States and the other great powers. It is also the target of the strongest international sanctions regime ever assembled, with help from China and Russia. The Obama administration's diplomacy with Iran may or may not succeed, but it is not clear what Mead would do differently to prevent the country from acquiring nuclear weapons. U.S. President Barack Obama's approach has the virtue of offering Tehran a path by which it can move from being a hostile regional power to becoming a more constructive, nonnuclear member of the international community—a potential geopolitical game changer that Mead fails to appreciate.

## REVISIONISM REVISITED

Not only does Mead underestimate the strength of the United States and the order it built; he also overstates the degree to which China and Russia are seeking to resist both. (Apart from its nuclear ambitions, Iran looks like a state engaged more in futile protest than actual resistance, so it shouldn't be considered anything close to a revisionist power.) Without a doubt, China and Russia desire greater regional influence. China has made aggressive claims over maritime rights and nearby contested islands, and it has embarked on an arms buildup. Putin has visions of reclaiming Russia's dominance in its "near abroad." Both great powers bristle at U.S. leadership and resist it when they can.

But China and Russia are not true revisionists. As former Israeli Foreign Minister Shlomo Ben-Ami has said, Putin's foreign policy is "more a reflection of his resentment of Russia's geopolitical marginalization than a battle cry from a rising empire." China, of course, is an actual rising power, and this does invite dangerous competition with U.S. allies in Asia. But China is not currently trying to break those alliances or overthrow the wider system of regional security governance embodied in the Association of Southeast Asian Nations and the East Asia Summit. And even if China harbors ambitions of eventually doing so, U.S. security partnerships in the region are, if anything, getting stronger, not weaker. At most, China and Russia are spoilers. They do not have the interests—let alone the ideas, capacities, or allies—to lead them to upend existing global rules and institutions.

In fact, although they resent that the United States stands at the top of the current geopolitical system, they embrace the underlying logic of that framework, and with good reason. Openness gives them access to trade, investment, and technology from other societies. Rules give them tools to protect their sovereignty and interests. Despite controversies over the new idea of "the responsibility to protect" (which has been applied only selectively), the current world order enshrines the age-old norms of state sovereignty and nonintervention. Those Westphalian principles remain the bedrock of world politics—and China and Russia have tied their national interests to them (despite Putin's disturbing irredentism).

It should come as no surprise, then, that China and Russia have become deeply integrated into the existing international order. They are both permanent members of the UN Security Council, with veto rights, and they both participate actively in the World Trade Organization, the International Monetary Fund, the World Bank, and the G-20. They are geopolitical insiders, sitting at all the high tables of global governance.

China, despite its rapid ascent, has no ambitious global agenda; it remains fixated inward, on preserving party rule. Some Chinese intellectuals and political figures, such as Yan Xuetong and Zhu Chenghu, do have a wish list of revisionist goals. They see the Western system as a threat and are waiting for the day when China can reorganize the international order. But these voices do not reach very far into the political elite. Indeed, Chinese leaders have moved away from their earlier calls for sweeping change. In 2007, at its Central Committee meeting, the Chinese Communist Party replaced previous proposals for a "new international economic order" with calls for more modest reforms centering on fairness and justice. The Chinese scholar Wang Jisi has argued that this move is "subtle but important," shifting China's orientation toward that of a global reformer. China now wants a larger role in the International Monetary Fund and the World Bank, greater voice in such forums as the G-20, and wider global use of its currency. That is not the agenda of a country trying to revise the economic order.

China and Russia are also members in good standing of the nuclear club. The centerpiece of the Cold War settlement between the United States and the Soviet Union (and then Russia) was a shared effort to limit atomic weapons. Although U.S.-Russian relations have since soured, the nuclear component of their arrangement has held. In 2010, Moscow and Washington signed the New START treaty, which requires mutual reductions in long-range nuclear weapons.

Before the 1990s, China was a nuclear outsider. Although it had a modest arsenal, it saw itself as a voice of the nonnuclear developing world and criticized arms control agreements and test bans. But in a remarkable shift, China has since come to support the array of nuclear accords, including the Nuclear Nonproliferation Treaty and the Comprehensive Nuclear Test Ban Treaty. It has affirmed a "no first use" doctrine, kept its arsenal small, and taken its entire nuclear force off alert. China has also played an active role in the Nuclear Security Summit, an initiative proposed by Obama in 2009, and it has joined the "P5 process," a collaborate effort to safeguard nuclear weapons.

Across a wide range of issues, China and Russia are acting more like established great powers than revisionist ones. They often choose to shun multilateralism, but so, too, on occasion do the United States and other powerful democracies. (Beijing has ratified the UN Convention on the Law of the Sea; Washington has not.) And China and Russia are using global rules and institutions to advance their own interests. Their struggles with the United States revolve around gaining voice within the existing order and manipulating it to suit their needs. They wish to enhance their positions within the system, but they are not trying to replace it.

## HERE TO STAY

Ultimately, even if China and Russia do attempt to contest the basic terms of the current global order, the adventure will be daunting and self-defeating. These powers aren't just up against the United States; they would also have to contend with the most globally organized and deeply entrenched order the world has ever seen, one that is dominated by states that are liberal, capitalist, and democratic. This order is backed by a U.S.-led network of alliances, institutions, geopolitical bargains, client states, and democratic partnerships. It has proved dynamic and expansive, easily integrating rising states, beginning with Japan and Germany after World War II. It has shown a capacity for shared leadership, as exemplified by such forums as the G-8 and the G-20. It has allowed rising non-Western countries to trade and grow, sharing the dividends of modernization. It has accommodated a surprisingly wide variety of political and economic models—social

democratic (western Europe), neoliberal (the United Kingdom and the United States), and state capitalist (East Asia). The prosperity of nearly every country—and the stability of its government—fundamentally depends on this order.

In the age of liberal order, revisionist struggles are a fool's errand. Indeed, China and Russia know this. They do not have grand visions of an alternative order. For them, international relations are mainly about the search for commerce and resources, the protection of their sovereignty, and, where possible, regional domination. They have shown no interest in building their own orders or even taking full responsibility for the current one and have offered no alternative visions of global economic or political progress. That's a critical shortcoming, since international orders rise and fall not simply with the power of the leading state; their success also hinges on whether they are seen as legitimate and whether their actual operation solves problems that both weak and powerful states care about. In the struggle for world order, China and Russia (and certainly Iran) are simply not in the game.

Under these circumstances, the United States should not give up its efforts to strengthen the liberal order. The world that Washington inhabits today is one it should welcome. And the grand strategy it should pursue is the one it has followed for decades: deep global engagement. It is a strategy in which the United States ties itself to the regions of the world through trade, alliances, multilateral institutions, and diplomacy. It is a strategy in which the United States establishes leadership not simply through the exercise of power but also through sustained efforts at global problem solving and rule making. It created a world that is friendly to American interests, and it is made friendly because, as President John F. Kennedy once said, it is a world "where the weak are safe and the strong are just."

# The New Population Bomb: The Four Megatrends That Will Change the World

JACK A. GOLDSTONE

Forty-two years ago, the biologist Paul Ehrlich warned in *The Population Bomb* that mass starvation would strike in the 1970s and 1980s, with the world's population growth outpacing the production of food and other critical resources. Thanks to innovations and efforts such as the "green revolution" in farming and the widespread adoption of family planning, Ehrlich's worst fears did not come to pass. In fact, since the 1970s, global economic output has increased and fertility has fallen dramatically, especially in developing countries.

The United Nations Population Division now projects that global population growth will nearly halt by 2050. By that date, the world's population will have stabilized at 9.15 billion people, according to the "medium growth" variant of the UN's authoritative population database World Population Prospects: The 2008 Revision. (Today's global population is 6.83 billion.) Barring a cataclysmic climate crisis or a complete failure to recover from the current economic malaise, global economic output is expected to increase by two to three percent per year, meaning that global income will increase far more than population over the next four decades.

But twenty-first-century international security will depend less on how many people inhabit the world than on how the global population is composed and distributed: where populations are declining and where they are growing, which countries are relatively older and which are more youthful, and how demographics will influence population movements across regions.

These elements are not well recognized or widely understood. A recent article in *The Economist*, for example, cheered the decline in global fertility without noting other vital demographic developments. Indeed, the same UN data cited by *The Economist* reveal four historic shifts that will fundamentally alter the world's population over the next four decades: the relative demographic weight of the world's developed countries will drop by nearly 25 percent, shifting economic power to the developing nations; the developed countries' labor forces will substantially age and decline, constraining economic growth in the developed world and raising the demand for immigrant workers; most of the world's expected population growth will increasingly be concentrated in today's poorest, youngest, and most heavily Muslim countries, which have a dangerous lack of quality education, capital, and employment opportunities; and, for the first time in history, most of the world's population will become urbanized, with the largest urban centers being in the world's poorest countries, where policing, sanitation, and health care are often scarce.

Taken together, these trends will pose challenges every bit as alarming as those noted by Ehrlich. Coping with them will require nothing less than a major reconsideration of the world's basic global governance structures.

## EUROPE'S REVERSAL OF FORTUNES

At the beginning of the eighteenth century, approximately 20 percent of the world's inhabitants lived in Europe (including Russia). Then, with the Industrial Revolution, Europe's population boomed, and streams of European emigrants set off for the Americas. By the eve of World War I, Europe's population had more than quadrupled. In 1913, Europe had more people than China, and the proportion of the world's population living in Europe and the former European colonies of North America had risen to over 33 percent.

But this trend reversed after World War I, as basic health care and sanitation began to spread to poorer countries. In Asia, Africa, and Latin America, people began to live longer, and birthrates remained high or fell only slowly. By 2003, the combined populations of Europe, the United States, and Canada accounted for just 17 percent of the global population. In 2050, this figure is expected to be just 12 percent—far less than it was in 1700. (These projections, moreover, might even understate the reality because they reflect the "medium growth" projection of the UN forecasts, which assumes that the fertility rates of developing countries will decline while those of developed countries will increase. In fact, many developed countries show no evidence of increasing fertility rates.)

The West's relative decline is even more dramatic if one also considers changes in income. The Industrial Revolution made Europeans not only more numerous than they had been but also considerably richer per capita than others worldwide. According to the economic historian Angus Maddison, Europe, the United States, and Canada together produced about 32 percent of the world's GDP at the beginning of the nineteenth century. By 1950, that proportion had increased to a remarkable 68 percent of the world's total output (adjusted to reflect purchasing power parity).

This trend, too, is headed for a sharp reversal. The proportion of global GDP produced by Europe, the United States, and Canada fell from 68 percent in 1950 to 47 percent in 2003 and will decline even more steeply in the future. If the growth rate of per capita income (again, adjusted for purchasing power parity) between 2003 and 2050 remains as it was between 1973 and 2003—averaging 1.68 percent annually in Europe, the United States, and Canada and 2.47 percent annually in the rest of the world—then the combined GDP of Europe, the United States, and Canada will roughly double by 2050, whereas the GDP of the rest of the world will grow by a factor of five. The portion of global GDP produced by Europe, the United States, and Canada in 2050 will then be less than 30 percent—smaller than it was in 1820.

These figures also imply that an overwhelming proportion of the world's GDP growth between 2003 and 2050—nearly 80 percent—will occur outside of Europe, the United States, and Canada.

By the middle of this century, the global middle class—those capable of purchasing durable consumer products, such as cars, appliances, and electronics—will increasingly be found in what is now considered the developing world. The World Bank has predicted that by 2030 the number of middle-class people in the developing world will be 1.2 billion—a rise of 200 percent since 2005. This means that the developing world's middle class alone will be larger than the total populations of Europe, Japan, and the United States combined. From now on, therefore, the main driver of global economic expansion will be the economic growth of newly industrialized countries, such as Brazil, China, India, Indonesia, Mexico, and Turkey.

## AGING PAINS

Part of the reason developed countries will be less economically dynamic in the coming decades is that their populations will become substantially older. The European countries, Canada, the United States, Japan, South Korea, and even China are aging at unprecedented rates. Today, the proportion of people aged 60 or older in China and South Korea is 12–15 percent. It is 15–22 percent in the European Union, Canada, and the United States and 30 percent in Japan. With baby boomers aging and life expectancy increasing, these numbers will increase dramatically. In 2050, approximately 30 percent of Americans, Canadians, Chinese, and Europeans will be over 60, as will more than 40 percent of Japanese and South Koreans.

Over the next decades, therefore, these countries will have increasingly large proportions of retirees and increasingly small proportions of workers. As workers born during the baby boom of 1945–65 are retiring, they are not being replaced by a new cohort of citizens of prime working age (15–59 years old). Industrialized countries are experiencing a drop in their working-age populations that is even more severe than the overall slowdown in their population growth. South Korea represents the most extreme example. Even as its total population is projected to decline by almost 9 percent by 2050 (from 48.3 million to 44.1 million), the population of working-age South Koreans is expected to drop by 36 percent (from

32.9 million to 21.1 million), and the number of South Koreans aged 60 and older will increase by almost 150 percent (from 7.3 million to 18 million). By 2050, in other words, the entire working-age population will barely exceed the 60-and-older population. Although South Korea's case is extreme, it represents an increasingly common fate for developed countries. Europe is expected to lose 24 percent of its prime working-age population (about 120 million workers) by 2050, and its 60-and-older population is expected to increase by 47 percent. In the United States, where higher fertility and more immigration are expected than in Europe, the working-age population will grow by 15 percent over the next four decades—a steep decline from its growth of 62 percent between 1950 and 2010. And by 2050, the United States' 60-and-older population is expected to double.

All this will have a dramatic impact on economic growth, health care, and military strength in the developed world. The forces that fueled economic growth in industrialized countries during the second half of the twentieth century—increased productivity due to better education, the movement of women into the labor force, and innovations in technology—will all likely weaken in the coming decades. College enrollment boomed after World War II, a trend that is not likely to recur in the twenty-first century; the extensive movement of women into the labor force also was a one-time social change; and the technological change of the time resulted from innovators who created new products and leading-edge consumers who were willing to try them out—two groups that are thinning out as the industrialized world's population ages.

Overall economic growth will also be hampered by a decline in the number of new consumers and new households. When developed countries' labor forces were growing by 0.5–1.0 percent per year, as they did until 2005, even annual increases in real output per worker of just 1.7 percent meant that annual economic growth totaled 2.2–2.7 percent per year. But with the labor forces of many developed countries (such as Germany, Hungary, Japan, Russia, and the Baltic states) now shrinking by 0.2 percent per year and those of other countries (including Austria, the Czech Republic, Denmark, Greece, and Italy)

growing by less than 0.2 percent per year, the same 1.7 percent increase in real output per worker yields only 1.5–1.9 percent annual overall growth. Moreover, developed countries will be lucky to keep productivity growth at even that level; in many developed countries, productivity is more likely to decline as the population ages.

A further strain on industrialized economies will be rising medical costs: as populations age, they will demand more health care for longer periods of time. Public pension schemes for aging populations are already being reformed in various industrialized countries—often prompting heated debate. In theory, at least, pensions might be kept solvent by increasing the retirement age, raising taxes modestly, and phasing out benefits for the wealthy. Regardless, the number of 80- and 90-year-olds—who are unlikely to work and highly likely to require nursing-home and other expensive care—will rise dramatically. And even if 60- and 70-year-olds remain active and employed, they will require procedures and medications—hip replacements, kidney transplants, blood-pressure treatments—to sustain their health in old age.

All this means that just as aging developed countries will have proportionally fewer workers, innovators, and consumerist young households, a large portion of those countries' remaining economic growth will have to be diverted to pay for the medical bills and pensions of their growing elderly populations. Basic services, meanwhile, will be increasingly costly because fewer young workers will be available for strenuous and labor-intensive jobs. Unfortunately, policymakers seldom reckon with these potentially disruptive effects of otherwise welcome developments, such as higher life expectancy.

## YOUTH AND ISLAM IN THE DEVELOPING WORLD

Even as the industrialized countries of Europe, North America, and Northeast Asia will experience unprecedented aging this century, fast-growing countries in Africa, Latin America, the Middle East, and Southeast Asia will have exceptionally youthful populations. Today, roughly nine out of ten children under the age of 15 live in developing countries. And these are the countries that will continue to have the world's highest birthrates. Indeed, over 70 percent of the world's population growth between now and 2050 will occur in 24 countries, all of which are classified by the World Bank as low income or lower-middle income, with an average per capita income of under $3,855 in 2008.

Many developing countries have few ways of providing employment to their young, fast-growing populations. Would-be laborers, therefore, will be increasingly attracted to the labor markets of the aging developed countries of Europe, North America, and Northeast Asia. Youthful immigrants from nearby regions with high unemployment—Central America, North Africa, and Southeast Asia, for example—will be drawn to those vital entry-level and manual-labor jobs that sustain advanced economies: janitors, nursing-home aides, bus drivers, plumbers, security guards, farm workers, and the like. Current levels of immigration from developing to developed countries are paltry compared to those that the forces of supply and demand might soon create across the world.

These forces will act strongly on the Muslim world, where many economically weak countries will continue to experience dramatic population growth in the decades ahead. In 1950, Bangladesh, Egypt, Indonesia, Nigeria, Pakistan, and Turkey had a combined population of 242 million. By 2009, those six countries were the world's most populous Muslim-majority countries and had a combined population of 886 million. Their populations are continuing to grow and indeed are expected to increase by 475 million between now and 2050—during which time, by comparison, the six most populous developed countries are projected to gain only 44 million inhabitants. Worldwide, of the 48 fastest-growing countries today—those with annual population growth of two percent or more—28 are majority Muslim or have Muslim minorities of 33 percent or more.

It is therefore imperative to improve relations between Muslim and Western societies. This will be difficult given that many Muslims live in poor communities vulnerable to radical appeals and many see the West as antagonistic and militaristic. In the 2009 Pew Global Attitudes Project survey, for example, whereas 69 percent of those Indonesians and Nigerians surveyed reported viewing the

United States favorably, just 18 percent of those polled in Egypt, Jordan, Pakistan, and Turkey (all U.S. allies) did. And in 2006, when the Pew survey last asked detailed questions about Muslim-Western relations, more than half of the respondents in Muslim countries characterized those relations as bad and blamed the West for this state of affairs.

But improving relations is all the more important because of the growing demographic weight of poor Muslim countries and the attendant increase in Muslim immigration, especially to Europe from North Africa and the Middle East. (To be sure, forecasts that Muslims will soon dominate Europe are outlandish: Muslims compose just three to ten percent of the population in the major European countries today, and this proportion will at most double by midcentury.) Strategists worldwide must consider that the world's young are becoming concentrated in those countries least prepared to educate and employ them, including some Muslim states. Any resulting poverty, social tension, or ideological radicalization could have disruptive effects in many corners of the world. But this need not be the case; the healthy immigration of workers to the developed world and the movement of capital to the developing world, among other things, could lead to better results.

## URBAN SPRAWL

Exacerbating twenty-first-century risks will be the fact that the world is urbanizing to an unprecedented degree. The year 2010 will likely be the first time in history that a majority of the world's people live in cities rather than in the countryside. Whereas less than 30 percent of the world's population was urban in 1950, according to UN projections, more than 70 percent will be by 2050.

Lower-income countries in Asia and Africa are urbanizing especially rapidly, as agriculture becomes less labor intensive and as employment opportunities shift to the industrial and service sectors. Already, most of the world's urban agglomerations—Mumbai (population 20.1 million), Mexico City (19.5 million), New Delhi (17 million), Shanghai (15.8 million), Calcutta (15.6 million), Karachi (13.1 million), Cairo (12.5 million), Manila (11.7 million), Lagos (10.6 million), Jakarta (9.7 million)—are found in low-income countries. Many of these countries have multiple cities with over one million residents each: Pakistan has eight, Mexico 12, and China more than 100. The UN projects that the urbanized proportion of sub-Saharan Africa will nearly double between 2005 and 2050, from 35 percent (300 million people) to over 67 percent (1 billion). China, which is roughly 40 percent urbanized today, is expected to be 73 percent urbanized by 2050; India, which is less than 30 percent urbanized today, is expected to be 55 percent urbanized by 2050. Overall, the world's urban population is expected to grow by 3 billion people by 2050.

This urbanization may prove destabilizing. Developing countries that urbanize in the twenty-first century will have far lower per capita incomes than did many industrial countries when they first urbanized. The United States, for example, did not reach 65 percent urbanization until 1950, when per capita income was nearly $13,000 (in 2005 dollars). By contrast, Nigeria, Pakistan, and the Philippines, which are approaching similar levels of urbanization, currently have per capita incomes of just $1,800-$4,000 (in 2005 dollars).

According to the research of Richard Cincotta and other political demographers, countries with younger populations are especially prone to civil unrest and are less able to create or sustain democratic institutions. And the more heavily urbanized, the more such countries are likely to experience Dickensian poverty and anarchic violence. In good times, a thriving economy might keep urban residents employed and governments flush with sufficient resources to meet their needs. More often, however, sprawling and impoverished cities are vulnerable to crime lords, gangs, and petty rebellions. Thus, the rapid urbanization of the developing world in the decades ahead might bring, in exaggerated form, problems similar to those that urbanization brought to nineteenth-century Europe. Back then, cyclical employment, inadequate policing, and limited sanitation and education often spawned widespread labor strife, periodic violence, and sometimes—as in the 1820s, the 1830s, and 1848—even revolutions.

International terrorism might also originate in fast-urbanizing developing countries (even more than it already does). With their neighborhood networks, access to the Internet and digital communications technology, and concentration of valuable targets, sprawling cities offer excellent opportunities for recruiting, maintaining, and hiding terrorist networks.

## DEFUSING THE BOMB

Averting this century's potential dangers will require sweeping measures. Three major global efforts defused the population bomb of Ehrlich's day: a commitment by governments and nongovernmental organizations to control reproduction rates; agricultural advances, such as the green revolution and the spread of new technology; and a vast increase in international trade, which globalized markets and thus allowed developing countries to export foodstuffs in exchange for seeds, fertilizers, and machinery, which in turn helped them boost production. But today's population bomb is the product less of absolute growth in the world's population than of changes in its age and distribution. Policymakers must therefore adapt today's global governance institutions to the new realities of the aging of the industrialized world, the concentration of the world's economic and population growth in developing countries, and the increase in international immigration.

During the Cold War, Western strategists divided the world into a "First World," of democratic industrialized countries; a "Second World," of communist industrialized countries; and a "Third World," of developing countries. These strategists focused chiefly on deterring or managing conflict between the First and the Second Worlds and on launching proxy wars and diplomatic initiatives to attract Third World countries into the First World's camp.

## CREATIVE REFORMS AT HOME

The aging industrialized countries can also take various steps at home to promote stability in light of the coming demographic trends. First, they should encourage families to have more children. France and Sweden have had success providing child care, generous leave time, and financial allowances to families with young children. Yet there is no consensus among policymakers—and certainly not among demographers—about what policies best encourage fertility.

# Critical Thinking and Discussion Questions for Part III (Sections 8–11)

## SECTION 8

1. **Theorists wrote twenty years ago about emerging environmental changes as causes of acute international conflict. In your view, how can environmental problems cause conflicts?**

2. **Do you support the idea of environmental and natural resource equality?**
   - Do you think that the world should have an agreement guaranteeing all countries "fair access" to natural resources?
   - How would you define fairness in this case?

3. **Specifically, do you believe that other countries, like China or India, that have no access to the Arctic Sea should have an international mandate to establish such access? Explain your opinion.**

4. **How does oil, according to Amory Lovins (on the companion website), "contribute" to dictatorships, corruption, terrorism, conflict, and war?**
   - Do you believe that the scope of corruption and incidences of war may diminish if the world turns to nuclear energy instead of oil? Explain.
   - Would corruption and violence significantly diminish if most fossil fuel resources were under international control? Do you agree? Explain.

5. **Should a moratorium on commercial whaling be lifted since the number of whales is increasing again globally? Search the Web and discuss this question in class.**

6. **Imagine that environmentalism (the ideology that we need to provide urgent help for the environment) and environmental skepticism (the ideology that most environmental problems are exaggerated as a result of financial and political interests) are on the opposite ends of an imaginable spectrum. Where do you place your personal views of global environment and environmental policies? Explain your choice.**
   - Environmentalism +3 +2 +1 0 -1 -2 -3 Skepticism

7. **How important are renewable energy strategies for international relations?**
   - India has a central ministry in charge of renewables. Should all governments have similar government ministries and why?
   - What will be the major economic and political obstacles to global renewable energy policies?

8. **Do you believe that countries should continue to have total environmental sovereignty over their territories and natural resources?**
   - Could you suggest scenarios under which such sovereignty should be lifted, at least temporarily?
   - Could such sovereignty be lifted without the use of force? How?

9. **Imagine that affordable alternative energy sources have finally emerged and fossil fuels such as oil and coal have become too expensive and thus almost obsolete. How could these changes affect the United States' foreign policy and international relations? As an expert in international energy policies, prepare a policy brief to the US Congress. What is a policy brief? In general terms, it is a relatively short summary of an expert's opinion (or several expert's views) on a specific issue that has or may have implications on a country's security, economic, or political situation. A policy brief usually offers a forecast and discusses the government's policy options for dealing with the issue in focus. Some suggestions on the best option are offered as well. Policy briefs are either solicited or offered to government policy makers and others who are interested in formulating or influencing policy (foreign policy in our case). In your brief, discuss the following:**
   - How plausible is it that affordable alternative energy sources finally emerge and are ready for distribution in five years? In ten years? Later? Explain your view.
   - Assume that affordable alternative energy sources appear in several years. Which country or countries could be the biggest producers of such sources? Could it be China producing solar panels? Or maybe Brazil with its ethanol fuel? Could it be the United States or the European Union? Or maybe other countries?

## SECTION 9

1. **John Stuart Mill, a prominent thinker of the nineteenth century, argued that any foreign intervention, however benign its proclaimed intent was, could be judged by others as an act of violence driven by cynical self-interest.**
   - Discuss contemporary examples that prove this assertion.
   - Discuss contemporary examples that disprove this assertion.
   - Which international factors can affect one country's perceptions of other countries' actions?

2. **What specific political steps should be implemented by the United States and its allies to make sure that the key provisions of the Convention on the Prevention and Punishment of the Crime of Genocide are working? (See the companion website.)**
   - If some of the provisions are violated, do you think that the United States has a right to impose those provisions for moral reasons?

3. **Discuss legal arguments surrounding the implementation of the responsibility-to-protect (R2P, RtoP) concept.**

4. **In your view, under what circumstances (if any) may the R2P concept be applied unilaterally, that is, by one country, without a broad international consensus?**

5. **The concept of R2P is evolving. Its definitions may change. However, R2P proponents maintain that its evolving definitions should clearly state that R2P leads to humanitarian actions and not aggressive wars.**
   - Discuss the differences between humanitarian actions and aggression.
   - Is it necessary for any country to have the approval of the United Nations to carry out a humanitarian intervention with the use of armed forces?

6. **Imagine that an authoritarian country, acting without international approval, uses the R2P arguments to violate the sovereignty of another country. How would you react as president of the United States?**
   - Consider Russia's military interference in Syria after 2015. Ask your professor, if necessary, to provide the details.
   - Compare Russia's actions with the war in Kosovo in the 1990s, where NATO carried out a humanitarian intervention against Yugoslavia. Ask your professor, if necessary, to provide the details.
   - Think (hypothetically) of and discuss the situation in and around the United States or Canada that would allow other countries like China to apply the R2P concept toward North America.

7. **Peter Singer (see the companion website) uses a metaphor of a drowning child to justify the necessity of humanitarian interventions. Discuss this analogy in the context of international relations.**
   - Why does this analogy appear strong under some circumstances, and why is it weak in other contexts?
   - What other behavioral analogy would you personally suggest to defend R2P?

8. **Peter Singer (see the companion website) writes that "it is wrong to spend anything at all on any luxury as long as there are people starving in the world." Do you personally agree with this statement?**
   - How would the strategy of spending less help starving people? Suggest several ways for this strategy's implementation.
   - Critics disagree with this strategy and maintain that even if we all stop buying luxuries, the world will not change for the better. What is your view?
   - Do you think it would be a good idea to introduce a global luxury tax and use the funds for humanitarian assistance? Which products would you tax and how much?

9. **According to Singer, how would lower fertility rates help the extremely poor globally?**

10. **Dan Bulley (see the companion website) writes about moral factors in foreign policy. Describe these factors.**
    - What should an "ethical" foreign policy be in your view?
    - Is this policy practically achievable?
    - Should the United States or the United Kingdom adhere to strict ethical rules in their foreign policy even when many other countries break them?

11. **Would you support the idea of universal heath rights (such as the right of every person on the planet to have access to medical care)? Can this idea be implemented? Explain your review.**
    - Would you endorse the United Nations as the distributor of universal health benefits?
    - Would you endorse several independent healthcare companies to be in charge of universal health benefits?
    - Would you give the right to local governments to manage the new program?

# SECTION 10

1. **Discuss the reasons why the nationalistic, xenophobic, misogynistic, and explicitly anti–human rights agenda of many populist political leaders has appeared in the twenty-first century.**

2. **Why does culture matter in international relations?**
   - In which ways are cultural and political factors connected?
   - In your view, how do cultural factors affect foreign policy and vice versa?

3. **Describe a *culture of fear*, according to Holger Mölder.**
   - How does this culture result in specific foreign policy actions?
   - What can be done to change the culture of fear?

4. **The culture of fear, practiced by powerful international actors, can affect international relations and destabilize international systems.**
   - Discuss two or three examples of such cultures of fear in history. Ask your professor for help. How did these cultures of fear affect policies?

5. **How does Jerry Muller understand nationalism? How do you personally define nationalism? Discuss in class.**

6. **How did European nationalism, according to Muller, differ from non-European forms of nationalism?**
   - What are some examples of different ethnic groups living peacefully together within a nation-state?
   - What conditions are necessary to avoid ethnic tension and violence?

7. **How would you describe memory wars in the post-Soviet space discussed by Torbakov?**
   - What role do security fears and economic interests play in the disputes about historical narratives and history textbooks?
   - Why and how can memory wars aggravate regional crises and interstate conflicts, such as the Russian–Ukrainian conflict that started in 2014?
   - Can similar memory wars be observed in other parts of the world? Search for examples.

8. **How would religion, according to Scott Thomas (on the companion website), change global politics?**
   - What is your view on the role of religion in international relations today: Is it mostly positive, mostly negative, or mixed?
   - Will religious tensions increase, decrease, or remain the same in ten years?

9. **Do you see the forthcoming clash of civilizations and religions (see Huntington, Section 1) or do you see the detachment of religion from particular territories, as Thomas claims?**

# SECTION 11

1. **Do you personally support or oppose the idea of a global government? Explain your arguments.**

2. **What role should the United States play in such a government if it is established in ten or twenty years or so?**

3. **How would demographic factors change world politics according to Goldstone?**
   - What is the most significant demographic change, in your opinion, that would impact international relations in five to ten years? In twenty years?
   - How, and in which ways, would this change impact international relations?

4. **Do you see particular tendencies of global authoritarian revival today that resemble George Orwell's descriptions in *1984*? (See the companion website.)**
   - Investigate (use, for example, the Freedom House criteria) how many countries were considered authoritarian in 2000.
   - How many countries are authoritarian today? Several think tanks use *democracy indexes* to rank countries. Discuss your findings.
   - Can modern authoritarian countries manipulate information in the same way as Orwell described in his novel?

5. **Do you agree or disagree with Ikenberry's thesis that the age of geopolitics may be over soon? Explain why.**

6. **Why do Deudney and Ikenberry (on the companion website) believe that the liberal model of international relations should prevail in the future?**
   - Do you agree or disagree with this prediction and why?
   - Do you see the signs that the liberal model is winning today?

7. **Discuss Fred Bergsten's claims that any country that needs to be an economic superpower must be large, vibrant, and globally integrated, not isolated. (See the companion website.)**
   - Which country or countries fit this profile now?
   - Which country or countries may fit this profile in ten years?

8. **Consider and discuss the situation in which Russia and China challenge the existing liberal order.**
   - Which actions would you qualify as a challenge to the existing liberal order?
   - What will be the response of the United States and NATO to the challenge?
   - Would you call Russia's behavior today a challenge to the liberal order? Why?
   - Would you call China's behavior today a challenge to the liberal order? Why?
   - What will be the consequences of a strategic partnership between Russia and China in support for the liberal order?

9. **Which practices, policies, or traditions could China offer to other countries so that they follow China's global lead and eventually accept it?**

10. **Have these predictions and discussions strengthened (we hope) your interest in international relations? If yes, how?**